T0155783

Communications
in Computer and Information Science   **1846**

Editorial Board Members

Joaquim Filipe ⓘ, *Polytechnic Institute of Setúbal, Setúbal, Portugal*
Ashish Ghosh ⓘ, *Indian Statistical Institute, Kolkata, India*
Raquel Oliveira Prates ⓘ, *Federal University of Minas Gerais (UFMG),*
Belo Horizonte, Brazil
Lizhu Zhou, *Tsinghua University, Beijing, China*

Rationale

The CCIS series is devoted to the publication of proceedings of computer science conferences. Its aim is to efficiently disseminate original research results in informatics in printed and electronic form. While the focus is on publication of peer-reviewed full papers presenting mature work, inclusion of reviewed short papers reporting on work in progress is welcome, too. Besides globally relevant meetings with internationally representative program committees guaranteeing a strict peer-reviewing and paper selection process, conferences run by societies or of high regional or national relevance are also considered for publication.

Topics

The topical scope of CCIS spans the entire spectrum of informatics ranging from foundational topics in the theory of computing to information and communications science and technology and a broad variety of interdisciplinary application fields.

Information for Volume Editors and Authors

Publication in CCIS is free of charge. No royalties are paid, however, we offer registered conference participants temporary free access to the online version of the conference proceedings on SpringerLink (http://link.springer.com) by means of an http referrer from the conference website and/or a number of complimentary printed copies, as specified in the official acceptance email of the event.

CCIS proceedings can be published in time for distribution at conferences or as postproceedings, and delivered in the form of printed books and/or electronically as USBs and/or e-content licenses for accessing proceedings at SpringerLink. Furthermore, CCIS proceedings are included in the CCIS electronic book series hosted in the SpringerLink digital library at http://link.springer.com/bookseries/7899. Conferences publishing in CCIS are allowed to use Online Conference Service (OCS) for managing the whole proceedings lifecycle (from submission and reviewing to preparing for publication) free of charge.

Publication process

The language of publication is exclusively English. Authors publishing in CCIS have to sign the Springer CCIS copyright transfer form, however, they are free to use their material published in CCIS for substantially changed, more elaborate subsequent publications elsewhere. For the preparation of the camera-ready papers/files, authors have to strictly adhere to the Springer CCIS Authors' Instructions and are strongly encouraged to use the CCIS LaTeX style files or templates.

Abstracting/Indexing

CCIS is abstracted/indexed in DBLP, Google Scholar, EI-Compendex, Mathematical Reviews, SCImago, Scopus. CCIS volumes are also submitted for the inclusion in ISI Proceedings.

How to start

To start the evaluation of your proposal for inclusion in the CCIS series, please send an e-mail to ccis@springer.com.

Xiaofeng Meng · Yang Chen · Liming Suo ·
Qi Xuan · Zi-Ke Zhang

Editors

Big Data and Social Computing

8th China National Conference, BDSC 2023
Urumqi, China, July 15–17, 2023
Proceedings

Editors
Xiaofeng Meng
Renmin University of China
Beijing, China

Liming Suo
Nankai University
Tianjin, China

Zi-Ke Zhang
Zhejiang University
Hangzhou, China

Yang Chen
Fudan University
Shanghai, China

Qi Xuan
Zhejiang University of Technology
Hangzhou, China

ISSN 1865-0929   ISSN 1865-0937 (electronic)
Communications in Computer and Information Science
ISBN 978-981-99-3924-4   ISBN 978-981-99-3925-1 (eBook)
https://doi.org/10.1007/978-981-99-3925-1

This Springer imprint is published by the registered company Springer Nature Singapore Pte Ltd.
The registered company address is: 152 Beach Road, #21-01/04 Gateway East, Singapore 189721, Singapore

Preface

With the development of mobile Internet applications and big data, the volume of data is seeing explosive growth. So how to dig out insightful information from big data becomes a crucial matter. In general, big data analysis includes capturing data, data storage, data analysis, search, sharing, transfer, visualization, querying, updating, and information privacy. Moreover, with the popularization of artificial intelligence algorithms and big data technology in the last decade, social computing has emerged, which is a field of computer science that is concerned with the intersection of social behavior and computational systems. For example, blogs, email, instant messaging, social network services, wikis, online gaming, and other instances of what is often called social software illustrate ideas from social computing. Nowadays, big data technology and the idea of social computing have been gradually extended to more and more industries including Internet searches, fintech, healthcare analytics, genomics, geographic information systems, urban informatics, and business informatics. We believe that in the future, big data will become a part of everyday life.

This volume contains the papers presented at the China National Conference on Big Data & Social Computing (BDSC 2023). This conference was held as the 8th in its series with an emphasis on state-of-the-art advances in big data and social computing. The main conference received 141 paper submissions, out of which 26 papers were accepted as regular papers. All papers underwent a rigorous peer review process in which each paper was double-blind reviewed by 2 to 3 experts. The accepted papers, together with our invited posters and flash mob videos, led to a vibrant technical program. Meanwhile, we also invited leading scholars in the field to deliver keynote speeches based on the theme of the conference, Digital Transformation and Sustainable Development. Besides, we organized a variety of academic events, including the Social Computing Innovation Competition, the Rising Star Forum, and the Frontier Workshop. These activities played a positive role in promoting academic progress and dissemination. We are looking forward to future events in this conference series.

The conference would not have been successful without the help of so many people. We would like to thank the Organizing Committee for their hard work in putting together the conference. First, we would like to express our sincere thanks for the guidance from the general assembly co-chairs: Wushouer Silamu and Jiayin Qi. We would like to express our deep gratitude to organizing chair Jiabo Xu for his support and promotion of this event. We would also like to thank the program committee co-chairs: Yang Chen, Liming Suo, and Suran Wu supervised the review process of the technical papers and compiled a high-quality technical program. We greatly appreciate the excellent support and hard work of tutorial chair Zi-Ke Zhang, Rising Star Forum chair Xiaoming Li; Social Computing Innovation Competition chairs Chao Wu, Feiyu Xiong, and Huajian Cai; publicity chairs Shuo Yu and Qingyuan Gong; publication chair Qi Xuan; membership/committee development chair Yong Li; registration chair Yipitihaer

Tayier and special session chairs Luning Liu and Peng Lu. Most importantly, we would like to thank the authors for submitting their papers to BDSC 2023.

We believe that the BDSC conference provides a good forum for both academic researchers and industrial practitioners to discuss advanced topics in big data and social computing. We also expect that future BDSC conferences will be as successful as indicated by the contributions presented in this volume.

May 2023

Xiaofeng Meng
Yang Chen
Liming Suo
Qi Xuan
Zi-Ke Zhang

Organization

Steering Committee Chair

Xiaofeng Meng   Renmin University of China

General Co-chairs

Wushouer Silamu   Xinjiang University, China
Jiayin Qi   Shanghai University of International Business and
                              Economics, China

Program Committee Co-chairs

Yang Chen   Fudan University, China
Liming Suo   Nankai University, China
Suran Wu   Harbin Engineering University, China

Organizing Committee Chair

Jiabo Xu   Xinjiang Institute of Technology, China

Tutorial Chair

Zi-Ke Zhang   Zhejiang University, China

Rising Star Forum Chair

Xiaoming Li   Peking University, China

Social Computing Innovation Competition Chairs

Chao Wu	Zhejiang University, China
Feiyu Xiong	Alibaba, China
Huajian Cai	Institute of Psychology, Chinese Academy of Sciences, China

Special Session Chairs

Luning Liu	Harbin Institute of Technology, China
Peng Lu	Chinese Academy of Social Sciences, China

Publication Chair

Qi Xuan	Zhejiang University of Technology, China

Publicity Chairs

Shuo Yu	Dalian University of Technology, China
Qingyuan Gong	Fudan University, China

Membership/Committee Development Chair

Yong Li	Northwest Normal University, China

Registration Chair

Yipitihaer Tayier	Xinjiang Institute of Technology, China

Paper Award Chairs

Jianguo Liu	Shanghai University of Finance and Economics, China
Peng Lv	Central South University, China

Vision Paper Chair

Ye Wu   Beijing Normal University, China

Program Committee

Zhidong Cao	Chinese Academy of Sciences, China
Huashan Chen	Chinese Academy of Social Sciences, China
Xuezhong Chen	University of Jinan, China
Yang Chen	Fudan University, China
Jiangao Deng	Hohai University, China
Ying Fan	Beijing Normal University, China
Shizheng Feng	Renmin University of China, China
Xiaoming Fu	University of Göttingen, Germany
Danhuai Guo	Chinese Academy of Sciences, China
Li He	Xi'an Jiaotong University, China
Kuangshi Huang	China Population and Development Research Center, China
Tao Jia	Southwest University, China
Ding Li	Renmin University of China, China
Yong Li	Northwest Normal University, China
Yucheng Liang	Sun Yat-sen University, China
Xianghong Lin	Northwest Normal University, China
Huan Liu	Arizona State University, USA
Ji Liu	Xinjiang University of Finance, China
Jianguo Liu	Shanghai University of Finance and Economics, China
Luning Liu	Harbin Institute of Technology, China
Yi Liu	Tsinghua University, China
Tun Lu	Fudan University, China
Jiade Luo	Tsinghua University, China
Peng Lv	Chinese Academy of Social Sciences, China
Peng Lv	Central South University, China
Youzhong Ma	Luoyang Normal University, China
Tianguang Meng	Tsinghua University, China
Xiaofeng Meng	Renmin University of China, China
Jiayin Qi	Guangzhou University, China
Xiaofan Wang	Shanghai University, China
Feiyue Wang	Chinese Academy of Sciences, China
Xiao Wang	Chinese Academy of Sciences, China
Chao Wu	Zhejiang University, China

Ye Wu	Beijing Normal University, China
Feng Xia	Dalian University of Technology, China
Jinghong Xu	Beijing Normal University, China
Lei Xu	Beijing Institute of Technology, China
Wei Xu	Renmin University of China, China
Xiaoke Xu	Dalian Minzu University, China
Qi Xuan	Zhejiang University of Technology, China
Hu Yang	Central University of Finance and Economics, China
Miaoyu Yang	Kwai, China
Yan Yu	Renmin University of China, China
Yong Yuan	Renmin University of China, China
Hui Zhang	Tsinghua University, China
Jiang Zhang	Beijing Normal University, China
Lun Zhang	Beijing Normal University, China
Changping Zhang	Guilin University of Technology, China
Dajun Zeng	Chinese Academy of Sciences, China
Lu Zheng	Tsinghua University, China
Junfeng Zhou	Donghua University, China
Tao Zhou	University of Electronic Science and Technology of China, China
Xiaolin Zhou	Peking University, China
Jinqing Zhu	Bytedance, China
Jianhua Zhu	City University of Hong Kong, China
Huajun Chen	Zhejiang University, China
Weifeng Dai	Fudan University, China
Bo Fan	Shanghai Jiao Tong University, China
Haipo Hu	East China University of Science and Technology, China
Yang Yue	Shenzhen University, China
Bo Li	Peking University, China
Ruiqi Li	Beijing University of Chemical Technology, China
Zi Li	Chongqing Technology and Business University, China
Jia Liu	Beijing Dongfang Guoxin Technology Co., Ltd., China
Yijie Peng	Peking University, China
Jun Su	Tsinghua University, China
Heli Sun	Xi'an Jiaotong University, China
Liming Suo	Nankai University, China
Tao Wu	Chongqing University of Posts and Telecommunications, China

Wuqing Wu	Renmin University of China, China
Guanghui Yan	Lanzhou Jiaotong University, China
Lan You	Hubei University, China
Wen Zhang	Beijing University of Technology, China
Yiming Zhang	Chinese Academy of Labour and Social Security, China
Zi-Ke Zhang	Zhejiang University, China
Yan Zhao	Harbin Engineering University, China
Xiaoxue Gao	East China Normal University, China
Qingyuan Gong	Fudan University, China
Weiwei Gu	Beijing University of Chemical Technology, China
Haimeng Liu	Chinese Academy of Sciences, China
Jiaqi Liu	Chinese Academy of Social Sciences, China
Quanhui Liu	Sichuan University, China
Shuo Wang	Hebei University, China
Bin Zhou	Jiangsu University of Science and Technology, China
Xin Lu	National University of Defense Technology, China
Xiangjie Kong	Zhejiang University of Technology, China
Jingjing Qu	Shanghai AI Lab, China
Biao Huang	Zhejiang University, China
Shuai Xu	Nanjing University of Aeronautics and Astronautics, China
Xien Liu	Tsinghua University, China
Chuang Liu	Hangzhou Normal University, China
Yingnan Cong	China University of Political Science and Law, China
Shuo Yu	Dalian University of Technology, China
Yuan Gao	Northwest University, China
Hongke Zhao	Tianjin University, China
Jinyin Chen	Zhejiang University of Technology, China
Mingjie Lv	Zhejiang Lab, China
Qi Su	University of St. Andrews, UK
Jichao Li	National University of Defense Technology, China
Lei Dong	Peking University, China
Lizhen Wang	Yunnan University, China
Haochao Ying	Zhejiang University, China
Xiao Zhang	Shandong University, China
Haoyin Lv	Longdong University, China
Xueliang Fu	Inner Mongolia Agricultural University, China

Contents

Digital Society and Public Security

Artificial Intelligence and Cognitive Science

Internet Intelligent Algorithm Governance

Digital Technology and Sustainable Development

A Power Consumption Forecasting Method Based on Knowledge Embedding Under the Influence of the COVID-19 Pandemic

Qifan Zhang[✉] and Xiu Cao

Shanghai Key Lab of Intelligent Information Processing,
Department of Computer Science, Fudan University, Shanghai 200433, China
20210240154@fudan.edu.cn

Abstract. This paper addresses the new challenges of power consumption forecasting under the COVID-19 pandemic by proposing a knowledge embedding-based method (PEC-19). This method constructs a multi-source enterprise knowledge graph by analyzing and combining the specific impact of COVID-19 on power consumption, and designs the Connection Count Calculation of PEC-19 (3CP) algorithm and Similarity Degree Calculation of PEC-19 (SDCP) algorithm based on the graph to measure the similarity between different users affected by the COVID-19 pandemic and enable knowledge transfer and embedding among them. Moreover, the PEC-19 framework introduces a SEIR-based caáźǦse number prediction module and a comprehensive feature extraction module to account for the trend of the COVID-19 pandemic and increase the variety of time series features. Compared with existing baseline methods, the PEC-19 framework can significantly improve the power consumption forecasting performance in both univariate and multivariate time series forecasting tasks, and each module contributes differently to the proposed method. The framework also has some applicability and provides a new solution for various public health emergencies, which helps to reduce power operation cost, coordinate supply and demand, and conduct accurate scheduling.

Keywords: the COVID-19 pandemic · power consumption forecasting · knowledge embedding · knowledge graph · transfer learning

1 Introduction

Power consumption forecasting is a fundamental step in power system operation and decision-making problems such as unit commitment, reserve management, and maintenance scheduling [1], which affect the cost and reliability of system operation [2]. To ease the power supply and demand imbalance and ensure safe and stable power supply, China is promoting market-oriented electricity prices [3]. Industrial and commercial users who do not directly purchase electricity from the electricity market rely on power supply companies to purchase electricity for them, which requires higher precision and finer-grained power consumption forecasts from power supply companies. However, the COVID-19 pandemic [4,5] has significantly impacted the electricity demand in many countries and regions [6–8], and posed new challenges to the power consumption forecasting task, especially for non-residential power consumption. Ignoring the obvious and sudden impact of the pandemic on power consumption will greatly reduce the accuracy of electricity forecasting, prevent effective adjustments of power supply strategy, and increase operating costs and system risk. In addition, non-residential power consumption accounts for a large proportion of total power consumption and brings more economic benefits to power supply enterprises [9]. Therefore, research on forecasting non-residential power consumption under the circumstances of the COVID-19 pandemic is a very important and yet to be resolved work.

The existing power consumption forecasting algorithm cannot handle the changes in power consumption caused by the COVID-19 pandemic. The forecasting model is built and validated based on historical data, and the main input features of the standard power consumption forecasting algorithm are weather, time information and previous power consumption [1]. The COVID-19 pandemic has violated the assumption that power consumption forecasts rely on similar load patterns at similar times of the year. This is because such events are rare in history since the current grid infrastructure was established. Therefore, it is not surprising that the power consumption forecasting algorithms used by electricity operators will produce larger forecast errors during the pandemic. For the short-term power consumption forecast in daily units, this part of the forecast error can be reduced by manually setting the characteristics of each day as weekends, but this is not enough to close the accuracy gap, and it cannot be applied to the medium and long-term power consumption forecasting task [10]. Some scholars have studied the adaptive learning scheme [11] of power consumption in different regions or seasons, but few research have considered the power consumption forecasting task in emergencies. Moreover, when the pandemic is under control, the user's power consumption behavior will change rapidly again. This fact makes the challenge posed by the pandemic to the power consumption forecasting task more complicated [12].

This paper proposes a solution PEC-19 for these challenges. The solution uses instance-based homogeneous transfer learning to add other users' historical power consumption samples affected by the pandemic to expand the training set, which solves the problem of insufficient data. The sample similarity is the similarity of the degree of impact of the pandemic among different users, but information related to the impact of the pandemic, such as policies, streets, and personnel, and their relationship with each other are knowledge-based, and it is hard to achieve such knowledge-intensive goals only by data-driven methods. The knowledge graph [13] is suitable for accomplishing these goals. It can also meet visualization requirements, handle searches involving relationships and data diversity, and solve the problem of data islands. The network knowledge is well connected and embedded in the power consumption forecasting model. The solution also considers the pandemic development trend of the forecast month through SEIR infectious disease dynamics, and adds pandemic-related features to expand the data types.

This paper makes the following contributions:

(1) It proposes a graph similarity calculation module to enable knowledge transfer and embedding between multiple users. This module constructs a knowledge graph by analyzing and combining the specific impact of the COVID-19 pandemic on power consumption, and uses the 3CP algorithm and the SDCP algorithm to distinguish between different users who are affected by the pandemic. The knowledge about the similarity of users affected by the pandemic can be embedded in the power consumption forecasting model to increase the number of time series samples and improve the accuracy of power consumption forecasting under the pandemic situation. It also has advantages in terms of deep relationship mining ability.

(2) It proposes a SEIR-based case number prediction module to consider the development trend of the COVID-19 pandemic. This module uses the SEIR infectious disease dynamics model considering the incubation period factor to predict the number of daily existing confirmed cases, and then combines the calculation of the identification threshold and classification threshold to determine the pandemic development trend in the month to be predicted for power consumption. The domain knowledge determined comprehensively by the pandemic development trend and affected similarity will be transformed into constraints in the loss function of the regressor of the forecasting value output module. This module designs model penalties and rewards to give more attention to the samples constructed from other users who are more similarly affected and have a more severe epidemic trend during the training process.

(3) A comprehensive feature extraction module that extracts pandemic-related features such as the number of confirmed cases in addition to conventional power consumption forecasting features such as time data and meteorological data. This module increases the type of time series data and provides more information for the forecasting value output module to improve the forecasting effect.

2   Related Work

This section introduces the background knowledge and related work on power consumption forecasting, transfer learning and knowledge embedding.

2.1   Power Consumption Forecasting

Power consumption forecasting is a vital part of power operations and planning, especially under the influence of COVID-19 on grid load and demand [2]. Time series forecasting methods are widely used in this task [14], as well as in other fields such as weather forecasting [15] and inventory control [16]. Machine learning methods have made significant progress in time series forecasting [17], but they face challenges such as non-stationarity [18] and model selection [19]. Existing methods can be classified into statistical methods and machine learning-based methods [20]. Statistical methods such as ARIMA [21,22] and ETS [23,24] can predict a single sequence. Machine learning-based methods use deep neural networks to learn complex patterns [25] from diverse time series data. LSTM [26] and Transformers [27] are popular deep neural networks for time series forecasting due to their ability to model non-linear temporal patterns. Ensemble Learning is also a machine learning-based method that can improve forecasting accuracy [28,29]. Examples of Ensemble Learning are Random Forest Regressor [30], AdaBoost Regressor [31], Bagging Regressor [32] and XGBoost Regressor [33].

2.2 Transfer Learning

This paper proposes an instance-based homogeneous transfer learning scheme that combines other users' historical power consumption data affected by the pandemic to obtain enough and diverse training samples. Transfer learning transfers knowledge from related source domains to improve learning performance in the target domain [34]. The scheme uses instance-based transfer learning, which adjusts and transforms data, and instance weighting, which assigns weights to source domain instances in the loss function. The weight parameters can be obtained by reweighting source domain instances based on instance weight and domain weight [35], or by iteratively adjusting the weights to reduce the negative impact of distribution differences [31,36]. Heuristic methods such as Jiang and Zhai's [37] general weighting framework can implement instance weighting strategies to minimize the cross-entropy loss for different types of instances. However, this paper requires a transfer learning solution that can handle knowledge-intensive goals related to epidemic information, such as policies, streets, and personnel.

2.3 Knowledge Embedding

The knowledge graph is a way of expressing and managing knowledge that facilitates knowledge interconnection in the "Web3.0" era. It was first proposed in May 2012 to improve search engine performance [13]. Since 2013, it has been widely applied in various fields. This paper focuses on the penalty and reward design method, which converts domain knowledge into constraints in the loss function. For example, PgNN [38] and PINN [39] embed domain knowledge into neural networks by introducing physical mechanisms or equations. TgNN [40] extends PINN to exploit prior information as domain knowledge in hydrology and petroleum engineering. Zhu et al. [41] showed that domain knowledge alone can train a model without labeled data. By embedding domain knowledge into machine learning models, this paper aims to combine pandemic knowledge with power consumption forecasting using a transfer learning approach.

3   PEC-19

The overall structure of the Power Consumption Forecasting Method Based on Knowledge Embedding Under the Influence of the COVID-19 Pandemic (PEC-19) proposed in this study is shown in the Fig. 1:

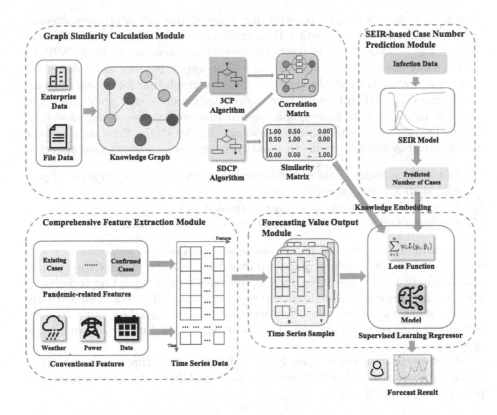

Fig. 1. PEC-19

This paper presents a framework for power consumption forecasting under the COVID-19 pandemic (PEC-19), which consists of four modules: graph similarity calculation, SEIR-based case number prediction, comprehensive feature extraction and forecasting value output. The graph similarity calculation module uses enterprise data and user profile data to construct a multi-source enterprise knowledge graph, and applies 3CP and SDCP algorithms to measure the similarity of users' power consumption affected by the pandemic. The SEIR-based case number prediction module uses the SEIR model to predict the infection cases, and combines the similarity to assign sample weights to different user data in the loss function of the forecasting model. The comprehensive feature extraction module extracts pandemic-related features in addition to conventional features, and organizes them as time series data for the forecasting value output module.

The forecasting value output module processes the time series data into samples for model training, and modifies the loss function according to sample weights, to obtain the power consumption forecast under the pandemic.

3.1   Graph Similarity Calculation Module

This module has two tasks: constructing a knowledge graph of users affected by the pandemic and calculating their similarity using 3CP and SDCP algorithms. The main challenge of power consumption forecasting under COVID-19 is the lack of historical data for each user. To incorporate other users' data, this paper builds a multi-source enterprise knowledge graph that focuses on the pandemic impact, based on standby power consumption data, user profile data and Internet data. The knowledge graph construction involves knowledge modeling, knowledge extraction and knowledge storage. In this study, three data sources with completely different structures and types are used for extraction, namely:

(1) Enterprises disclose data according to law, such as company type, legal person, shareholders, executives, etc.
(2) User profile data in the power company system.
(3) Policies about the COVID-19 pandemic collected on the Internet.

To acquire data, we use hyperlink-based traversal crawler technology and extract entities, relationships, and attributes from semi-structured data and natural language texts using table parsing and information extraction techniques. We also use business rules to form and represent knowledge. When an attribute value contains a hyperlink to another entry, we analyze the linked entity to establish inter-entity relationships and obtain a structured and networked knowledge system.

We store the knowledge in Neo4j graph database for future search tasks. The graph database also makes the knowledge more scalable and flexible. The overall process is illustrated in Fig. 2:

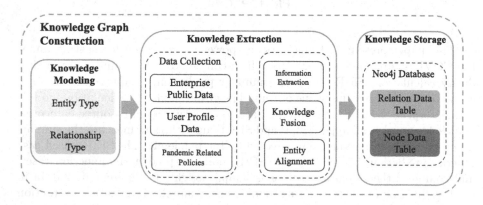

Fig. 2. The overall process of knowledge graph construction

Algorithm 1. 3CP Algorithm

Input: *weightThreshold* : Weight threshold
nodeList : User node list
n : Total number of users
KG : Knowledge graph
Output: *connectionCount* : Correlation matrix

1: Initialize the correlation matrix *connectionCount* values are all -1
2: $i \leftarrow 0$, $j \leftarrow 0$
3: **for** $node1 \in nodeList$ **do**
4:     **for** $node2 \in nodeList$ **do**
5:         **if** $i = j$ **then**
6:             $connectionCount_{ij} \leftarrow 0$
7:         **if** $i \neq j$ and $connectionCount_{ij} = -1$ **then**
8:             $count \leftarrow$ The number of paths with weighted length $\leq$ *weightThreshold* between node1 and node2 in KG
9:             $connectionCount_{ij} \leftarrow count$
10:            $connectionCount_{ji} \leftarrow count$
11:        $j \leftarrow j + 1$
12:    $i \leftarrow i + 1$
13:    $j \leftarrow 0$
14: **return** *connectionCount*

This paper measures the impact of the pandemic on users based on the knowledge graph. The Connection Count Calculation of PEC-19 (3CP) algorithm, inspired by the graph node classification algorithm, computes the user node associations for the SDCP algorithm to calculate the similarity degree. The "association" definition is: two nodes are associated if there is a path with a weight length less than or equal to the weight threshold *weightThreshold*. The *weightThreshold* can be adjusted dynamically according to the situation and results.

The connection count calculation requires the above definition to compute the *connectionCount* between each user. Algorithm 1 shows the algorithm flow:

$connectionCount_{ij}$ denotes the connections between node i and node j. Lines 5 and 6 set the self-connections to 0. Line 8 applies the "association" definition. Since the knowledge graph ignores the relationship direction, the *connectionCount* matrix is diagonal-symmetric, so lines 7, 9, and 10 optimize the time complexity. They update $connectionCount_{ij}$ and $connectionCount_{ji}$ simultaneously, and skip the calculation if $connectionCount_{ij}$ is not -1.

The Similarity Degree Calculation of PEC-19 (SDCP) algorithm computes the *similarityDegree* of different users affected by COVID-19 after obtaining the *connectionCount* matrix. Algorithm 2 shows the similarity calculation algorithm flow:

This algorithm normalizes the *similarityDegree* to [0,1]. The larger the value, the more similar the impact of COVID-19. It also handles the case when

---

Algorithm 2. SDCP Algorithm

Input: $connectionCount$: Correlation matrix
α : Importance of other users
n : Total number of users
Output: $similarityDegree$: Similarity matrix
1: Initialize the similarity matrix $similarityDegree$ values are all -1
2: **for** $i \in 1, \ldots, n$ **do**
3:     max_i=Max($connectionCount_i$)
4:     **for** $j \in 1, \ldots, n$ **do**
5:         **if** $i = j$ **then**
6:             $similarityDegree_{ij} \leftarrow 1$
7:         **if** $i \neq j$ and $max_i = 0$ **then**
8:             $similarityDegree_{ij} \leftarrow 0$
9:         **if** $i \neq j$ and $max_i \neq 0$ **then**
10:            $similarityDegree_{ij} \leftarrow \alpha - \alpha \frac{max_i - connectionCount_{ij}}{max_i}$
11: **return** $similarityDegree$

---

a user node has 0 associations with itself and others. The self-association is 0, but the similarity is 1. The other-association is 0, but the similarity is 0.

3.2   SEIR-Based Case Number Prediction Module

The SEIR-based case number prediction module of the PEC-19 framework embeds knowledge into the model to improve the prediction accuracy under COVID-19. It considers the monthly severity of the pandemic, which varies in different cities and periods. For example, for city S, January 2020 is the start month, February is the worst month, March is the second worst month, and April to June are less severe. The monthly severity affects the power consumption prediction. This study designs a knowledge acquisition and embedding scheme with clear steps and quantitative calculations.

This module uses the SEIR infectious disease dynamics model to predict the confirmed cases and the pandemic trend in the power consumption forecast month. It combines the predicted cases with the graph similarity calculation module to determine the sample weight for different user data, and changes the loss function of the power consumption forecasting model. Moreover, this module also performs pandemic identification. When the forecast result is below the identification threshold, it skips the relevant calculations, saving time and resources.

The process is to build an SEIR model based on the epidemiological data and the historical daily cases of the COVID-19 strain, and use it to predict the daily cases in the forecast month, and compute the average daily cases. Then, according to the estimated average daily cases, the identification threshold, and the classification threshold, the severity is classified and the impact coefficient is given to improve the loss function. Fig. 3 shows the process:

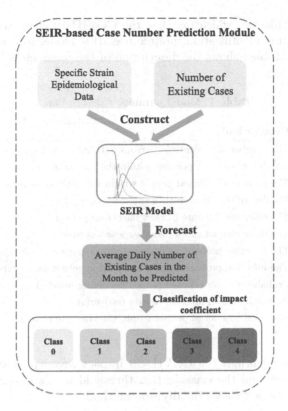

Fig. 3. The overall process of the SEIR-based case number prediction module

This module predicts the confirmed infections and the power consumption impact of COVID-19 in the forecast month using the SEIR infectious disease model. Its differential equation is:

$$\frac{dS}{dt} = -\frac{r_1\beta_1SI}{N} - \frac{r_2\beta_2SE}{N} \tag{1}$$

$$\frac{dE}{dt} = \frac{r_1\beta_1SI}{N} + \frac{r_2\beta_2SE}{N} - \alpha E \tag{2}$$

$$\frac{dI}{dt} = \alpha E - \gamma I \tag{3}$$

$$\frac{dR}{dt} = \gamma I \tag{4}$$

The infectious disease model is a key mathematical model for studying infectious diseases. Common models are SI, SIR and SEIR, depending on the disease type. The SI model splits the population into susceptible and infected people, while the SIR model adds the recovered people to the SI model. The SEIR model adds the exposed people to the SIR model. These people do not show symptoms immediately, but can infect others as pathogen carriers. This model considers the exposed population, which matches the COVID-19 characteristics. Therefore, this pandemic identification module uses this model to predict the cases and the impact. Table 1 shows the description of the parameters involved in the SEIR model:

Table 1. Model parameter description

Parameter	Description
S	The number of susceptible persons within the contagious range
E	Number of exposed persons within the contagious range
I	The number of infected people within the contagious range
R	Number of recoveries within the contagious range
r_1	The daily contact rate of each infectious person
r_2	The daily contact rate of each exposed person
β_1	The infection probability of a susceptible person by an infected person
β_2	The infection probability of a susceptible person by an exposed person
α	Probability of an exposed person becoming infected
γ	Probability of an infected person recovering
N	The total number of people within the contagious range

This module quantifies the COVID-19 impact severity by comparing the average daily cases and the classification threshold in the power consumption forecast month. Table 2 shows the division method:

Table 2. Classification of COVID-19 infection severity

Severity	The Interval of The Number of Existing Cases	Influence Coefficient
Class 0	less than the recognition threshold a	0
Class 1	greater than or equal to a, less than b	1
Class 2	greater than or equal to b, less than c	2
Class 3	greater than or equal to c, less than d	3
Class 4	greater than or equal to d, less than e	4

This study divided the range between the recognition threshold a and the average daily cases e in the worst pandemic month into four grades, and obtained five pandemic severity classes: class 0, class 1, class 2, class 3 and class 4. Class 4 is the most severe, and the sample weights of other users calculated by the graph similarity calculation module will be multiplied by 4; while class 0 means no pandemic impact, and the sample weights of other users will be multiplied by 0, ignoring them; the other three classes are similar.

The recognition threshold a is the average daily cases for about 5 days when the power consumption in the area starts to drop. The upper limit e is the average daily cases in the worst pandemic month. The grading thresholds b, c, and d are calculated as follows:

$$b = a + \frac{(e - a)}{4} \tag{5}$$

$$c = a + \frac{2(e - a)}{4} \tag{6}$$

$$d = a + \frac{3(e - a)}{4} \tag{7}$$

3.3 Comprehensive Feature Extraction Module

The PEC-19 framework's comprehensive feature extraction module extracts conventional power consumption forecasting features and adds pandemic-related features to capture the pandemic situation. They are combined as time series data and passed to the forecasting value output module. This way, the regressor model can learn pandemic-related knowledge to improve the power consumption forecasting accuracy under COVID-19 and the existing method. The pandemic-related features in the sample input at each time point are the average daily cases and the average daily confirmed cases in city S. The data source is S City Health Committee.

3.4 Forecasting Value Output Module

The PEC-19 framework outputs the final power consumption forecasting result through the forecasting value output module, using the sample weights from the graph similarity calculation module and the SEIR-based case number prediction module, and the time series data from the comprehensive feature extraction module. This module preprocesses the time series data into time series samples, and uses the supervised machine learning regression method for sample training and expected continuous value output. This module is compatible with various regressors for different data situations. The experiment in this paper uses XGBoost as the regressor. The data preprocessing includes preliminary data analysis, data cleaning, data deformation and feature engineering. This study firstly analyzes the data type, average value, median and other information of each feature, and observes some data distribution and relationship by plotting. Then, it removes the missing and outlier data, and converts the time-series data into time-series samples by the sliding window method. It also performs zero-mean normalization to make the data have 0 mean and 1 standard deviation, which accelerates parameter convergence during training. Feature engineering enables machines to obtain more effective features. The features in this study are mainly numerical features, which can be directly input to the model.

This study incorporates the domain knowledge into the loss function as constraints. This module modifies the loss function of the conventional regressor using the sample weights. The PEC-19 framework's regressor multiplies the improved sample weights to each sample's loss function to get the final cost function. This improved loss function uses the similarity information of different users and the pandemic severity in different months to embed knowledge for the forecasting model. The regressor finds the optimal parameters by minimizing the following cost function through the training samples:

$$CostFunction = \sum_{i=1}^{n} w_i l\left(y_i, \hat{y}_i\right) \tag{8}$$

Among them, n is the total number of training samples, w_i is the weight of the i-th training sample, $l\left(y_i, \hat{y}_i\right)$ is the loss function of y_i and $\hat{y}_i$.

4   Experimental Results and Analysis

This section evaluates the PEC-19 framework for power consumption forecasting under COVID-19, compares it with baseline models, and examines its parameter sensitivity. It also adds ablation studies for each module to demonstrate the research effectiveness.

4.1   Experiment Settings

To verify the power consumption forecasting effect of the PEC-19 framework proposed in this study during the COVID-19 pandemic, this chapter compares it with various power consumption forecasting models such as XGBoost Regressor [33], LSTM [26] and Informer [27]. The power consumption forecasting model requires that the input at time point t be historical multivariate time series data of length T $X^t = \left\{x_1^t, x_2^t, \ldots, x_T^t \mid X_i^t \in R^{d_x}\right\}$, the output is the future value $y^t = \left\{y_1^t, y_2^t, \ldots, y_H^t \mid y_i^t \in R^{d_y}\right\}$, where R^{d_x} and R^{d_y} are the dimensions of the input/output data, and H is the forecast horizon. The forecasting task's input data dimension is greater than 1, meaning that there are multiple features such as power and weather at each time point, which belongs to Multivariate Time Series Forecasting (MTSF). When the input data dimension is equal to 1, every A time point that only has the feature of power consumption belongs to Univariate Time Series Forecasting (UTSF).

Given the forecasting sequence $\{\hat{y}_{t+1}, \ldots, \hat{y}_{t+H}\}$ of length H and the observed sequence $\{y_{t+1}, \ldots, y_{t+H}\}$, the following metrics are usually used to evaluate the forecasting performance:

$$MSE = \frac{1}{H}\sum_{i=1}^{H}(y_{t+i} - \hat{y}_{t+i})^2 \tag{9}$$

$$MAE = \frac{1}{H}\sum_{i=1}^{H}|y_{t+i} - \hat{y}_{t+i}| \tag{10}$$

$$MAPE = \frac{100}{H}\sum_{i=1}^{H}\frac{|y_{t+i} - \hat{y}_{t+i}|}{|y_{t+i}|} \tag{11}$$

$$sMAPE = \frac{200}{H}\sum_{i=1}^{H}\frac{|y_{t+i} - \hat{y}_{t+i}|}{|y_{t+i}| + |\hat{y}_{t+i}|} \tag{12}$$

The forecasting performance of a model can be evaluated using various indicators such as mean square error (MSE), mean absolute error (MAE), mean absolute percentage error (MAPE), and symmetric mean absolute percentage error (sMAPE). The value range of MSE, MAE, and MAPE is $[0, +\infty)$, while sMAPE has a value range of [0,2]. A smaller value of these indicators indicates better forecasting performance of the model. In this experiment, forecasting performance was evaluated using MSE, MAE, and sMAPE. MAPE was not used to avoid errors caused when the true value is close to zero.

The time step of the time series forecasting model in this experiment is 1 month. The length T of the historical time series data X^t input by the model is gradually extended from 3, 6, 12, and the forecasting range H is 1. The experimental operating environment is described in Table 3:

Table 3. Experimental Operating Environment Description

Environment	Configuration
Operating System	Windows10
GPU	NVIDIA GeForce GTX 1660 Ti
CPU	Intel i7-11700F CPU @ 2.50 GHz
Memory	16 GB

4.2 Main Experiment Results and Analysis

Table 4 summarizes the univariate/multivariate input power consumption time series forecasting and evaluation results of various methods under different input step sizes. The first column represents the forecasting method, the second column represents different input step sizes, and the third to fifth columns represent the MSE, MAE, and sMAPE of the corresponding forecasting method under the corresponding input step size in the case of univariate time series forecasting. The last three columns indicate the MSE, MAE, and sMAPE in the case of multivariate time series forecasting. The best results are highlighted with darker fonts.

The PEC-19 framework proposed in this study significantly improves power consumption forecasting under various input step sizes compared with other methods in the univariate input time series forecasting task performance, as shown in the third to fifth columns of Table 4. This result demonstrates the success of the method in improving power consumption forecasting in the context of COVID-19. In terms of parameter sensitivity of the univariate time series forecasting task on input step size, the PEC-19 framework has an average decrease of 0.033 in MSE, 0.050 in MAE, and 0.050 in sMAPE compared to other baseline methods when the input step size is 3.16.50. At an input step size of 6, MSE drops by 0.039 on average, MAE by 0.043 on average, and sMAPE by 14.96 on average. At an input step size of 12, MSE drops by 0.033 on average, MAE by 0.051 on average, and sMAPE by 15.93 on average. Overall, under the univariate time series forecasting task, input step size has no obvious effect on improving

Table 4. Forecast results of power consumption under the influence of the COVID-19 pandemic

Method	Input Step	UTSF			MTSF		
		MSE	MAE	sMAPE	MSE	MAE	sMAPE
PEC-19	3	**0.0036**	**0.043**	**8.996**	**0.0029**	**0.040**	**8.752**
	6	**0.0075**	**0.055**	**12.141**	**0.0061**	**0.049**	**11.461**
	12	**0.0052**	**0.047**	**10.392**	**0.0021**	**0.034**	**7.199**
Linear Regression	3	0.0208	0.070	20.301	0.1404	0.226	42.581
	6	0.0292	0.087	27.259	1.3622	0.698	83.626
	12	0.0163	0.084	19.731	0.1827	0.252	46.480
SVR	3	0.0564	0.129	31.990	0.0642	0.186	56.810
	6	0.0668	0.137	32.033	0.0596	0.179	53.576
	12	0.0645	0.146	35.083	0.0457	0.144	41.260
Random Forest	3	0.0239	0.070	20.942	0.0208	0.063	20.469
	6	0.0537	0.093	26.084	0.0314	0.084	24.045
	12	0.0354	0.075	24.694	0.0285	0.074	23.191
AdaBoost	3	0.0417	0.100	28.170	0.0348	0.090	27.223
	6	0.0567	0.101	26.801	0.0468	0.099	25.517
	12	0.0395	0.096	27.978	0.0385	0.088	26.131
XGBoost	3	0.0546	0.116	31.450	0.0424	0.112	30.343
	6	0.0577	0.114	28.589	0.0343	0.091	27.126
	12	0.0296	0.095	28.631	0.0293	0.081	25.796
MLP	3	0.0492	0.112	28.640	0.0671	0.195	34.883
	6	0.0417	0.119	30.865	0.0689	0.223	41.477
	12	0.0535	0.141	33.789	0.1304	0.291	62.104
LSTM	3	0.0224	0.096	22.395	0.0168	0.061	19.680
	6	0.0463	0.084	23.210	0.0119	0.077	17.298
	12	0.0323	0.081	24.821	0.0153	0.080	18.503
Informer	3	0.0385	0.078	23.300	0.0290	0.067	22.702
	6	0.0316	0.073	23.388	0.0222	0.076	21.224
	12	0.0165	0.061	16.134	0.0146	0.060	15.427

PEC-19 forecasting effect. MSE drops the most when input step size is 6; MAE drops the most when input step size is 12; sMAPE drops the most when input step size is 3.

The PEC-19 framework proposed in this research has improved power consumption forecasting performance under various input step sizes in the multivariate input time series forecasting task, as shown in the last three columns of Table 4. When the input step length is 12, the forecasting error represented by each evaluation index is the smallest. Linear Regression and SVR methods here are relatively univariate in multivariate input time series tasks and have significantly worse performance, indicating that they have not trained well and learned the rules when facing more feature inputs. In terms of parameter sensitivity of the multivariate time series forecasting task on input step size, the

PEC-19 framework has an average decrease of 0.045 in MSE, 0.079 in MAE, and 21.99 in sMAPE compared to other baseline methods when the input step size is 3. When the input step size is 6, the average decrease of MSE is 0.179, the average decrease of MAE is 0.129, and the average decrease of sMAPE is 23.86. When the input step size is 12, MSE drops by 0.054 on average, MAE drops by 0.092 on average, and sMAPE drops by 24.01 on average. Under multivariate time series forecasting task, MSE and MAE indexes of PEC-19 method decrease most when input step size is 6; sMAPE index decreases most when input step size is 12.

4.3 Ablation Study Results and Analysis

To better understand the impact of each module in the PEC-19 framework proposed in this paper and to further illustrate the effectiveness and uniqueness of the research results, this paper conducted ablation study for the graph similarity calculation module, SEIR-based case number prediction module, and comprehensive feature extraction module. The evaluation results are shown in Table 5. The first column indicates whether the forecasting type is univariate input or multivariate input, and the input length is 12. The second to fourth columns indicate the ablation of each model, and the last three columns indicate MSE, MAE, and sMAPE of PEC-19 framework after corresponding ablation. For appearance purposes, in the table, the graph similarity calculation module is referred to as the graph module, SEIR-based case number prediction module is referred to as SEIR module, and comprehensive feature extraction module is referred to as comprehensive module.

Table 5. Power consumption forecasting ablation study under the influence of the COVID-19 pandemic

Forecast Type	Graph	SEIR	Comprehensive	MSE	MAE	sMAPE
UTSF	✓			0.0053	0.059	12.52
		✓		0.0091	0.052	12.54
			✓	0.0374	0.084	25.14
	✓	✓		0.0152	0.063	16.26
	✓		✓	**0.0049**	0.056	11.97
	✓	✓		0.0071	0.048	11.17
	✓	✓	✓	0.0052	**0.047**	**10.39**
MTSF	✓			0.0043	0.051	10.90
		✓		0.0066	0.047	10.82
			✓	0.0355	0.082	24.35
	✓	✓		0.0135	0.060	16.10
	✓		✓	0.0034	0.046	9.70
	✓	✓		0.0026	0.042	8.66
	✓	✓	✓	**0.0021**	**0.034**	**7.20**

The experimental results are carried out from the perspective of univariate and multivariate forecasting tasks, and the performance of all module ablation schemes is explained. Various indicators show that on the whole, each module is helpful to improve forecasting accuracy, especially the graph similarity calculation module and SEIR-based case number forecasting module. The performance degradation caused by ablation of these two modules at the same time will be very obvious, while the role of comprehensive feature extraction module is relatively weak. From the perspective of forecasting types, performance improvement of each module will be more obvious in case of multivariate power consumption forecasting. In summary, PEC-19 framework proposed in this paper makes full use of characteristics of various power consumption changes during pandemic period and improves accuracy of power consumption forecasts for power users during this period.

5   Conclusion

This paper proposes a power consumption forecasting method PEC-19 based on knowledge embedding and transfer learning to face the problem of a sharp drop in the accuracy of power consumption forecasting caused by sudden changes in the power consumption pattern under the COVID-19 pandemic. This method aims at the problem of insufficient data during the pandemic period. The paper proposes a graph similarity calculation module to enable knowledge transfer and embedding among multiple users. This module also has advantages in terms of sexuality and deep relationship mining ability. In addition, the paper proposes a SEIR-based case number prediction module to consider development trend of COVID-19 pandemic. The knowledge about the development trend of the pandemic and the knowledge of affected similarity comprehensively determine sample weights of samples corresponding to different user data, thereby changing calculation method of regression loss function in forecasting value output module. This paper proposes a comprehensive feature extraction module, so as to further extract pandemic-related features such as number of confirmed cases on basis of conventional power consumption forecasting features such as time data and meteorological data. In this paper, aiming at above three main works, through comparison and ablation studies to verify their actual correction effect on power consumption forecasting in case of COVID-19 pandemic. Both tasks and multivariate time series forecasting tasks can significantly improve forecasting effect of power consumption, and each module contributes to improvement of effect to varying degrees.

This research aims to explore and research emerging problem of decline in accuracy of power consumption forecasting under influence of COVID-19 pandemic, and proposes comprehensive and innovative solution. Some modules still have room for improvement. Regarding prediction of number of confirmed cases, although SEIR infectious disease dynamics model used in this study can meet basic objectives of pandemic identification and severity grading in this study, if you need to further improve prediction accuracy in future, you can try other prediction models for number of cases. In knowledge modeling link of knowledge graph, current research plan considers total of 11 types of entity types and 13 types of relationship types. In future, existing model structure can be further supplemented and improved based on knowledge of epidemiology or impact of policies and regulations.

References

1. Gross, G., Galiana, F.D.: Short-term load forecasting. In: Proceedings of the IEEE 75.12, pp. 1558–1573 (1987)
2. Hobbs, B.F., et al.: Analysis of the value for unit commitment of improved load forecasts. IEEE Trans. Power Syst. **14**(4), 1342–1348 (1999)
3. Development and Reform Commission. Notice of the National Development and Reform Commission on further deepening the market-oriented reform of on-grid power prices for coal-fired power generation, 11 October 2021. http://www.gov. cn/zhengce/zhengceku/2021-10/12/content_5642159.htm. Accessed 10 Nov 2021
4. Li, Q., et al.: Early transmission dynamics in Wuhan, China, of novel coronavirus-infected pneumonia. N. Engl. J. Med. **382**(13), 1199–1199 (2020)
5. Huang, C., et al.: Clinical features of patients infected with 2019 novel coronavirus in Wuhan, China. Lancet **395**(10223), 497–506 (2020)
6. Leach, A., Rivers, N., Shaffer, B.: Canadian electricity markets during the COVID-19 pandemic: an initial assessment. Can. Publ. Policy **46**(2), 145–159 (2020)
7. Fezzi, C., Fanghella, V.: Real-time estimation of the short-run impact of COVID-19 on economic activity using electricity market data. Environ. Resourc. Econ. **76**(4), 885–900 (2020)
8. DiSavino, S.: COVID-19: America hasn't used this little energy in 16 years. https://www.weforum.org/agenda/2020/04/united-states-eneregy-electricity-power-coronavirus-covid19
9. Guo, Z., et al.: Residential electricity consumption behavior: influencing factors, related theories and intervention strategies. Renew. Sustain. Energy Rev. **81**, 399–412 (2018)
10. Fiot, J.-B., Dinuzzo, F.: Electricity demand forecasting by multi-task learning. IEEE Trans. Smart Grid **9**(2), 544–551 (2016)
11. Grady, W.M., et al.: Enhancement, implementation, and performance of an adaptive short-term load forecasting algorithm. IEEE Trans. Power Syst. **6**(4), 1404–1410 (1991)
12. Barker, T., Dagoumas, A., Rubin, J.: The macroeconomic rebound effect and the world economy. Energy Efficiency **2**(4), 411–427 (2009)
13. Singhal, A.: Introducing the knowledge graph: things, not strings. https://blog. google/products/search/introducing-knowledgegraph-things-not/
14. Miller, C., et al.: The ASHRAE great energy predictor III competition: overview and results. Sci. Technol. Built Environ. **26**(10), 1427–1447 (2020)
15. Liang, Y., et al.: Geoman: multi-level attention networks for geosensory time series prediction. In: Proceedings of the 27th International Joint Conference on Artificial Intelligence, pp. 3428–3434. AAAI (2018)
16. Seeger, M., Salinas, D., Flunkert, V.: Bayesian intermittent demand forecasting for large inventories. In: Proceedings of the 30th Annual Conference on Neural Information Processing Systems, pp. 4653–4661. MIT Press (2016)

17. Lim, B., Zohren, S.: Time-series forecasting with deep learning: a survey. Philos. Trans. Roy. Soc. A **379**(2194), 28 (2021)
18. Tanaka, K.: Time Series Analysis: Nonstationary and Noninvertible Distribution Theory, vol. 4. Wiley, Hoboken (2017)
19. Wolpert, D.H.: The lack of a priori distinctions between learning algorithms. Neural Comput. **8**(7), 1341–1390 (1996)
20. Fawaz, H.I., et al.: Deep learning for time series classification: a review. Data Min. Knowl. Discov. **33**(4), 917–963 (2019)
21. Zhang, G.P.: Time series forecasting using a hybrid ARIMA and neural network model. Neurocomputing **50**, 159–175 (2003)
22. Pai, P.-F., Lin, C.-S.: A hybrid ARIMA and support vector machines model in stock price forecasting. Omega **33**(6), 497–505 (2005)
23. Hyndman, R., et al.: Forecasting with Exponential Smoothing: The State Space Approach. Springer, Heidelberg (2008). https://doi.org/10.1007/978-3-540-71918-2
24. Durbin, J., Koopman, S.J.: Time series analysis by state space methods. OUP Oxford (2012)
25. Rangapuram, S.S., et al.: Deep state space models for time series forecasting. In: Proceedings of the 32nd Annual Conference on Neural Information Processing Systems, pp. 7796–7805. MIT Press (2018)
26. Lai, G., et al.: Modeling long-and short-term temporal patterns with deep neural networks. In: Proceedings of the 41st International ACM SIGIR Conference on Research and Development in Information Retrieval, pp. 95–104. ACM (2018)
27. Zhou, H., et al.: Informer: beyond efficient transformer for long sequence time-series forecasting. In: Proceedings of the AAAI Conference on Artificial Intelligence, pp. 11106–11115. AAAI (2021)
28. Taylor, J.W., McSharry, P.E. Buizza, R.: Wind power density forecasting using ensemble predictions and time series models. IEEE Trans. Energy Convers. **24**(3), 775–782 (2009)
29. Makridakis, S., Spiliotis, E., Assimakopoulos, V.: The M4 competition: results, findings, conclusion and way forward. Int. J. Forecast. **34**(4), 802–808 (2018)
30. Breiman, L.: Random forests. Mach. Learn. **45**(1), 5–32 (2001)
31. Freund, Y., Schapire, R.E.: A decision-theoretic generalization of on-line learning and an application to Boosting. J. Comput. Syst. Sci. **55**(1), 119–139 (1997)
32. Drucker, H.: Improving regressors using boosting techniques. In: Proceedings of the 14th International Conference on Machine Learning. Morgan Kaufmann, pp. 107–115 (1997)
33. Chen, T., Guestrin, C.: XGBoost: a scalable tree boosting system. In: Proceedings of the 22nd ACM SIGKDD International Conference on Knowledge Discovery and Data Mining, ACM, pp. 785–794 (2016)
34. Pan, S.J., Yang, Q.: A survey on transfer learning. IEEE Trans. Knowl. Data Eng. **22**(10), 1345–1359 (2009)
35. Sun, Q., et al.: A two-stage weighting framework for multi-source domain adaptation. In: Proceedings of the 25th Annual Conference on Neural Information Processing Systems, pp. 505–513. MIT Press (2011)
36. Dai, W., et al.: Boosting for transfer learning. In: Proceedings of the International Conference on Machine Learning, pp. 193–200. ACM (2007)
37. Jiang, J., Zhai, C.X.: Instance weighting for domain adaptation in NLP. In: Proceedings of the 45th Annual Meeting of the Association of Computational Linguistics, pp. 264–271. The Association for Computational Linguistics (2007)

38. Karpatne, A., et al.: Physics-guided Neural Networks (PGNN): an application in lake temperature modeling. CoRR abs/1710.11431 (2017). arXiv: 1710.11431. http://arxiv.org/abs/1710.11431
39. Raissi, M., Perdikaris, P., Karniadakis, G.E.: Physics-informed neural networks: a deep learning framework for solving forward and inverse problems involving nonlinear partial differential equations. J. Comput. Phys. **378**, 686–707 (2019)
40. Wang, N., et al.: Deep learning of subsurface flow via theory-guided neural network. J. Hydrol. **584**, 1247–1247 (2020)
41. Zhu, Y., et al.: Physics-constrained deep learning for high-dimensional surrogate modeling and uncertainty quantification without labeled data. J. Comput. Phys. **394**, 56–81 (2019)

An Efficient Regional Co-location Pattern Mining Algorithm Over Extended Objects Based on Neighborhood Distribution Relation Computation

Jinpeng Zhang[1,5], Lizhen Wang[1,3]($\boxtimes$), Vanha Tran[4], and Wenlu Lou[2]($\boxtimes$)

[1] The School of Computer Science and Engineering, Yunnan University, Kunming 650091, Yunnan, China
zjp@ynufe.edu.cn, lzhwang@ynu.edu.cn

[2] The School of Business, Yunnan University of Finance and Economics, Kunming 650221, Yunnan, China
wenlu_lou@163.com

[3] Dianchi College of Yunnan University, Kunming 650228, Yunnan, China

[4] Department of Information Technology Specialization, FPT University, Hanoi 155514, Vietnam
hatv14@fe.edu.vn

[5] The School of Information, Yunnan University of Finance and Economics, Kunming 650221, Yunnan, China

Abstract. Regional co-location patterns (RCPs) indicate the feature sets that generally co-occur within sub-regions but rarely co-occur in the whole study area. Spatial features have different densities and neighbor relationships in different regions, which poses great challenges to the two core steps of RCPs—regional partitioning and prevalence computation of RCPs in the sub-regions. Moreover, the existing RCPs mining methods are limited to point instances, while RCPs over extended spatial instances have not yet been explored. To address these challenges, this study develops a feature transaction method to detect RCPs and their prevalent regions. We first draw the radiation range of instances with distance buffers and generate feature transactions at buffer intersections between instances. Second, transactions are categorized into global prevalent and non-global prevalent. The locations of the non-global prevalent feature transactions are used to imply the range of candidate RCPs. In the local range, the distribution relation of the features is calculated to mine RCPs. We denote this process as neighborhood distribution relation computation. Experimental evaluations illustrate our proposed approach can capture more detailed RCPs information over extended instances and has better efficiency than the comparison algorithms.

Keywords: Spatial data mining · Regional co-location pattern · Neighborhood distribution relation computation · Feature transaction · Extended instances

© The Author(s), under exclusive license to Springer Nature Singapore Pte Ltd. 2023
X. Meng et al. (Eds.): BDSC 2023, CCIS 1846, pp. 22–36, 2023.
https://doi.org/10.1007/978-981-99-3925-1_2

1 Introduction

Spatial co-location pattern mining [1] finds the subsets of features (co-locations) often co-occur in geographic space. It has been widely applied in many fields, such as species distribution analysis [2, 3], geoscience [4], location-based services [5, 6], intelligent crime data analysis [7], environmental management [8] and urban region profiling [9, 10]. Taking species distribution analysis as an example, the prevalent co-occurrence of certain plants and the infrequent occurrence of others in the studied area provides an important basis for agricultural production, forestry protection and so on.

As proposed by Michael Goodchild [11], because of spatial heterogeneity, spatial isolation creates spatial differences between features among distant regions. Unlike the first law of geography states the similarity of nearby areas, the Michael Goodchild's law reveals the spatial differences among distant regions. Thus, the spatial co-location pattern is variable within different sub-regions. Some spatial co-location patterns probably occurred frequently in some local areas, but rarely happened in the whole study area. This type of co-location pattern is called Regional co-location patterns (RCPs). The lack of a priori knowledge of sub-regions and the variation of instance density lead to a series of challenges in RCPs mining.

Figure 1 displays a dataset containing spatial extended events of four sub-regions (sub-areas). The distribution of spatial features is unbalanced in the four sub-areas. In sub-area 1, feature A has an instance A4 adjacent to C's instance C2, A4 occupies 4 cells but C2 owns 1. Obviously, two extended instances are neighbors, but how to measure the neighbor relationship between them is a challenge. In sub-regions 2, 3 and 4, A's instances are close to B's instances. However, this neighbor relationship does not appear in sub-area 1. Counting the patterns of each sub-region, {A, C} in sub-area 1, {A, B} in sub-area 2, {A, B, C}, {A, B}, {A,C} and {B, C} in sub-area 3 and {A, B} in sub-area 4. In each sub-area, the co-occurring feature types and their distribution shapes are different.

Based on Fig. 1, we propose three key issues of mining RCPs with extended instances.

First, as instances' form is more diverse, the neighbor relationship between extended instances should be addressed, such as A1 and B1. In addition, since the form of instances is rich and variable, how to calculate the prevalence of co-locations in sub-regions is the second challenge. Third, the regional scope of the co-location pattern is difficult to specify.

To tackle the above challenges, this paper proposes a neighborhood distribution relation-based RCPs mining algorithm. For the first difficulty, a neighbor relationship between instances is judged by the existence of the overlap portion between buffers of extended instances. For the second challenge, the prevalence of patterns in the sub-region is measured by the degree of intersection of buffers of different instances. The more overlap portion reflects the higher the local prevalent of a pattern. For the third, non-global prevalence co-locations' locations are utilized to indicate the potential local RCPs' prevalent regions and distribution relations are employed to filter the RCPs' regional scopes.

The remainder of this paper is organized as follows. Section 2 covers related work. Section 3 introduces the related concepts and the flow of our algorithm. Section 4

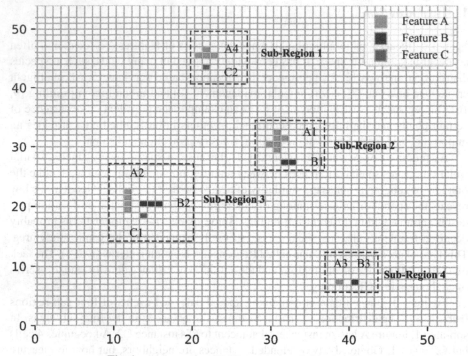

Fig. 1. An example of RCPs over extended instances.

presents the experimental evaluation. Section 5 concludes the paper and outlines our future research priorities.

2 Related Work

Many algorithms has been proposed for RCPs mining according to the relation of patterns and regions. These algorithms can be divided into two types:

The first type named division-based approach, which first identifies the RCPs' regions and then mine RCPs in the regions. At first, the division-based method needs to specify division rules. Then, the entire research area is divided into several local sub-regions according to the rules. Finally, algorithms detect the prevalent RCPs of each sub-region separately. Eick et al. [12] adopted a quad-tree-based method, which divides the global area into four equal parts and then uses a recursive method to further subdivide the divided areas until to achieve the desired effect. Qian et al.[13, 14] developed a k-nearest neighbor graph (KNNG) partitioning method that partitions the mining area into several homogenous sub-regions. In each sub-region, the authors assume that the region exhibits relatively uniform neighborhood distances. Consequently, the weights of the edges in the KNNG vary slightly. Subgraphs that satisfy constraints on parameters are merged. Clique instances in the graph of each sub-region are searched to identify prevalent RCPs.

The second type first detects RCPs and then searches the regions where their instances locate in. Deng et al. presented a multi-level method for discovery of RCPs [15]. The multi-level method made discovery of sub-regions of RCPs as a special clustering problem. This method utilizes global non-prevalent co-location patterns as candidate RCPs. Each RCP adopts an adaptive spatial clustering scheme to identify its prevalent sub-areas. They also proposed an overlap method for deducing the sub-regions of $(k + 1)$-size RCPs from k-size patterns to avoid exhausting all possible RCPs. [16] constructs the natural neighborhood for each spatial feature instance, the neighbor relationship of the instances of each candidate RCP is modeled utilizing the Delaunay triangulation network. Then the whole plane will be segmented into several sub-graphs, in each sub-graph, the prevalence of each candidate RCP is evaluated and RCPs can be generated. Moreover, a multi-direction optimization algorithm is proposed to check RCPs in sub-graph.

The above methods work well in RCPs mining for point instances, but they are not applicable to extended instances. Since the algorithms are rooted in constraints on statistical parameter and it is difficult to measure the distribution of instances in regions with various densities in fixed parameters. Besides, during the iterative computation from k-size to $(k + 1)$-size co-location pattern, some overlapping regions are repeatedly searched, this leads to worse efficiency of these methods.

To overcome the aforementioned shortcomings, we developed a neighborhood distribution relation computation method to discover RCPs over extended instances. We use distance buffers to express the distance range of extended instances and generate feature transactions through buffer overlap operations. Based on the feature transactions, disjoint local pattern regions are mined to generate RCPs. Experiments show our method is more effective and efficient than the existing methods.

3 Method

In this section, we first propose the related concepts. Then we give the formal description of mining RCPs over extended instances.

3.1 Basic Concepts

Definition 1. (Cell spatial dataset) A **cell spatial dataset** S is a regular cell array representing the distribution of spatial instances. Each cell specifies the feature to which the cell's position belongs, and its position is implicitly expressed through the horizontal and vertical coordinates of the cell.

Definition 2. (Spatial feature) A spatial feature fi refers to the type of a set of spatial instances with commonality.

For example, institution species, landcover types, and business types are different spatial features.

Definition 3. (Extended instance) In a cell spatial dataset, several consecutive cells form an **extended instance** I_k, which represents the occurrence of a feature in a certain position range.

As Fig. 2 illustrates, Ik is expressed by the red. The extended instance owns 6 cells, so the area of it is 6.

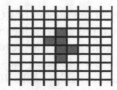

Fig. 2. An example of extended instance I_k.

Definition 4. (Size-d buffer of a cell) For a cell, its neighbor scope is some cells set in which cells are completely covered within its d distance. We denoted the neighbor range as the size-d buffer of this cell.

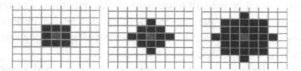

Fig. 3. Buffers of a cell under buffer size 1, 2 and 3.

For example, a cell's size-1 buffer is placed in a locality where the distance from the cell is not greater than 1. As shown in Fig. 3, red is the cell, the green is the size-1, size-2, and size-3 buffers of the cell.

Definition 5. (Instance's size-d buffer) The size-d buffer of an instance is the set of size-d buffers of the cells that make up the instance. We denoted it as $buffer(I_j, d)$, where d is the buffer size and the radiation buffer represents the range of the effect of this instance. The union of size-d buffer of each cell that makes up the instance formed the **size-d radiation buffer of the instance** ($d > 0$).

Definition 6. (Neighbor relationship between instances, feature transaction and feature transaction instance) Extended instances have a **neighbor relationship** if their buffers intersect. Given two extended instances I_i and I_j, $buffer(I_i, d)$ is I_i's size-d radiation buffer, $buffer(I_j, d)$ is I_j's size-d radiation buffer, $buffer(\{I_i, I_j\}, d)$ is defined as the shared buffer region between I_i and I_j, $buffer(\{I_i, I_j\}, d) = buffer(I_i, d) \cap buffer(I_j, d)$. If $buffer(\{I_i, I_j\}, d) > 0$, there exists a shared cell between I_i and I_j, which illustrates they have a **neighbor relationship**.

If a cell $Cell_i$ locates in the buffer of instances of a feature f_i, the cell's position generates a feature transaction $\{f_i\}$. Moreover, if cell $Cell_i$ locates in the intersection of buffers of I_i, I_j......and I_k, $Cell_i$ generate a feature transaction $\{f_i, f_j...f_k\}$. If a cell $Cell_i$ has a feature transaction t_i, the concatenated cells of the same feature transaction as t_i form the feature transaction instance, I_{t_i}.

Take Fig. 4 as an example, in the arrow pointing position, the number represents the id of the cell, and the content of the brackets stands for the cell's feature transaction. $Cell_1$ and $Cell_2$ generate feature transaction $\{A, B\}$, $Cell_3$ generate feature transaction

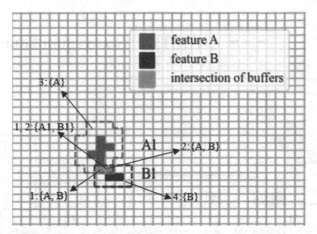

Fig. 4. An example of the neighbor relationship between extended instances and feature transaction.

{A}, and $Cell_4$ has transaction {B}. For $Cell_1$ and $Cell_2$, they form feature transaction instance {A1, B1}.

Definition 7. (Co-location pattern, participation ratio and participation index) The spatial co-location pattern c ($c \subseteq F$) is a subset of feature set F, where the size of c is the number of features in c. The participation ratio $PI(c, f_i)$ measures the participating state of a feature f_i in the m-size co-location pattern $c = \{f_1, \dots, f_m\}$. It is the ratio of the number of cells whose transaction contains f_i to the total number of cells whose transaction contains f_i namely:

$$PR(f_i, c) = \frac{Num(c)}{Num(f_i)} \tag{1}$$

The minimum **participation rate** among all spatial features of c is called participation index $PI(c)$ of c, that is:

$$PI(c) = min_{i=1}^{m}\{PR\_R(f_i, c)\} \tag{2}$$

Definition 8. (Feature transaction instance's region, regional participation ratio and participation index) Feature transaction instance's **region** indicates the size-d buffer of the transaction instance. The size of region is consistent with the buffer size d of the extended instances. The region contains the location where the transaction instance appears and the distance constraint range around the location. The **regional participation ratio** of a feature f_i in $c = \{f_1, \dots, f_m\}$ in a region R, $Pr\_R(f_i, c)$ is the ratio of the number of cells whose transaction contains c to the number of cells whose transaction contains f_i:

$$PR\_R(f_i, c) = \frac{Num(c, R)}{Num(f_i, R)} \tag{3}$$

The instance's **regional participation index** in a region R (PI_R) reflects the prevalence of row instances in the local area and denoted as:

$$PI\_R(c) = min_{i=1}^{m}\{PR\_R(f_i, c)\} \tag{4}$$

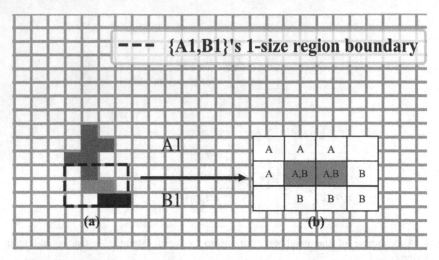

Fig.5. Example of A1 and B1's 1-size region and feature transaction in the region.

The dotted line in Fig. 5 (a) displays the size-1 region range of the transaction instance, and Fig. 5 (b) shows each cell's feature transactions in the local range. The PR_R of A in c is the ratio of the number of cells containing c in the feature transaction to the number of cells contained A in the feature transaction, that is, Num(c)/Num(A) $= 2/6 = 0.333$. Similarly, the participation rate of B is Num(c)/Num(B) $= 0.333$. The $PI\_R(c)$ is the minimum value of PR_R of A and B in c, i.e., min$\{0.333, 0.333\} = 0.333$.

Definition 9. (Coordinates set of a cell's buffer) For a user specified buffer size d, the coordinates set within its buffer range is denoted as coordinates set of a $Cell_i$'s buffer,$buffer(Cell_i, d)$. Suppose cell $Cell_i$'s coordinates are x and y, since the cell positions are all integers, we can calculate the set of coordinates satisfying the buffer size d distance constraint to avoid repeated Euclidean distance operations to improve the efficiency.

$$buffer(Cell_i, d) = \{(x+i, y+j)|\sqrt{i^2 + j^2} \le d \& i, j \in N\} \tag{5}$$

For example, suppose $d = 2$, $Cell_i$'s coordinates are (x, y), $buffer(Cell_i, 2) = \{(x, y), (x, y+1), (x, y-1), (x, y+2), (x, y-2), (x+1, y), (x+1, y+1), (x+1, y-1), (x-1, y), (x-1, y+1), (x-1, y-1), (x+2, 0), (x-2, 0)\}$. For different cells, input their coordinates can get their buffer cell coordinate range without calculation.

3.2   The Overall Mining Framework

As described in Fig. 6, the algorithm first mining the global co-location patterns. In the mining global co-location stage, the neighbor relationships between extended instances are materialized as feature transactions of cells, and global co-location patterns are achieved by FP-growth. In the mining RCPs stage, the feature transaction of each cell is evaluated whether it is a global non-prevalent transaction and if so, the region distribution relationship is calculated for the local range where the non-global transaction occurs. Finally, the RCPs and their prevalent regions are generated.

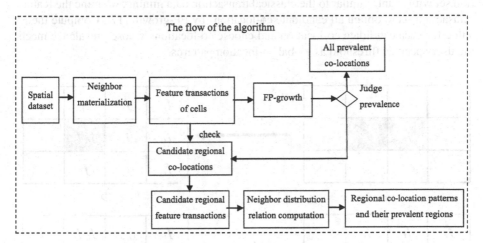

Fig. 6. The flow of the algorithm.

3.3 Mining Global Co-locations

Neighbor Materialization: Algorithm first materialization the neighbor relationship between extended instances by feature transactions. In a cell-structure dataset, the neighbor instances generate instance transactions at the intersection of buffers. In order to extract neighbor relationships, we can construct a buffer intersection between instances and calculate the coincidence relationships between buffers. To quickly calculate the buffer location of an instance, by Definition 5, we equate the buffer calculation of an extended instance to the buffer calculation of the set of cells that make up the instance. Moreover, we use Definition 9 to facilitate the buffer calculation for each cell.

With Definition 9, we can quickly find the cells within current cell $Cell_i$'s size-d buffer. These cells' feature transactions are updated with feature f_i of the $Cell_i$ owns, move to the next cell position, repeat the operation until all positions are manipulated, each cell is covered by the buffer of all cells within its neighborhood and add corresponding feature information. Finally, since all the buffers of $Cell_i$'s neighbor overlap, the transaction formed on $Cell_i$ is a maximal transaction.

Figure 7 illustrates the cell feature transaction generation process. In the plane, the red cell $cell_r$ with feature f_i, the blue cell $cell_b$ with feature f_j, other cells have no features. In Fig. 7(a), current position is $cell_r$, the red dashed line depicts the size-1 buffer range of $cell_r$. Then the cells' transaction within the dashed line are updated with f_i. Figure 7(b) demonstrates the results. When moving to the $cell_b$ position in Fig. 7 (c), its size-1 buffer range as shown in the blue dashed line. Within the blue dashed line, the transactions are updated with $cell_b$'s feature f_j. Figure 7(d) illustrates the results.

Mining Global Co-locations by FP-Growth: We count the number of all cells' maximal feature transactions generated in the previous section to generate a feature transaction set with count. Similar to the classical transaction data mining, we mine the feature transaction set to obtain all candidate co-locations by FP-growth [17]. Compute the PI value for each candidate co-location and choose co-locations whose prevalence meets the user-specified threshold as global co-location patterns.

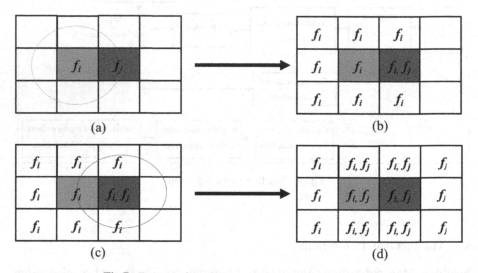

Fig.7. Example for cells' transaction generation process.

3.4 Mining RCPs

We take the global non-prevalent patterns captured in the previous section as candidate RCPs, scan the spatial plane to check whether each cell's feature transaction is global pattern. If so the cell is the location of the global pattern occurrence and skip, otherwise the cell is the potential RCPs occurrence. The cell is denoted as a candidate and the concatenated cells of the same feature transaction as the candidate RCP cell form the feature transaction instance.

The local range of this feature transaction instance is considered as a sub-dataset of the whole spatial cell dataset, on which FP-growth is used again to mine the RCPs. In the local range, the regional prevalence of each candidate is calculated. Next, the patterns that satisfy the prevalence requirement are filtered, and their local range is one of regions in which the RCPs are prevalent.

The purpose of this process is mainly to mine the RCPs that may be prevalent in the local range of non-global feature transaction instances. The transaction instance arises from the intersection of the distribution of feature buffers in that local area, which is essentially a distribution relation calculation. By Definition 8, the region can satisfy arbitrarily shaped feature transaction instances. We defined this process as **neighborhood distribution relation calculation**, which is the key step of proposed algorithm.

Taking Fig. 8 as an example, the green is the cells with feature transaction {A, B}, Other transactions are shown in the legend in Fig. 8. Based on these feature transactions, the candidate global co-location patterns are mined in the way of Sect. 3.3. They are {A, B} with prevalence 0.117, {A, C} 0.0735, {B, C} 0.083 and {A, B, C} 0.014. If the user specifies a threshold value of 0.05, {A, B}, {A, C} and {B, C} are global co-location patterns, {A, B, C} is a candidate RCP. Since there is no {A, B, C} feature transaction in the transactions of the cells adjacent to the black cell, the transaction instance of {A, B, C} only cover on the black cell. Neighborhood distribution relation calculation is employed in the sub-region of the cell with feature transaction {A, B, C}. The black cell radiates size-1 buffer to form the sub-region of candidate RCP {A, B, C}, which is shown by the black dashed range in Fig. 8. The black arrows point to the distribution of feature transactions of cells in the sub-region. RCP {A, B, C} owns 1 cell, A has 5 cells, B has 4 and C has 4. By Definition 7, the regional prevalence of {A, B, C} in the sub-region is the minimum value of the ratio of the number of cells of RCP to the number of cells of feature in RCP. Therefore, it is min{1/5, 1/4, 1/4} = 0.2, which is greater than the user specified threshold 0.05. {A, B, C} is a RCP in the sub-region. The other subregions are calculated in this way to obtain all RCPs.

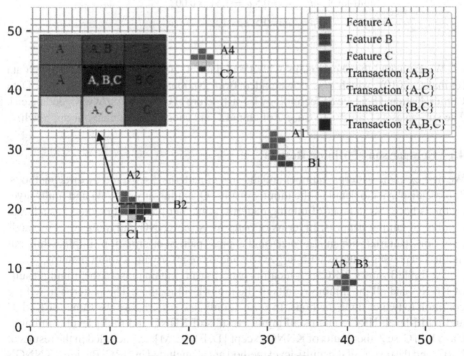

Fig. 8. Examples of mining RCPs.

4   Experimental Evaluation

In this section, we assess the mining effectiveness and efficiency of our neighborhood distribution relation calculation method. We use NRC to denote our presented algorithm for simplicity. Due to the lack of RCPs mining algorithms on extended instances, we apply the classical point instance algorithm, KNNG [13, 14], and the multi-level approach [15] to extended instance mining for comparison. By abstracting extended instances into point instances by geometric center, the traditional distance threshold measures the neighbor relationships between instances, comparison methods are employed to mine RCPs over extended instances. Three methods' experimental parameters setting is listed in Table 1. All experiments are done in Python 3.7 on a computer with a Windows 10 operating system, Intel i5-4288U CPU, and 12G RAM.

Table 1. Experimental parameters setting.

Experiment No	Method	Parameters
		buffer size b, minimum distance d, prevalence thresholds min_pi, Distance variation threshold ε, ratio threshold α, abundance threshold si
4.1, 4.2	KNNG	$min\_pi = 0.5$, $\varepsilon = 0.45$, $\alpha = 0.02$
	Multi-level	$min\_pi = 0.5$, $d = 1$, si $= 0.002$
	NRC	$min\_pi = 0.5$, $b = 1$,

We evaluated the experiments with a real dataset, 2010 China land cover type data (chinaLC 2010), which was downloaded from National Earth System Science Data Center, National Science & Technology Infrastructure of China (http://www.geodata.cn). The sub-datasets Case 1 and Case 2 of chinaLC are chosen to evaluate our approach.

4.1   Comparison of Mining Results

We first examine patterns' number and the size of patterns discovered by three methods. Table 2 displays the detail of the mining results. Quantitatively, KNNG and multi-layer methods have less number of mining patterns, while our presented method has a larger number of mining patterns. In terms of patterns' size, KNNG and multi-level methods only mine patterns with smaller sizes and express pattern information simply, while our method expresses patterns with larger size and more information about patterns.

As Table 3 shows, NRC's co-location patterns can contain most of the mining results of KNNG and all the mining results of the multi-level method. The patterns in red are common to two or three methods. In Case 1, only two patterns are the same for KNNG and multi-level. NRC contains all mining results of KNNG and multi-level. Similar to Case 1, in Case 2, the results of KNNG except {D, F},{E, M} are included in the results of NRC, and the results of the multi-level method are all included in NRC. Besides, KNNG's {D, F} and {E, M} (blue in Table 3) are not covered by the other two methods. Moreover, NRC's co-location patterns provide additional spatial information on features than

Table 2. The number of mining results on KNNG, Multi-level and NRC.

Methods	Case 1					Case 2				
	Size-2	Size-3	Size-4	Size-5	Pattern	Size-2	Size-3	Size-4	Size-5	Pattern
KNNG	7	0	0	0	7	8	0	0	0	8
Multi-level	15	0	0	0	15	18	0	0	0	18
NRC	62	86	38	3	189	66	76	21	2	165

Table 3. The effect of mining results on KNNG, Multi-level and NRC.

methods	Mining co-location pattern results	
	Case 1	Case 2
KNNG	{E, F} {N, S} {N, R} {G, S} {J, S} {D, E} {M, R}	{G, J} {G, P} {D, F} {E, M} {J, S} {P, S} {G, S} {P, Q}
Multi-level	{A, E} {A, J} {A, S} {D, N} {D, S} {E, J} {E, N} {E, S} {F, J} {J, N} {K, N} {M, R} {N, Q} {N, R} {R, S}	AN CJ DE DJ DO EF EJ EO FJ FS GQ JL JO JP JQ LO OQ PQ
NRC	{A, D} {A, E} {A, F} {A, J} {A, M} {A, N} {A, Q} {A, R} {A, S} {B, D} {B, K} {B, M} {B, R} {B, S} {D, E} {D, F} {D, J} {D, M} {D, N}] {D, R} {D, S} {E, F} {E, G} {E, J} {E, M} {E, N} {E, O} {E, S} {F, J} {F, M} {F, N} {F, S} {G, J} {G, M} {G, P} {G, Q} {G, S} {J, K} {J, M} {J, N} {J, O} {J, P} {J, Q} {J, R} {J, S} {K, M} {K, N} {K, Q} {K, R} {K, S} {M, N} {M, P} {M, Q} {M, R} {M, S} {N, Q} {N, R} {N, S} {P, S} {Q, R} {Q, S} {R, S} {A, D, E} {A, D, E, F} {A, D, E, F, N} { A, J, N}...	{A, E} {A, F} {A, J} {A, K} {A, N} {A, O} {A, Q} {C, D} {C, E} {C, J} {C, L} {C, N} {C, O} {C, S} {D, E} {D, G} {D, J} {D, L} {D, N} {D, O} {D, P} {D, Q} {D, S} {E, F} {E, J} {E, L} {E, N} {E, O} {E, S} {F, J} {F, L} {F, M} {F, N} {F, O} {F, Q} {F, S} {G, J} {G, M} {G, N} {G, P} {G, Q} {G, S} {J, K} {J, L} {J, M} {J, N} {J, O} {J, P} {J, Q} {J, S} {K, Q} {L, O} {M, P} {M, Q} {M, S} {N, O} {N, P} {N, Q} {N, S} {O, P} {O, Q} {O, S} {P, Q} {P, S} {Q, S} {A, N, Q} {C, J, L} {C, J, O} {C, J, S} {D, E} {D, E, J} {D, E, J, L} {P, Q, S} {G, J, P, Q, S}...

KNNG and multi-level methods. For example, the co-location of KNNG and multi-level method in Case2, {P, Q}. NRC's result is {P, Q}, {P, Q, S}, {G, J, P, Q, S}.

Analyze the results, since NRC divides the plane more finely and divides more localities, while KNNG and multi-level divide more brutally and divide less localities, NRC reflects the details of spatial distribution more comprehensively, while KNNG and multi-level will ignore some distributions of features. As consequence, the results of NRC mining are the most abundant, and the multi-level method is slightly better than KNNG.

4.2 Efficiency Evaluation

The efficiency of KNNG, Multi-level and our NRC of discovering RCPs over extended instances is evaluated in this experiment. We employ sub-datasets of the chinaLC with instance numbers ranging from 10K to 30K (K = 1,000) to test the scalability. To be as objective as possible, all run times are the average of ten runs.

From Fig. 9 we can see the execution time of our NRC method increases linearly as the number of instances grows, showing a good computational performance. NRC is relatively flat as the number of instances increases, while KNNG and multi-layer methods fluctuate more. In terms of different number of instances, the running time of NRC is better than other methods. The running time of NRC is better than other methods when it comes to different number of instances. Our method has higher efficiency, slightly better than the multi-level method, and has a greater advantage over the KNNG.

Analyze the reason, the KNNG and multi-level method iteratively mine the co-location pattern from k to $k + 1$, while some sub-regions are involved in multiple operations, such as KNNG's region merging and multi-level's region intersection and union operations. Unlike the two methods, our NRC divides regions independently of each other. Global co-location pattern information helps NRC reduce the number of sub-regions of candidate RCPs need to search. FP-growth is executed on each sub-region to avoid iterative operations, which reduces the running time to some extent.

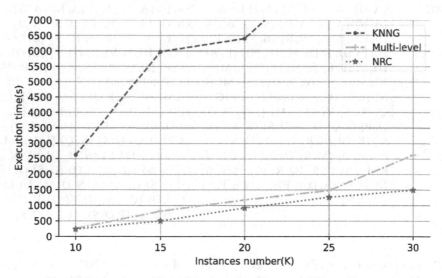

Fig. 9. Comparison of execution times for different numbers of instances.

5 Conclusion

We propose an NRC algorithm to mine RCPs over extended instances. Neighbor relationships between extended instances are materialized as feature transactions of cells. Depending on the feature transactions, global co-location patterns are achieved by FP-growth. We use the global non-prevalent co-locations as candidate RCPs to check the regions where RCPs occur. Neighborhood distribution relation computation is implemented on the instance region of global non-prevalent transactions to generate RCPs. The experiment on real data sets demonstrates NRC's effectiveness and efficiency.

We intend to further improve the efficiency of NRC to meet the demand for spatial applications, such as the survey of water distribution in arid areas and the analysis of medical resources in the regions where COVID-19 occurs.

Acknowledgments. This work is supported by the National Natural Science Foundation of China (62276227, 61966036), the Yunnan Fundamental Research Projects (202201AS070015), the Project of Innovative Research Team of Yunnan Province (2018HC019) and Yunnan University of Finance and Economics Scientific Research Fund (2022B03).

References

1. Huang, Y., Shekhar, S., Xiong, H.: Discovering colocation patterns from spatial data sets: a general approach. IEEE Trans. Knowl. Data Eng. **16**, 1472–1485 (2004). https://doi.org/10.1109/TKDE.2004.90
2. Wang, L.: Preference-Based Spatial Co-location Pattern Mining. Springer, Singapore (2022). https://doi.org/10.1007/978-981-16-7566-9
3. Zhang, J., Wang, L., Tran, V., Zhou, L.: Spatial co-location pattern mining over extended objects based on cell-relation operations. Expert Syst. Appl. **213**, 119253 (2023). https://doi.org/10.1016/j.eswa.2022.119253
4. Chen, S., Wang, F., Zhang, C.: Simultaneous heterogeneous data clustering based on higher order relationships. In: Seventh IEEE International Conference on Data Mining Workshops (ICDMW 2007), pp. 387–392. IEEE, Omaha, NE, USA (2007). https://doi.org/10.1109/ICDMW.2007.44
5. Chang, X., Ma, Z., Lin, M., Yang, Y., Hauptmann, A.G.: Feature interaction augmented sparse learning for fast kinect motion detection. IEEE Trans. Image Process. **26**, 3911–3920 (2017). https://doi.org/10.1109/TIP.2017.2708506
6. Yu, W.: Spatial co-location pattern mining for location-based services in road networks. Expert Syst. Appl. **46**, 324–335 (2016). https://doi.org/10.1016/j.eswa.2015.10.010
7. Phillips, P., Lee, I.: Mining co-distribution patterns for large crime datasets. Expert Syst. Appl. **39**, 11556–11563 (2012). https://doi.org/10.1016/j.eswa.2012.03.071
8. Akbari, M., Samadzadegan, F., Weibel, R.: A generic regional spatio-temporal co-occurrence pattern mining model: a case study for air pollution. J. Geogr. Syst. **17**(3), 249–274 (2015). https://doi.org/10.1007/s10109-015-0216-4
9. Kong, X., Xia, F., Ma, K., Li, J., Yang, Q.: Discovering transit-oriented development regions of megacities using heterogeneous urban data. IEEE Trans. Comput. Soc. Syst. **6**, 943–955 (2019). https://doi.org/10.1109/TCSS.2019.2919960
10. Hou, M., Xia, F., Gao, H., Chen, X., Chen, H.: Urban region profiling with spatio-temporal graph neural networks. IEEE Trans. Comput. Soc. Syst. **9**, 1736–1747 (2022). https://doi.org/10.1109/TCSS.2022.3183570
11. Goodchild, M.F.: The Fundamental Laws of GIScience. Invited talk at University Consortium for Geographic Information Science, University of California, Santa Barbara (2003)
12. Eick, C.F., Parmar, R., Ding, W., Stepinski, T.F., Nicot, J.-P.: Finding Regional Co-location Patterns for Sets of Continuous Variables. 11
13. Qian, F., Chiew, K., He, Q., Huang, H.: Mining regional co-location patterns with kNNG. J. Intell. Inf. Syst. **42**(3), 485–505 (2013). https://doi.org/10.1007/s10844-013-0280-5

14. Qian, F., Chiew, K., He, Q., Huang, H., Ma, L.: Discovery of regional co-location patterns with k-nearest neighbor graph. In: Pei, J., Tseng, V.S., Cao, L., Motoda, H., Xu, G. (eds.) PAKDD 2013. LNCS (LNAI), vol. 7818, pp. 174–186. Springer, Heidelberg (2013). https://doi.org/10.1007/978-3-642-37453-1_15
15. Deng, M., Cai, J., Liu, Q., He, Z., Tang, J.: Multi-level method for discovery of regional co-location patterns. Int. J. Geogr. Inf. Sci. **31**, 1846–1870 (2017). https://doi.org/10.1080/13658816.2017.1334890
16. Liu, Q., Liu, W., Deng, M., Cai, J., Liu, Y.: An adaptive detection of multilevel co-location patterns based on natural neighborhoods. Int. J. Geogr. Inf. Sci. **35**, 556–581 (2021). https://doi.org/10.1080/13658816.2020.1775235
17. Han, J., Pei, J., Yin, Y., Mao, R.: Mining frequent patterns without candidate generation: a frequent-pattern tree approach. Data Min. Knowl. Disc. **8**, 53–87 (2004). https://doi.org/10.1023/B:DAMI.0000005258.31418.83

Research on Multi-objective Optimization Algorithm for Coal Blending

Xiaojie Li[1,2], Runlong Yu[1], Guiquan Liu[1], Lei Chen[3], Enhong Chen[1(✉)],
and Shengjun Liu[2]

[1] School of Computer Science and Technology, University of Science and Technology of China,
Hefei 230027, China
cheneh@ustc.edu.cn
[2] Hefei City Cloud Data Center Co., LTD., Hefei 230088, China
[3] Anhui Zhenxin Internet Technology Co., LTD., Wuhu 241000, China

Abstract. Coal blending optimization presents a complex and challenging task, as it encompasses multiple competing objectives, such as quality, cost, and environmental considerations. This study specifically targets coal blending for coking applications and offers a comprehensive approach to tackle these challenges. We employ Miceforest to accurately fill in missing data and introduce an enhanced lightweight Transformer network architecture for constructing a coke index prediction model. Based on the predicted outcomes, we develop a multi-objective and multi-constraint coal blending optimization model, allowing us to calculate the maximum allocation for individual coals and minimize the algorithm's search space. Furthermore, we suggest a universal repair method that corrects unreasonable solutions while preserving the algorithm's evolutionary trend throughout the iterative process. To assess the efficacy of our approach, we integrate these technological advancements with traditional multi-objective algorithms. Experimental results reveal that these modified algorithms yield superior performance in generating more efficient and effective coal blending solutions for coking plants, as compared to their original counterparts.

Keywords: Coal Blending · Coke Index Prediction · Multi-objective Optimization · Constrained Optimization Problem · Transformer

1 Introduction

Coal blending and coking [1] is the core process segment of the coking industry. Here, coal blending refers to the mixing of a variety of single-coals into mixed-coal according to complex process constraints, and the composition and proportion of different single-coals in the mixed-coal is the coal blending scheme. The process of producing coke after placing the mixed-coal in a furnace and distilling it at a high temperature of 1000 °C is coking. The advantages and disadvantages of the coal blending scheme not only determine the quality of the coke, but also affect the environmental protection indicators and the cost of the coke, so the optimization of coal blending schemes has always been

X. Meng et al. (Eds.): BDSC 2023, CCIS 1846, pp. 37–60, 2023.
https://doi.org/10.1007/978-981-99-3925-1_3

the focus of the process optimization in the coking industry. Improving quality, reducing cost and environmental protection are multiple objectives that are closely related but competing, so coal blending is also a multi-objective optimization problem, which is called the Multi-objective Optimization of Coal Blending (MOP-CB).

In recent years, a lot of work has been done in the field of coal blending for coking has in the direction of machine learning and deep learning [2–7]. For example, Baozi Qi et al. [8] proposed a coke quality prediction model based on a chaotic sparrow search algorithm to optimize the support vector regression machine (SVR), and the results show that it has good accuracy and adaptability. Wenhua Tao et al. [9] used the difference algorithm to optimize the initial weight and threshold of the neural networks, and established a coke quality prediction model based on DE-BP optimization. The model has fast convergence accuracy and high prediction accuracy. Jianwen Lu et al. [10] adopted a multi-layer neural network to predict coke quality and the prediction accuracy met the national error requirements. Libang Liu et al. [11] used the improved whale optimization algorithm and long short-term memory (LSTM [12–14]) neural network for comprehensive modeling to predict coke quality, with high accuracy and fast running speed. The above works mainly focus on two directions. The first direction is on the coke quality prediction model and its improvement algorithm, and its objective is to improve the prediction accuracy of coke quality [8]. However, these researches have blind spots on how to optimize the coal blending scheme. The second direction is about the coal blending optimization algorithm, and the main objective of this direction is to reduce the cost by optimizing the coal blending schemes. However, when coal blending optimization becomes a MOP-CB problem that should consider quality, cost and environmental protection at the same time, these reported algorithms cannot deal with it effectively.

In the MOP-CB problem, the main technical difficulty lies in the performance challenge posed to the multi-objective optimization algorithm. The mechanism of coal blending for coking is complex [15], as strict constraints are imposed on various indicators of the mixed-coal fed into the furnace during production. Therefore, the main challenge in the MOP-CB problem is that each objective function has many constraints. Classical multi-objective optimization algorithms such as the NSGA-II [16], GDE3 [17], SMPSO [18], and CCMO [19] algorithms are inadequate to deal with multi-objective optimization problems with multiple constraints, which leads to a serious decline in optimization performance.

In this paper, we first use Miceforest to fill in the missing data in the data set. Then, we make light improvements based on the network structure of Transformer [20–23] to build the coke index prediction model. According to the prediction results, we build a multi-objective and multi-constraint coal blending optimization model. We use the model to calculate the upper allocation limit of a single coal and to reduce the search space of the algorithm. We propose a universal repair method that repairs unreasonable solutions while maintaining the trend of algorithm evolution during the process of algorithm iteration process. Finally, we combine the proposed method with four classical multi-objective optimization algorithms and each modified-algorithm achieves better experimental results, resulting in a better coal blending scheme for the coking plants.

We summarize our main contributions as follows:

- We propose an improved Transformer network model that captures the complex relationships between various features of mixed-coal. Compared to previous work, our model improves the accuracy of coking prediction.
- We formulate a multi-objective optimization problem for coal blending, taking into account quality, cost, and environmental protection objectives. Our approach enables the identification of the global optimal decision for coal blending schemes.
- We present two technical innovations to improve the performance of multi-objective optimization algorithms: a method for solving the upper limit of allocation and a universal repair method. These innovations can be integrated into any classical multi-objective optimization algorithm.
- Experimentally, we combine our technical innovative with four classical multi-objective optimization algorithms, NSGA-II, GDE3, SMPSO and CCMO, and the result shows that our strategy significantly improves the performance of classical multi-objective optimization algorithms under complex process constraints.

Overview. This paper is organized as follows. Section 2 describes the data preprocessing. In Sect. 3, we present a coke index prediction model based on an improved lightweight Transformer network. In Sect. 4, we describe a multi-objective optimization algorithm for coal blending combined with upper limit calculation and result repair. Section 5 provides the simulation experimental results and analysis. Finally, a summary is presented in Sect. 6.

2 Data Preprocessing

Our data preprocessing work consists of two parts, data cleaning and data filling.

2.1 Data Cleaning

The data used in this work are provided by a coking plant, and a total of 330 historical production data after desensitization. After data preprocessing, 263 pieces of data are relatively available, and the missing rate of some data is within an acceptable range. Missing data will have a negative impact on the subsequent research work, so in order to eliminate the negative impact, this work carried out data filling processing for missing values in this batch of data.

2.2 Data Filling

The coking industry adopts the sampling test method to obtain key index data, and operators often have the problem of missing detection, missing registration. Therefore, missing data is a common problem in the coke industry data set. This work adopted Miceforest [24–27] data filling method to eliminate missing data.

Miceforest Data Filling Method. Miceforest performs Multiple Imputation by Chained Equations (MICE) through random forests [28]. A series of iterative prediction models were used to fill in the missing data in the data set. In each iteration, each specified variable in the data set is estimated against the other variables in the data set. These iterations should run until convergence occurs. That is, the missing value is filled many times by using the existing data in the incomplete data set. The detailed steps of the Miceforest data filling method are as follows:

- Initialization. For each feature with missing values, we will randomly select some values from the complete values in these features and replace the missing values in the feature with them to obtain an initial complete data set.
- Iteration. Select one feature at a time, take the missing value in the current feature as the prediction target, and the remaining values as labels, use the random forest model to model the remaining value data, and then enter the remaining features corresponding to the missing value and obtain the missing value prediction result, and fill in the missing value. Do the same for any missing feature columns. Repeat these steps several times until the total number of iterations is reached or the difference in the data set after two consecutive iterations is less than a certain threshold (i.e., convergence).
- Output. We can output the data set obtained by the last iteration, or we can combine the data obtained by several iterations. In this game the former is chosen.

The specific procedure is shown in Fig. 1.

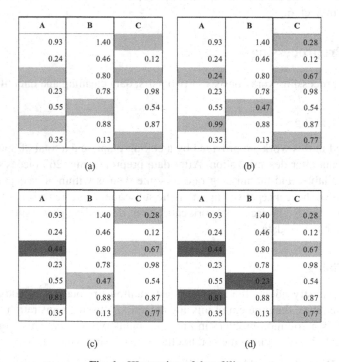

(a) (b) (c) (d)

Fig. 1. Illustration of data filling.

Figure 1a shows an example of a missing data set with three features, and the orange area is the missing data. Figure 1b shows the empty part filled with random numbers. The red part of the Fig. 1c shows the data after filling with a random forest model for feature A. Figure 1d shows that the same is done for feature B.

Data Filling Evaluation Index. This work uses three indexes to evaluate the effectiveness of data filling. They are Raw Bias (RB), Percent Bias (PB) and Root Mean Square Error (RMSE) [23].

The difference between the expectation of the estimated value after data filling and the expectation of the true value before data filling is the RB. The formula is as follows. The closer RB is to zero, the smaller the gap.

$$RB = \left| E\left(Q'\right) - Q \right| \tag{1}$$

Here, $E(Q')$ is the expectation of the estimate. Q is the expected true value.

The formula for the percentage error PB is as follows:

$$PB = 100 \times \left| \frac{\left(E\left(Q'\right) - Q\right)}{Q} \right| \tag{2}$$

If the PB value is within 5%, it is considered acceptable.

The root mean square error RMSE [29] also considers the mean and standard deviation of the eigenvalues before and after filling. The formula is as follows:

$$RMSE_1 = \sqrt{\left(E(Q') - Q\right)^2} \tag{3}$$

Q is the eigenvalue before filling, Q' is the eigenvalue after filling.

Data Filling Effect Analysis. Table 1 shows the index analysis before and after the partial data filling. It can be seen that before and after the data filling, the difference between the means values is small, and the variance is also small. The PB value is less than 5%. The RMSE takes into account the changes in mean and variance at the same time, and its value is also very small, close to 0.

From the contents of Table 1, it can be seen that the data filling did not significantly change the mean variance of the original data. From this point of view, the data set after the filling in this work is valid.

Table 1. Index analysis before and after filling.

Index	A_d	S_{td}	V_d	Coke_A_d	Coke_CRI	Coke_M_{40}
Missing ratio	0.167	0.167	0.167	0.232	0.51	0.559
Mean before complement	9.579	0.7	0.7	12.408	24.137	87.989

(*continued*)

Table 1. (*continued*)

Index	A_d	S_{td}	V_d	Coke_A_d	Coke_CRI	Coke_M_{40}
Supplementary mean	9.578	0.703	26.283	12.404	24.279	87.985
Standard deviation before complement	0.199	0.076	1.105	0.229	2.698	2.132
Supplementary standard deviation	0.195	0.076	1.105	0.22	2.523	1.931
PB	0.007	0.495	0.239	0.029	0.628	0.005
RB	0.001	0.003	0.063	0.004	0.142	0.004
RMSE	6.91E-04	3.46E-03	6.30E-02	3.69E-03	1.52E-01	4.00E-03

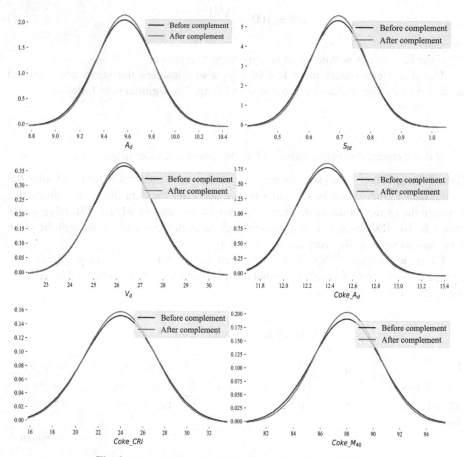

Fig. 2. Data density graph before and after feature filling.

Data Set Difference Analysis Before and After Data Filling. In this work, six features are selected, they are ash (A_d), sulphur (S_{td}), dry base volatile (V_d) of mixed-coal and coke ash (Coke_A_d), coke reactivity (Coke_CRI) and coke crushing strength (Coke_M_{40}) of coke. Figure 2 shows the data density of these six properties before and after data filling.

It can be seen that the data distribution after filling is basically consistent with that before filling, i.e., the data distribution of the original data set is almost unchanged after data filling, which verifies the effectiveness of data filling in this work.

Data Normalization. In order to make the subsequent training of the prediction model more stable, standard data normalization is performed on the filled data, which can scale the data to a certain range to ensure numerical stability. The formula is as follows:

$$x_i' = \frac{x_i - mean(x)}{std(x)} \tag{4}$$

Here, x is the feature population to be normalized, x_i is a sample of the population, x_i' is the value of this sample after standard normalization, $mean(x)$ is the mean value, $std(x)$ is the standard deviation.

3 Coke Index Prediction Model

In this section, we first describe the problem for coke index prediction. Then we improve the Transformer network model. The model will predict coke index in later sections.

3.1 Description of the Problems for Coke Index Prediction

The input parameters of the coke index prediction model in this paper are the five important characteristics of the mixed-coal entering the furnace, which are the ash (A_d), sulfur (S_{td}), dry base volatile (V_d), G value and dry ashless volatile (V_{daf}) before entering the furnace. The output parameters are nine important characteristics of the furnace coke, which are coke ash (Coke_A_d), coke sulfur (Coke_S_{td}), dry base volatile (Coke_V_{daf}), dry ashless volatile (Coke_V_d), coke crush strength (Coke_M_{40}), coke wear resistance (Coke_M_{10}), coke reactivity (Coke_CRI), coke reaction strength (Coke_CSR) and coking time (Dur).

In this paper, four factors need to be considered in the model design. First, due to the actual situation of the data set, such as less input feature dimension and less data, we need to pay attention to prevent overfitting problems in the model design. Second, because the input features of mixed-coal are composed of a variety of single-coal doping ratios, the relationship between the input features is complex, so it is necessary to fully express the dependence between the input features. Third, the correlation between the input features and the indicators to be predicted is strong, and the mapping relationship needs to be effectively established. Fourth, combined with the characteristics of industrial sites with high timeliness requirements, this work hopes that the model will occupy fewer computing resources and obtain accurate prediction results in a faster time.

Transformer [23] is a general model architecture based on the attention mechanism that has been widely used to solve a variety of problems, but has rarely been tried for prediction tasks [30, 31]. Transformer has three advantages: it can capture long-range dependencies between any two locations in the input sequence; it can generate a context-sensitive representation vector for each location; it can realize parallel computation and improve computational efficiency. Therefore, we believe that the Transformer network model can also be used to build a coke index prediction model.

3.2 Improvement of Transformer Network Model

According to the above requirement, in this work, simplifications and modifications have been made for Transformer, details are as follows.

- Due to less feature dimension and less data of the input data set, we reduce the number of Self-attention layers and Feed-forward layers in the model.
- Since our problem does not involve sequence order information, we remove the part of the model related to positional coding.
- Since we do not need to embed discrete symbols into continuous space, we simplify the parts of the model related to the embedding layer.
- Since we do not need to normalize the inputs and outputs, we remove these parts from the model that are related to normalization operations.

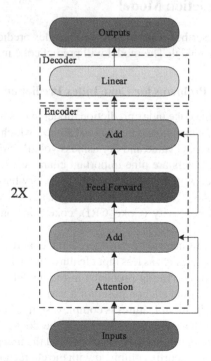

Fig. 3. General framework of the predictive model.

In summary, a lightweight Transformer network structure is proposed to train predictive models, and the overall network structure is mainly composed of Encoder and Decoder, as shown in Fig. 3.

Encoder. In the Transformer network in this article, the encoder section consists of two Transformer Encoder blocks. Its specific structure is shown on the left side of Fig. 3. The first layer is an attention layer, the second layer is the residual connection (Add), the third layer is a feed forward layer (Feed Forward), and the fourth layer is a residual connection (Add).

The attention layer in this work uses scaled dot-production attention [23], and the reason is that this attention can be achieved using highly optimized matrix operations in the computer, and the speed can be greatly improved. It is calculated as shown in formula (5):

$$Attention(Q, K, V) = softmax\left(\frac{QK^T}{\sqrt{d_k}}\right)V \tag{5}$$

In this work, the input feature is a one-dimensional vector consisting of five features of the mixed-coal. After normalization, the vector is sent directly to the self-attention layer. The self-attention layer can learn the complex and nonlinear dependencies between these features and generate a representation vector that is contextually relevant and rich in semantic information for each feature. These representation vectors are fed into a Predictor (linear layer) that predicts coke parameters after coking.

In this work, the ReLU activation function is used to form a feed forward layer to enhance the large-value part of the feature, suppress the small-value part, and thus to strengthen the expression ability of the feature. Its calculation process can be represented by formula (6):

$$FFN(x) = max(0, xW_1 + b_1)W_2 + b_2 \tag{6}$$

Here, W_1, W_2, b_1 is model parameter, x is the input.

Decoder. In this work, a regression model is constructed through a decoder of a linear fully connected layer, and its main function is to transform the features extracted by Encoder into the features to be predicted, and map them to the output layer to obtain the predicted values. It is calculated as shown in formula (7):

$$Decoder(x) = xW_3 + b_3 \tag{7}$$

Here, W_3, b_3 is model parameter, x is the continuous value obtained by the coding layer, and $Decoder(x)$ is the predicted output after regression.

4 Design of Multi-objective Optimization Algorithm for Coal Blending

In the previous section, the coke index prediction model can be used to predict the coke indicators after coking. These indicators affect the quality of coke, the cost of coal blending, and environmental goals.

In this section, we first show how to use the results of the quality prediction model to construct a multi-objective optimization algorithm for coal blending, and then proposes a new allocation upper limit calculate method and a new repair method for the algorithm based on the model.

The proposed methods can be combined with all multi-objective optimization algorithms to improve their performance. The specific steps are: firstly, the calculated upper limit is combined with the initialization step of the multi-objective optimization algorithm, that is, solution searching is only performed within the upper limit, so as to reduce the search space of the algorithm; Then we can use the proposed repair method in the process of algorithm stacking, that is, in each iteration, if the solution violates the constraints, then the repair method will be used to fix the scheme.

4.1 Multi-objective Optimization Model for Coal Blending

Multi-objective Optimization Model. In this paper, the MOP-CB problem is characterized based on three objectives: coke quality, coal blending cost and environmental protection. Based on the coke index prediction model, a multi-objective optimization model for coal blending is proposed, and the model is constructed as follows:

$$
\begin{aligned}
&\max f(x) = (Q, E, -C) \\
&s.t.\ x = (x_1, x_2 \ldots, x_n) \in [0, 1] \\
&x_1 + x_2 \cdots + x_n = 1
\end{aligned}
\tag{8}
$$

Among them, $\widehat{y}_i$ is the coal blending scheme, $x_i \in [0, 1]$ is the ratio of single-coal to the total coal in the furnace, $Q \in \mathbb{R}_0^+$ is the coke quality target, which can be derived from the following formula (9):

$$
Q = \sum_{i=1}^n w_i p_i
\tag{9}
$$

Here, p_i is the coke index parameter obtained after full combustion of coal into the furnace, w_i is its mass weight coefficient. Specific values are derived from historical experience, as shown in Table 2.

$E \in [0, 1]$ is an environmental protection indicator, and its value can be determined by the sulfur content in the coke composition. The higher the sulfur content, the higher the sulfur retention content, and the less sulfur-containing pollution emitted. $C \in \mathbb{R}_0^+$ is the cost target, which can be expressed by the following formula (10):

$$
C = \sum_{i=1}^n c_i x_i
\tag{10}
$$

Here, $c_i \in \mathbb{R}_0^+$ is the market unit price of the ith type of single-coal into the furnace, the specific value is shown in Table 3.

Constraint. In addition to the constraints in formula (8), this work also has strict process constraints on other indicators of coal blended into the furnace, as shown in Table 4:

Table 2. Coke index parameters.

Coke index	Interpretation	Weight coefficient of quality
Coke_A_d	Coke ash	0.15
Coke_S_{td}	Coke sulfur	0.15
Coke_V_d	Coke dry ashless volatile	0.05
Coke_V_{daf}	Coke dry base volatile	0.05
Coke_M_{40}	Coke crush strength	0.15
Coke_M_{10}	Coke wear resistance	0.15
Coke_CRI	Coke reactivity	0.05
Coke_CSR	Coke reaction Strength	0.15
Dur	Coking time	0.10

Table 3. Unit price of single-coal.

type of single-coal	Unit price per ton
LH coking coal	2400
GB coking coal	2500
DL coking coal	3500
HN ordinary ash coking coal	2500
GJ coking coal	3800
High sulfur high heat strong coking coal	3300
LH Low ash and fat coal	2570
HN 1/3 coking coal	2340
LH1/3 coking coal	2360
DT gas coal	2230
BK coke lean coal	3000
Lean coal	2900

The index value of the furnace mixed-coal shown in Table 4 is multiplied by the proportion of different types of single-coal and its corresponding industrial index value, and the calculation process is as follows:

$$P_i = \sum_{j=1}^{n} x_j P_j^i \tag{11}$$

Here, $x_i \in [0, 1]$ is the proportion of jth single-coal to the total coal in the furnace, p_j^i refers to the ith industrial index value of the jth single-coal. Table 5 lists all the industrial index values of different single-coals.

Table 4. Process index constraint of mixed-coal.

Symbol	Index	Lower limit of proportion (%)	Upper limit of proportion (%)
p_1	moisture	10.00	12.00
p_2	A_d	9.75	9.82
p_3	V_d	25.60	27.10
p_4	V_{daf}	28.50	30.00
p_5	S_{td}	0.65	0.72
p_6	G value	80.00	82.00

Table 5. Industrial index value of single-coal.

Type of single-coal	p_1	p_2	p_3	p_4	p_5	p_6
LH coking coal	10.73	10.70	23.70	26.56	0.50	90.9
GB coking coal	11.47	10.70	20.60	23.12	0.40	87.63
DL coking coal	10.84	10.40	19.60	21.87	0.78	80.41
HN ordinary ash coking coal	12.25	10.30	19.90	22.17	0.60	80.83
GJ coking coal	12.02	11.10	16.60	18.72	1.52	74.09
High sulfur high heat strong coking coal	11.52	9.92	20.00	22.21	1.94	82.01
LH Low ash and fat coal	9.52	9.77	29.20	32.31	0.37	90.16
HN 1/3 coking coal	10.75	6.60	33.80	36.19	0.33	83.35
LH1/3 coking coal	9.475	9.10	31.30	34.44	0.40	88.95
DT gas coal	10.48	7.84	34.10	37.01	0.58	79.39
BK coke lean coal	10.77	6.18	18.30	19.51	0.71	83.06
Lean coal	9.662	9.91	15.10	16.80	0.46	49.35

4.2 Acquisition of the Upper Limit of the Proportion of Single-Coal

A closer look at Tables 4 and 5 suggests that every single-coal should have its own allocation limit, because too high a single-coal allocation ratio will cause some indicators of the mixed-coal into the furnace to exceed the process constraints. For example, if LH coking coal accounts for more than 77.8% of the mixed-coal, the G value of the mixed-coal will exceed the upper limit, regardless of the proportion of other single-coals.

Therefore, we believe that each single-coal has its own allocation limit, marked as U_j here, and its ratio to the mixed-coal cannot exceed this upper limit. As long as the upper limits of different types of single-coal can be calculated, the search space of the algorithm can be significantly reduced, so as to reduce the number of invalid solutions generated by the algorithm.

Based on the above considerations, the first necessary step is to calculate the maximum and minimum values of each industrial index for all single-coals, which are recorded here as p_{max}^i and p_{min}^i, and the calculation process is shown in Algorithm 4.1, where n is the number of indicators and m is the number of single-coal types.

Algorithm 4.1 Algorithm flow to obtain the extreme value of each industrial indicator in all single-coals.
1.   for $i := 1$ to n do
2. $p_{max} \leftarrow 1.0e14, p_{min} \leftarrow 0$;
3.   for $j := 1$ to m do
4. $p_{max} \leftarrow \min(p_j^i, p_{max})$;
5. $p_{min} \leftarrow \max(p_j^i, p_{min})$;
6.   end for
7. $p_{max}^i \leftarrow p_{min}, p_{min}^i \leftarrow p_{max}$
8.   end for

Then the algorithm goes through all the p_j^i and compare it with the lower and upper limits of the corresponding index of the single-coal (denoted as p_{low}^i and p_{high}^i in this article). If $p_j^i < p_{low}^i$, it is obvious that the proportion of the single-coal x_i is allocated too much, then the ith industrial index value of the single-coal will not meet the proportion requirement. Hence we can get the formula (12):

$$p_j^i U_j^i + p_{max}^i \left(1 - U_j^i \right) = p_{low}^i \qquad (12)$$

U_j^i is the upper limit of the jth single-coal under the constraints of the ith industrial index, and the formula (13) can be derived:

$$U_j^i = \frac{p_{low}^i - p_{max}^i}{p_j^i - p_{max}^i} \qquad (13)$$

At the same time, if $p_j^i > p_{high}^i$, we can easily draw from the above conclusions:

$$U_j^i = \frac{p_{high}^i - p_{min}^i}{p_j^i - p_{min}^i} \qquad (14)$$

The upper limit of the proportion allocated for each single-coal U_j is the minimum of all U_j^i. The specific process of obtaining is shown in Algorithm 4.2.

Algorithm 4.2 Algorithm flow to obtain the upper limit of allocation proportion of each single-coal.

1. for $j := 1$ to m do
2. $U_j \leftarrow 1.0$
3.   for $i := 1$ to n do
4.   if $p_j^i < p_{low}^i$ then
5. $U_j^i \leftarrow \dfrac{p_{low}^i - p_{max}^i}{p_j^i - p_{max}^i}$
6.   end if
7.   if $p_j^i > p_{high}^i$ then
8. $U_j^i \leftarrow \dfrac{p_{high}^i - p_{min}^i}{p_j^i - p_{min}^i}$
9.   end if
10. $U_j \leftarrow \min(U_j, U_j^i)$
11.   end for
12. end for

4.3 A New Repair Method

After obtaining the allocation limit of every single-coal through the above method, the upper limit can be brought into the MOP-CB problem to obtain a specific solution, but this may produce an unreasonable solution. The reason is the value of the decision variable $(x_1, x_2 \ldots, x_n)$ is frequently changed by the evolutionary operator during the search process of classical multi-objective optimization algorithms. In order to make good use of the upper limit obtained and move the unfeasible solution back to the correct space, in this section, we propose a universal repair method (URM). This method can be combined with any multi-objective optimization algorithm to obtain the corrected solution within the correct space. This gives a greater chance of being translated into viable solutions.

In general, for a pending solution $(x_1, x_2 \ldots, x_n)$, possible violations of constraints can be summarized in the following two points:

- single x_i exceeds the new limit, i.e., $x_i > U_i$.
- the sum of all x_i does not satisfy the constraint, $\sum_{i=1}^{n} x_i \neq 1.0$.

Therefore, whenever a new solution is generated, we need to check whether it satisfies the above two constraints. If not, we need to fix it with URM (the specific method is shown in Algorithm 4.3), and to meet $x_i \leq U_i$ and $\sum_{i=1}^{n} x_i = 1.0$. For convenience, $x_i^{'}$ indicates the value of x_i after the last iteration, which has been checked and fixed, so that the constraint has not been violated, that is, $x_i^{'} \leq U_i$. In addition, x_i^0 represents the value of x_i that was fixed by our URM in the current iteration. If $x_i > U_i$, in order to maintain its increasing trend, we make:

$$x_i^0 \leftarrow rand\left(x_i', U_i\right) \tag{15}$$

Algorithm 4.3 Universal repair method.
1.　　$sum \leftarrow 0, sum' \leftarrow 0, sum_{low}' \leftarrow 0$
2.　　for $i := 1$ to m do
3.　　　if x_i has changed do
4.　　　　if $x_i > U_i$ then
5.　　　　　$x_i^0 \leftarrow rand(x_i', U_i)$
6.　　　　end if
7.　　　end if
8.　　end for
9.　　for $i = 1$ to m do
10.　　$sum \leftarrow sum + x_i$
11.　　if x_i has changed do
12.　　　$sum' \leftarrow sum' + x_i^0$
13.　　　$sum_{low}' \leftarrow sum_{low}' + x_i'$
14.　　end if
15.　　end for
16.　　if $sum \neq 1.0$
17.　　　for $i := 1$ to m do
18.　　　if x_i has changed do
19.　　　$x_i^0 \leftarrow x_i \dfrac{\left(x_i^0 - x_i'\right) * \left(1.0 - (sum - sum') - sum_{low}'\right)}{sum' - sum_{low}'}$
20.　　　end if
21.　　end for
22.　end if

In addition to this, we use *sum* to represent the sum of all x after checking and fixing formula (15). If *sum* $\neq 1.0$, we need to use formula (16) to fix all changed x_i uniformly.

$$x_i^0 \leftarrow x_i' + \frac{\left(x_i^0 - x_i'\right) * \left(1.0 - (sum - sum') - sum_{low}'\right)}{sum' - sum_{low}'} \tag{16}$$

where *sum'* represents the sum of all changed x_i and sum_{low}' represents the sum of all x'. When all changed x_i have been fixed according formula (16), the sum of all x_i will equal 1.0, as evidenced below:

$$
\begin{aligned}
sum_{new} &= \sum_{i=1}^{n} x_i' + sum - sum' \\
&= \sum_{i=1}^{n} \left[x_i' + \frac{\left(x_i^0 - x_i'\right) * \left(1.0 - (sum - sum') - sum_{low}'\right)}{sum' - sum_{low}'} \right] \\
&\quad + sum - sum' \\
&= sum_{low} + \frac{\left(sum' - sum_{low}\right) * \left(1.0 - (sum - sum') - sum_{low}'\right)}{sum' - sum_{low}'} \\
&\quad + sum - sum' \\
&= sum - sum' + sum_{low} + 1.0 - (sum - sum') - sum_{low}' \\
&= 1.0
\end{aligned}
\tag{17}
$$

5   Simulation Experimental Results and Analysis

In this section, we describe two experiments and analyze the results. First, we compare the other three models with the coke index prediction model established by the improved Transformer proposed in this article, and provide a comparison of the four models on three evaluation metrics.

Then, we combine our scheme with four classical multi-objective optimization algorithms and provide experimental results before and after optimization, verifying its effectiveness on three evaluation metrics.

5.1   Hardware Environment

All of the code for this comparison experiment was implemented in Python and C++ and tested on a computer using Intel(R) Core(TM) i5-4460 CPU @ 3.20 GHz, 8.0 GB DDR4 RAM @ 2400 MHz.

5.2   Coke Index Prediction Model Experiment Results and Analysis

Experimental Parameters. In this paper, the improved lightweight Transformer network is used to build a coke index prediction model. The model can well represent the differences and connections between different features and translate them into desired predictions. In the hyper parameters design of the model, the batch size is set to 16, the learning rate is 1E−2, the weight decay is 1E−3, the optimization method is Adam [32], and the training round epoch is 5.

Model Evaluation Metrics. To evaluate the effectivity of the coke index prediction model, MSE (mean square error), RMSE (root mean square error), and MAE (mean absolute error) are used in this work. The specific calculation formulas are as follows:

$$MSE = \frac{1}{n} \sum_{i=1}^{n} (\hat{y}_i - y_i)^2$$

$$RMSE_2 = \sqrt{\frac{1}{n} \sum_{i=1}^{n} (\hat{y}_i - y_i)^2} \tag{18}$$

$$MAE = \frac{1}{n} \sum_{i=1}^{n} |\hat{y}_i - y_i|$$

where n is the number of test samples, $\hat{y}_i$ is the predicted value, y_i is the true value. MSE, RMSE, and MAE are all common indicators for evaluating regression problems, intuitively comparing the difference between predicted and true values, so the smaller the value of all three, the better.

Comparison of Prediction Performance. In this paper, random forest [33] and ridge regression [34] in the field of machine learning, and the multi-layer perception machine in the field of deep learning are used to build coke prediction models respectively, and compare with the coke index prediction model built by improved Transformer proposed in this work. Experiments show that when using the random forest for regression tasks, overfitting is easy to occur because its predicted values cannot exceed the range of training data. Ridge regression may have an underfitting problem. Multilayer perception is prone to overfitting problem. The improved Transformer method proposed in this article effectively avoids the above problems. Table 6 shows a comparison of the three evaluation metrics of the four models.

Table 6. Comparison of prediction performance

	MSE	MAE	RMSE
Random forest	0.768	0.704	0.877
Ridge regression	0.697	0.662	0.835
Multi-layer perception machine	0.740	0.681	0.860 .
Transformer (Ours)	0.692	0.660	0.832

The smaller the values in Table 6, the better the model fits the distribution of the data. It can be seen that the performance of the improved Transformer prediction model proposed in this work is better than that of other models, that to say it is more effective and feasible.

5.3 Experimental Results and Analysis of Multi-objective Optimization Algorithm for Coal Blending

Experimental Parameters. In order to verify the effectiveness of the proposed allocation upper limit scheme and the new constraint treatment scheme, in this work, these schemes were combined with a variety of classical multi-objective optimization algorithms and the results are compared individually, such as NSGA-II [16] algorithm, GDE3 [17] algorithm, SMPSO [18] algorithm and CCMO [19] algorithm. The experimental parameters of each algorithm are set as follows: the crossover rate of the NSGA-II algorithm is 0.9, and the mutation rate is $1.0/n$ (n is the population size). The probability of differential compilation of the GDE3 algorithm is 0.5. For SMPSO, the maximum and minimum values for each learning factor are set to 2.5 and 1.5, respectively, and the velocity of each particle is limited to 0.1. The crossover rate of CCMO is 0.9 and the mutation rate is $1.0/n$. In order to ensure the fairness of the comparison, the population size of each algorithm is 200, and each population is iterated 150 times.

Evaluation Indicators

Capacity Value. The work uses the capacity value [35, 36] metric to evaluate the performance of the algorithm. The capacity value refers to the number of non-dominated solutions that each algorithm finally obtains, and as with the evaluation metric mentioned above, for each instance, we combine the solution sets obtained by 10 independent runs and remove duplicate solutions.

Coverage Value. This work also uses the coverage value (Cv) [37] to evaluate the advantages and disadvantages between solution sets, and Cv can visually reflect how many solutions in the solution set obtained by an algorithm are dominated by the comparison algorithm, so it can be used as a convergence index to compare the quality of solution sets of different algorithms. Suppose we now have two solution sets A and B obtained by different algorithms, and if any target value in a solution in A is not worse than another set of solutions in B, then we can assume that this set of solutions in A overrides the solution in B. Cv(A,B) represents the percentage of A covering B, and if Cv(A,B) > Cv(B,A), it means that the algorithm corresponding to A is better than the algorithm corresponding to B. In order to prove the superiority of the proposed method, we need to combine the solution sets obtained by each algorithm running independently, remove the duplicate solutions, and then compare the coverage values between the merged solution sets [17].

Hypervolume Value. In addition to the above two evaluation indicators, in order to compare the performance between algorithms more comprehensively, this work also compares the hypervolume values [38] of the solution sets obtained by different algorithms. The hypervolume can reflect the volume of the target space between the non-dominated solution set and the reference point, which can well reflect the diversity of solutions in the solution set. In general, a larger hypervolume value indicates a higher quality of the solution set.

However, it is important to note that a reasonable reference point must be found. In order to determine the appropriate reference point, this paper combines the solutions obtained by each algorithm and removes the dominant solutions, and then picks out the worst value of each target among the remaining solutions, and 1.1 times of the value is set as the required reference point [39]. This method has been demonstrated able to effectively balance the convergence and diversity of solution sets.

Experimental Results. *Analysis of Capacity Value.* For the convenience of description, we label the solution sets obtained by conventional NSGA-II, GDE3, SMPSO and CCMO algorithms as A, B, C and D respectively, and label the solution set obtained by these four algorithms the corresponding combined with our method as A+, B+, C+ and D+ respectively. It is worth noting that the capacity value of the solution set obtained by the SMPSO algorithm is 0, that is, it does not produce an effective solution. The reason may be the SMPSO algorithm does not make full use of the information obtained in the calculation process, i.e. only the group optimal and individual optimal information is used in each iteration, and the MOP-CB problem studied in this paper has too many constraints, resulting in the decline of the algorithm's search ability, so the performance of the algorithm itself cannot produce an effective solution. It can be seen from Table 7, in the multi-objective optimization of coal blending, the search performance of the classic multi-objective optimization algorithm combined with our proposed method, is significantly improved. Specifically, the capacity values of the solution sets obtained by the original NSGA-II algorithm, GDE3 algorithm, SMPSO algorithm and CCMO algorithm are 405, 1202, 0 and 929, respectively, while the capacity values obtained by the four algorithms improved by the method proposed in this paper are 3891, 4462, 214 and 929. These results show that the proposed method can effectively enhance the exploration ability of classical multi-objective optimization algorithms, so that they can adapt well to the demand for coal blending and obtain more feasible non-dominated solutions.

Table 7. Results of capacity value.

Example	|A|	|A+|	|B|	|B+|	|C|	|C+|	|D|	|D+|
1	180	**3557**	1237	**4723**	0	**608**	0	**1001**
2	495	**3913**	1268	**4881**	0	**126**	0	**748**
3	316	**3948**	1268	**4328**	0	**302**	42	**1103**
4	310	**4562**	1283	**4314**	0	**263**	156	**996**
5	466	**3491**	1220	**3766**	0	**180**	21	**770**
6	409	**4035**	1090	**4707**	0	**201**	57	**1012**
7	268	**3207**	1127	**4186**	0	**154**	20	**1196**
8	378	**3930**	1027	**4221**	0	**116**	0	**554**
9	763	**3762**	1255	**4559**	0	**157**	1	**1207**
10	466	**3810**	1247	**4938**	0	**31**	93	**704**
Average value	405	**3821**	1202	**4462**	0	214	39	**929**

Analysis of Coverage Value. Table 8 shows the coverage values of various multi-objective optimization algorithms in the field of coal blending optimization on 10 instances. It can be seen that after the optimization by our proposed method, the coverage value of the optimized multi-objective optimization algorithm is better than the original one. Overall, the coverage values of the solution sets obtained by the original NSGA-II algorithm, GDE3 algorithm, SMPSO algorithm and CCMO algorithm are 6.99%, 44.31%, 0.00% and 30.21%, respectively. After the optimization by the method proposed in this work, the coverage values of these four algorithms are 58.91%, 99.62%, 100.00% and 89.94%, respectively. That is, the overall coverage values are increased by about 53%, 55%, 100% and 60%, respectively. The above results show that the multi-objective optimization algorithm optimized by the proposed method has better convergence and can find better non-dominated solutions.

Table 8. Results of coverage values.

Example	|A|	|A+|	|B|	|B+|	|C|	|C+|	|D|	|D+|
1	0.00	**82.22**	39.17	**100.00**	0.00	**100.00**	0.00	**100.00**
2	3.94	**44.65**	53.66	**99.61**	0.00	**100.00**	0.00	**100.00**
3	0.00	**72.15**	44.96	**99.68**	0.00	**100.00**	24.12	**42.86**
4	2.52	**87.10**	27.82	**99.77**	0.00	**100.00**	55.02	**98.08**
5	0.00	**94.42**	49.89	**99.75**	0.00	**100.00**	14.42	**100.00**
6	53.93	**57.46**	30.08	**100.00**	0.00	**100.00**	49.31	**68.42**
7	0.09	**37.69**	50.24	**100.00**	0.00	**100.00**	77.59	**90.00**
8	1.83	**51.06**	48.52	**99.42**	0.00	**100.00**	0.00	**100.00**
9	7.66	**50.59**	46.35	**98.01**	0.00	**100.00**	21.87	**100.00**
10	0.00	**11.80**	52.37	**99.92**	0.00	**100.00**	59.80	**100.00**
Average value	6.99	**58.91**	44.31	**99.62**	0.00	**100.00**	30.21	**89.94**

Analysis of Hypervolume Value. Table 9 shows the Hypervolume results of four multi-objective optimization algorithms on 10 instances in the field of coal blending optimization. It can be seen from the table that the Hypervolume values obtained by the multi-objective optimization algorithm combined with our proposed method are much better than the original multi-objective optimization algorithm. In particular, The HV obtained by the original CCMO algorithm are all 0, indicating that the solutions in the solution set are dominated by reference points or no feasible solutions can be found.

To visualize the distribution of non-dominant solutions and the results of hypervolume results, Fig. 4 shows the performance results of the four groups of algorithms in Example 4. The reason we chose example 4 is that the hypervolume obtained in this example is closest to the overall hypervolume mean value. As can be seen from Fig. 4, compared to the original multi-objective optimization algorithms, the solutions obtained by the optimized algorithms distribute more widely in the objective space and provide more diversity.

From the comparison results of the above indicators, it can be seen that compared with the classic multi-objective optimization algorithm, the algorithm optimized by the

Table 9. Results of hypervolume (mean and standard deviation).

Example	|A|	|A+|	|B|	|B+|	|C|	|C+|	|D|	|D+|
1	53.43 (168.90)	**2284.00 (1667.00)**	952.40 (437.50)	**1129.00 (817.40)**	0.00 (0.00)	**32.29 (72.02)**	0.00 (0.00)	**114.70 (285.10)**
2	2.05 (6.48)	**1701.00 (808.80)**	12.15 (37.46)	**32.94 (96.95)**	0.00 (0.00)	**3.142 (9.936)**	0.00 (0.00)	**603.70 (829.60)**
3	253.40 (521.70)	**2804.00 (1089.00)**	**577.20 (740.70)**	367.60 (683.60)	0.00 (0.00)	**2.592 (8.196)**	0.00 (0.00)	**113.70 (333.80)**
4	2.02 (6.38)	**1876.00 (986.50)**	762.70 (827.10)	**859.40 (742.00)**	0.00 (0.00)	**2.037 (6.44)**	2.04 (6.45)	**37.39 (114.50)**
5	208.60 (354.40)	**1627.00 (1335.00)**	256.20 (334.50)	**333.00 (519.50)**	0.00 (0.00)	**3.124 (9.879)**	0.00 (0.00)	**98.97 (181.30)**
6	103.10 (318.70)	**955.00 (861.80)**	**455.00 (585.60)**	217.60 (379.40)	0.00 (0.00)	**76.72 (235.6)**	136.70 (432.20)	**282.30 (483.60)**
7	205.70 (455.80)	**2304.00 (1659.00)**	92.87 (175.20)	**423.00 (381.00)**	0.00 (0.00)	**10.13 (32.03)**	81.14 (256.60)	**207.10 (273.70)**
8	2.04 (6.45)	**1443.00 (716.00)**	0.17 (0.23)	**50.74 (106.90)**	0.00 (0.00)	**11.23 (31.8)**	0.00 (0.00)	**19.25 (54.19)**
9	42.75 (119.30)	**1545.00 (1126.00)**	1.75 (1.40)	**332.30 (500.30)**	0.00 (0.00)	**2.07 (6.545)**	0.00 (0.00)	**156.50 (254.10)**
10	104.10 (329.30)	**2606.00 (1514.00)**	89.82 (274.60)	**170.90 (304.40)**	0.00 (0.00)	**2.018 (6.381)**	0.00 (0.00)	**316.90 (431.80)**
Average value	97.72 (228.74)	**1914.50 (1176.31)**	320.03 (341.43)	**391.65 (453.15)**	0.00 (0.00)	**15.02 (34.17)**	21.99 (76.53)	**195.05 (324.17)**

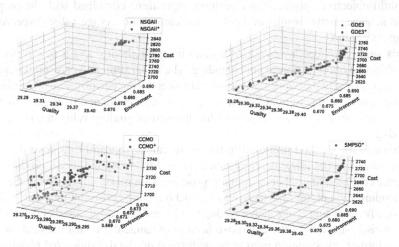

Fig. 4. The non-dominated solutions obtained by algorithms in example 4.

new upper limit and a universal repair method proposed in this work can better meet the coal blending needs of enterprises and provide more and better coal blending solutions for coking plants.

This is because, by calculating the allocation upper limit of each single-coal, we can generate the allocation interval during the initialization of the multi-objective optimization algorithm, which can greatly reduce the exploration space of the multi-objective optimization algorithm.

This paper also proposes a universal repair method, which fixes the values that change in the iteration process of the multi-objective optimization algorithm, and can maintain the evolutionary trend of the algorithm during the repair process.

At the same time, the above experimental results also show that when solving some special multi-objective optimization problems, we can fully make use of the information of the problem itself, to effectively narrow the search interval of the algorithm population, reduce the invalid search in the wrong search range, and significantly improve the ability of the multi-objective optimization algorithm to solve special problems.

6 Summary

Multi-objective optimization of coal blending is a research hotspot of process optimization in coking industry, and its fundamental goal is to study how to effectively match various raw coal without reducing the quality of coke, so as to reduce coal blending costs and reduce pollution. Taking a coking plant as an example, this work first constructs a quality prediction model through Miceforest and Transformer, and then establishes a multi-objective and multi-constraint coal blending optimization model according to the prediction results. Based on the model, a new upper limit and constraint processing scheme is proposed for multi-objective optimization algorithm. Compared with classical multi-objective optimization algorithm, algorithms combined with the proposed method achieves better results in the three indicators of coverage value, hypervolume and capacity value.

This study provides a new idea for coke index prediction and a new method for multi-objective optimization of coal blending. The upper limit and constraint treatment methods proposed in this work can significantly improve the performance of the classical multi-objective optimization algorithm, so as to provide more and better coal blending solutions for coal enterprises. This work has theoretical guiding value in coal blending for coking.

Although the method proposed in this work can significantly improve the ability of multi-objective optimization algorithm to solve MCP-CB, and it will produce more and better coal blending schemes for enterprise decision makers, however, in the actual coal blending and coking of enterprises, the coal blending constraint index may change dynamically according to the actual coking results and the current market demand, that is, the decision-makers of the enterprise need to dynamically adjust the coal blending ratio, so further investigation need to be performed on the dynamic coal blending and the coking problem of the enterprise.

References

1. Pang, K.L., Zheng, Y.Z.: Application of intelligent coal blending for coking in coking industry and its prospect. Angang Technol. **438**, 101–106 (2022)
2. Yuan, Y., Qu, Q., Chen, L., et al.: Modeling and optimization of coal blending and coking costs using coal petrography. Inf. Sci. **522**, 49–68 (2020)
3. Shen, Y., Hu, Y., Wang, M., et al.: Speciation and thermal transformation of sulfur forms in high-sulfur coal and its utilization in coal-blending coking process: a review. Chin. J. Chem. Eng. **35**, 70–82 (2021)
4. Zi, J., Jin, F., Zhao, J., et al.: A multi-objective simulated annealing algorithm-based coal blending optimization approach in coking process. In: 2020 IEEE International Conference on Dependable, Autonomic and Secure Computing, International Conference on Pervasive Intelligence and Computing, International Conference on Cloud and Big Data Computing, International Conference on Cyber Science and Technology Congress (DASC/PiCom/CBDCom/CyberSciTech), pp. 103–109. IEEE (2020)
5. Janiesch, C., Zschech, P., Heinrich, K.: Machine learning and deep learning. Electron. Mark. **31**(3), 685–695 (2021). https://doi.org/10.1007/s12525-021-00475-2
6. Guo, P., Liu, Q., Yu, S., et al.: A transformer with layer-cross decoding for remaining useful life prediction. J. Supercomput. (2023). https://doi.org/10.1007/s11227-023-05126-1
7. Liu, Y., Zhang, J., Fang, L., et al.: Multimodal motion prediction with stacked transformers. In: Proceedings of the IEEE/CVF Conference on Computer Vision and Pattern Recognition, pp. 7577–7586 (2021)
8. Bao, Z.Q., Lu, C.W., Zhang, S., et al.: Research on coke quality prediction model based on TSSA-SVR model. China Min. Mag. **31**(6), 86–92 (2022)
9. Tao, W.H., Yuan, Z.B.: Prediction model of coke quality based on DE-BP neural network. J. Syst. Simul. **30**(05), 1650–1656 (2018)
10. Lu, J.W., Lu, P.S., Jiang, X., et al.: Prediction of coke quality with multi-layer neural network. Sci. Technol. Baotou Steel **46**(1), 14–17 (2020)
11. Liu, L.B., Yang, S., Wang, Z.J., et al.: Prediction of coke quality based on improved WOA-LSTM. CIESC J. **73**(3), 1291–1299 (2022)
12. Gers, F.A., Schmidhuber, J., Cummins, F.: Learning to forget: continual prediction with LSTM. Neural Comput. **12**(10), 2451–2471 (2000)
13. Yu, Y., Si, X., Hu, C., et al.: A review of recurrent neural networks: LSTM cells and network architectures. Neural Comput. **31**(7), 1235–1270 (2019)
14. Greff, K., Srivastava, R.K., Koutník, J., et al.: LSTM: a search space odyssey. IEEE Trans. Neural Netw. Learn. Syst. **28**(10), 2222–2232 (2016)
15. Jia, X.Z., Chen, Y., Lu, J.W.: Analysis on reasons affecting predictive effects of coke quality. Sci. Technol. Baotou Steel **46**(2), 5–24 (2020)
16. Deb, K., Pratap, A., Agarwal, S., et al.: A fast and elitist multiobjective genetic algorithm: NSGA-II. IEEE Trans. Evol. Comput. **6**(2), 182–197 (2002)
17. Kukkonen, S., Lampinen, J.: GDE3: the third evolution step of generalized differential evolution. In: 2005 IEEE Congress on Evolutionary Computation, pp. 443–450 (2005)
18. Nebro, A.J., Durillo, J.J., Garcia-Nieto, J., etal.: A new PSO-based metaheuristic for multi-objective optimization. In: Proceedings of the IEEE Symposium on Computational Intelligence in Multi-criteria Decision-Making, pp. 66–73 (2009)
19. Tian, Y., Zhang, T., Xiao, J., et al.: A coevolutionary framework for constrained multi-objective optimization problems. IEEE Trans. Evol. Comput. **25**(1), 102–116 (2021)
20. Han, K., Xiao, A., Wu, E., et al.: Transformer in transformer. Adv. Neural. Inf. Process. Syst. **34**, 15908–15919 (2021)

21. Popel, M., Bojar, O.: Training tips for the transformer model. Comput. Lang. (2018). https://doi.org/10.2478/pralin-2018-0002
22. Xiong, R., Yang, Y., He, D., et al.: On layer normalization in the transformer architecture. In: International Conference on Machine Learning, pp. 10524–10533 (2020)
23. Vaswani, A., Shazeer, N., Parmar, N., et al.: Attention is all you need. In: NIPS'17: Proceedings of the 31st International Conference on Neural Information Processing Systems, pp. 6000–6010 (2017)
24. Wilson, S.V., Cebere, B., Myatt, J., et al.: Another Sam Wilson/miceforest: Release for Zenodo (2022). https://doi.org/10.5281/zenodo.7428632
25. Duchesnay, E., Lofstedt, T., Younes, F.: Statistics and Machine Learning in Python. Engineering School, France. ffhal-03038776v3f (2021)
26. Mishra, P., Mani, K.D., Johri, P., et al.: FCMI: feature correlation based missing data imputation. arXiv preprint, arXiv:2107.00100 (2021)
27. de Goeij, M.C.M., van Diepen, M., Jager, K.J., et al.: Multiple imputation: dealing with missing data. Nephrol. Dial. Transplant. 28(10), 2415–2420 (2013)
28. Stekhoven, D.J., Bühlmann, P.: MissForest-non-parametric missing value imputation for mixed-type data. Bioinformatics 28(1), 112–118 (2012)
29. Chai, T., Draxler, R.R.: Root mean square error (RMSE) or mean absolute error (MAE)?-Arguments against avoiding RMSE in the literature. Geosci. Model Dev. 7(3), 1247–1250 (2014)
30. Kim, N.W., Lee, H.Y., Lee, J.G., et al.: Transformer based prediction method for solar power generation data. In: 2021 International Conference on Information and Communication Technology Convergence (ICTC), pp. 7–9. IEEE (2021)
31. Cholakov, R., Kolev, T.: Transformers predicting the future. Applying attention in next-frame and time series forecasting. arXiv preprint arXiv:2108.08224 (2021)
32. Kingma, D.P., Ba, J.: Adam: a method for stochastic optimization. arXiv preprint arXiv:1412.6980 (2014)
33. Rigatti, S.J.: Random forest. J. Insurance Med. 47(1), 31–39 (2017)
34. McDonald, G.C.: Ridge regression. Wiley Interdisc. Rev. Comput. Stat. 1(1), 93–100 (2009)
35. Li, M., Chen, T., Yao, X.: How to evaluate solutions in pareto-based search-based software engineering? A critical review and methodological guidance. IEEE Trans. Softw. Eng. 99, 1 (2020)
36. van Veldhuizen, D.A., Lamont, G.B.: On measuring multiobjective evolutionary algorithm performance. In: Proceedings of the IEEE Congress on Evolutionary Computation, pp. 204–211 (2000)
37. Zitzler, E., Thiele, L.: Multiobjective evolutionary algorithms: a comparison case study and the strength pareto approach. IEEE Trans. Evol. Comput. 3(4), 257–271 (1999)
38. Zitzler, E., Thiele, L.: Multiobjective optimization using evolutionary algorithms-a comparative case study. In: Proceedings of the 5th International Conference on Parallel Problem Solving from Nature, pp. 292–301 (1998)
39. Li, M., Yao, X.: Quality evaluation of solution sets in multiobjective optimisation: a survey. ACM Comput. Surv. 52(2), Article no. 26 (2019)

Social Network and Group Behavior

Research on the Public Value of Government Social Media Content and Communication Strategies Under "Infodemic"

Lianren Wu[1](✉), Yanan Hu[2], Jinjir Li[3], Panwei Xiang[2], and Jiayin Qi[1]

[1] School of Cyberspace Security, Guangzhou University, Guangzhou 510006, China
Lianrenwu@suibe.edu.cn
[2] Shanghai University of International Business and Economics, Shanghai 200336, China
[3] School of Tourism Management, Shanghai Normal University, Shanghai 200233, China

Abstract. After the outbreak of the COVID-19, there is an overload of misinformation related to the epidemic, causing the dangerous phenomenon of "infodemic" where it is impossible to distinguish the true from the false. The current problem faced is that the public is viciously involved in the spread of rumors, as well as disinformation that spreads much faster and more widely than correct information. False information is more likely to promote public engagement because of its high emotional intensity and its ability to fill the public's information needs in a timely manner. Government social media, such as microblogging and WeChat accounts of official agencies, serve as the main sources for releasing information on the progress of the epidemic, dispelling rumors, popularizing science and spreading positive energy. How should government social media promote public engagement to achieve infodemic management? this study takes 2827 tweets related to the epidemic posted by official government microblogging account, "Wuhan Publishing", and examines the factors and mechanisms that promote public engagement from the perspective of public value management theory and public sentiment. The theoretical contributions of this study are (1) further exploring the influencing factors and mechanisms of public engagement in government social media from the perspective of public value preferences and social emotional safety, and (2) expanding the application of public value management theory and social emotional safety theory in emergency management.

Keywords: Infodemic · Government Social Media · Public Engagement · Public Value · Public Sentiment · Communication Strategies

1 Introduction

At the beginning of COVID-19, the negative public opinion topics triggered by public engagement were constantly and exceedingly hot, adding to the burden of the government in carrying out public crisis management. Many unscrupulous elements with bad intentions and attempts to destabilize society took advantage of the situation to spread disturbing conspiracy theories. Netizen in extreme anxiety and lack of professional knowledge are more likely to believe rumors and spread them, generating a large number of vicious public engagement behaviors, thus increasing social instability. It is gratifying to see that the public not only supports the fight against the epidemic in terms of human, financial and material resources, but also plays a very important role in the fight against the "infodemic" (Lazer et al. 2018).

Although different conclusions have been proposed (Juul and Ugander 2021), disinformation is more likely to promote public engagement in information dissemination because of its high emotional intensity and its ability to fill the public's information needs in a timely manner (Chen et al., 2020). How should government social media (GSM), which publishes official information and accurate information, promote benign public engagement and improve the effectiveness of GSM crisis communication? This question has been an important concern for scholars and practice managers.

To achieve benign public engagement in GSM and reach the governance of disinformation, first, it is necessary to analyze the public value of the content provided by GSM and its satisfaction of public value preferences, and on this basis, explore the mechanism of public engagement in GSM.

In recent years, although studies related to public engagement in social media have received extensive attention (Chen et al. 2020; Li, et al. 2022), especially studies on the antecedents of public engagement in social media, for example, Chen et al. (2020) analyzed the effects of media richness, dialogic loop, content type and emotional valence on public engagement. In the context of the COVID-19 crisis, this paper investigates the key factors and mechanisms of public engagement in GSM from the perspectives of public value management theory, persuasion theory and public sentiment, combining elaboration likelihood model (ELM) and heuristic systematic model (HSM), and proposes strategies to promote public engagement in GSM to achieve soft governance of "infodemic". Specifically, this paper focuses on addressing the following three questions. (1) What are the public value characteristics of GSM content in COVID-19 crisis communication? (2) What is the impact of public value types of GSM content on public engagement? (3) Does public sentiment play a moderating role between public value types and public engagement? That is, does the initial public sentiment toward GSM content promote subsequent public engagement behavior (retweets, comments, and likes), and does it create an information cascade or herding effect?

2   Review of Related Research

2.1   Research on GSM and Crisis Management

During public crises, government agencies around the world have historically used social media to disseminate information, observe public behavior and opinions, channel and dispel rumors, build social cohesion, and mobilize resource flows (Zhang et al. 2019; Chon and Kim 2022). For example, Graham et al. (2015) used survey data collected from more than 300 local government agencies in the United States to study the role of social media tools for crisis communication. The results showed that the degree of social media use, rather than the number of tools used, was positively associated with the ability of local government agencies to control crisis situations. In particular, GSM also played an important role during this COVID-19 crisis. For example, Li et al. (2022) studied the role of GSM for crisis coordination during COVID-19 in Wuhan and found that social media can provide a venue for the government to not only address information overload, but also to mitigate friction between levels of government. Tang et al. (2021) studied how GSM protects against fraud during COVID-19 and showed that concerned GSM users influence their information security behavior through perceived severity and perceived vulnerability. Baniamin (2021) analyzed different initiatives taken by citizens based on social media during the COVID-19 crisis in Bangladesh. Górska et al. (2022) analyzed more than 3000 postings by local governments in Poland on social media and found three types of rhetorical strategies that easily resonate with the public and thus enhance communication.

2.2 Public Engagement in GSM

In the "infodemic" context, the purpose of GSM is to disseminate information about government agencies' actions and strategies to combat COVID-19, to communicate the latest COVID-19 news, to effectively control the spread of disinformation, and to provide a favorable public opinion environment for the fight against of COVID-19. The premise of all these purposes is the need for public engagement in GSM, not for the public to engagement in other social media platforms full of disinformation. Current research on public engagement in GSM can be divided into two aspects.

One aspect is the study of the effectiveness of public engagement in GSM, which assesses the effectiveness of public engagement in GSM by using quantitative indicators from social media platforms, such as the number of shares or retweets, likes and comments (Agostino and Arnaboldi 2016). However, scholars have different insights on the contribution of the three behaviors of retweeting, commenting, and liking, as well as the level of individual effort. Some scholars believe that liking is the behavior with the lowest contribution and individual effort, called low level of engagement (LLoE), commenting is the behavior with medium contribution and individual effort, called medium level of engagement (MLoE), and retweeting is the behavior with the highest contribution and individual effort, called high level of engagement (HLoE) (Kim and Yang 2017).

Some scholars hold the opposite view (Yoon et al., 2018), arguing that "liking" implies approval and "retweeting" aims to share with others, and they are both characterized as "shallow engagement". This is because clicking on the "like" or "retweet" button does not require much effort and is merely evidence that the user has viewed or browsed the social media content. However, the term "comment" is based on concepts such as interpretation and creation, and is considered to be a form of "profound engagement"; it can be used as real evidence of effort, proving that the user has not only seen the social media content and also have enough enthusiasm to take action. On the other hand, there is the study of the factors and mechanisms influencing public engagement in GSM. Especially in the context of COVID-19, this issue has again received extensive attention from scholars in different disciplines (Yang et al. 2021; Kim et al. 2022). Among them, information timeliness (Li et al. 2022), information type and media richness (Chen et al. 2020), Trusting-Building Strategies (Ngai et al., 2022), information sources credibility (Shah and Wei 2022) and emotions (Wu et al. 2022a, 2022b; Ngai et al. 2022; Hagemann and Abramova 2023) are important antecedents that influence public engagement in GSM. Table 1 below lists representative literature in the field of public engagement in GSM in recent years.

Table 1. Summary of representative literature in the field of public engagement in GSM

Authors & year	Research Background	Research Variables & Theory & Model
Chen et al. (2023)	COVID-19; public engagement; conspiracy theories	SIDE, social identity theory
Li et al. (2022)	COVID-19; public engagement; false information	Information timeliness; information richness; breath; depth; NLP model
Dong et al. (2022)	COVID-19; public engagement	Online official information; participation of entertainers
Ngai et al. (2022)	COVID-19; public engagement; Trust-Building strategies	Accessibility to external links; provision of emotional support; information on skills and resources
He (2022)	COVID-19;youth; engagement in government-generated videos	Entertainment education; collaborative governance; content topic; emotion valence
Feng (2021)	Diffusion of government micro-blogs	City names; content topic; emotional words content richness the homogeneity of texts .
Luo (2021)	COVID-19;Public engagement; People's Daily	Emotional valence; post content
Islm (2021)	COVID-19;Public engagement; comparative study	Information-seeking; political benefits; self-development; altruism; perceived reciprocity; perceived connectivity
Guo (2021)	2015 Tianjin explosions; citizens participate; civic voluntarism	Perceived reciprocity; emotional support; external political efficacy; rumor control; civic shills; mobilization
Pang (2021)	COVID-19; public engagement; Facebook; Macao	Word frequency and content analysis
Chen (2020)	COVID-19; citizen engagement; Healthy China	Media richness; dialogic loop; content type; emotional valence

3   Research Hypotheses and Model

3.1   Public Values and Public Engagement in GSMA

Facing the sudden outbreak of public crisis events, how the government can promote public engagement through social media so as to improve the effectiveness of crisis communication is an urgent practical problem and an important theoretical proposition.

Numerous scholars have explored this issue from different theoretical perspectives. Among them, the public value theory paradigm has been proposed to provide a new way of thinking to explain this issue (Rosenbloom, 2017). In recent years, the public value approach has been used to measure the success of e-government. Meanwhile, social media, as a public value domain, has gained extensive scholarly attention (Irfan et al., 2019). How GSM serves the public and creates public value is a concern for government agencies. Therefore, the classification of public value types is the premise of this study. Referring to existing studies, this paper classifies the types of public values provided by GSM postings during the COVID-19 crisis into mission-based public values and non-mission-based public values.

Mission-based public values are the core activities and main objectives of government agencies, which are generally derived from policy and regulatory documents and are mandatory. Nonmission-based public values are those that are not mandated by policy and are additional values that the public expects a "good government" to provide. Based on the above definition, mission-based public values are divided into three dimensions of responsibility, efficiency, and truth, which are reflected in four action indicators: anti-epidemic defense, living services, epidemic briefing, and truth release. The nonmission-based public values were categorized into two dimensions of caring and helping, which are reflected in four action indicators: emotional support, morale boosting, scientific knowledge, and social concern.

Mission-based public values are the basic requirements that government agencies need to achieve and should meet the public value preferences. In public health crisis events, the public will access relevant information through official GSM accounts or government agency social networking sites (Shah and Wei 2022; Li et al. 2022).

At this point, if the GSMA does not provide authoritative information on crisis response and management, there will be a lot of rumors and false information in cyberspace, leading to the phenomenon of "infodemic" (Kreps and Kriner 2022). This will cause public anxiety and panic and make it more difficult for government agencies to deal with crisis events (Kim et al. 2022).

Reading and sharing GSMA postings enables the public to get the latest news and alleviate anxiety and panic. Therefore, GSMA postings based on mission-based public values promote public motivation to engage (e.g., motivation to retweet, comment, and like). Nonmission-based public values, which are "soft requirements" beyond policy prescriptions, also resonate with the public and trigger positive reactions and engagement behaviors (Wu et al., 2022). Based on the above analysis, this paper proposes hypothesis H1.

Hypothesis 1: Types of Public Value in GSM postings will have significantly differentiated effects on public engagement in retweeting (H1a), commenting (H1b), and liking(H1c).

3.2 The Language of GSM Postings

The impact of linguistic features of postings on social media engagement has received attention and research in the marketing field, e.g. linguistic features on B2B brand engagement on social media (Pitt et al. 2019; Deng et al. 2021a, 2021b), express certainty (Pezzuti et al. 2021). If the posting is in the form of a video, the tone of voice also affects the user's engagement and final decision (Oh and Ki 2019).

The linguistic characteristics of GSM postings are also important. Among them is the informal and less complex relationship-oriented (or socially oriented) type (Otterbacher et al. 2017), which can be used to soften hierarchical power relations, convey a sense of intimacy, and reduce social distance. There is also a formal and complex information-oriented (or task-oriented) type, where the language is more similar to written language. It has been concluded in the field of marketing and business management that relationship-oriented language types can positively influence consumer engagement (Rennekamp and Witz 2020; Gesselman et al. 2019). Therefore, this study proposes the following hypothesis 2 for the language of GSM postings.

Hypothesis 2: Types of language in GSMA postings will have significantly differentiated effects on public engagement in retweeting (H2a), commenting (H2b), and liking(H2c).

3.3   The Source of GSM Postings

The source and credibility of information has a critical impact on user behavior and decision making. For example, in consumer decisions, expert reviews are more helpful for consumers to make purchase decisions compared to consumer reviews (Filieri et al. 2018), and the credibility of the information source affects e-WOM adoption and consumer purchase intentions (Ismagilova et al. 2020). The source of information is also very important in public crisis communication. Reliable sources of information can help the public to have an accurate understanding of the crisis situation (Qazi et al. 2020).

In China, administrative regions or management levels are generally divided into central, provincial and municipal levels, and more detailed ones such as district (county) levels. Is there a difference between GSM postings originating from different levels of management for the same event in terms of promoting public engagement? This question has not been explored by scholars.

Local governments will have more detailed information about an event due to their proximity to the event location. Therefore, local government social media postings serve as an important source of information and facilitate public engagement. The authors argue that local-level GSM postings (provincial and municipal) promote public engagement more than central-level GSM postings in crisis event contexts. Therefore, we propose hypothesis 3 and 4.

Hypothesis 3: The source of GSMA postings will have significantly differentiated effects on public engagement in retweeting (H3a), commenting (H3b), and liking(H3c).

Hypothesis 4: The level of GSMA posting will negatively affect public engagement in retweeting (H4a), commenting (H4b) and liking (H4c).

3.4   Media Richness and Public Engagement

The posting of GSM is usually presented in the style of texts, pictures or videos, and their media richness ranges from low to high (Yue et al. 2019). Media richness theory has been widely studied in various fields. (Chen and Chang 2018; Lee and Borah 2020).Regarding the relationship between media richness and public engagement, the existing results are quite controversial (Chen et al., 2020; Li et al., 2022). Some scholars argue that as the media richness of postings increases, there is a corresponding increase in the number of retweets and a subsequent decrease in the number of comments and likes (Ji et al. 2019), or no effect (Kim and Yang 2017). Other scholars argue that low media-rich postings (e.g., text) are more likely to attract users' attention and sharing (Lee and Xu 2018). Under a crisis event, the public is more concerned about whether the information satisfies their needs and reduces uncertainty.

In COVID-19 crisis, the authors argue that as the richness of the media increases, the more content is provided, the more public uncertainty is removed and thus public sharing is facilitated. However, the textual format is more accurate in conveying key information and describing government crisis management measures. In this case, postings in text form are more likely to promote public comments and likes than those containing images or videos. Based on this, this paper proposes hypothesis 5.

Hypothesis 5. The style of GSMA postings will have significantly differentiated effects on public engagement in retweeting (H5a), commenting (H5b) and liking (H5c).

3.5 Dialogue Strategies and Public Engagement

GSM is widely used as a tool for government agencies to disseminate information. However, through social media, the interaction between government agencies and the public is inadequate (Zheng and Zheng 2014). It is currently unknown whether government agencies interacting with the public on social media will promote public engagement. However, it has been shown that the quality of government agencies' responses to public issues is important and promotes the public's shift to GSM (Gintova 2019), and the adoption of dialogic strategies has a positive impact on public engagement (Chen et al. 2020). Establishing dialogue with the public through dialogic communication framework is increasingly valued by various organizations (Wang and Yang 2020). Government agencies also use dialogic communication as an effective social media strategy (Lai et al. 2020). Therefore, we propose hypothesis 6.

Hypothesis 6: The adoption of dialogue strategies in GSMA will positively influence public engagement in retweeting (H6a), commenting (H6b), and liking(H6c).

3.6 The Moderating Effect of Public Sentiment (PS)

The sentiments embedded in social media postings are contagious, especially negative sentiments. Research findings from multiple disciplines have indicated the presence of negative bias in informational decision making (Yin et al. 2014). According to the social sharing theory of emotions, people who experience sentiments tend to be more eager to share and talk. Sentiments trigger social sharing: individuals can regulate their emotional state through sentiments sharing. Moreover, the diffusion of sentiments can lead to group polarization and information cascading phenomena (Tokita et al. 2021). It has been more consistently argued in the literature that content containing sentiments promotes public social media engagement behavior. More critically, studies have discussed the sentiments contained in the content of postings (Xu and Zhang 2018; Chen et al. 2020), and few studies have explored the sentiments generated by the public in response to GSM postings and the impact of sentiments on subsequent public engagement behavior. This paper will systematically investigate this issue, and further, the authors argue that mission-based public value GSM postings are more likely to promote public engagement in positive public sentiments (i.e., public information need preferences are met) (Wu et al. 2022a, 2022b). In negative public sentiments (i.e., public information need preferences are not met), the public reflects dissatisfaction with government agencies by discussing non-mission-based topics such as caring and helping more often. The government is accused of not only failing to meet public needs in mission-based public values, but also failing to fulfill even non-mission-based public values. At this point, the GSMA postings of non-mission public values caused more public engagement. We found an interaction effect between public value types and public sentiments, so we propose the following hypothesis 7 and 8.

Hypothesis 7: The public sentiment of GSMA postings will have significantly differentiated effects on public engagement in retweeting (H7a), commenting (H7b) and liking (H7c).

Hypothesis 8: The public sentiment of GSMA postings has a moderating effect between public values and public engagement in retweeting (H8a), commenting (H8b) and liking (H8c).

Based on the above theories and assumptions, the research model of this paper is shown in Fig. 1.

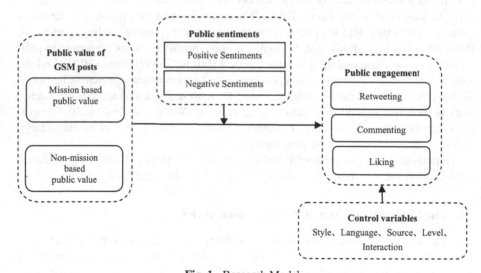

Fig. 1. Research Model

4   Study Design and Hypothesis Testing

4.1   Data Collection and Processing

This study collected the COVID-19 related microblogs posted by the official Sina Weibo account of Wuhan City, Hubei Province from January 1, 2020 to April 30, 2020. A total of 2827 tweets were collected. For each tweet, the information collected includes: text content, number of retweets, comments and likes, etc. Also, the URL of the image or video is captured to determine the media type of the posting (i.e., text, image, or video). The hashtag "#topic" and mentions of other Weibo accounts "@somebody" for each tweet were also identified and extracted.

In addition, because this study was to calculate public sentiment through public comments on GSM tweets, information on the top 10 hottest comments of each tweet was also collected. This includes information such as the time the comment was posted, the content of the comment, and the number of likes on the comment.

A total of 26,895 comments were collected. The data were pre-processed to eliminate microblogs with less than 10 comments, and 2,552 microblogs were retained after processing the data from "Wuhan Publishing". These microblogs contain a total of 6,272 topics, including 2,430 non-mission based topics and 3,822 mission based topics. The number of topics in each action indicator and the mean value of public sentiment are shown in Fig. 2.

(The specific calculation process of the public sentiment value is described in Sect. 4.2). The COVID-19 epidemic in Wuhan was divided into four phases, namely, the warning phase, the outbreak phase, the persistent phase, and the recovery phase, and the mean value of positive and negative public sentiment in each phase are shown in Fig. 2.

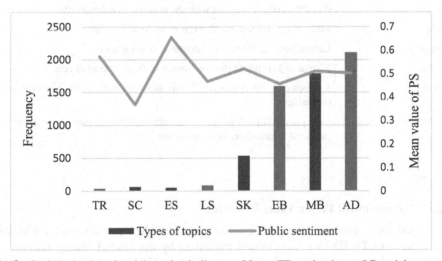

Fig. 2. Statistical values for eight action indicators (Notes: TR-truth release, SC-social concern, ES-emotional support, LS-Living services, SK-scientific knowledge, EB-epidemic briefing, MB-morale boosting, AD - anti-epidemic defense)

Figure 2 shows the eight action indicators for mission-based public values and non-mission-based public values, as well as the frequency of topics related to each action indicator and the mean value of public sentiment. The four red bars (TR, LS, EB, and AD) represent mission-based public values, and their topic frequencies are 37,85,1595 and 2105, respectively. The four blue bars (SC, ES, SK, and MB) represent non-mission-based public values, and their topic frequencies are 60,49,533 and 1788, respectively.

Public comments on tweets related to emotional support (ES) are positive, with the highest mean value of public sentiment at 0.656. Public comments on tweets related to social concern (SC) are negative, with the lowest mean value of public sentiment at 0.368.

4.2 Variable Description

Table 2 describes the main variables of this study.

Table 2. Description of main variables

Variables	Description and measurement
Retweeting Commenting Liking	Number of retweets received by GSM postings Number of comments received by GSM postings Number of likes received by GSM postings
Public Sentiment (PS)	PS = 1, indicating positive PS for GSM postings; PS = 0, indicating negative PS
Public Value (PV)	PV = 1, when the GSM posting is consistent with the mission-based PV; PV = 0 is consistent with the non-mission-based PV
Style	Style = 1, text; Style = 2, Figure; Style = 3, video
Language	Language = 1, formal; Language = 0, informal。
Source	Source = 1, original tweets; Source = 0, retweeted tweets
Level	1 indicates municipal level; 2 indicates provincial level; 3 indicates central level
Dialogue	1 means the GSMA adoption interactive dialogue strategy with the public, 0 means there is no adoption

4.2.1 Calculation of Public Value Variables

First, a validation analysis of the public value types of GSMA postings was conducted. The topics of COVID-19 related tweets published by the official Weibo account of "Wuhan Publishing" were counted and classified into public value types, and the results are shown in Appendix 1. The results verified the completeness and mutual exclusivity of the mission-based and non-mission-based public value sets constructed in Table 1, and the constructed public value sets were appropriate.

Second, the public value consistency of GSMA postings is calculated and determined. According to the topics contained in GSMA postings, if only one topic is contained, it can be determined according to Table 1. When it is a task-based public value topic, then GSMA postings are consistent with task-based public value, and thus the variable PV = 1. Similarly, non-task-based public value can be determined. This study used four graduate students, one in each group of two, and two groups to analyze and determine the public value of GSMA postings. If the GSMA postings contain multiple topics, the cosine similarity measure, which is commonly used to calculate text similarity for text classification (Xia et al. 2015; Park et al. 2020), is used. The initial feature vector of task-based and non-task-based public values of GSMA postings is set as $X(0) = (1, 1, 1, 1)$. The actual mission-based public value feature vector $X_{mission}(i) = (x_{i1}, x_{i2}, x_{i3}, x_{i4})$ and the non-mission-based public value feature vector $Xnonmission(i) = (x_{i1}, x_{i2}, x_{i3}, x_{i4})$ are obtained based on the topics contained in the GSMA postings.

Finally, Eq. (1) was used to calculate the consistency of GSMA postings with mission-based public values, and Eq. (2) was used to calculate the consistency of GSMA postings with non-mission-based public values.

$$\text{Cos}_{mission}(X(0), X(i)) = \frac{X(0) \cdot X_{mission}(i)}{\|X(0)\| \|X_{mission}(i)\|} \tag{1}$$

$$\text{Cos}_{nonmission}(X(0), X(i)) = \frac{X(0) \cdot X_{nonmission}(i)}{\|X(0)\| \|X_{nonmission}(i)\|} \tag{2}$$

Results between 0 and 1, comparing the values of $\text{Cos}_{mission}(X(0), X(i))$ and $\text{Cos}_{nonmission}(X(0), X(i))$, determine the type of public value of GSMA postings.

4.2.2 Calculation of Public Sentiment Variables

In this study, 10 popular comments received by GSMA postings were collected, and the data collected included the content of the comments, the timing of the comments, and the number of likes on the comments. Among the collected data, we found that the public comments on GSMA postings were short and contained more implicit and sarcastic words. The accuracy of the calculated results is low when using the sentiment analysis method of machine learning. Considering the small size of the dataset in this study, a manual annotation method was used to classify public sentiment into "positive", "neutral" and "negative". Four graduate students were used to process the data, with two groups of two each. Then, for each GSMA tweet, the total number of likes for the "positive" comments is $Likes(positive)$, and the total number of likes for the tweet is $Likes(total)$, then the "positive" public sentiment value of the GSMA tweet is.

$$PS = Likes(positive)/Likes(total) \tag{3}$$

The value of PS ranges from 0 to 1, the closer the value is to 1, the more "positive" the public sentiment is. On the contrary, the closer the value is to 0, the more "negative" the public sentiment is. In the example in Table 5, the number of likes for the "positive" comments is 759 and the total number of likes for the comments on the tweet is 1333. Therefore, the public sentiment of the tweet is 759/1333 = 0.5694 and the public sentiment of the tweet is positive.

4.3 Hypothesis Test

Since the number of retweets, comments and likes received by GSMA postings do not obey a normal distribution, a negative binomial regression model is used in this paper. Table 3 shows the estimation results of the negative binomial regression model, and according to the Omnibus test, models 1 to 6 pass the test, indicating that it is appropriate to use the negative binomial regression model.

The results from Models 1, 3 and 5 show that the type of public value of GSMA postings has a significant effect on public retweets ($\beta = 0.154$, $p < 0.01$) and public comments ($\beta = -0.369$, $p < 0.001$), while the effect on public comments ($\beta = -0.019$, $p > 0.05$) is not significant. **Hypothesis 1 was partially supported**. Mission-based public values promote high levels of public engagement (retweeting behavior) more than non-mission-based public values, non-mission-based public values promote low levels of engagement (liking behavior) more than mission-based public values, while for medium levels of engagement (commenting behavior), mission-based public values are not significantly different from non-mission-based public values.

The type of language of GSMA postings had a significant effect on public retweeting behavior ($\beta = 0.575$, $p < 0.001$), public commenting behavior ($\beta = 0.484$, $p < 0.001$), and public liking behavior ($\beta = 0.281$, $p < 0.001$), and **hypothesis 2 was supported**. The informal and less complex socially oriented communication approach has clear advantages for promoting public engagement.

The source of GSMA postings had a significantly differentiated effect on public retweeting ($\beta = 0.165$, $p < 0.01$), commenting ($\beta = 0.385$, $p < 0.001$) and liking ($\beta = 0.235$, $p < 0.001$). **Hypothesis 3 was supported** and original postings promote better public engagement than retweeted postings. The level of GSMA posting will negatively affect public engagement in retweeting ($\beta = -0.841$, $p < 0.001$), commenting ($\beta = -0.403$, $p < 0.001$) and liking ($\beta = -0.507$, $p < 0.001$), **Hypothesis 4 was supported.**

The style of GSMA postings had a significantly differentiated effects on public retweeting ($\beta = -0.111$, $p < 0.01$) and commenting ($\beta = -0.616$, $p < 0.001$) and liking (H5c), while the effect on public comments ($\beta = -0.017$, $p > 0.05$) is not significant. **Hypothesis 5 was partially supported**. Furthermore, in COVID-19 pandemics crisis, the number of retweets are positively correlated with the media richness of GSMA postings. The number of comments is negatively correlated with the media richness of GSM postings.

The adoption of dialogue strategies in GSMA had positively influence public engagement in retweeting ($\beta = -0.606$, $p < 0.001$), commenting ($\beta = -0.308$, $p < 0.001$), and liking ($\beta = -0.561$, $p < 0.001$), **Hypothesis 6 was supported.**

The public sentiment of GSMA postings had a significantly differentiated effects on public engagement in retweeting ($\beta = -0.825$, $p < 0.001$), commenting ($\beta = -0.639$, $p < 0.001$) and liking ($\beta = -1.414$, $p < 0.001$), **Hypothesis 7 was supported.** Negative public sentiment brings more retweets, comments and likes. In the negative public sentiment, mean (retweets) $= 42$, mean (comments) $= 81.5$, mean (likes) $= 368.2$. In the positive public sentiment, mean (retweets) $= 37$, mean (comments) $= 69.4$, mean (likes) $= 211.4$.

The public sentiment of GSMA postings has a moderating effect between public values and public engagement in retweeting ($\beta = -0.877$, $p < 0.001$), commenting $\beta = -0.620$, $p < 0.01$) and liking ($\beta = -1.280$, $p < 0.001$), **Hypothesis 8 was supported.** In the positive public sentiments, mission-based public value GSMA postings promote more public engagement than non-mission-based public value GSMA postings. In negative public sentiments, non-mission-based public value GSMA postings promote more public engagement than mission-based public value GSMA postings.

Table 3. Negative binomial regression model estimation results

	Retweeting		Commenting		Liking	
	Model 1	Model 2	Model 3	Model 4	Model 5	Model 6
Intercept	3.049*** (0.1111)	3.089*** (0.1117)	4.248*** (0.1059)	4.273*** (0.1065)	5.575*** (0.1094)	5.583*** (0.1101)
PV	0.154** (0.0708)	0.071 (0.0823)	−0.019 (0.0703)	−0.036 (0.0822)	−0.369*** (0.0703)	−0.278** (0.0836)
Language	0.575*** (0.0631)	0.539*** (0.0638)	0.484*** (0.0548)	0.461*** (0.0553)	0.281*** (0.0572)	0.239*** (0.0576)
Source	0.165** (0.0665)	0.186** (0.0667)	0.385*** (0.0654)	0.397*** (0.0663)	0.235*** (0.0664)	0.246*** (0.0666)
Level (reference group Level = 1 City)						
Level = 2	−0.841*** (0.0532)	−0.847*** (0.0535)	−0.403*** (0.0537)	−0.411*** (0.0538)	−0.507*** (0.0541)	−0.528*** (0.0543)
Level = 3	−1.335*** (0.0610)	−1.298*** (0.0621)	−0.806*** (0.0597)	−0.771*** (0.0610)	−1.271*** (0.0599)	−1.190*** (0.0612)
Style (reference group Style = 1: Text)						
Style = 2 Figure	0.111** (0.0482)	0.094* (0.0488)	−0.616*** (0.0466)	−0.815*** (0.0603)	−0.017 (0.0490)	−0,057 (0.0495)
Style = 3 Video	0.389*** (0.0618)	0.386*** (0.0617)	−0.812*** (0.0602)	−0.633*** (0.0476)	−0.040 (0.0625)	−0.046 (0.0624)
Dialogue	0.606*** (0.0730)	0.616*** (0.0746)	0.308*** (0.0654)	0.326*** (0.0669)	0.561*** (0.0675)	0.641*** (0.0697)
PS		−0.825*** (0.1888)		−0.639*** (0.1813)		−1.414*** (0.1801)
PV × PS		0.877*** (0.1936)		0.620** (0.1860)		1.280*** (0.1848)
Log likelihood	−11384.02	−11375.21	−13101.04	−13095.62	−16442.93	−16414.76
Omnibus test	1149.40***	1167.01***	953.19***	964.04***	1053.51***	1109.85***
df	8	10	8	10	8	10

Note: *, **, *** denote significance levels of 0.05, 0.01, 0.001, respectively. N = 2552

4.4 Multivariate ANOVA

In order to verify the above moderating model, this paper subjected the number of retweets, comments and likes to logarithmic variation, and then conducted multivariate ANOVA. The interaction between public values and public sentiment has a significant effect on public retweeting behavior, commenting behavior and liking behavior. It indicates that there is a significant moderating effect of public sentiment between public values and public engagement.

Mean effects analysis of subgroups showed (Fig. 3) that under negative public sentiment, GSMA postings with non-mission-based public values received significantly more retweets (M(non-mission) = 2.42 > M(mission) = 2.31, F = 5.994, P = 0.018), comments (M(non-mission) = 3.31 > M(mission) = 2.90, F = 22.598, P < 0.001) and likes (M(non-mission) = 4.23 > M(mission) = 3.98, F = 7.258, P = 0.007) than mission-based public value GSMA postings. Under positive public sentiment, mission-based public value GSMA postings received significantly more retweets (M(mission) = 2.42 > M(non-mission) = 2.15, F = 7.849, P = 0.014), comments (M(mission) = 2.87 > M(non-mission) = 2.41, F = 7.358, P = 0.035), and likes than non-mission-based public value GSMA postings.

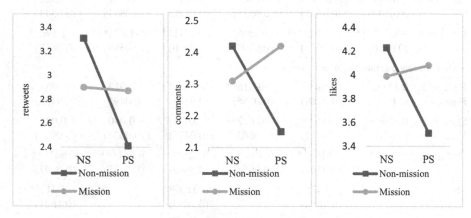

Fig. 3. Mean effects analysis

5   Research Contributions and Management Insights

5.1   Theoretical Contributions

The theoretical implications of this study are twofold. First, the promotion of public engagement through GSM in crisis communication has been widely studied, especially the antecedents of public engagement in GSMAs have been investigated. However, most existing studies have looked at factors such as the form of GSM postings (text, images, and videos), content type, or content sentiment. There is a lack of perspective on the balance between public information needs and information supply from government agencies. More importantly, what public values are provided by GSMAs during crisis events, do they satisfy the value preferences of netizens, and does the type of public value have a significant impact on public engagement? These questions have not been systematically studied.

In fact, in crisis communication, the public's demand for information has both quantitative and qualitative requirements. From the perspective of information flow management, government response is mainly about how to deal with the contradiction between information demand and information supply. In order to ensure the quality and quantity of information supply, it is necessary to understand the information demand of the public first. Based on public value management theory, this paper explores the influence mechanism on public engagement from the perspective of consistency between the content of government response and public value. The findings show that the alignment of government response content with public values significantly and positively influences public engagement in the early stage of public health emergencies. These results extend the study of public value management theory in emergency management and emergency communication.

Second, the "content sentiment" of government social media posts is an important factor influencing public engagement in existing studies (Chen et al. 2020). However, few scholars have studied public engagement from the perspective of public sentiment, i.e., the sentiment of public comments on posts. In online platforms, potential users' behaviors are influenced by initial users' views or commenting behaviors, resulting in an information cascade, also known as herding behavior. And, emotions are also contagious, with negative collective emotions generating larger information cascades.

5.2 Management Implications

(1) Based on the findings of this study, strategies for using social media during government crises and strategies for enhancing benign public engagement behavior can be improved from the perspective of public value management theory and information flow management.

The release of government information during a sudden public crisis event mainly deals with the contradiction between the demand for information and the supply of information. In order to ensure information supply, it is first necessary to grasp public information demand. Therefore, the government can make full use of various databases of online public opinion on this COVID-19 epidemic to analyze the value supply and public information demand. The purpose is to explore the establishment of a public value content library for public health emergencies, to accurately grasp the public values behind the events, to achieve accurate responses to public opinion.

(2) In crisis communication, the government should pay attention to social emotional safety, grasp public sentiment in a timely manner and actively carry out interaction strategies. The results of this study show that negative public sentiment can have a cascading effect on subsequent netizens' participation. To prevent greater negative effects on inappropriate or failed government responses, government departments should handle and respond to netizens' comments in a timely manner. Timely communication and interaction between the government and netizens are the main measures to eliminate misunderstandings and prevent secondary public opinion incidents.

Acknowledgements. This work was supported by the Natural Science Foundation of China [grant number: 72274119; 72293583].

References

Agostino, D., Arnaboldi, M.: A measurement framework for assessing the contribution of social media to public engagement: an empirical analysis on Facebook. Publ. Manag. Rev. **18**(9), 1289–1307 (2016)

Bakker, M.H., van Bommel, M., Kerstholt, J.H., Giebels, E.: The interplay between governmental communications and fellow citizens' reactions via twitter: experimental results of a theoretical crisis in the Netherlands. J. Contingencies Crisis Manag. **27**(3), 265–271 (2019)

Baniamin, H.M.: Citizens' initiatives for crisis management and the use of social media: an analysis of COVID-19 crisis in Bangladesh. Publ. Organ. Rev. **21**(4), 797–813 (2021). https://doi.org/10.1007/s11115-021-00534-4

Barberá, P., et al.: Who leads? Who follows? Measuring issue attention and agenda setting by legislators and the mass public using social media data. Am. Polit. Sci. Rev. **113**(4), 883–901 (2019)

Bonsón, E., Royo, S., Ratkai, M.: Citizens' engagement on local governments' Facebook sites. an empirical analysis: the impact of different media and content types in Western Europe. Gov. Inf. Q. **32**(1), 52–62 (2015)

Bonsón, E., Perea, D., Bednárová, M.: Twitter as a tool for citizen engagement: an empirical study of the Andalusian municipalities. Gov. Inf. Q. **36**(3), 480–489 (2019)

Brown, P.R.: Public value measurement vs. public value creating imagination–the constraining influence of old and new public management paradigms. Int. J. Publ. Admin. 1–10 (2021)

Chatfield, A.T., Reddick, C.G.: All hands on deck to tweet# sandy: networked governance of citizen coproduction in turbulent times. Gov. Inf. Q. **35**(2), 259–272 (2018)

Chen, Q., Min, C., Zhang, W., Wang, G., Ma, X., Evans, R.: Unpacking the black box: how to promote citizen engagement through government social media during the COVID-19 crisis. Comput. Hum. Behav. **110**, 106380 (2020)

Chen, A., Chen, K., Zhang, J., Meng, J., Shen, C.: When national identity meets conspiracies: the contagion of national identity language in public engagement and discourse about COVID-19 conspiracy theories. J. Comput.-Mediat. Commun. **28**(1), zmac034 (2023)

Chen, C.C., Chang, Y.C.: What drives purchase intention on Airbnb? Perspectives of consumer reviews, information quality, and media richness. Telematics Inform. **35**(5), 1512–1523 (2018)

Chon, M.G., Kim, S.: Dealing with the COVID-19 crisis: theoretical application of social media analytics in government crisis management. Publ. Relat. Rev. **48**(3), 102201 (2022)

Cinelli, M., et al.: The COVID-19 social media infodemic. Sci. Rep. **10**(1), 1–10 (2020)

Deng, Q., Hine, M.J., Ji, S., Wang, Y.: Understanding consumer engagement with brand posts on social media: the effects of post linguistic styles. Electron. Commer. Res. Appl. **48**, 101068 (2021)

Deng, Q., Wang, Y., Rod, M., Ji, S.: Speak to head and heart: the effects of linguistic features on B2B brand engagement on social media. Ind. Mark. Manag. **99**, 1–15 (2021)

Díaz-Díaz, R., Pérez-González, D.: Implementation of social media concepts for e-government: case study of a social media tool for value co-creation and citizen participation. J. Organ. End User Comput. (JOEUC) **28**(3), 104–121 (2016)

Di Gangi, P.M., Wasko, M.M.: Social media engagement theory: exploring the influence of user engagement on social media usage. J. Organ. End User Comput. (JOEUC) **28**(2), 53–73 (2016)

Dong, X., Lian, Y.: The moderating effects of entertainers on public engagement through government activities in social media during the COVID-19. Telematics Inform. **66**, 101746 (2022)

Elbanna, A., Bunker, D., Levine, L., Sleigh, A.: Emergency management in the changing world of social media: framing the research agenda with the stakeholders through engaged scholarship. Int. J. Inf. Manag. **47**, 112–120 (2019)

Feng, X., Hui, K., Deng, X., Jiang, G.: Understanding how the semantic features of contents influence the diffusion of government microblogs: moderating role of content topics. Inf. Manag. **58**(8), 103547 (2021)

Filieri, R., McLeay, F., Tsui, B., Lin, Z.: Consumer perceptions of information helpfulness and determinants of purchase intention in online consumer reviews of services. Inf. Manag. **55**(8), 956–970 (2018)

Gesselman, A.N., Ta, V.P., Garcia, J.R.: Worth a thousand interpersonal words: emoji as affective signals for relationship-oriented digital communication. PLoS ONE **14**(8), e0221297 (2019)

Gintova, M.: Understanding government social media users: an analysis of interactions on immigration, refugees and citizenship Canada Twitter and Facebook. Gov. Inf. Q. **36**(4), 101388 (2019)

Górska, A., Dobija, D., Grossi, G., et al.: Getting through COVID-19 together: understanding local governments' social media communication. Cities **121**, 103453 (2022)

Graham, M.W., Avery, E.J., Park, S.: The role of social media in local government crisis communications. Publ. Relat. Rev. **41**(3), 386–394 (2015)

Gretry, A., Horváth, C., Belei, N., van Riel, A.C.: "Don't pretend to be my friend!" When an informal brand communication style backfires on social media. J. Bus. Res. **74**, 77–89 (2017)

Guo, J., Liu, N., Wu, Y., Zhang, C.: Why do citizens participate on government social media accounts during crises? A civic voluntarism perspective. Inf. Manag. **58**(1), 103286 (2021)

Han, X., Wang, J., Zhang, M., Wang, X.: Using social media to mine and analyze public opinion related to COVID-19 in China. Int. J. Environ. Res. Publ. Health **17**(8), 2788 (2020)

Hagemann, L., Abramova, O.: Sentiment, we-talk and engagement on social media: insights from Twitter data mining on the US presidential elections 2020. Internet Research, (ahead-of-print) (2023)

He, C., Liu, H., He, L., Lu, T., Li, B.: More collaboration, less seriousness: investigating new strategies for promoting youth engagement in government-generated videos during the COVID-19 pandemic in China. Comput. Hum. Behav. **126**, 107019 (2022)

Henrich, N., Holmes, B.: What the public was saying about the H1N1 vaccine: perceptions and issues discussed in on-line comments during the 2009 H1N1 pandemic. PLoS ONE **6**(4), e18479 (2011)

Hsu, Y.C., Chen, Y.L., Wei, H.N., Yang, Y.W., Chen, Y.H.: Risk and outbreak communication: lessons from Taiwan's experiences in the post-SARS era. Health Secur. **15**(2), 165–169 (2017)

Hu, X., et al.: Understanding the impact of emotional support on mental health resilience of the community in the social media in Covid-19 pandemic. J. Affect. Disord. **308**, 360–368 (2022)

Irfan, A., Rasli, A., Sulaiman, Z., Sami, A., Qureshi, M.I.: The influence of social media on public value: a systematic review of past decade. J. Publ. Value Admin. Insight **2**(1), 1–6 (2019)

Islm, T., et al.: Why DO citizens engage in government social media accounts during COVID-19 pandemic? A comparative study. Telematics Inform. **62**, 101619 (2021)

Ismagilova, E., Slade, E., Rana, N.P., Dwivedi, Y.K.: The effect of characteristics of source credibility on consumer behaviour: a meta-analysis. J. Retail. Consum. Serv. **53**, 101736 (2020)

Ji, Y.G., Chen, Z.F., Tao, W., Li, Z.C.: Functional and emotional traits of corporate social media message strategies: behavioral insights from S&P 500 Facebook data. Publ. Relat. Rev. **45**(1), 88–103 (2019)

Jozani, M., Ayaburi, E., Ko, M., Choo, K.K.R.: Privacy concerns and benefits of engagement with social media-enabled apps: a privacy calculus perspective. Comput. Hum. Behav. **107**, 106260 (2020)

Juul, J.L., Ugander, J.: Comparing information diffusion mechanisms by matching on cascade size. Proc. Natl. Acad. Sci. **118**(46), e2100786118 (2021)

Kaur, W., Balakrishnan, V., Rana, O., Sinniah, A.: Liking, sharing, commenting and reacting on Facebook: user behaviors' impact on sentiment intensity. Telematics Inform. **39**, 25–36 (2019)

Kreps, S.E., Kriner, D.L.: The COVID-19 Infodemic and the efficacy of interventions intended to reduce misinformation. Publ. Opin. Q. **86**(1), 162–175

Kim, C., Yang, S.U.: Like, comment, and share on Facebook: how each behavior differs from the other. Publ. Relat. Rev. **43**(2), 441–449 (2017)

Kim, H.M., et al.: How public health agencies break through COVID-19 conversations: a strategic network approach to public engagement. Health Commun. **37**(10), 1276–1284 (2022)

Lai, C.H., Ping, Y.R., Chen, Y.C.: Examining government dialogic orientation in social media strategies, outcomes, and perceived effectiveness: a mixed-methods approach. Int. J. Strateg. Commun. **14**(3), 139–159 (2020)

Lazer, D.M.J., Baum, M.A., Benkler, Y., et al.: The science of fake news. Science **359**(6380), 1094–1096 (2018)

Li, K., Zhou, C., Luo, X.R., Benitez, J., Liao, Q.: Impact of information timeliness and richness on public engagement on social media during COVID-19 pandemic: an empirical investigation based on NLP and machine learning. Decis. Support Syst. 113752 (2022)

Lee, D.K.L., Borah, P.: Self-presentation on Instagram and friendship development among young adults: a moderated mediation model of media richness, perceived functionality, and openness. Comput. Hum. Behav. **103**, 57–66 (2020)

Lee, J., Xu, W.: The more attacks, the more retweets: Trump's and Clinton's agenda setting on Twitter. Publ. Relat. Rev. **44**(2), 201–213 (2018)

Li, Y., Chandra, Y., Kapucu, N.: Crisis coordination and the role of social media in response to COVID-19 in Wuhan, China. Am. Rev. Publ. Admin. **50**(6–7), 698–705 (2020)

Li, J., et al.: The continued use of social commerce platforms and psychological anxiety—the roles of influencers, informational incentives and FoMO. Int. J. Environ. Res. Publ. Health **18**(22), 12254 (2021)

Lin, X., Lachlan, K.A., Spence, P.R.: Exploring extreme events on social media: a comparison of user reposting/retweeting behaviors on Twitter and Weibo. Comput. Hum. Behav. **65**, 576–581 (2016)

Liu, W., Lai, C.H., Xu, W.W.: Tweeting about emergency: a semantic network analysis of government organizations' social media messaging during hurricane Harvey. Publ. Relat. Rev. **44**(5), 807–819 (2018)

Luo, L., Duan, S., Shang, S., Lyu, W.: Understanding citizen engagement and concerns about the COVID-19 pandemic in China: a thematic analysis of government social media. Aslib J. Inf. Manag. **73**(6), 865–884 (2021)

Mansoor, M.: Citizens' trust in government as a function of good governance and government agency's provision of quality information on social media during COVID-19. Gov. Inf. Q. **38**(4), 101597 (2021)

Meltzer, M., Ştefănescu, L., Ozunu, A.: Keep them engaged: Romanian county inspectorates for emergency situations' Facebook usage for disaster risk communication and beyond. Sustainability **10**(5), 1411 (2018)

Moynihan, D.P., Pandey, S.K., Wright, B.E.: Prosocial values and performance management theory: Linking perceived social impact and performance information use. Governance **25**(3), 463–483 (2012)

Mousavizadeh, M., Koohikamali, M., Salehan, M., Kim, D.J.: An investigation of peripheral and central cues of online customer review voting and helpfulness through the lens of elaboration likelihood model. Inf. Syst. Front. **24**, 211–231 (2022)

Neely, S.R., Collins, M.: Social media and crisis communications: a survey of local governments in Florida. J. Homeland Secur. Emergency Manag. **15**(1) (2018)

Ngai, C.S.B., Singh, R.G., Lu, W., Yao, L., Koon, A.C.: Exploring the relationship between trust-building strategies and public engagement on social media during the COVID-19 outbreak. Health Commun. 1–17 (2022)

Oh, J., Ki, E.J.: Factors affecting social presence and word-of-mouth in corporate social responsibility communication: tone of voice, message framing, and online medium type. Publ. Relat. Rev. **45**(2), 319–331 (2019)

Otterbacher, J., Ang, C.S., Litvak, M., Atkins, D.: Show me you care: trait empathy, linguistic style, and mimicry on Facebook. ACM Trans. Internet Technol. (TOIT) **17**(1), 1–22 (2017)

Park, K., Hong, J.S., Kim, W.: A methodology combining cosine similarity with classifier for text classification. Appl. Artif. Intell. **34**(5), 396–411 (2020)

Page, B.I., Shapiro, R.Y.: Effects of public opinion on policy. Am. Polit. Sci. Rev. **77**(1), 175–190 (1983)

Pang, P.C.I., Cai, Q., Jiang, W., Chan, K.S.: Engagement of government social media on Facebook during the COVID-19 pandemic in Macao. Int. J. Environ. Res. Publ. Health **18**(7), 3508 (2021)

Pezzuti, T., Leonhardt, J.M., Warren, C.: Certainty in language increases consumer engagement on social media. J. Interact. Mark. **53**, 32–46 (2021)

Pitt, C.S., Plangger, K.A., Botha, E., Kietzmann, J., Pitt, L.: How employees engage with B2B brands on social media: word choice and verbal tone. Ind. Mark. Manag. **81**, 130–137 (2019)

Qazi, A., et al.: Analyzing situational awareness through public opinion to predict adoption of social distancing amid pandemic COVID-19. J. Med. Virol. **92**(7), 849–855 (2020)

Rennekamp, K.M., Witz, P.D.: Linguistic formality and audience engagement: investors' reactions to characteristics of social media disclosures. Contemp. Account. Res. (2020)

Rosenbloom, D.H.: Beyond efficiency: value frameworks for public administration. Chin. Publ. Admin. Rev. **8**(1), 37–46 (2017)

Shah, Z., Wei, L.: Source credibility and the information quality matter in public engagement on social networking sites during the COVID-19 crisis. Front. Psychol. **13** (2022)

Sharif, M.H.M., Troshani, I., Davidson, R.: Determinants of social media impact in local government. J. Organ. End User Comput. (JOEUC) **28**(3), 82–103 (2016)

Su, Z., et al.: Mental health consequences of COVID-19 media coverage: the need for effective crisis communication practices. Glob. Health **17**(1), 1–8 (2021)

Tang, Z., Miller, A.S., Zhou, Z., Warkentin, M.: Does government social media promote users' information security behavior towards COVID-19 scams? Cultivation effects and protective motivations. Gov. Inf. Q. **38**(2), 101572 (2021). https://doi.org/10.1016/j.giq.2021.101572

Tokita, C.K., Guess, A.M., Tarnita, C.E.: Polarized information ecosystems can reorganize social networks via information cascades. Proc. Natl. Acad. Sci. **118**(50), e2102147118 (2021)

Wang, Y., Yang, Y.: Dialogic communication on social media: how organizations use Twitter to build dialogic relationships with their publics. Comput. Hum. Behav. **104**, 106183 (2020). https://doi.org/10.1016/j.chb.2019.106183

Wang, W.J., Haase, T.W., Yang, C.H.: Warning message elements and retweet counts: an analysis of tweets sent during hurricane irma. Nat. Hazard. Rev. **21**(1), 04019014 (2020)

Wu, L., Li, J., Qi, J., Shi, N., Zhu, H.: How to promote public engagement and enhance sentiment through government social media during the COVID-19 crisis: a public value management perspective. J. Organ. End User Comput. (JOEUC) **34**(6), 1–24 (2022)

Wu, L., Qi, J., Shi, N., Li, J., Yan, Q.: Revealing the relationship of topics popularity and bursty human activity patterns in social temporal networks. Physica A **588**, 126568 (2022)

Wu, L., Li, J., Qi, J., Kong, D., Li, X.: The role of opinion leaders in the sustainable development of corporate-led consumer advice networks: evidence from a Chinese travel content community. Sustainability 13(19), 11128 (2021)

Wu, L., Li, J., Qi, J.: Characterizing popularity dynamics of hot topics using micro-blogs spatio-temporal data. J. Big Data 6(1), 1–16 (2019). https://doi.org/10.1186/s40537-019-0266-4

Xia, P., Zhang, L., Li, F.: Learning similarity with cosine similarity ensemble. Inf. Sci. 307, 39–52 (2015)

Xie, L., Pinto, J., Zhong, B.: Building community resilience on social media to help recover from the COVID-19 pandemic. Comput. Hum. Behav. 134, 107294 (2022)

Yang, Y., Deng, W., Zhang, Y., Mao, Z.: Promoting public engagement during the COVID-19 crisis: how effective is the Wuhan Local Government's information release? Int. J. Environ. Res. Publ. Health 18(1), 118 (2021)

Yin, D., Bond, S.D., Zhang, H.: Anxious or angry? Effects of discrete emotions on the perceived helpfulness of online reviews. MIS Q. 38(2), 539–560 (2014)

Yoon, G., Li, C., Ji, Y., North, M., Hong, C., Liu, J.: Attracting comments: digital engagement metrics on Facebook and financial performance. J. Advert. 47(1), 24–37 (2018)

Yue, C.A., Thelen, P., Robinson, K., Men, L.R.: How do CEOs communicate on Twitter? A comparative study between Fortune 200 companies and top startup companies. Corp. Commun. Int. J. 24(3), 532–552 (2019)

Yuniarto, D., Khozinaturrohmah, H.N., Rahman, A.B.A.: Effectiveness of Covid-19 information through social media based on public intention. Appl. Inf. Syst. Manag. (AISM) 4(1), 37–44 (2021)

Zhang, H., Li, Y., Dolan, C., Song, Z.: Observations from Wuhan: an adaptive risk and crisis communication system for a health emergency. Risk Manag. Healthc. Policy 14, 3179 (2021)

Zhang, C., Fan, C., Yao, W., et al.: Social media for intelligent public information and warning in disasters: an interdisciplinary review. Int. J. Inf. Manag. 49, 190–207 (2019)

Zhou, C., Li, K., Lu, Y.: Linguistic characteristics and the dissemination of misinformation in social media: the moderating effect of information richness. Inf. Process. Manag. 58(6), 102679 (2021)

Zheng, L., Zheng, T.: Innovation through social media in the public sector: information and interactions. Gov. Inf. Q. 31, S106–S117 (2014)

Location Recommendations Based on Multi-view Learning and Attention-Enhanced Graph Networks

Junxin Chen[1,2], Kuijie Lin[1], Xiang Chen[1,2(✉)], Xijun Wang[1], and Terng-Yin Hsu[3]

[1] School of Electronics and Information Technology, Sun Yat-sen University, Guangzhou 511400, China

[2] Guangdong Provincial Key Laboratory of Big Data Computing, The Chinese University of Hong Kong, Shenzhen 518000, China

{chenjx248,linkj25}@mail2.sysu.edu.cn,
{chenxiang,wangxijun}@mail.sysu.edu.cn

[3] Department of Computer Science, National Chiao Tung University, Hsinchu 30013, Taiwan

yhsu@cs.nctu.edu.tw

Abstract. Personalized location recommendation plays a very important role in location-based social networks, from which both users and service providers can benefit from. In spite of the significant endeavors that have been made towards acquiring knowledge on location attributes and user inclinations, it is still faced with serious data sparsity problems. In this paper, we propose a personalized location recommendation model based on graph neural networks with multi-view learning to obtain effective representations of mobile users and locations from different heterogeneous graphs. We also design an attention-enhanced mechanism to explore the implicit interactions between mobile users and locations themselves. Conducting adequate comparative experiments on two real-world telecom datasets has demonstrated that our model achieves superior performance. Additionally, our model has been proven effective in addressing data sparsity issues.

Keywords: Location Recommendation · Multi-view Learning · Graph Neural Networks · Data Sparsity

1 Introduction

Today, with the advancement of technologies, electronic footprints have been widely used in our life. Check-ins, calling details, or GPS coordinates accumulated by our mobile phones have enabled the rapid development of location-based social networks (LBSNs), such as Gowalla[1], Yelp[2], Foursquare[3], etc. [1]. Network

---

[1] https://blog.gowalla.com/.
[2] http://www.yelp.com/.
[3] https://foursquare.com/.

X. Meng et al. (Eds.): BDSC 2023, CCIS 1846, pp. 83–95, 2023.
https://doi.org/10.1007/978-981-99-3925-1_5

operators and companies can use these data to make personalized location recommendations, which can promote the development of urban tourism and enrich people's lives. In LBSNs, how to suggest locations that align with users' interests when they visit an unfamiliar city is one of the significant research topics all the time. However, location recommendations especially lack the feedbacks [2], which differs from other recommendations that can get users' feedback from behaviors directly. It's hard to tell from the check-in data whether users are satisfied with their visits. In addition, since the locations visited by a user only account for a very small part of each city, the interactions of user-location are extremely sparse [3]. All these problems have a great negative impact on accurate personalized location recommendations, so it is urgent to be solved.

Existing methods often utilize side information to release data sparsity. Geographical characters are used as regularizations in [4] or are fused with user interests to obtain latent features [5]. Personal information and social relationships are also used to explore implicit preferences [6–8]. In fact, in addition to these attributes of users and places themselves, other behaviors can also reflect their characteristics, such as app usage data coming from mobile networks [9,10]. Users' daily routines and space characteristics they stay in can be hinted at from app usage information. For example, people are more likely to use mail or call apps when they are in the office, while they are more frequently using cameras in tourist attractions. Different mobile users also have different app usage behaviors. Socialists turn to social apps more often than others, while fitness enthusiasts use fitness apps more frequently. Therefore, we propose a multi-view learning method aiming at capturing multifaceted semantic information from telecommunication data. Besides users' preferences and visiting patterns of locations, it also learns mobile users' app usage behaviors in different locations to enrich their characteristics, which can also help network service providers to learn user mobility.

With the powerful representation abilities of graph neural network, it is a model applied in recommender systems to find structural relationships and get better recommendations [11–13]. To fully learn inherent information about user-app-location, we design an attention-enhanced graph neural network based on different heterogeneous graphs. It not only obtains users' activities and locations' features but also mines the relationships between users and locations themselves to enhance the representations. The fundamental contributions can be summarized as follows:

1. We propose a multi-view learning model based on graph representation networks to learn different semantic information from several heterogeneous graphs, which can enrich the representations of users and locations.
2. We design an attention-enhanced mechanism with graph neural networks to fully explore multifaceted relationships between graph nodes.
3. Adequate experiments are conducted on two real-world datasets. The results are proved that our model outperforms other the state-of-art methods. Besides, This model has shown to be a viable solution for addressing the challenge of data sparsity.

The rest of the paper is organized as follows. Section 2 describes the related work. Section 3 introduces our proposed model. Section 4 introduces the experiment setting and evaluates model performances. Section 5 is the conclusion of the paper.

2 Related Work

Early works usually apply collaborative filtering on location recommendations. The conventional approach for recommendation is Matrix Factorization (MF), which is used to decompose a user-location interaction matrix so that it can get representations to realize recommendations [14]. In [15,16], geographical features are integrated with MF together. In [10], temporal information and app usage are incorporated into high-dimensional tensor decomposition to release data sparsity and cold start problems. Recently, various neural networks are gradually applied to location recommendations. In [17], the recurrent neural network is implemented for tourist attraction recommendations. In [18], long-short term memory combined with social influences and location popularity is used to recommend locations. In [19], a convolutional neural network combined with MF is used to obtain users' potential location preferences. Since graph-based methods have shown their great power in many fields and achieved impressive improvements in recommendations [11], graph-based recommendations are proposed with high-order signals aggregated by graph convolution structures [20,21]. In [22], the user's movements with temporal patterns are integrated into the graph attention network to improve the next point-of-interest (POI) recommendations. In [23], a cross-graph neural network is designed to obtain time-aware user activities to realize location recommendations. However, these models are either limited in their representation abilities or don't provide solutions to the data sparsity problem with telecom data.

3 Proposed Model

The overall framework of our proposed model is shown in Fig. 1. Details are introduced as follows.

3.1 Heterogeneous Graph Construction

The users' app usage records are firstly extracted into three interaction matrices, then three heterogeneous graphs are constructed according to them. The user-location graph is defined as $G_{ul} = (\mathcal{V}_{ul}, \mathcal{E}_{ul}, \mathbf{X}_{ul})$. $\mathcal{V}_{ul}$ is the set of user and location nodes. $\mathcal{E}_{ul}$ is the set of undirect edges defined by visiting frequencies. The user-app graph and the location-app graph are also defined as $G_{ua} = (\mathcal{V}_{ua}, \mathcal{E}_{ua}, \mathbf{X}_{ua})$ and $G_{la} = (\mathcal{V}_{la}, \mathcal{E}_{la}, \mathbf{X}_{la})$. $\mathcal{V}_{ua}$ is the set of user and app nodes. $\mathcal{E}_{ua}$ is the set of undirect edges defined by the users' usage frequencies of apps. Similarly, $\mathcal{V}_{la}$ is node sets of location and app. $\mathcal{E}_{la}$ is the set of undirect edges defined by apps' used frequencies in each location. $\mathbf{X}_{ul}$, $\mathbf{X}_{ua}$ and $\mathbf{X}_{la}$ are the graphs' origin attributes, separately.

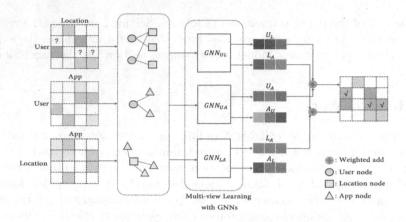

Fig. 1. The Overall Framework of Our Proposed Model

3.2 The Multi-view Learning Based Graph Neural Network

Since the graph convolution network (GCN) has powerful feature aggregation capabilities, it is commonly employed in recommender systems. We first use it to find the representations of each graph's nodes. Then three different views of node embeddings are learned by three independent networks, GCN_{ul}, GCN_{ua}, and GCN_{la}. GCN_{ul} can learn users' activities and locations' visited patterns from G_{ul}. Users' app habits U_a and locations' app usage pattern L_a can be learned by GCN_{ua} and GCN_{la}, respectively.

Suppose the output of k_{th} layer is $\mathbf{H}^{(k)} = \left(h_1^{(k)}, h_2^{(k)}, \ldots, h_{|\mathcal{V}|}^{(k)} \right)$, $|\mathcal{V}|$ means nodes number. The input of our model is defined as

$$H^{(0)} = \mathbf{X}, \tag{1}$$

where $\mathbf{X}$ is attribute matrix. Then the output of k_{th} GCN layer is

$$H^{(k)} = ReLU \left(\tilde{\mathbf{D}}^{-\frac{1}{2}} \tilde{\mathbf{A}} \tilde{\mathbf{D}}^{-\frac{1}{2}} H^{(k-1)} \mathbf{W}^{(k)} \right), \tag{2}$$

where $\tilde{\mathbf{A}} = \mathbf{A} + \mathbf{I}$, $\mathbf{I}$ is identity matrix. $\tilde{\mathbf{D}}$ is degree matrix calculated by $\mathbf{A}$, $\mathbf{D}_{ii} = \sum_j \tilde{\mathbf{A}}_{ij}$. $\mathbf{A}$ is the adjacent matrix of G. We use the ReLU activation function, but we won't apply it in the last layer [21].

After that, we can get users' visiting behavior $\mathbf{U}_l$ and locations' visited pattern $\mathbf{L}_u$, users' app habits $\mathbf{U}_a$ and apps' usage pattern $\mathbf{L}_a$ on various locations. $\mathbf{U}_l \in \mathbf{R}^{N_U \times d_{ul}}$, $\mathbf{L}_u \in \mathbf{R}^{N_L \times d_{ul}}$, $\mathbf{U}_a \in \mathbf{R}^{N_U \times d_{ua}}$, $L_a \in \mathbf{R}^{N_L \times d_{la}}$. d_{ul}, d_{ua}, and d_{la} are the latent dimension of GCNs' final outputs, respectively. N_U and N_L are the numbers of users and locations.

However, GCN only treats neighbor nodes with the same weight. Moreover, the similarity between homogeneous nodes is ignored in heterogeneous graphs. Thus we designed an attention-enhanced layer to find correlations between entities. Important parts that should be focused on the self-attention mechanism are also captured as the formula (3)–(6) shown. The same operation is performed on location representations X which stands for $\mathbf{U}_l$ and $\mathbf{L}_u$.

$$X_{attn} = softmax(\frac{Q_x K_x}{\sqrt{h_K}})V_x, \tag{3}$$

$$Q_x = W_{Qx}X, \tag{4}$$

$$K_x = W_{Kx}X, \tag{5}$$

$$V_x = W_{Vx}X. \tag{6}$$

Then we can get attention-enhanced representations $\mathbf{U}_l'$ and $\mathbf{L}_u'$ as formula (7) (8), where $bn()$ is batch normalization operation.

$$\mathbf{U}_l' = bn(\mathbf{U}_l + \mathbf{U}_{l-attn}), \tag{7}$$

$$\mathbf{L}_u' = bn(\mathbf{L}_u + \mathbf{L}_{u-attn}). \tag{8}$$

Considering different views have different contributions to the model, we use a weighted fusion method to get final representations. We map $\mathbf{U}_a$ and $\mathbf{L}_a$ to the same dimensions d_{ul} using linear layers. Then $\mathbf{U}_{final}$ and $\mathbf{L}_{final}$ are obtained as follows:

$$\mathbf{U}_a' = \sigma(W_u a\mathbf{U}_a + b_u a), \tag{9}$$

$$\mathbf{L}_a' = \sigma(W_l a\mathbf{L}_a + b_l a), \tag{10}$$

$$\mathbf{U}_{final} = \mathbf{U}_l' + \alpha\mathbf{U}_a, \tag{11}$$

$$\mathbf{L}_{final} = \mathbf{L}_u' + \beta\mathbf{L}_a. \tag{12}$$

where $\mathbf{U}_{final}$ is the users' representations, $\mathbf{U}_{final} \in \mathbf{R}^{N_U \times d_{ul}}$. $\mathbf{L}_{final}$ is the locations' representations, $\mathbf{L}_{final} \in \mathbf{R}^{N_L \times d_{ul}}$. Values of α and β range from 0 to 1.

3.3 Recommendations and Optimization

The final recommendations are based on ratings of each user i to location j where they haven't been to. The ratings are obtained by the inner product of $\mathbf{U}_{final}$ and $\mathbf{L}_{final}$ as,

$$\hat{S} = \mathbf{U}_{final} \circ \mathbf{L}_{final}^T, \tag{13}$$

where $\hat{S} \in \mathbf{R}^{N_U \times N_L}$. $\hat{s}_{ij} \in S$ means the preference score of user i to location j.

We apply mean squared error to our proposed model to optimize its parameters as,

$$L = \frac{1}{N_{Tr}} \sum_{(i,j) \in Tr} (s_{ij} - \hat{s}_{ij})^2, \tag{14}$$

where s_{ij} is the ground truth ranked by user-location pair (i, j). Tr is our trainset and N_{tr} is number of training samples.

4 Experiments

4.1 Datasets

We conduct experiments on two real-world telecommunication datasets. Details about the two datasets are introduced briefly.

Telecom Dataset: This dataset comprises app usage records from mobile networks and was collected by one of the largest telecom operators [24]. This dataset contains 10000 users' activities covering 11584 locations, and 1327 apps' usage records in Shanghai, China.

TalkingData: This dataset is published on the Kaggle website[25]. It records the users' app usage behavior with temporal and spatial information. This dataset contains 256 users' visiting records on 439 locations with their usage of 689 apps in Guangzhou, China.

Table 1 provides detailed information of Telecom and TalkingData datasets.

Table 1. Datasets and Statistics Information

Metrics	Telecom Dataset	TalkingData
Data Sources	Cellular network	Mobile application
City	Shanghai, China	Guangzhou, China
Time Duration	20th-26th, April, 2016	1st-7th, May, 2016
Users	10000	256
Locations	11584	439
Apps	1327	689
Records	40470865	180106

Table 2. Performance Comparison on Two Datasets Evaluated by Different Metrics. The optimal results are displayed in **bold** for each column.

Models	Telecom Dataset						TalkingData		
	HR@3	ACC@3	nDCG@3	HR@5	ACC@5	nDCG@5	HR@2	ACC@2	nDCG@2
MF	0.6988	0.3828	0.6510	0.9397	0.4135	0.6807	0.9203	0.7698	0.8912
KNN	0.6914	0.3784	0.6182	0.9184	0.5110	0.6533	0.9010	0.7623	0.8834
SVD	0.7373	0.4011	0.6380	0.9335	0.5180	0.6665	0.9292	0.7736	0.8884
SoRec	0.7498	0.4072	0.6490	0.9330	0.5287	0.6818	0.9279	0.7728	0.8855
SR	0.7462	0.4083	0.6494	0.9379	0.5239	0.6827	0.9316	0.7734	0.8924
NCGF	0.7404	0.3956	0.6389	0.9383	0.5258	0.6678	0.9363	0.7864	0.8851
CMF-UL	0.7395	0.4088	0.6802	0.9539	0.5458	0.7054	0.9356	0.7803	0.8969
ApGCN	0.8237	0.4764	0.7201	0.9689	0.5763	0.7449	0. 9768	0.8357	0.9515
Ours	0.8468	0.5010	0.7357	0.9747	0.5955	0.7525	0.9882	0.8667	0.9621

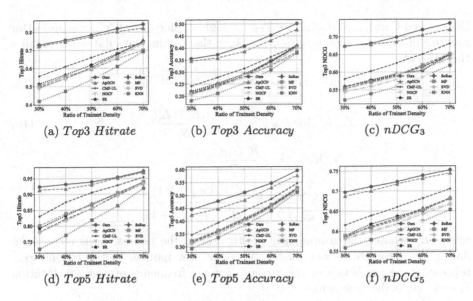

(a) *Top3 Hitrate*   (b) *Top3 Accuracy*   (c) *nDCG₃*

(d) *Top5 Hitrate*   (e) *Top5 Accuracy*   (f) *nDCG₅*

Fig. 2. Recommendation Performance Comparisons on Telecom Dataset under Different Sparsity

Table 3. Ablation Study on Two Datasets

Models	Telecom Dataset						TalkingData		
	HR@3	ACC@3	nDCG@3	HR@5	ACC@5	nDCG@5	HR@2	ACC@2	nDCG@2
Ours-N	0.8237	0.4764	0.7201	0.9689	0.5763	0.7449	0.9727	0.8357	0.9510
Ours-A	0.8305	0.4764	0.7209	0.9689	0.5768	0.7429	0.9804	0.8412	0.9523
Ours-U	0.8381	0.4907	0.7214	0.9709	0.5882	0.7408	0.9853	0.8497	0.9557
Ours-L	0.8370	0.4830	0.7174	0.9697	0.5814	0.7473	0.9848	0.8436	0.9522
Ours	0.8468	0.5010	0.7357	0.9747	0.5955	0.7525	0.9882	0.8667	0.9621

4.2 Settings

We use *TopK Hitrate* and *TopK Accuracy* to evaluate recommendation performances. The quality of recommend ranking results is evaluated using Normalized

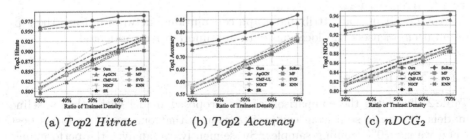

(a) *Top2 Hitrate*   (b) *Top2 Accuracy*   (c) *nDCG₂*

Fig. 3. Recommendation Performance Comparisons on Talking Dataset under Different Sparsity

Discounted Cumulative Gain $nDCG_K$. A higher value of $nDCG_K$ means better ranking quality. K value is various because the TalkingData dataset is smaller than the other.

$$TopK\ Hitrate = \frac{\sum_{i=1}^{N}(|L_i^p \cap L_i^t| \geqslant 1)}{N}, \tag{15}$$

$$TopK\ Accuracy = \frac{\sum_{i=1}^{N}(|L_i^p \cap L_i^t|/K)}{N}, \tag{16}$$

$$nDCG_K = \frac{DCG_K}{IDCG_K}$$
$$= \sum_{i=1}^{N} \frac{\sum_{j=1}^{K} rel_j^{p(i)}/log_2(j+1)}{N\sum_{j=1}^{K} rel_j^{t(i)}/log_2(j+1)}, \tag{17}$$

where L_i^t denotes the groundtruth of ith user in the testset. L_i^p is recommendation results given by our model. N is the user number in the testset. rel_k^p represents the prediction of the kth app's usage frequency of user i in location j, and rel_k^t is the true value.

In order to get more reliable results, we compare our model with the following baselines, including MF [14], SVD [26], KNN, SR-U [15], SoRec [16], NGCF [20], CMF-UL [10] and ApGCN [27]. Details are introduced below.

MF: It is a traditional method that user-location interactions are decomposed without any additional information to get latent features of users and locations.

SVD: It aims to recommend the most similar locations according to users' attributes with Singular Value Decomposition (SVD).

KNN: It identifies the k-most comparable users and then utilizes their browsing habits to generate recommendations.

SR-U: Social relationship between users is taken as a regularization term to optimize user embeddings in the latent space.

SoRec: User relationship is represented by their app usage records. Then it is incorporated into user-location matrix.

NGCF: It is designed to get high-order features of users and locations with signals propagated on a bipartite graph without other information.

CMF-UL: App pattern and temporal information are integrated into user-location matrix decomposition by combining users' online and offline behaviors with transfer learning.

ApGCN: It uses an attributed graph convolutional network to learn the representations of users and locations with app information considered.

4.3   Performances

Table 2 illustrates the comparison of the proposed model with other baseline models. It can be seen from comparison results that our model performs best when we use 70% training samples. Subsequently, we analyze the performance of our approach under varying levels of data sparsity. We randomly select the different ratios of trainset density as different data sparsity [10]. 30% density means we only use 30% samples of trainset to train our model, then the rest 70% to be tested. The results on two datasets are shown in Fig. 2 and Fig. 3. It can be seen that our model achieves the best performance among all provided baselines. This evaluation indicates that the multi-view learning method designed by us can capture more hidden information than the single-view learning, and the self-attention mechanism can learn and enhance the relevant semantics between the user and the location, which makes it perform better.

In addition, it can be observed that the two models, namely ApGCN and CMF-UL, exhibit the best performance among all the models evaluated alongside our proposed model. These two models are based on graph convolutional neural network and matrix decomposition respectively, but both mine user behavior preferences and location attribute representations contained in App data to make up for sparsity in user-location interaction. It reveals that App data can effectively make up for the missing relevant information of places and users, and relieve data sparsity problem, so as to improve the recommendation results.

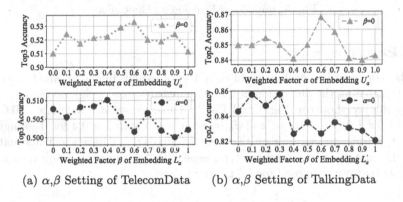

(a) α, β Setting of TelecomData   (b) α, β Setting of TalkingData

Fig. 4. Impacts of Weight Factors α and β

4.4   Ablation Study

To prove the effectiveness of multi-view learning, we make an ablation study to evaluate each part's contribution to our proposed model. Results are shown in Table 3. $Ours - N$ means we don't use any improvements to compensate for the embeddings of users and locations. $Ours - A$ means only the self-attention mechanism is applied. $Ours - U$ and $Ours - L$ are used additional information U'_a and L'_a. $Ours - all$ means every mentioned part is combined. It can be seen from the results that multi-view learning and self-attention-enhanced mechanism make visible contributions to inherent feature exploration about users and locations.

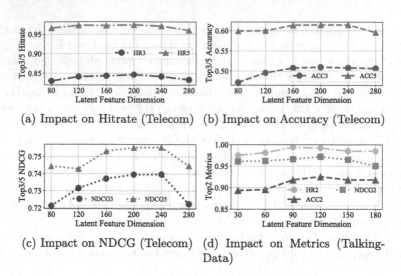

(a) Impact on Hitrate (Telecom)   (b) Impact on Accuracy (Telecom)

(c) Impact on NDCG (Telecom)   (d) Impact on Metrics (Talking-Data)

Fig. 5. Impacts of Embedding Dimension

4.5   Parameter Study

We also conducted an evaluation of the effect of various hyper-parameters on our model, including the dimension of latent representations, weighted factor α, and β. Results are shown in Fig. 4 and Fig. 5. Thus, we set $d_{ul} = 200, \alpha = 0.6$ and $\beta = 0.4$ for Telecom dataset and $d_{ul} = 90, \alpha = 0.6$ and $\beta = 0.4$ for TalkingData dataset. Besides, it can be seen that metric curves don't have great fluctuations with the change of hyper-parameters, especially for the embedding dimension. It shows that our proposed model is very robust.

5   Conclusions

In this paper, we introduces a novel multi-view learning approach that utilizes graph neural network to extract effective representations from diverse aspects of telecommunication records. Mobile users' preferences for locations and visiting patterns of locations are learned by graph convolutional network with an attention-enhanced mechanism. Moreover, app usage behavior of different mobile users and locations are obtained to enhance representations. Adequate experiments are conducted on various recommendation methods and our proposed model performed best with successfully alleviating data sparsity problems. For future research, we aim to integrate temporal features to capture both short-term and long-term changes in mobile users' location preferences, paving the way for more comprehensive analysis in this domain.

Acknowledgements. This research is supported partly by the National Key Research and Development Program of China under Grant 2019YFE0196400, and partly by the Open Research Fund under Grant No. B10120210117-OF09 from the Guangdong Provincial Key Laboratory of Big Data Computing, The Chinese University of Hong Kong, Shenzhen.

References

1. Werneck, H., Silva, N., Viana, M.C., Mourão, F., Pereira, A.C.M., Rocha, L.: A survey on point-of-interest recommendation in location-based social networks. In: Proceedings of the Brazilian Symposium on Multimedia and the Web, pp. 185–192. Association for Computing Machinery, New York, NY, USA (2020). https://doi.org/10.1145/3428658.3430970
2. Natarajan, N., Shin, D., Dhillon, I.S.: Which app will you use next? Collaborative filtering with interactional context. In: Proceedings of the 7th ACM Conference on Recommender Systems, pp. 201–208. ACM, Hong Kong, China (2013)
3. Huang, Z., Chen, H., Zeng, D.D.: Applying associative retrieval techniques to alleviate the sparsity problem in collaborative filtering. ACM Trans. Inf. Syst. 22(1), 116–142 (2004)
4. Ye, M., Yin, P., Lee, W.C., Lee, D.L.: Exploiting geographical influence for collaborative point-of-interest recommendation. In: Proceedings of the 34th International ACM SIGIR Conference on Research and Development in Information Retrieval. SIGIR '11, pp. 325–334. Association for Computing Machinery, New York, NY, USA (2011). https://doi.org/10.1145/2009916.2009962
5. Zhou, F., Yin, R., Zhang, K., Trajcevski, G., Zhong, T., Wu, J.: Adversarial point-of-interest recommendation. In: The World Wide Web Conference. WWW '19, pp. 3462–34618. Association for Computing Machinery, New York, NY, USA (2019). https://doi.org/10.1145/3308558.3313609
6. Saleem, M.A., Lee, Y.-K., Lee, S.: Dynamicity in social trends towards trajectory based location recommendation. In: Biswas, J., Kobayashi, H., Wong, L., Abdulrazak, B., Mokhtari, M. (eds.) ICOST 2013. LNCS, vol. 7910, pp. 86–93. Springer, Heidelberg (2013). https://doi.org/10.1007/978-3-642-39470-6_11
7. Zhao, W.X., Zhou, N., Sun, A., Wen, J.-R., Han, J., Chang, E.Y.: A time-aware trajectory embedding model for next-location recommendation. Knowl. Inf. Syst. 56(3), 559–579 (2017). https://doi.org/10.1007/s10115-017-1107-4
8. Yang, D., Zhang, D., Yu, Z., Wang, Z.: A sentiment-enhanced personalized location recommendation system. In: 24th ACM Conference on Hypertext and Social Media (Part of ECRC), pp. 119–128. ACM, Paris, France (2013)
9. Lee, Y., Park, I., Cho, S., Choi, J.: Smartphone user segmentation based on app usage sequence with neural networks. Telematics Inform. 35(2), 329–339 (2018)
10. Tu, Z., Fan, Y., Li, Y., Chen, X., Su, L., Jin, D.: From fingerprint to footprint: cold-start location recommendation by learning user interest from app data. Proc. ACM Interact. Mob. Wearable Ubiquitous Technol. 3(1), 26:1–26:22 (2019). https://doi.org/10.1145/3314413
11. Wang, S., et al.: Graph learning based recommender systems: a review. In: IJCAI, pp. 4644–4652. ijcai.org (2021)

12. Su, Y., et al.: HRec: heterogeneous graph embedding-based personalized point-of-interest recommendation. In: Gedeon, T., Wong, K.W., Lee, M. (eds.) ICONIP 2019. LNCS, vol. 11955, pp. 37–49. Springer, Cham (2019). https://doi.org/10.1007/978-3-030-36718-3_4

13. Hu, X., Xu, J., Wang, W., Li, Z., Liu, A.: A graph embedding based model for fine-grained POI recommendation. Neurocomputing **428**, 376–384 (2021)

14. Sarwar, B.M., Karypis, G., Konstan, J.A., Riedl, J.T.: Application of dimensionality reduction in recommender system - a case study. In: In ACM WebKDD Workshop (2000)

15. Lian, D., Zhao, C., Xie, X., Sun, G., Chen, E., Rui, Y.: Geomf: joint geographical modeling and matrix factorization for point-of-interest recommendation. In: The 20th ACM SIGKDD International Conference on Knowledge Discovery and Data Mining, KDD '14, New York, NY, USA, 24–27 August 2014, pp. 831–840. ACM (2014). https://doi.org/10.1145/2623330.2623638

16. Lian, D., Zheng, K., Ge, Y., Cao, L., Chen, E., Xie, X.: Geomf++: scalable location recommendation via joint geographical modeling and matrix factorization. ACM Trans. Inf. Syst. **36**(3), 33:1–33:29 (2018). https://doi.org/10.1145/3182166

17. Qi, M., Ma, W., Shan, R.: Design and implementation of tourist location recommendation system based on recurrent neural network. Electron. Technol. Softw. Eng. **01**, 184–185 (2020)

18. Zhong, C., Zhu, J., Xi, H.: PS-LSTM: popularity analysis and social network for point-of-interest recommendation in previously unvisited locations. In: CNIOT 2021: 2nd International Conference on Computing, Networks and Internet of Things, Beijing, China, 20–22 May 2021, pp. 28:1–28:6. ACM (2021). https://doi.org/10.1145/3468691.3468720

19. Ameen, T., Chen, L., Xu, Z., Lyu, D., Shi, H.: A convolutional neural network and matrix factorization-based travel location recommendation method using community-contributed geotagged photos. ISPRS Int. J. Geo Inf. **9**(8), 464 (2020). https://doi.org/10.3390/ijgi9080464

20. Wang, X., He, X., Wang, M., Feng, F., Chua, T.: Neural graph collaborative filtering. In: Piwowarski, B., Chevalier, M., Gaussier, É., Maarek, Y., Nie, J., Scholer, F. (eds.) Proceedings of the 42nd International ACM SIGIR Conference on Research and Development in Information Retrieval, SIGIR 2019, Paris, France, 21–25 July 2019, pp. 165–174. ACM (2019). https://doi.org/10.1145/3331184.3331267

21. He, X., Deng, K., Wang, X., Li, Y., Zhang, Y., Wang, M.: LightGCN: simplifying and powering graph convolution network for recommendation. In: Proceedings of the 43rd International ACM SIGIR Conference on Research and Development in Information Retrieval, pp. 639–648. ACM, Virtual Event, China (2020)

22. Wang, C., et al.: Cthgat: category-aware and time-aware next point-of-interest via heterogeneous graph attention network. In: 2021 IEEE International Conference on Systems, Man, and Cybernetics (SMC), pp. 2420–2426 (2021). https://doi.org/10.1109/SMC52423.2021.9658805

23. Wang, X., Liu, X., Li, L., Chen, X., Liu, J., Wu, H.: Time-aware user modeling with check-in time prediction for next poi recommendation. In: 2021 IEEE International Conference on Web Services (ICWS), pp. 125–134 (2021). https://doi.org/10.1109/ICWS53863.2021.00028

24. Yu, D., Li, Y., Xu, F., Zhang, P., Kostakos, V.: Smartphone app usage prediction using points of interest. Proc. ACM Interact. Mob. Wearable Ubiquitous Technol. **1**(4), 174:1–174:21 (2017). https://doi.org/10.1145/3161413

25. Talkingdata: Talkingdata mobile user demographics. https://www.kaggle.com/c/talkingdata-mobile-user-demographics. Accessed 11 Oct 2018

26. Koren, Y., Bell, R., Volinsky, C.: Matrix factorization techniques for recommender systems. Computer **42**(8), 30–37 (2009)
27. Chen, X., Chen, J., Lian, X., Mai, W.: Resolving data sparsity via aggregating graph-based user-app-location association for location recommendations. Appl. Sci. **12**(14) (2022). https://doi.org/10.3390/app12146882

Driving Style Classification and Dynamic Recognition Considering Traffic State

Han Xing[1], Gangqiao Wang[2], Yi Liu[1(✉)], and Hui Zhang[1]

[1] Institute of Public Safety Research, Department of Engineering Physics,
Tsinghua University, Beijing 100084, China
liuyi@tsinghua.edu.cn
[2] College of Management, Shenzhen University, Shenzhen 518060, China

Abstract. Identifying aggressive driving styles and assisting in providing driving behavior recommendations is necessary to reduce traffic accidents and improve traffic safety. However, driving behaviours reflect driving intentions that vary with traffic states, resulting in uncertainty in the classification of driving styles. In this paper, the driving behavior is evaluated comprehensively from two dimensions of speed and headway, and then the driving intention is fully recognized to lay the foundation for solving the driving style ambiguity. The driving style is divided into five categories by using k-means clustering method. The results of variance test showed that 11 parameters are significantly different between groups. This shows that the driving style classification method proposed in this paper can distinguish different driving styles.

Keywords: Driving Intention · Traffic State · Driving Style Classification · K-Means · NGSIM

1 Introduction

Driving style refers to the accumulated driving habits of an individual in the process of driving [1, 8, 14]. If an individual often adopts aggressive or dangerous driving behaviors, it is aggressive driving style; otherwise, it is safe driving style. At present, the research results of driving style can be applied to tasks such as adaptive cruise system [17], fuel consumption prediction [9], vehicle insurance pricing [3], and dangerous driving identification [11], which has great application value.

The methods for studying driving style are mainly divided into two categories, one is to use questionnaires, the other is to use vehicle track data. The driving style classification is achieved by calculating the similarity between individuals. When calculating the similarity between individuals, most of them calculate the similarity of attributes or speed curves between two individuals. This ignores the impact of traffic environment and individual driving intentions in different environments.

In this paper, we combine the traffic environment, evaluate the driving behavior from two dimensions of speed and headway respectively, and get the driving

X. Meng et al. (Eds.): BDSC 2023, CCIS 1846, pp. 96–106, 2023.
https://doi.org/10.1007/978-981-99-3925-1_6

style characteristics of individuals by analyzing the driving intention of each individual driving behavior, so as to realize the driving style classification.

The sections of this paper are organized as follows, Sect. 2 is the research works. Section 3 is data processing. Section 4 is the driving intention and driving style classification, and Sect. 5 is the conclusion.

2   Research Works

The questionnaire method is to measure individual personality, emotion and other sociological information, and then distinguishes the individual's driving style. Moreover, driving behavior can be measured at the same time to establish the relationship between personality or emotion and driving behavior. The widely concerned work is the Multidimensional Driving Style Inventory (MDSI) questionnaire, which contains 44 items and divides driving styles into 8 categories [12], namely, dissociative, anxious, risky, angry, high-velocity, distress reduction, patient, and careful. The questionnaire shows the correlation between driving style and gender, age, race, car ownership and experience [13]. On the basis of the MDSI questionnaire, Hanneke [6] simplified the MDSI's 44 questions to 24 items using the maximum factor rotation method, and changed the driving style from 8 categories to 6 categories, namely, dissociative driving, anxious driving, risky driving, angry driving, distress reduction driving, and careful driving. In addition, driving simulator was used to collect individual driving behavior data, and it was found that there was a certain correlation between self-reported driving style and driving behavior data, which proved that the improved MDSI questionnaire could serve as a driving style classification tool for driving simulation [5].

The applied camera can collect trajectory data, including information on driving speed, position, and acceleration, without interference to the individual [7]. In the process of completing the driving task, the driving direction and acceleration are the driving behavior output after receiving the environmental information, so they can fully express the individual driving style. Vygandas collected urban public transportation trajectory data, extracted longitudinal acceleration, lateral acceleration, vertical acceleration and other features, and classified driving styles into aggressive and normal [15]. Evgenia collected instantaneous fuel consumption, vehicle speed, and accelerator pedal amplitude data, and applied a recursive Bayesian algorithm to cluster driving styles into seven categories [10]. Bing used KL (Kullback-Leibler) to calculate the similarity between different drivers based on space headway, relative speed and acceleration, and divided driving styles into three categories: aggressive, normal and cautious [17]. Laura defined the safety zone, and identified unsafe behaviors by the values of kinematic parameters (speed and acceleration) that do not conform to the safety zone [2]. In a period of time, the proportion of unsafe behaviors was used as the criteria for judging driving styles, which are divided into two categories: cautious and aggressive. Qiuyi divided highway traffic states into 12 operational categories (maneuver states), in which the five categories of free driving, approaching, near following, and constrained left and right lane changes can effectively classify driving styles into high risk, medium risk, and low risk [4]. Maria distinguished different positions, applied the clustering algorithm to distinguish different numbers of driving styles, and pointed out the trend of driving style switching in different positions [16].

3 Data Processing

The Next Generation Simulation Program (NGSIM) project collected vehicle trajectories on the US 101 freeway on June 15, 2005. The information collected includes: vehicle number, time, horizontal and vertical coordinates, lane number, vehicle length, speed, acceleration, headway, headway time, etc., which can meet the needs of driving style classification and recognition.

In driving tasks, the car-following behavior is the most important and common behavior, which occupies most of the individual's driving time and can fully reflect the individual's driving style. Therefore, this paper selects the individual's car-following behavior data as the base data for driving style classification and identification. Data pre-processing is divided into the following steps.

- Individuals need a certain reaction time to react to the current traffic state. The reaction time is denoted as $\Delta\tau$, and in this paper, $\Delta\tau$ is set equal to 1 s. To facilitate data exploration and analysis, the original data are re-sampled with an interval equal to $\Delta\tau$.
- Apply data such as vehicle number, time, lane number and horizontal and vertical coordinates to match the information of leading and following vehicles to the same line.
- Intercepting the car-following clips with time greater than or equal to 20 s.
- When the headway is greater than 100 m, the following vehicle is in a free-running state, so car following clips with headway less than or equal to 100 m are selected.

Applying the above rules, the data set consisting of the selected car following segments is denoted as $\mathbf{D}$, where i-th car following segment is denoted as $\mathbf{D}_i$, and the start time and end time of $\mathbf{D}_i$ is denoted as T_i^1 and T_i^n, respectively, and the descriptive statistics of $\mathbf{D}$ are shown in Table 1.

Table 1. Description Statistics of $\mathbf{D}$

Number of car following segments	Average car following time (s)	Average velocity (m/s)
4715	52.8660	8.8612
Variance of velocity	Average headway (m)	Variance of headway
4.2802	20.6455	10.1127

4 Driving Intention and Driving Style Classification

4.1 Driving Intention

Under different traffic states, the same driving behavior may represent different intentions, which is the difficulty in analyzing driving style. In the process of car-following, individuals are affected by headway and driving speed at the same time. This paper evaluates driving behaviors from two dimensions, driving speed and headway spacing, respectively, to fully identify the driving intentions of individuals.

In existing studies of car-following behavior, such as the Gipps model, it is assumed that the desired headway distance (s_d) of individual is equal to the minimum safe distance (s_m), which leads to the ideal acceleration (a_s) that an individual should adopt. If the individual adopts an acceleration greater than a_s, it is aggressive or dangerous. If the acceleration adopted by the individual is less than a_s, it is conservative or safe.

However, in the actual car-following process, the individual desired headway is often not equal to s_m. Based on data set D, the Pearson correlation coefficients between $s(t + \Delta\tau)$ and $s_m(t)$, $s(t) - s_m(t)$ are calculated to be equal to 0.3443 and 0.8829, respectively, and the Spearman correlation coefficients are equal to 0.4244 and 0.7781, respectively. This indicates that there is a weakly correlation between $s(t+\Delta\tau)$ and $s_m(t)$, while there is a strong correlation between $s(t+\Delta\tau)$ and $s(t) - s_m(t)$, as in Fig. 1(A). Therefore, we define s_d as in Eq. 1.

$$s_d(t + \Delta\tau) = w_s^1 * s_m(t) + w_s^2 * (s(t) - s_m(t)) + \lambda_s \tag{1}$$

$$s_m(t) = \frac{v_f^2(t)}{2b_f} + v_f(t) * \Delta\tau + L_l - \frac{v_l^2(t)}{2b_l} \tag{2}$$

where, w_s^1=0.8785; w_s^2=0.1615; λ_s=1.4321; b_f and b_l represent the maximum deceleration of the following car and leading car, respectively, and they are set equal to 5 m/s^2; L_l represents the body length of the leading vehicle.

Take s(t) into $s_d(t+\Delta\tau)$ in Eq. 1 to calculate the velocity $v_s(t)$ that should be adopted from the headway dimension at this time, as shown in Eq. 3. Then the theoretical optimal acceleration $a_s(t)$ that should be adopted from the headway dimension is obtained, as shown in Eq. 4.

$$v_s(t) = [2b_f(\frac{(1 - w_s^2)s(t) - \lambda_s}{w_s^1 - w_s^2} + \frac{v_l^2(t)}{2b_l} - L_l) + (b_f\Delta\tau)^2]^{\frac{1}{2}} - b_f\Delta\tau \tag{3}$$

$$a_s(t) = \frac{v_s(t) - v_f(t)}{\Delta\tau} \tag{4}$$

It has been pointed out that the individual desired driving speed (v_d) is similar to the speed (v_l) of the leading vehicle [17]. Therefore, the Pearson correlation coefficients between $v_f(t + \Delta\tau)$ and $v_l(t)$, $v_l(t) - v_f(t)$ are calculated to be equal

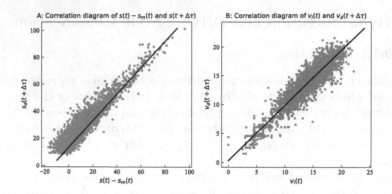

Fig. 1. Correlation diagram between $s(t + \Delta\tau)$ and $s(t) - s_m(t)$, $v_f(t + \Delta\tau)$ and $v_l(t)$

to 0.9656 and 0.0249, respectively, and the Spearman correlation coefficients are equal to 0.9647 and 0.0333, respectively. The scatter plot between $v_f(t + \Delta\tau)$ and $v_l(t)$ is shown in Fig. 1(B). Similarly, $v_d(t)$ is defined as in Eq. 5, and then the theoretical optimal acceleration $a_v(t)$ is defined from the perspective of the desired velocity as in Eq. 6.

$$v_d(t) = w_v^1 v_l(t) + w_v^2 t(v_l(t) - v_f(t)) + \lambda_v \tag{5}$$

$$a_v(t) = \frac{v_d^t - v_f(t)}{\Delta\tau} \tag{6}$$

The a_s and a_v represent the theoretical desired acceleration. If the actual acceleration a_f adopted by an individual is greater than a_s or a_v, the individual's intended headway is less than s_m, or the speed is greater than v_d, which means that the individual's driving intention is aggressive or dangerous. If a_f is less than a_s or a_v, the individual intends that the headway is greater than s_m, or the speed is less than v_d, which means that the individual's driving intention is safe or conservative.

4.2   Driving Style Classification

After specifying an individual's driving intention, it is not convenient enough to express the driving style features. Therefore, driving behavior benefits and categories are proposed.

In an arbitrary traffic state, if a_f is closer to a_s and a_v, the individual will approach desired car-following state. If a_f deviates more from a_s and a_v, the more it deviates from the desired following state. Therefore, the Gaussian function is applied to calculate the driving behavior gain as in Eq. 7.

$$R(t) = \begin{cases} R_s(t) = \frac{1}{\sqrt{2\pi}\sigma_s} e^{-\frac{[a_f(t)-a_s(t)]^2}{2\sigma_s^2}} \\ R_v(t) = \frac{1}{\sqrt{2\pi}\sigma_v} e^{-\frac{[a_f(t)-a_v(t)]^2}{2\sigma_v^2}} \end{cases} \tag{7}$$

where σ_s, σ_v represent the standard deviation of $a_s(t)$, $a_v(t)$ in the dataset $\mathbf{D}$, respectively.

Define the dataset formed by the acceleration a_f adopted by an individual as $\mathbf{D}_a$, and let $\delta \in \mathbf{D}_a$. It is known that

$$\int_{-\infty}^{+\infty} R_v da_f(t) = \int_{-\infty}^{+\infty} R_s da_f(t) = 1.$$

Define the driving behavior categories as in Eq. 8. Let $b = 1, \cdots, 7$.

$$B(t) = \begin{cases} B_s(t) = \begin{cases} b & \frac{b-1}{7} \le \int_{-\infty}^{\delta} R_s(t) da_f(t) < \frac{b}{7} \\ 7 & \int_{-\infty}^{\delta} R_s(t) da_f(t) = 1 \end{cases} \\ B_v(t) = \begin{cases} b & \frac{b-1}{7} \le \int_{-\infty}^{\delta} R_v(t) da_f(t) < \frac{b}{7} \\ 7 & \int_{-\infty}^{\delta} R_v(t) da_f(t) = 1 \end{cases} \end{cases} \tag{8}$$

In total, $B(t)$ divides the driving behavior of individuals in all traffic states into seven categories, and $B(t)$ represents the driving behavior features at moment t. Taking the states of $v_f(t) < v_d(t)$ and $v_f(t) < v_s(t)$ as examples, the distributions of $B_v(t)$ and $B_s(t)$ are drawn in Fig. 2.

In Fig. 2, when $a_f(t)$ is close to $a_v(t)$ or $a_s(t)$, it indicates that the vehicle will follow in the desired state, so it is judged that such driving behavior is neutral, corresponding to the categories of $B_v = 4$ and $B_S = 4$. When $a_f(t)$ is less than $a_v(t)$ or $a_s(t)$, this type of driving behavior is conservative, corresponding to the categories of $B_v = 1, 2, 3$ and $B_S = 1, 2, 3$, where category 1 represents the most conservative category. When $a_f(t)$ is greater than $a_v(t)$ or $a_s(t)$, such driving behavior is radical, corresponding to the categories of $B_v = 5, 6, 7$ and $B_S = 5, 6, 7$, where category 7 represents the most aggressive driving behavior category.

The individual driving behavior category can represent the driving style features within a period of time. The frequency f_v^b and f_s^b of the driving behavior category B_v and B_s within the $[T_i^1, T_i^n]$ period are counted. For the $i - th$ car following segment $\mathbf{D}_i$, its driving style feature F_i is composed of f_v^b and f_s^b, as shown in Eq. 9.

$$F_i = f_v^b || f_s^b \tag{9}$$

$$\begin{cases} f_v^b = \frac{1}{n} countif(B_v = b) \\ f_s^b = \frac{1}{n} countif(B_s = b) \end{cases} \tag{10}$$

where, $||$ represents the splicing of two vectors, $F_i \in R^{1*(2*7)}$, $i = 1, 2, 3, \ldots, N$, N represents the number of car-following segments, $N=4715$.

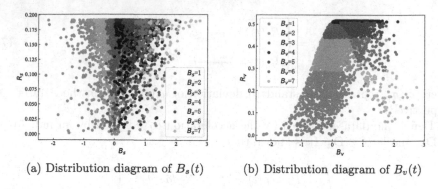

(a) Distribution diagram of $B_s(t)$ (b) Distribution diagram of $B_v(t)$

Fig. 2. Distribution of $B_s(t)$ and $B_v(t)$ under $v_f(t) < v_d(t)$ and $v_f(t) < v_s(t)$

In this paper, K-means method is applied to realize driving style classification, and the classification results when the number of clusters k is within the interval [3,9] are compared. The Calinski-harabasz index is used to evaluate the clustering results. If the Calinski-harabasz index value is higher, the clustering effect is better.

Before applying the K-means algorithm, the PCA algorithm is applied to achieve orthogonality between features, and the first three features, which contain 93% of the feature information, are extracted as the input features of driving style classification. When the number of clusters k is taken within the interval [3,9], the Calinski-harabasz index is shown in Fig. 3. It can be seen that when $k = 5$ is selected, the Calinski harabasz index is the largest. Therefore, the driving style is divided into five categories, and the features distribution of different categories are shown in Fig. 4.

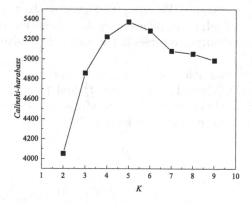

Fig. 3. Calinski-harabasz index value when $k \in [3, 9]$

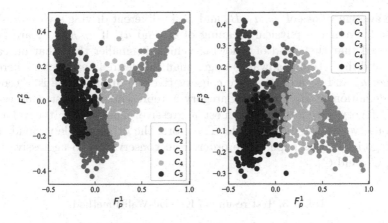

Fig. 4. Distribution of driving style classification features

Test whether the following 11 variables have significant differences among different driving style groups. If the differences are significant, it indicates that the driving style classification is effective. The Shapiro-Wilk and Kolmogorov-Smirnovtest methods are used to test the normal distribution of variables, and the Levene is used to test the homogeneity of variance of parameters. The test results are shown in Table 2. The test results show that the p value is less than 0.01, so the 11 variables to be tested do not obey the Gaussian distribution, and the variances do not have homogeneity. Therefore, Kruskal-Wallis is selected to test the differences between different driving style categories, and the test results are shown in Table 3. The test results show that among different driving style categories, the 11 variables in the above tests have significant differences. This proves that the driving style classification method proposed in this paper can fully extract the driving style features from the trajectory data, and has the ability to distinguish different individual driving styles.

Table 2. Test results of Shapiro-Wilk and Kolmogorov-Smirnovtest methods

	v_f	a_f	s	v_s	a_s	v_d
Levene	1.9705E-245	4.1634E-29	0.0000	0.0000	0.0000	0.0000
Shapiro-Wilk	0.0000	0.0000	0.0000	0.0000	0.0000	0.0000
Kolmogorov-Smirnovtest	0.0000	0.0000	0.0000	0.0000	0.0000	0.0000
	a_v	R_v	R_s	B_v	B_s	
Levene	0.0000	0.0000	0.0000	0.0000	0.0000	
Shapiro-Wilk	0.0000	0.0000	0.0000	0.0000	0.0000	
Kolmogorov-Smirnovtest	0.0000	0.0000	0.0000	0.0000	0.0000	

The average values of a_v, a_s, B_v and B_s in different driving styles are shown in Table 4. From the physical meaning of a_v and a_s, if a_v and a_s are larger, it is proved that the speed of following vehicle is smaller than that of leading vehicle, and the actual headway is larger than the desired headspace. Therefore, the larger a_v and a_s are, the more conservative the driving style is. According to the definition of B_v and B_s, Category 1 represents the most conservative, while Category 7 represents the most aggressive. The smaller the value, the more conservative the driving style. Therefore, the driving style is divided into five categories in this paper. The order from conservative to aggressive is C_1, C_4, C_2, C_5, and C_3.

Table 3. Test results of Kruskal-Wallis method

	v_f	a_f	s	v_s	a_s	v_d
Statistical value	10803.2914	48.5140	46007.5124	10688.4779	87876.4707	9999.7221
p	0.0000	7.3739E-10	0.0000	0.0000	0.0000	0.0000
	a_v	R_v	R_s	B_v	B_s	
Levene	0.0000	0.0000	0.0000	0.0000	0.0000	
Statistical value	1473.8025	9278.5954	50838.3695	1701.6234	106999.7887	
p	0.0000	0.0000	0.0000	0.0000	0.0000	

Table 4. Statistics of Driving Style Classification Results

	Number of driving style groups	mean(a_v)	mean(a_s)	mean(B_v)	mean(B_s)
C_1	415	0.4717	3.9579	3.5010	1.3935
C_2	1325	0.0865	0.9116	3.9175	3.0533
C_3	737	0.0246	−1.1607	4.0538	5.3430
C_4	892	0.1918	1.9684	3.7918	2.2166
C_5	1346	0.0679	−0.0974	3.9643	4.1766

5   Conclusion

This paper proposes a driving style classification and identification method. Firstly, combining with the real-time traffic environment, the driving intention of individuals is fully recognized from two dimensions of speed and headway. Secondly, the driving styles are divided into five categories, and all 11 parameters in different categories are significantly different between groups.

For individuals with the most aggressive C_3 driving style, providing advice on deceleration driving behavior can reduce the probability of traffic accidents. For individuals with the most conservative C_1 driving style, providing stable driving behavior suggestions can reduce the phenomenon of traffic turbulence and improve the traffic efficiency of the road. Under different traffic conditions, the next step is to study the impact of different driving styles on traffic safety and traffic efficiency.

Acknowledgments. Funded by National Key R&D Program of China (No. 2021YFC3001500) and National Natural Science Foundation of China (No. 72174102, No. 72004141).

Conflict of Interest Statement. The authors declare that they have no conflict of interest.

References

1. Blander, J., West, R., French, D.: Behavioral correlates of individual differences in road-traffic crash risk: an examination of methods and findings. Psychol. Bull. **113**, 279–294 (1993)
2. Eboli, L., Mazzulla, G., Pungillo, G.: How drivers' characteristics can affect driving style. Transp. Res. Procedia **27**, 945–952 (2017)
3. Eboli, L., Mazzulla, G., Pungillo, G.: The influence of physical and emotional factors on driving style of car drivers: a survey design. Travel Behav. Soc **7**, 43–51 (2017)
4. Guo, Q., Zhao, Z., Shen, P., Zhan, X., Li, J.: Adaptive optimal control based on driving style recognition for plugin hybrid electric vehicle. Energy **186**, 115824 (2019)
5. Huysduynen, H.H.V., Terken, J., Eggen, B.: The relation between self-reported driving style and driving behaviour. A simulator study. Transp. Res. Part F Traff. Psychol. Behav. **56**, 245–255 (2018)
6. Huysduynen, H.H.V., Terken, J., Martens, J.B., Eggen, B.: Measuring driving styles: a validation of the multidimensional driving style inventory. In: Proceedings of the 7th International Conference on Automotive User Interfaces and Interactive Vehicular Applications, pp. 257–264 (2015)
7. Nes, N.V., Bärgman, J., Christoph, M., Schagen, I.V.: The potential of naturalistic driving for in-depth understanding of driver behavior: Udrive results and beyond. Saf. Sci. **119**, 11–20 (2019)
8. Sagberg, F., Piccinini, F.B., Sweden, Engström, J.: A review of research on driving styles and road safety. Accid. Anal. Prevent. **57**, 1248–1275 (2015)
9. Javanmardi, S., Bideaux, E., Trégouët, J.F., Trigui, R., Tattegrain, H., Bourles, E.: Driving style modelling for eco-driving applications. ScienceDirect **51**, 13866–13871 (2017)
10. Suzdaleva, E., Nagya, I.: An online estimation of driving style using data-dependent pointer model. Transp. Res. Part C **86**, 23–36 (2018)
11. Suzdaleva, E., Nagy, I.: Two-layer pointer model of driving style depending on the driving environment. Transp. Res. Part B **128**, 254–270 (2019)
12. Taubman-Ben-Ari, O., Mikulincer, M., Gillath, O.: The multidimensional driving style inventory-scale construct and validation. Accid. Anal. Prevent. **36**(3), 323–332 (2004)
13. Taubman-Ben-Ari, O., Skvirsky, V.: The multidimensional driving style inventory a decade later: review of the literature and re-evaluation of the scale. Accid. Anal. Prevent. **93**, 179–188 (2016)

14. Taubman-Ben-Ari, O., Yehiel, D.: Driving styles and their associations with personality and motivation. Accid. Anal. Prev. **45**, 416–422 (2012)
15. Vaitkus, V., Lengvenis, P., Žylius, G.: Driving style classification using long-term accelerometer information. In: 19th International Conference on Methods and Models in Automation and Robotics, vol. 9, pp. 641–644 (2014)
16. de Zepeda, M.V.N., Meng, F., Su, J., Zeng, X.J., Wang, Q.: Dynamic clustering analysis for driving styles identification. Eng. Appl. Artif. Intell. **97**, 104096 (2021)
17. Zhu, B., Jiang, Y., Zhao, J., He, R., Bian, N., Deng, W.: Typical-driving-style-oriented personalized adaptive cruise control design based on human driving data. Transp. Res. Part C Emerg. Technol. **100**, 274–288 (2015)

Who Connects Wikipedia? A Deep Analysis of Node Roles and Connection Patterns in Wikilink Network

Hongyu Dong[✉] and Haoxiang Xia

Institute of Systems Engineering, Dalian University of Technology, Dalian, Liaoning 116024, China
dlsp@mail.dlut.edu.cn

Abstract. Wikipedia is not only an online encyclopedia, but also a spontaneously formed network of knowledge. Its important information is contained not only in the content of the pages, but also in the links between them. The larger the network, the more complex its internal hierarchy. This study analyses the role of nodes in the Wikipedia link network and the linking patterns of the network, and finds that the network is composed of a few highly core nodes and a large number of edge nodes populating it. These high nodes are not tightly connected to each other, often in different knowledge communities, and are connected through a plurality of club nodes across communities, which play an integral role in the transfer and flow of information throughout the network. This study reveals the roles and information transfer mechanisms of key nodes in the network and provides a reference for building more efficient knowledge networks.

Keywords: Wikipedia · Complex Network · Community Structure · Diverse Club · Connection Patterns

1 Introduction

Knowledge innovation and growth are vital to human social and economic development, and the development of the information age poses new challenges to the integration of knowledge and the need for new forms of knowledge organization. As one of the world's largest self-organizing knowledge communities, Wikipedia's content entries are compiled collaboratively by volunteers and organized on the basis of group intelligence and a self-organizing development process. Wikipedia's reliance on group intelligence provides a model for the study of self-organized creation in the growth of scientific knowledge, and its linking structure and knowledge construction model are important for the construction and integration of group knowledge.

Lizorkin et al. divided the Wikipedia network into communities and found that there are semantically closely related entries between different communities in the network, which play an important role in connecting and communicating between different communities [1]. Brandes et al. analyzed the cooperation between editors by relationships, they found that the side relationships of the link network were related to the quality of

X. Meng et al. (Eds.): BDSC 2023, CCIS 1846, pp. 107–118, 2023.
https://doi.org/10.1007/978-981-99-3925-1_7

the lexical content [2]. Simulation of network dynamics [3] and growth models using the edge relations of Wikilink networks [4] is also one of the hot research topics, and these studies fully illustrate the vast amount of information hidden in the structure of Wikipedia link networks.

The information in Wikipedia's knowledge network is contained in the content of the entries and the links between them. The structure of the link network directly affects the efficiency of knowledge integration and the development pattern of Wikipedia. However, there is a lack of in-depth research on the structural form and formation process of Wikipedia's link networks. In order to grasp the mechanism of efficient organization of knowledge in the current information age, this study examines the changes in the key structure of Wikipedia link networks from the perspective of complex networks, using the English Wikipedia from 2002–2018 as the research object.

2 Methods

2.1 Nodes Connectivity in Community

The larger the network, the more complex the internal hierarchy. Guimerà and Amaral proposed a method for characterising the role of nodes in the context of the presence of a network community in 2005 [5]. The role of a node in a network is mainly determined by the strength of its connectivity within a community and the breadth of its connectivity between communities [5, 6], which are denoted using Z_i and P_i, respectively.

The within-module degree Z_i measures the strength of connectivity between node i and other nodes within its community.

$$Z_i = \frac{K_i - \overline{K}_{S_i}}{\sigma_{K_{S_i}}} \tag{1}$$

where K_{S_i} is the number of neighbouring nodes of node i in community s, $\overline{K}_{S_i}$ is the mean of the K values of all nodes in community s, and $\sigma_{K_{S_i}}$ is the standard deviation of the K values of all nodes in community s. From the above equation, Z_i is the quantile of z-score in the whole community and is the normalised level of the strength of the node's connection to the community within its community. Values generally range from -2 to 10, with nodes of higher degree generally having higher Z-scores.

The participation coefficient measures the communication role of a node with other communities and ranges from 0 to 1. The more concentrated the edges of a node are in one community the smaller the value, and conversely the more evenly distributed it is across multiple communities the larger the value [5]. P can be expressed as

$$P_i = 1 - \sum_{s=1}^{N_M} \left(\frac{K_{is}}{K_i}\right)^2 \tag{2}$$

where N_M represents the total number of communities in the network, K_i is the degree of node i, and K_{is} the number of edges of node i in community s.

2.2 Network Role Segmentation

The P and Z values determine a node's connectivity role in its community and in other communities. Guimerà et al. proposed a method for classifying nodes' roles based on their P and Z values, and in this study nodes with Z values greater than 2.5 were classified as core nodes and nodes with Z values less than 2.5 were classified as non-core nodes with reference to the former. The specific division and its distribution in the Z-P parameter space are shown in the figure below. We can define the nodes in the wiki link network as different roles according to the above metrics, analyse their distribution and the connection methods between nodes in the Z-P space, and compare them with the random network to obtain the connection information between the nodes with different roles in the network [5] (Fig. 1)

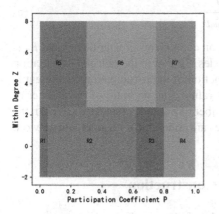

$$Z \geq 2.5, \begin{cases} P \leq 0.3, \text{ provincial hubs} \\ 0.3 < P \leq 0.75, \text{ connector hubs} \\ P > 0.75, \text{ kinless hubs} \end{cases}$$

$$Z < 2.5, \begin{cases} P \leq 0.05, \text{ ultra - peripheral nodes} \\ 0.05 < P \leq 0.62, \text{ peripheral nodes} \\ 0.62 < P \leq 0.8, \text{ non - hub connector} \\ P > 0.8, \text{ non - hub kinless nodes} \end{cases}$$

(a) Regional distribution of node roles in Z-P space   (b) Node role division based on Z-P value

Fig. 1. Division of node roles in the network

2.3 Clubness of Complex Network

In order to describe the characteristics of nodes that are more connected to each other, the concept of rich-club was introduced by Colizza et al. in 2006 [7]. There exists a high degree of nodes in the network with strong connectivity between them, which can be measured by the rich-club coefficient, which is calculated as follows

$$\phi(k) = \frac{2E_k}{N_k(N_k - 1)} \tag{3}$$

$$\phi_{norm} = \frac{\phi}{\phi_{rand}} \tag{4}$$

where N_k is the number of nodes with degree greater than k and E_k is the number of connected edges between these nodes. The rich club factor is calculated by sorting the nodes in reverse order of their degree values, then removing them one at a time and calculating the ratio of the number of contiguous edges in the network to the maximum possible number of contiguous edges. The rich club is a relative concept and to obtain a quantitative description requires generating a random network with the same degree distribution and dividing the two to obtain the normalised rich club coefficient.

In 2017 Bertolero et al. introduced the concept of the diverse-club [8], which measures the connectivity between nodes using a ranking of participation coefficients. A network with the phenomenon of diverse-club contains a group of nodes spanning multiple communities, connected to each other by multiple edges and simultaneously having a high level of mediated centrality. This is calculated as follows:

$$\theta(p) = \frac{2E_p}{N_p(N_p - 1)} \tag{5}$$

$$\theta_{norm} = \frac{\theta}{\theta_{rand}} \tag{6}$$

where N_p is the number of nodes with participation coefficients greater than P and E_p is the number of connected edges between these nodes. Similar to the rich club calculation process, the multivariate club coefficient is a function of the participation coefficient P. The nodes are sorted from smallest to largest P values, and the ratio of the number of remaining connected edges to the maximum number of possible connected edges in the network is removed and calculated, and the values are compared with a random network of the same size.

3   Data Pre-processing and Network Construction

Cristian et al. crawled and processed Wikipedia data from complete dumps prior to that year in 2019 to obtain highly formatted Wikipedia link network data by parsing and regular matching of xml files to obtain node and link data [9]. This dataset was used in this study to obtain link data from the establishment of Wikipedia in 2001 until March 1st, 2018. The dataset contains a complete snapshot of the Wikipedia link network for each year.

Based on the network created after data cleaning and removal of redirected links, this study analysed the relationship between the number of nodes and the number of edges of the English Wikipedia link network. We find that the nodes and edges of the linked network show an approximate linear growth over time. According to the study, the relationship between the number of edges E(t) and the number of nodes N(t) in a time-evolving network can be expressed as $E(t) \propto N(t)^\alpha$ [10][11], where $1 \le \alpha \le 2$. When $\alpha = 1$ the network shows a sparse growth pattern, at which time the new connected edges of the network cannot maintain the link strength between the new nodes and the average degree of the network remains unchanged; when $\alpha = 2$ the network is a fully connected network, where the added nodes are connected to all previous nodes; $1 < \alpha < 2$ corresponds to the case in between.

Plotting the number of nodes versus the number of edges for each year of Wikipedia to obtain Fig. 2, it can be found that Wikipedia shows a highly fitted linear growth relationship with $\alpha = 1$, at which point the network will become increasingly sparse over time. The slope of the line with the redirected node data removed is 11, i.e. every additional 1 node in the network is connected to 11 nodes in the network, while in the original data this number is 1.8. It can be seen that about 80% of the connected edges in Wikipedia are redirected connected edges.

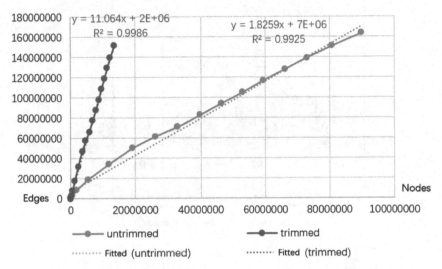

Fig. 2. Growth between the number of edges and nodes in Wikilink network

4 Node Role Classification and Distribution Characteristics

The underlying information is not sufficient for a complete portrayal of the network properties. In this section we take the 2002 network as an example, and will analyse the role and distribution of nodes in the Wikipedia link network. In this paper, the nodes in the network are divided into seven categories, and a scatter plot and density plot of the distribution of nodes in the linked network in 2002 are plotted in Z-P space, as shown in figure (a) below. The blue line in the figure represents the density distribution of nodes, the red on the right and upper side represents the density distribution of node attributes on each axis, and the grey bars and curves are the distribution box plots and density curves. We also labelled the nodes for each role in the network, as shown in figure (b) below. Nodes with a degree less than 20 have been removed from this figure, and the percentage marked is the proportion of nodes with a degree greater than 20 in the network (Fig. 3).

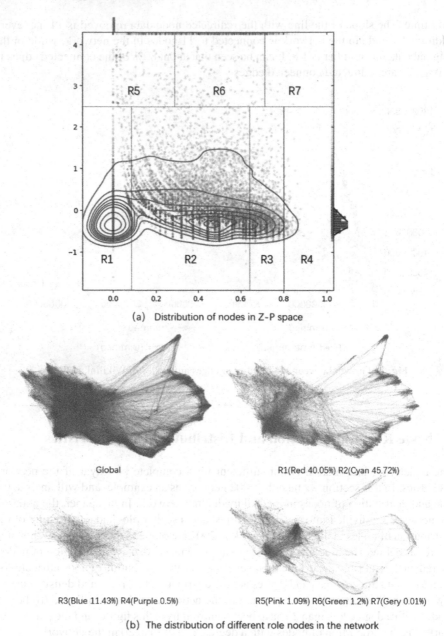

(a) Distribution of nodes in Z–P space

Global

R1(Red 40.05%) R2(Cyan 45.72%)

R3(Blue 11.43%) R4(Purple 0.5%)

R5(Pink 1.09%) R6(Green 1.2%) R7(Gery 0.01%)

(b) The distribution of different role nodes in the network

Fig. 3. Node role classification and distribution in 2002 Wikilink network

According to the density map we can find that the number of high Z-value R5-R7 nodes in the network is relatively small, while the low Z-value R1 and R2 types are relatively small. In terms of distribution, the edge nodes in the network show a roughly concentrated distribution and have less impact on the overall shape of the link network, but the percentage of these nodes in the network determines the overall size of the network. Combining the proportions of the different roles and their distribution in the network, we believe that the R3, R4, R5 and R6 nodes in the network mainly influence the overall connectivity characteristics of the network. The core nodes rely on their height values to connect a large number of nodes in their own communities, and have extensive links to other communities in the amateur world. The distribution of the height-valued nodes can be seen to be highly overlapping with R1 and R2 nodes and are centrally located. These core nodes are connected to other communities in the network, and are not particularly prominent in their own participation coefficients due to their height values, but their location determines the important role they play in the connectivity of the network. The high p-values R3 and R4 nodes are a series of bridge nodes with low degree values but widely present across communities, as can be seen from the distribution, and they are widely present across the clusters R1 and R2 nodes. In other words, the whole linking network is a network skeleton composed of core nodes with high Z-values. Their high values ensure the linking strength of the core structure of the network, and the rest of the nodes with high P-values populate the network skeleton to keep the different knowledge communities closely connected to each other, constituting a complex and ponderous knowledge network.

5 Clubness of Wikilink Network

In order to further analyse how nodes with high Z-value and high P-value are connected in the network, this paper analyses the club phenomenon in the network, and calculates the clubness coefficient in the network after removing nodes according to the percentage size of degree, P-value and Z-value respectively, and the results are shown in the figure below. It can be found that there is no obvious rich club and Z-club phenomenon in the network, and even the remaining link strength in the network is lower than that of a random network of the same size after the percentage of deleted nodes exceeds 80%. This may be related to the fact that the high-value and high-Z-value nodes are scattered in different knowledge communities in the network; for example, it is difficult for core nodes in the humanities to form connections with high-value nodes in the astronomy community, and although there may be more links between the two communities, these connections do not exist between the smaller number of high-value and high-Z-value nodes. This may be due to the fact that height-valued nodes in the network belong to separate domains of biology, for example anatomy and plants are difficult to directly relate to each other, so the connections between height nodes are not strong. A corresponding explanation can also be obtained from the division of node attributes in the Z-P space, where a higher proportion of core nodes are local core nodes, and such nodes tend to be connected only to nodes within the community, with fewer connections between local core nodes in different communities, again demonstrating that the connections between height nodes in the network are not strong. Due to the high correlation between node Z-values and degrees, rich clubs and Z-clubs show similar results (Fig. 4).

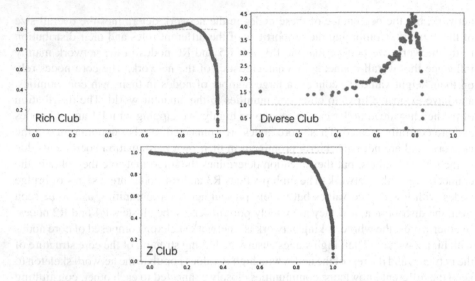

Fig. 4. The clubness coefficients for various clubs in 2002 Wikilink network

On the other hand, when nodes are removed in order of participation coefficient, the strength of connections in the network is consistently significantly higher than in a random network of the same size, with the remaining network being about four times stronger at 90% removal, after which an inflection point occurs, due to the large number of nodes with zero participation coefficients, whose neighbours are located in the same community and do not have connected edges across communities. After removing these nodes the remaining part of the network is very tightly linked. The existence of the plural club phenomenon suggests that nodes spanning different communities play an important role in linking knowledge in Wikipedia, mainly referring to R3, R4 and R7 nodes in the node classification. Combining the distribution of nodes with high participation coefficients in the network, as indicated in Fig. 3.11, with the distribution of nodes in the R3 and R4 categories in Fig. 3.12, we find that these nodes are in a position between communities and play an important role in the connectivity of the communities.

6   How Nodes of Different Role are Connected

Following an analysis of the connectivity patterns between the global nodes of the network, this study analyses the connectivity patterns between the various types of nodes in the network. This study proposes a random network generation algorithm that maintains the same distribution of network neutrality and modularity for random networks for comparison.

The number of nodes of each role in the network was first counted and compared with the random network generated by the same degree distribution and the algorithm in this paper, where each type of random network was generated 10 times to reduce the error and the average was taken as the final result, as shown in the figure below. When comparing the two, it can be seen that the number of nodes in networks with the same degree distribution can vary depending on the structure and nature of the network. The number of R3 and R4 nodes in the random network is significantly higher than that of the original and reconstructed networks, while the number of R1 and R2 nodes is lower. This is due to the fact that random networks are selected with equal probability from among all nodes of the network when performing edge rearrangement, whereas the algorithm used in this paper is a random selection of nodes within and across communities in which they are located, placing restrictions on the connectivity range connections of knowledge lexemes that are more realistic (Fig. 5).

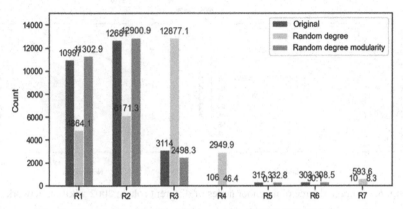

Fig. 5. Number of nodes for different roles in 2002 Wikilink network

The paper then analyses the average degree of the neighbouring nodes of each role node, as shown below. In order, the original network in 2002, the random network in igraph and the network generated by the algorithm used in this paper. The horizontal axis is the degree value of each type of node, the vertical axis is the average degree of neighbouring nodes, and each line represents the different role nodes plotted in double logarithmic coordinates. It can be noticed that the results of the original network are relatively similar to those of the networks generated in this paper, while the results of the random network show another pattern. Specifically the results for the network as a whole are broadly similar due to the same degree distribution for all three networks, but the results for the nodes of each role are quite different. In the random network R1, R2 and R3 nodes all preferred to connect to nodes with higher degree values, showing some heterogeneity. Whereas in the wiki network the tendency for R1 role nodes to connect to high degree nodes is closer to the network overall, high participation coefficient nodes show a similar tendency, and overall there is little variability in the tendency to link across role nodes with different degree values (Fig. 6).

We then analysed the strength of the links between the actors in the network and compared it with the results of the reconfiguration network, where the junction of each actor node in the figure (a) below represents the ratio of the number of linked edges between them to the number of possible linked edges in the network, and regularised the results of the reconfiguration network of the same size. We found that the links between R1 and R3 and R4 nodes in the linked network are more sparse than in the random network, while the links with R5 and R6 nodes are stronger than in the random network.

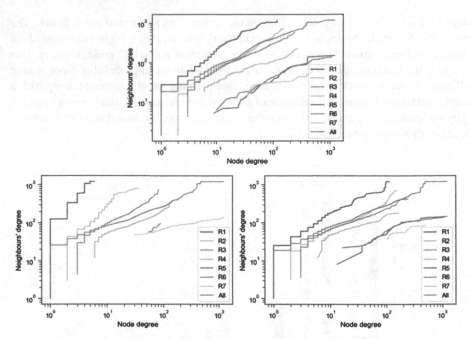

Fig. 6. Average degree of neighbor nodes of different role in 2002 wikilink network

That is, the general nodes in the community in the network are more connected to the central node of the community and less connected to the cross-community nodes, and the core nodes in the community of the explicit network are more connected to the bridge nodes between the communities, and it is through the nodes with high participation coefficients that the core nodes are connected to other nodes in the network. The number of R7 nodes is much less than in the random network, and thus the analysis of the strength of linked edges is not significant (Fig. 7).

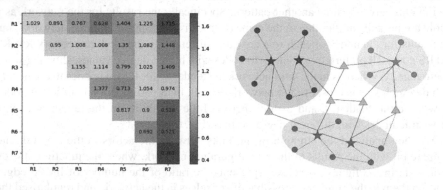

(a) Connection strength between different role nodes   (b) Schematic diagram of the structure between roles

Fig. 7. Connection patterns between different role nodes in 2002 Wikilink network

Putting the above analysis together, we can derive a broad picture about the connectivity patterns between the different actors in the network, with a schematic representation of the connectivity patterns shown in (b) above. Where circles represent the general low-degree value nodes in the network, these are the most numerous nodes in the network and represent general concepts in the knowledge community. These nodes are more numerous than a random network of the same size and have little impact on the structure of the network but influence the size of the network. The richness of the knowledge content expands the body of knowledge in Wikipedia and is an important part of the knowledge network. The pentagram represents the core nodes of the network, which are the core concepts of the knowledge community, and form the knowledge skeleton of the community in which they are located by linking to the general entries that make up the content of the community. The triangles represent the very few cross-community nodes in the network, which are connected more strongly than other role nodes in the network and bridge the inter-community connections by linking to the core nodes within the community, playing an important role in the knowledge integration of the network.

7 Conclusion

This study constructed an annual Wikipedia network by data pre-processing and cleaning the raw data of the English Wikipedia link network from 2002–2018. The node roles and linking patterns of the network were analysed and it was found that the network is composed of a small number of highly core nodes and a large number of edge nodes populating it. Highly valued nodes are often located in different knowledge communities and are not tightly connected to each other. There is no obvious rich club phenomenon in the network, but rather connections are made through a plurality of club nodes across communities, which play an integral role in the transfer and circulation of information throughout the network.

The results of this study help us to gain insights into the characteristics and evolutionary patterns of Wikilink network, reveal the roles and information transfer mechanisms of key nodes in the network, and provide useful references for building more robust and efficient knowledge networks.

References

1. Brandes, U., Kenis, P., Lerner, J., Van Raaij, D.: Network analysis of collaboration structure in Wikipedia. In: Proceedings of the 18th International Conference on World Wide Web, pp. 731–740 (2009)
2. Buriol, L.S., Castillo, C., Donato, D., Leonardi, S., Millozzi, S.: Temporal analysis of the Wikigraph. In: 2006 IEEE/WIC/ACM International Conference on Web Intelligence (WI 2006 Main Conference Proceedings) (WI'06), pp. 45–51 (2006)
3. Consonni, C., Laniado, D., Montresor, A.: WikiLinkGraphs: A Complete, Longitudinal and Multi-Language Dataset of the Wikipedia Link Networks (2019)
4. Csardi, G., Nepusz, T.: The igraph software package for complex network research. Int. J. Compl. Syst. **1695** (2006)
5. Guimera, R., Nunes Amaral, L.A.: Functional cartography of complex metabolic networks. Nature **433**(7028), 895–900 (2005)

6. Hagberg, A., Swart, P., Chult, D.S.: Exploring network structure, dynamics, and function using NetworkX. Los Alamos National Lab. (LANL), Los Alamos, NM (United States) (2008)
7. Leskovec, J., Kleinberg, J., Faloutsos, C.: Graphs over time: densification laws, shrinking diameters and possible explanations. In: Proceedings of the Eleventh ACM SIGKDD International Conference on Knowledge Discovery in Data Mining, pp. 177–187 (2005)
8. Lizorkin, D., Medelyan, O., Grineva, M.: Analysis of community structure in Wikipedia. In: Proceedings of the 18th International Conference on World Wide Web, pp. 1221–1222 (2009)
9. Masucci, A.P., Kalampokis, A., Eguíluz, V.M., Hernández-García, E.: Extracting directed information flow networks: an application to genetics and semantics. Phys. Rev. E **83**(2), 026103 (2011)
10. Porter, A., Mirzasoleiman, B., Leskovec, J.: Analytical models for motifs in temporal networks: discovering trends and anomalies. arXiv preprint arXiv:211214871 (2021)
11. Ravasz, E., Somera, A.L., Mongru, D.A., Oltvai, Z.N., Barabási, A.-L.: Hierarchical organization of modularity in metabolic networks. Science **297**(5586), 1551–1555 (2002)

Digital Infrastructure and the Intelligent Society

Social Behavior-Aware Driving Intention Detection Using Spatio-Temporal Attention Network

Pengfei Li, Guojiang Shen, Qihong Pan, Zhi Liu, and Xiangjie Kong[✉]

College of Computer Science and Technology, Zhejiang University of Technology, Hangzhou 310023, China
xjkong@ieee.org

Abstract. Driving intent detection represents a formidable challenge in the realm of intelligent transportation systems, as its accurate prediction is crucial for guaranteeing the safety and reliability of autonomous vehicles. The ability of autonomous vehicles to predict the driving intentions of surrounding vehicles can significantly enhance riding comfort and driving safety. However, current driving intent detection methods are limited in capturing the spatio-temporal dependencies between vehicles and the influence of driver's driving behavior on driving intentions. To address the above limitations, this paper proposes a Spatio-Temporal Interaction Graph Attention network model with Embedded vehicle Social behaviors (ES-STIGAT), which consists of three modules: Social Feature Extraction (SFE), Spatial Interaction Construction (SIC), and Temporal Prediction (TP). In the SFE module, we use the K-means clustering method and introduce the Social Value Orientation theory (SVO) to analyze the driving behavior of different vehicles. In the SIC module, we then use Graph Attention Network (GAT) to capture the spatial dependence of different vehicles throughout the time series. In the TP module, we capture the temporal dependencies in vehicle trajectories using an attention-based Long Short Term Memory network (LSTM), and obtain the probability of vehicle lane change intention through a Softmax layer. Finally, we conduct extensive experiments on real traffic datasets, and the experimental results validate the effectiveness of the framework.

Keywords: Driving intent detection · Social behavior · Graph attention network · Long short term memory · Social value orientation

1 Introduction

As the world becomes increasingly industrialized and the transportation network improves, the number of privately owned vehicles continues to rise. This increase in car ownership has brought with it growing concerns over road safety. Lane change behavior represents a significant high-risk driving action, as it requires a higher level of driver judgement and operational ability compared to simply

© The Author(s), under exclusive license to Springer Nature Singapore Pte Ltd. 2023
X. Meng et al. (Eds.): BDSC 2023, CCIS 1846, pp. 121–134, 2023.
https://doi.org/10.1007/978-981-99-3925-1_8

maintaining a lane. In mixed human-machine traffic scenarios, there is a high risk of traffic accidents if autonomous vehicles are unable to correctly identify the intentions of surrounding vehicles to change lanes. As such, the ability to accurately and quickly detect lane changes of surrounding vehicles is a crucial aspect of reducing road congestion, ensuring road safety, and enhancing the overall travel experience.

In recent years, researchers have developed a range of models to study vehicle lane change behavior, primarily based on rules and regulations. One of the earliest models, the Gipps model [1], produces a binary classification as the outcome and expresses lane change as a set of rules. However, rule-based models like this often oversimplify driving conditions and fail to consider a driver's behavior. To address this limitation, machine learning methods like Support Vector Machines (SVM) and Hidden Markov Models (HMM) have been employed for more accurate prediction of lane change behavior. These models predict maneuver as a function of vehicle location, speed, and other inputs, but suffer from low accuracy and robustness.

The development of graph neural networks has brought us a better idea to solve this problem. The nature and characteristics of the graph structure make it possible to more comprehensively and accurately represent the potential interaction relationships that exist between different adjacent vehicles. Our work presents a novel deep learning model, Embedded Spatio-Temporal Interaction Graph Attention Network Model with Driving Style, for vehicle lane change prediction. This model incorporates the driving styles of different vehicles into the pre-prediction analysis process, which is important for safety and efficiency improvement. The model first analyzes driving styles using K-means and SVO theory and assigns influence weights to vehicles. Then, it captures the spatial dependencies of vehicles using GAT and models the temporal dependencies between the sequence outputs from the spatial module using an attention mechanism-based LSTM. This enables the model to adaptively extract the temporal dependent features of vehicles for prediction. Following is a list of our work's key contributions:

(1) We propose a vehicle lane change prediction framework that combines driving style and attention mechanism, mining the spatial dependence of vehicles through GAT and the temporal dependence of vehicles through LSTM containing attention mechanism to solve vehicle lane change prediction in complex traffic scenarios.
(2) We introduce SVO theory into the model to analyze the social preferences of different drivers, which improves the model's ability to forecast outcomes by allowing it to more intuitively represent and reveal the process of vehicle social interaction.
(3) We have conducted extensive experiments on two publicly available traffic data, HighD and NGSIM, and the outcomes demonstrate that, in terms of prediction accuracy, our model performs noticeably better than the state-of-the-art solutions.

The rest of the paper is organized as follows. Related research on the attention mechanism and vehicle lane change prediction is presented in Sect. 2. Section 3 goes into great detail about our suggested framework. Section 4 discusses our experimental setup and confirms the suggested framework's usefulness. Finally, Sect. 5 conclusion the paper.

2   Related Work

2.1   Attention Mechanism

The way the human brain concentrates attention on certain inputs while ignoring others serves as the model for the attention mechanism in neural networks. This allows the model to concentrate on relevant information for a particular task. Attention mechanisms have been widely used in sequence-based tasks [2] and have proven to be effective in various machine learning applications, such as machine translation and machine reading. In addition to sequence-based tasks, attention mechanisms have also been applied to graph structure models. For example, the GAT introduced by Velickovic et al. [3] uses a self-attentive layer to define the relationship between nodes in a graph based solely on the node's feature data, without prior knowledge of the graph structure.

2.2   Rule-Based Vehicle Lane Change Detection

Vehicle lane change intention refers to the driver's driving intention based on the current vehicle status and the surrounding environment, which is derived from a series of cognitive processes including perception, decision-making, and evaluation [4]. Accurate perception of surrounding vehicle driving behavior and anticipation of possible dangers can significantly reduce traffic accidents caused by lane changes during high-speed driving, improve the decision-making capabilities of intelligent vehicles, and enhance driving comfort and safety [5,6]. Studies on vehicle lane change intention can be broadly categorized into two types: rule-based approaches [7,8] and model-based approaches [9–12].

The study of lane change strategies based on rule-based models primarily involves the definition of a set of lane change decision rules. For instance, Wang et al. [13] studied the issue of collaborative lane changes among multiple vehicles, proposed a collaborative lane change strategy based on Model Predictive Control (MPC), and established a lane change feasibility criterion that took into account the surrounding vehicle's ability to accommodate the main vehicle's acceleration and deceleration. Wan et al. [8] filtered the lane change data in a traffic dataset and proposed a new sequential combination lane change decision model that covers lane change waiting strategies such as gap generation, lane change location selection, and lane change speed selection. While rule-based approaches are simple to implement and robust, they have limitations in that they can only be applied to specific traffic scenarios.

2.3   Model-Based Vehicle Lane Change Detection

In the model-based approach. Liu *et al.* [14] proposed a HMM to predict driver intentions, but the model fails to consider the correlation between contextual time series features. Multiple Gated Recurrent Units (GRUs) were used by Ding *et al.* [15] to describe the pairwise relationships among the target vehicle and the nearby cars. By taking into account many facets of lane change behavior, Xie *et al.* [16] suggested using an LSTM network as a way to predict lane change decisions and lane change realization.

Based on the aforementioned study, it can be concluded that current methods for detecting lane changes in vehicles have limitations in capturing the spatiotemporal relationships between vehicles and considering the effect of driving styles. To address these limitations, this study proposes a spatiotemporal interaction graph attention model with incorporated driving styles. Our approach builds a spatiotemporal dependency module utilizing an attention mechanism that takes into account the driver's driving style to more effectively leverage the interaction information between vehicles, resulting in improved lane change recognition accuracy.

3   Methodology

3.1   Overview

We suggest the ES-STIGAT framework for lane change intention detection in this study. As shown in Fig. 2, the framework is comprised of three main modules: the SFE module, the SIC module, and the TP module. Using the SVO theory and k-means clustering techniques, the SFE module assesses the driving habits of the cars in its immediate vicinity. The SIC module builds a graph of the vehicles in the scenario and incorporates the influence weights of the driving styles. The GAT is used to calculate the features of each graph node by focusing on neighboring nodes, capturing the spatial dependencies of the vehicles. The TP module, equipped with an attention-based LSTM, updates the spatial properties of the vehicle network and calculates the probability of various lane change intents for each vehicle. The probability of various lane change intents for each vehicle is then calculated using the Softmax function, and the largest value of the probability is used as the outcome of the vehicle lane change intention recognition (Fig. 1).

3.2   Model Architectures

Social Feature Extraction Module The SFE module combines a K-means clustering algorithm as well as social value orientations. Social value orientation is a theory in social psychology. The theory refers to individuals' specific preferences for the distribution of their own and others' benefits in interdependent situations, and describes the individual variability in the extent to which decision

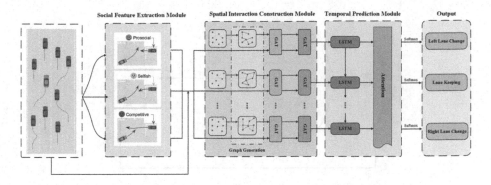

Fig. 1. Architecture of the proposed ES-STIGAT.

makers pay attention to the interests of others in interdependent decision situations. It argues that there are six interpersonal orientations of cooperation, equality, altruism, selfishness, competition, and aggression in social interactions. In realistic traffic scenarios, vehicles are steered by human drivers, and the driver's driving style preference has a greater impact on vehicle braking. In addition, to balance the model computational efficiency as well as the accuracy of driving style classification, as shown in Fig. 2, we team up automobiles in actual traffic situations to extract attributes and categorize them into three groups: prosocial, selfish, and competitive, and assign different weights to them (where α, β, γ are different weights). We specifically randomly group a set of items into k clusters, with the average of all the objects in each cluster serving as its center. Where the k averages are called the center of mass, and each remaining object is clustered around the nearest center of mass. The data points are then redistributed to the closest cluster once the new center of mass has been determined, based on the mean values of the data points in each of the modified clusters. Once the assignment is stable, the clustering process is finished by iteratively reassigning clustering centers and returning the clustering results. The final output is a set of clusters with centers of mass that minimizes the error function defined below:

$$L = \sum_{i=1}^{k} \sum_{x \in y_i} d(x, \mu(y_i)) \qquad (1)$$

where $y_1, y_2, ..., y_k$ are the k clusters, $\mu(y_i)$ is the center of mass of cluster y_i, and $d(x, \mu(y_i))$ denotes the distance between object x and the center of mass $\mu(y_i)$.

After clustering vehicles using a K-means clustering algorithm, driving styles are classified into three categories based on social value orientations: prosocial, selfish, and competitive. The impact of different driving styles on surrounding vehicles varies, thus different influence weights are assigned based on driving style and incorporated as prior knowledge in the subsequent spatial interaction construction module.

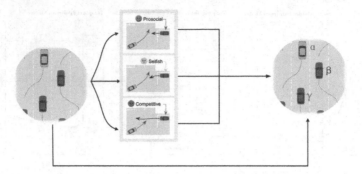

Fig. 2. Schematic diagram of driving style classification. We classify the driving styles of different vehicles into three categories: prosocial, selfish and competitive, and then assign different weights to them.

Spatial Interaction Construction Module. As shown in Fig. 2, we first treat all vehicles in a certain time interval as a node set V, where v_i denotes the i-th vehicle node. Then, since the graph structure input to the GAT layer is a graph structure composed of all the vehicle nodes mentioned above, the connection relationships of the nodes are different at different time intervals. Based on this, we further denote v_i^t as node v_i in time slice t. Then, we denote the feature of node v_i^t at layer l as $H_i^t \in \mathbb{R}^{d(l)}$, where $d(l)$ is denoted as the length of node v_i^t feature in layer l. The attention coefficient of node v_i^t and its neighboring node v_j^t in time slice t is then denoted as:

$$e_{ij}^t = a(WH_i^t, WH_j^t) \tag{2}$$

where $W \in \mathbb{R}^{F \times F}$ is a weight matrix of shared linear transformations (F is the H_i^t dimension and F' is the output dimension) and $a(\cdot)$ is a function that calculates the correlation between nodes v_i^t and v_j^t. A single-layer feedforward neural network is employed and trained in this paper, parameterized by the weight vector $a^T \in \mathbb{R}^{2d(l+1)}$, which can be expressed as:

$$e_{ij}^t = LeakyReLU(a^T[WH_i^t||WH_j^t]) \tag{3}$$

where $\bullet^T$ denotes the transpose operation, $||$ is the join operation, and $LeakyReLU$ is used as the activation function.

The collected attention coefficients were normalized using the softmax function to allow for visual comparison of the attention coefficients of other surrounding nodes:

$$\alpha_{ij}^t = softmax(e_{ij}^t) = \frac{exp(e_{ij}^t)}{\sum_{v_k \in N_{vi}^t} exp(e_{ik}^t)} \tag{4}$$

where N_{vi}^t denotes the set of all neighboring nodes of node v_i (Fig. 3).

After calculating the above coefficients, we calculate the new feature vector of node v_i^t at time slice t by weighted summation of the attention mechanism:

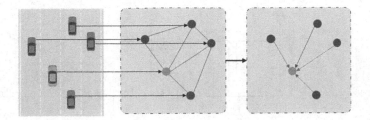

Fig. 3. Schematic diagram of the spatial graph construction of vehicles in a traffic scene. The graph structure is generated by sensing the state of the surrounding vehicles, where the different colored edges indicate the degree of their influence on the surrounding vehicles.

$$H_i^{t'} = \sigma\left(\sum_{v_j \in N_{vi}^t} \alpha_{ij}^t W H_j^t \right) \tag{5}$$

where $\sigma(\cdot)$ is a nonlinear function. The above equation describes how a single graph attention layer works. In this paper, we instead employ two graph attention layers that enhance the perceptual range between nodes.

Subsequently, we consider the aggregation of the feature vectors of all nodes updated at moment t of the time slice as the output of the GAT module. To be able to more easily input to the temporal prediction module, we convert the output vector to a feature vector $\beta^t \in \mathbb{R}^{Nd}$, and the whole output $O_{t+1} \in \mathbb{R}^{L \times Nd}$ can be represented as: indicates all spatial information that the spatial module has derived from the input demand sequence:

$$O_{t+1} = [\beta^n | n = t, t-1, t-2, ..., t-L+1] \tag{6}$$

Temporal Prediction Module. In addition to spatial interaction, traffic data also have significant temporal dependence. In this study, the LSTM network is employed as the primary architecture for the temporal prediction module. To further improve the validity of features at each time step and prevent the loss of network feature information, an attention mechanism is integrated into the LSTM network to assign varying weights to the outputs of the LSTM cells at each time step. The LSTM's structure is depicted in Fig. 4, and the input at time t consists of the layer input x_t, the previous layer output state h_{t-1}, and the previous cell output state C_{t-1}, while the output consists of C_t for the cell output state and h_t for the layer output. The three gates that make up an LSTM cell are the forgetting gate, the input gate, and the output gate. The forgetting gate controls how much of the cell state from the previous instant is maintained to the present moment, while the input gate chooses how much of the current input is saved to the cell state. The number of cell states that are conveyed to the current LSTM cell output is controlled by the output gate. Following is a definition of the particular equations:

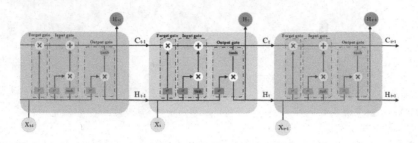

Fig. 4. LSTM structure schematic.

$$i_t = \sigma(W_{ii}x_t + b_{ii} + W_{hi}h_{t-1} + b_{hi}) \tag{7}$$

$$f_t = \sigma(W_{if}x_t + b_{if} + W_{hf}h_{t-1} + b_{hf}) \tag{8}$$

$$g_t = tanh(W_{ig}x_t + b_{ig} + W_{hg}h_{t-1} + b_{hg}) \tag{9}$$

$$o_t = \sigma(W_{io}x_t + b_{io} + W_{ho}h_{t-1} + b_{ho}) \tag{10}$$

$$c_t = f_t \circ c_{t-1} + i_t \circ g_t \tag{11}$$

$$h_t = o_t \circ tanh(c_t) \tag{12}$$

where f_t, g_t, and o_t are the input, forget, and output gate values, W_{ii}, W_{if}, W_{ig}, W_{io}, W_{hi}, W_{hf}, W_{hg}, and W_{ho} are the weight matrices connected to the three gates, respectively. $\circ$ denotes the Adama product.

Subsequently, the output matrix $H = [h_1, h_2, ..., h_l]$ is constructed by LSTM as the input information of Attention layer. Where h_i is the output of the implied node of the LSTM network at each moment. h_i accounts for the attention weight of the vehicle behavior using the score function S. The larger the score, the greater the weight of h_i contribution to the vehicle behavior representation.

$$S(h, h_i) = w^T tanh(Wh + Uh_i + b) \tag{13}$$

where w, W, and U are weight matrices, b is a bias, $tanh$ is a nonlinear activation function, and h can be considered as a vector of behavioral representations at a higher level of vehicle state information.

Model Output. Due of the variety and unpredictability of each vehicle's behavior in real-world traffic circumstances, the labels that directly output the behavior of surrounding target vehicles are often not effectively used by the decision module and may even mislead to cause wrong planning, so in order to provide complete information to ego vehicle, recognition models are needed to speculatively calculate the probabilities of different vehicle behaviors. We consider $S = (S_1, S_2, S_3)$ as the category vector for the surrounding target vehicle behavior recognition, S_1, S_2 and S_3 denote left lane change, keep straight and right lane change, respectively. The output of the model is denoted as

$Y = \{w_j^i | \forall i \in \{1, ..., N\}, j \in \{1, 2, 3\}\}$, N denotes the number of surrounding target vehicles, and w_j^i denotes the probability value of vehicle i behavior category j. Then the behavior probability of target vehicle i can be calculated as $w_j^i = P(S_j^i | I)$, and I denotes the original feature input.

4   Experiments

4.1   Dataset

To evaluate the effectiveness of our proposed technique, we conduct experiments using the German highway dataset (HighD) [17] and the real traffic dataset provided by the Federal Highway Administration (NGSIM) [18]. The HighD dataset consists of natural vehicle trajectory data collected by drones on German motorways and includes the trajectories of 110,500 vehicles recorded at six different points along a 420-meter section of road. The NGSIM dataset was obtained in 2005 through the use of multiple overhead cameras to observe freeway traffic dynamics. The data was obtained using visual tracking technology and includes information on vehicle type, speed, acceleration, front vehicle ID, and lane. The NGSIM segment is 640 m long with five lanes and was collected over 45 min at 10 Hz rate.

4.2   Evaluation Metrics

In line with other studies, we provide accuracy, precision, recall, and F1 ratings for each data sample in the test dataset. The F1 score, which has a maximum value of 1 and a minimum value of 0, is the average of accuracy and recall and is used as a statistic for the classification issue. Where recall indicates the percentage of samples from one class of the overall true samples of the class that the model correctly predicts, accuracy indicates the proportion of correctly predicted data to all data, precision indicates the percentage of true samples in the prediction results to all predicted samples, and precision indicates the percentage of true samples in the prediction results to all predicted samples. The following are the definitions of these parameters:

$$Accuracy = \frac{TP + TN}{TP + TN + FP + FN} \tag{14}$$

$$Precision = \frac{TP}{TP + FP} \tag{15}$$

$$Recall = \frac{FP}{FP + TN} \tag{16}$$

$$F1 = \frac{2 \times Precision \times Recall}{Precision + Recall} \tag{17}$$

where predictions of positive results are referred to as true positives (TP) and predictions of negative results as false negatives (FN). A negative projected to be negative is referred to as a true negative (TN), while a negative predicted to be positive is referred to as a false positive (FP).

Table 1. Results of Models Compared

Model	HighD				NGSIM			
	Precision	Recall	F1	Accuracy	Precision	Recall	F1	Accuracy
MLP [19]	0.742	0.523	0.612	0.596	0.805	0.811	0.805	0.772
LSTM [20]	0.814	0.840	0.823	0.788	0.802	0.920	0.857	0.812
CS-LSTM [21]	0.811	0.785	0.797	0.808	0.885	0.932	0.908	0.863
SIMP [22]	0.834	0.799	0.818	0.817	0.873	0.931	0.901	0.886
Dual [12]	0.856	0.851	0.853	0.831	0.925	0.895	0.910	0.901
ES-STIGAT	**0.907**	**0.866**	**0.878**	**0.908**	**0.967**	**0.959**	**0.960**	**0.963**

4.3   Experimental Environments and Parameter Settings

We will go through some model implementation specifics in this paragraph. Our model is implemented in the PyTorch framework and executed on a system with an NVIDIA GeForce RTX 3090 GPU. On LC/LK scenes that were taken from the training sets of the HighD and NGSIM datasets, we trained the suggested model and the re-implemented model. We utilized the Adam optimizer to train our suggested prediction model, using a learning rate of 0.001, 30 training periods, and 50 batch sizes. An early stopping technique with a validated loss function was used to avoid overfitting.

4.4   Experimental Results

Model Prediction Results. As shown in Table 1, we compare the performance of the ES-STIGAT prediction model with various baseline methods in two publicly available traffic datasets, HighD and NGSIM. Our proposed ES-STIGAT achieves the highest Precision, Recall, F1, and Accuracy among all methods at time stamp 2s. This is because in a complex and dynamic traffic environment, the lane change intention of a target vehicle not only depends on its historical trajectory, but is also influenced by other road participants, especially surrounding vehicles. Our model introduces attention mechanism and interaction information of target vehicles, which can effectively improve Precision, Recall, F1 and Accuracy for all types of vehicle intention recognition.

Comparison of Results with Different Timestamps. The behavior recognition algorithm of the surrounding cars should identify the behavior of the target vehicles as soon as feasible since it serves as both the front and rear ends of the autonomous driving system's vision module. This is because the on-board sensors and motion controllers can only meaningfully forecast the behavior of the target vehicle within a specific range. As shown in Fig. 5 and Fig. 6, we divide the prognostic time into four parts: 0.5s, 1s, 1.5s and 2s. The results on both datasets show that the prediction accuracy of all methods decreases to different degrees as the prediction time increases, but our proposed model still maintains a high accuracy, which demonstrates the robustness of our model and its potential for practical applications.

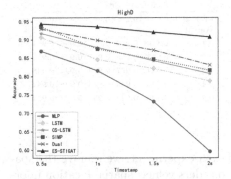 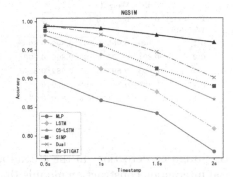

Fig. 5. Comparison of model accuracy at different timestamps in the HighD dataset.

Fig. 6. Comparison of model accuracy at different timestamps in the NGSIM dataset.

Impact of Different Driving Styles. We examine in this part how different driving behaviors affect the ability to forecast lane change intentions. As shown in Table 2 and Table 3, we conduct experiments on the effects of driving styles on two datasets. We categorized the three different vehicle driving styles as follows: prosocial, selfish, and competitive, and the weights of the three types were summed to 1. Also, we used pro-social and selfish as independent variables and competitive as dependent variables. The table shows that when the three driving styles are given weights of 0.1, 0.1, and 0.8, the model predicts outcomes with the maximum degree of accuracy. We believe this is due to the fact that in a real traffic scenario, when the driver is more aggressive, the greater the impact on the surrounding vehicles. Additionally, we discovered an intriguing phenomenon: when the selfish type is given larger weights than the pro-social type, the prediction accuracy of the model is also higher. This also confirms our above point from the side.

4.5 Ablation Study

Here we focus on validating the effectiveness of the model's social feature extraction module as well as the spatial interaction construction module. We will train two model variables with different modules: ES-STIGAT without the social feature extraction module and ES-STIGAT without the spatial interaction construction module, respectively, and the results are shown in Fig. 7 and Fig. 8. Compared to the removal of the social feature extraction module, the addition of the social feature extraction module improves each metric to a certain extent, which indicates that the embedding of the vehicle social features in our model is effective and the driving style of the vehicle has a certain enhancement effect on

Table 2. The effect of different driving style weights on accuracy in the HighD dataset.

Prosocial Weights	Selfish Weights				
	0.1	0.2	0.3	0.4	0.5
0.1	**0.908**	0.905	0.897	0.892	0.896
0.2	0.891	0.905	0.899	0.896	0.893
0.3	0.893	0.897	0.881	0.882	0.887
0.4	0.881	0.882	0.896	0.889	0.885
0.5	0.878	0.881	0.890	0.896	0.871

Table 3. The effect of different driving style weights on accuracy in the NGSIM dataset.

Prosocial Weights	Selfish Weights				
	0.1	0.2	0.3	0.4	0.5
0.1	**0.963**	0.960	0.959	0.956	0.951
0.2	0.953	0.958	0.957	0.948	0.951
0.3	0.944	0.957	0.949	0.942	0.948
0.4	0.942	0.949	0.944	0.938	0.942
0.5	0.936	0.946	0.938	0.933	0.931

the intention detection. In the second ablation experiment, we remove the spatial interaction construction module that considers vehicle spatial location information, and we see a significant decrease in accuracy from the results, which indicates that vehicle spatial location information is an important element to be considered when predicting vehicle intent to change lanes in dynamic traffic scenarios.

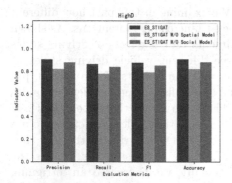

Fig. 7. Comparison of ES-STIGAT with its variants for various evaluation metrics in the HighD dataset.

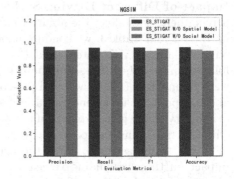

Fig. 8. Comparison of ES-STIGAT with its variants for various evaluation metrics in the NGSIM dataset.

5   Conclusion

In order to anticipate the intentions of cars to change lanes in traffic scenes, we present in this research a spatio-temporal interaction graph attention network model (ES-STIGAT) embedded with vehicle social behavior and including driving styles. The driving behaviors of vehicles are analyzed through k-means clustering and SVO, and assigned different weights based on their driving styles. Using GAT to combine spatial vehicle distribution and style-embedded features, the attention layer adaptively assigns weight coefficients to surrounding vehicles. In the temporal prediction module, LSTM with attention mechanism mines temporal feature information and outputs the lane change probability through the softmax layer. By integrating driving styles and attention mechanism, ES-STIGAT effectively captures temporal dependencies among vehicles and enhances the accuracy of lane change intention prediction. The efficacy of our suggested model has been tested and evaluated using genuine traffic datasets that are available to the public.

Acknowledgements. This work was supported in part by the "Pioneer" and "Leading Goose" R&D Program of Zhejiang under Grant 2022C01050, in part by the National Natural Science Foundation of China under Grant 62072409 and Grant 62073295, and in part by the Zhejiang Provincial Natural Science Foundation under Grant LR21F020003.

References

1. Gipps, P.G.: A model for the structure of lane-changing decisions. Transp. Res. Part B Methodol. **20**(5), 403–414 (1986)
2. Sa-Couto, L., Wichert, A.: Attention inspired network: steep learning curve in an invariant pattern recognition model. Neural Netw. **114**, 38–46 (2019)
3. Veličković, P., Cucurull, G., Casanova, A., Romero, A., Lio, P., Bengio, Y.: Graph attention networks. arXiv preprint arXiv:1710.10903 (2017)
4. Kong, X., Wu, Y., Wang, H., Xia, F.: Edge computing for internet of everything: A survey. IEEE Internet Things J. **9**(23), 23472–23485 (2022)
5. Song, R., Li, B.: Surrounding vehicles' lane change maneuver prediction and detection for intelligent vehicles: a comprehensive review. IEEE Trans. Intell. Transp. Syst. (2021)
6. Xing, Y., et al.: Driver lane change intention inference for intelligent vehicles: framework, survey, and challenges. IEEE Trans. Veh. Technol. **68**(5), 4377–4390 (2019)
7. Zhu, B., Liu, S., Zhao, J.: A lane-changing decision-making method for intelligent vehicle based on acceleration field. SAE Int. J. Passenger Cars-Electron. Electr. Syst. **11**(2018–01-0599), 219–230 (2018)
8. Wan, X., Jin, P.J., Gu, H., Chen, X., Ran, B.: Modeling freeway merging in a weaving section as a sequential decision-making process. J. Transp. Eng. Part A: Syst. **143**(5), 05017002 (2017)
9. Sarkar, A., Larson, K., Czarnecki, K.: Generalized dynamic cognitive hierarchy models for strategic driving behavior. In: Proceedings of the AAAI Conference on Artificial Intelligence, vol. 36, pp. 5173–5182 (2022)
10. Liao, X., et al.: Online prediction of lane change with a hierarchical learning-based approach. In: 2022 International Conference on Robotics and Automation (ICRA), pp. 948–954. IEEE (2022)
11. Li, Z.N., Huang, X.H., Mu, T., Wang, J.: Attention-based lane change and crash risk prediction model in highways. IEEE Trans. Intell. Transp. Syst. **23**(12), 22909–22922 (2022)
12. Mozaffari, S., Arnold, E., Dianati, M., Fallah, S.: Early lane change prediction for automated driving systems using multi-task attention-based convolutional neural networks. IEEE Trans. Intell. Veh. **7**(3), 758–770 (2022)

13. Wang, D., Hu, M., Wang, Y., Wang, J., Qin, H., Bian, Y.: Model predictive control-based cooperative lane change strategy for improving traffic flow. Adv. Mech. Eng. 8(2), 1687814016632992 (2016)
14. Liu, S., Zheng, K., Zhao, L., Fan, P.: A driving intention prediction method based on hidden Markov model for autonomous driving. Comput. Commun. 157, 143–149 (2020)
15. Ding, W., Chen, J., Shen, S.: Predicting vehicle behaviors over an extended horizon using behavior interaction network. In: 2019 International Conference on Robotics and Automation (ICRA), pp. 8634–8640. IEEE (2019)
16. Xie, D.F., Fang, Z.Z., Jia, B., He, Z.: A data-driven lane-changing model based on deep learning. Transp. Res. Part C Emerg. Technol. 106, 41–60 (2019)
17. Krajewski, R., Bock, J., Kloeker, L., Eckstein, L.: The HIGHD dataset: a drone dataset of naturalistic vehicle trajectories on German highways for validation of highly automated driving systems. In: 2018 21st International Conference on Intelligent Transportation Systems (ITSC), pp. 2118–2125. IEEE (2018)
18. DOT, U.: Next generation simulation (NGSIM) vehicle trajectories and supporting data. US Department of Transportation (2018)
19. Shou, Z., Wang, Z., Han, K., Liu, Y., Tiwari, P., Di, X.: Long-term prediction of lane change maneuver through a multilayer perceptron. In: 2020 IEEE Intelligent Vehicles Symposium (IV), pp. 246–252. IEEE (2020)
20. Wirthmüller, F., Klimke, M., Schlechtriemen, J., Hipp, J., Reichert, M.: Predicting the time until a vehicle changes the lane using LSTM-based recurrent neural networks. IEEE Robot. Autom. Lett. 6(2), 2357–2364 (2021)
21. Deo, N., Trivedi, M.M.: Convolutional social pooling for vehicle trajectory prediction. In: Proceedings of the IEEE Conference on Computer Vision and Pattern Recognition Workshops, pp. 1468–1476 (2018)
22. Hu, Y., Zhan, W., Tomizuka, M.: Probabilistic prediction of vehicle semantic intention and motion. In: 2018 IEEE Intelligent Vehicles Symposium (IV), pp. 307–313. IEEE (2018)

Intelligent Government Decision-Making: A Multidimensional Policy Text Visualization Analysis System

Chen Lan[1], Xuexi Wang[1], Junxia Ren[2], Xiaoxu Chen[3], and Siming Chen[1(✉)]

[1] School of Data Science, Fudan University, Shanghai 200433, China
simingchen@fudan.edu.cn
[2] Tiandao Fintech Co., Ltd., Zhejiang 310013, China
[3] Zhelixin Co., Ltd., Zhejiang 310013, China

Abstract. Government decision-making refers to the process of making decisions by government departments in various domains, such as politics, economics, and culture, based on national, ethnic, and public interests, as well as the current realities. The rationality and scientificity of government decisions are essential to social development and people's well-being. However, the increasing complexity of social and economic conditions requires comprehensive consideration of multiple factors and influences. Traditional decision-making methods, relying solely on expert experience and case studies, are insufficient to support effective government decision-making. They are time-consuming, subjective, and prone to limitations and uncertainties. Therefore, with the advent of the digital age, utilizing a large amount of digitized data has become a new challenge in government decision-making.

To overcome these limitations, this article proposes a policy text multidimensional visualization analysis system that incorporates natural language processing technology and data visualization technology. The system enables decision-makers from different regions to learn from each other and those in the same region to coordinate at a top-level, avoiding policy overlap and disconnection. This system mines a large-scale historical policy text set from a semantic and temporal-spatial perspective, allowing decision-makers to explore similar policy cases and gain insights. Through analyzing three similar policy cases, the effectiveness of the system in supporting government decision-making is validated.

Keywords: Government Governance · Visual Analysis · Artificial Intelligence · Visualization · Society

1 Introduction

Government decision-making involves making decisions by government departments in different domains based on various interests and situations. Policy documents are crucial documents that reflect the goals, principles, means, and implementation details of government decisions. They are essential for social governance and service work. However, traditional research-based decision-making has limitations, relying on expert experience and case studies, making it time-consuming and difficult to ensure objectivity and accuracy.

Information technology advancements have made it easier to collect, analyze, and disseminate large amounts of data from diverse sources, providing more scientific, accurate, and efficient support for government decision-making. The "14th Five-Year Plan for National Economic and Social Development and the Long-Term Goals Through the Year 2035" emphasizes the importance of digital government construction, which involves applying digital technology to government management services. To promote digital transformation, various government service platforms, such as "Zhe Li Ban," have been launched, enabling policy researchers and government decision-makers to access massive amounts of data, including policy texts and local statistical data. Data science technologies, including data mining, natural language processing, data visualization, and data visual analysis, can be utilized to optimize public policies based on the collected data.

Visualization technology is a field that transforms data into graphical or image forms, enabling interactive exploration by users. Information visualization and visual analytics are two branches of visualization technology. Visual analytics integrates computer computation and human cognitive ability to explore complex data sets, leading to new insights and actionable recommendations. The use of visualization and visual analytics technology in government decision-making is a nascent research area, which has started exploring how visualization technology can enhance the scientific and practical nature of decision-making and aid policymakers in addressing complex social problems. Ruppert et al. (2015) demonstrated that data visualization technology and visual analytics can assist decision-makers in policy analysis by implementing a scientific-policy interface through information visualization [1–3].

1.1 Problem Description

Policy-making requires policymakers to conduct in-depth research and analysis based on various information sources, including social environment, economic status, and livelihood needs. Policy texts provide essential information such as objectives, means, and implementation details. Analyzing policy texts can offer policymakers comprehensive information and facilitate the formulation of more scientific and rational policies. More scientific and reasonable policies.

The following is an example to illustrate the phenomenon of "multiple departments making policies".

1. In order to encourage the development of logistics companies (policy objective), the municipal government (department) of city A, a second-tier city (city feature), issued a policy to subsidize 30 yuan for each waterway container (policy measure).
2. In order to encourage logistics companies to transport more goods via waterway (policy objective), the finance bureau (department) of city A, a second-tier city (city feature), issued a policy to subsidize 25 yuan for each waterway container (policy measure).

3. In order to encourage the development of logistics companies (policy objective), the municipal government (department) of city B, a first-tier city (city feature), issued a policy to subsidize 30 yuan for each waterway container (policy measure).

The second data point, from a different department within the same city, has similar policy measures to the first. Is there policy redundancy? The third data point, from a different city, has similar policy goals to the first. Can the two policies learn from each other?

Policy text analysis is crucial in policy formulation and decision-making, but traditional methods are limited by the length and complexity of policy texts, making it difficult to handle large-scale data and prone to subjective bias. Improving efficiency and accuracy is crucial. Analyzing similar policy texts is especially important when multiple departments are involved, as duplication can lead to waste of resources and poor implementation. Therefore, exploring and analyzing similar policy texts is a critical part of policy formulation that policymakers must prioritize.

A policy text multi-dimensional visualization analysis system can have several benefits, including: avoiding policy duplication and redundancy, optimizing policy formulation and implementation mechanisms, avoiding cross-repetition or mutual detachment of policies formulated by different departments, enhancing policy transparency and credibility, and improving resource utilization efficiency. Additionally, similar policy text exploration methods based on machine learning algorithms and visual analysis technology can help decision-makers better understand policy text data, quickly find relevant policy text, and discover potential correlations, thereby providing better support for policy formulation and decision-making.

Therefore, using a multidimensional visual analysis system for exploring historical policy information, particularly similar policy texts, can enhance policy formulation and implementation efficiency and quality, while optimizing resource utilization, collaboration, and coordination among multiple departments. This can ultimately promote social stability.

2   Related Work

2.1   Government Decision-Making and Data Visualization

With the advent of the digital age, a large amount of data is digitized and the knowledge hidden in these datasets can be used to solve decision-making challenges [4]. In recent years, researchers have found that data visualization plays an extraordinary role in government decision-making. Data visualization interventions have an impact on attitudes, perceptions, and decisions [5], but there has been insufficient attention to the relationship with policy-making [6]. Ruppert et al. [7] proposed a method of bridging the knowledge gap through information visualization, which can improve the information transmission efficiency of policy analysts and thus better complete policy-making. The combination of human brains and data visualization in government decision-making has been demonstrated by researchers [8–10]. In addition, visualization technology can facilitate collaboration between scientists and politicians, providing more intuitive and understandable meanings behind data, helping policy makers better understand and master information, and incorporating citizens' needs and opinions into the policy-making process [3]. Burkhardt also proposed an information visualization-based policy modeling method to better accommodate citizens' opinions.

2.2 Visualization of Text Mining

Text visualization is a subfield of information visualization and visual analytics that aims to address challenges and analytical tasks within digital collections of text, including the ongoing proliferation of digital text sources and the increasing volume of data [11]. The challenges of evaluating methods for visual text analysis are becoming increasingly apparent, including data ambiguity, experimental design, user trust, and attention to the "big picture" [12]. Attribute-based text visualization, on the other hand, helps users understand relationships and interactions in text by automatically discovering common features between different attributes in the dataset [13–18]. In addition, Kang proposed an end-to-end system, Han addressed the difficulties of handling texts from multiple files by introducing Passages, and Fok studied the role of intelligent interfaces in assisting researchers to browse papers and proposed Scim [19–21].

2.3 Visual Analysis of Multidisciplinary Text Collections

Various text visualization techniques and methods have enriched the application prospects of text visualization across disciplines. Kavaz's method for analyzing hate speech annotations [22], Handler's solution for relationship summarization [23], Knittel's dynamic clustering algorithm for analyzing social media data streams [24], and Baumer's concept dimensions for political aspects of civic text visualization [25] are some examples. In epidemiology, Sondag introduced visual analysis methods to study the spread and control strategies of diseases on dynamic contact networks [26]. Additionally, tools such as the exploratory search concept model [27], Threddy for topic extraction [28], ClioQuery for newspaper archive analysis [29], and Paper Forager for research literature exploration [30] have driven the development of text mining visualization.

Overall, text visualization plays an important role in addressing challenges related to the analysis of digital text collections, and the emergence of various visualization techniques and methods has greatly enriched its application in different disciplinary fields. However, the challenges associated with evaluating visual text analysis methods must be carefully considered to ensure that these methods are effective and trustworthy.

3   Research Tasks and Research Ideas

3.1   Research Tasks

Therefore, in the process of policy-making, a multi-dimensional visual analysis system for policy text can be used to explore historical policy information, especially similar policy texts, which can not only improve the efficiency and quality of policy-making and implementation, but also fully utilize public resources, optimize the mechanism of policy-making and implementation, and promote collaboration and cooperation among multiple departments, thereby promoting stable social development.

To support government decision-making through the construction of a multi-dimensional visual analysis system for policy text, the following research tasks are proposed:

- **T1** Filter out interested text from a large text collection;
- **T2** Mine the semantics, temporal, and spatial information of individual policy texts;
- **T3** Explore the relationships between policy text collections from semantic, temporal, and spatial perspectives.

3.2   System Design Approach

According to the research tasks established in Chap. 3 3.1, in the construction of the visual analysis system, we will organize policy text data into two hierarchical levels: the geographic level of provinces, cities, and districts and the semantic level of themes, documents, titles, sentences, and keywords, utilizing these two types of information and daily time granularity for development. The specific data preparation work is implemented using natural language processing techniques in the Python language, which will be discussed in the next subsection. The specific design plan for the visual system views is as follows:

- **R1** Use a theme river chart to filter out a specific set of policy texts, and further screen semantically similar policy text sets in conjunction with the overview view.
- **R2** Support the exploration of the semantic, temporal, and other information of individual policy texts through linked maps, time views, force-directed graphs, time axes, and text views.
- **R3** Present the semantic relationships between sets of texts using overview views, text views, force-directed graphs, text comparison views, and display the spatial-temporal relationships between sets of texts using maps, labels, time views, etc.

4   Multidimensional Visual Analysis System for Policy Text

This paper designs and implements a multi-dimensional visual analysis system for policy text collections, using historical policy text collection data as the visualization object. Through a series of visualization views and view interaction functions, the system supports users to conduct large-scale policy text collection mining and enables decision makers to mine and compare individual policies and multiple policies to support government decision-making. The interactive system interface developed is shown in Fig. 1.

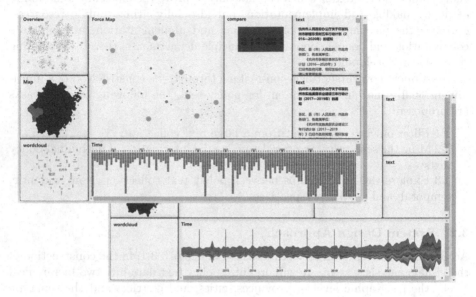

Fig. 1. The interface of the policy text multi-dimensional visual analysis system consists of a theme river chart, an overview view, a time view, a map, a force-directed graph, a text comparison view, a text view, and a word cloud.

4.1   Detailed Design of Key Views in the System

In the previous section, we discussed the visual analysis system's design ideas. In this section, we'll present the views individually from the perspectives of mapping and interaction, linkage with other views, and data preparation. Additionally, we'll cover certain views that are combined with natural language processing technology.

Theme Stream Graph. The system categorizes the Zhejiang Policy Document Library into 27 themes, such as "finance and audit," and employs a theme stream graph as the initial view to display the quantity changes and comparison relationships of different themes in the policy text collection over time. The horizontal axis represents time with monthly granularity, and years as tick marks. Each colored shape represents the temporal variation trend of a theme, with its width mapping to the number of a theme at a given time. The graph supports point selection and interaction, where hovering over a shape displays the specific theme name and fades out other shapes, and clicking on a shape switches to the corresponding time view and generates related views in the map and overview views.

The Overview View. After selecting any topic in the theme stream graph, the overview view reflects the semantic similarity relationships between the policy text titles in the policy document collection.

– **Data Preparation:** The overview view is generated by applying the Chinese-BERT-wwm-ext model [31] to each title in the policy document set to create a vector space of title representations. The vector space is then projected onto a two-dimensional space using Principal Component Analysis (PCA) and t-Distributed Stochastic Neighbor Embedding (t-SNE) algorithms. The system records the two-dimensional space projections for the document sets classified into 27 different themes.
– **Mapping:** Each point in the overview view represents a policy document, and points that are close to each other in the overview view indicate that the corresponding policy documents have similar semantic features in their titles.
– **Interaction:** The overview view supports a brush selection function, where a grey box records the selected area, and multiple selections are allowed.
– **Linking:** Selecting a specific theme in the theme river chart will display the corresponding document set information in the overview view. After a brush selection is applied to the overview view, the document set information represented by the points within the selected area will be further displayed in the map, timeline, force-directed graph, and word cloud.

Timeline View. The timeline view displays the time information of the document set and the changing trend of the number of theme documents selected by the river theme graph over time.

– **Mapping:** The horizontal axis represents time with a monthly granularity, and the publication date of policy documents determines their vertical position, with earlier documents at the top. The time scale is shown with circles labeled with the year and month, where January circles are larger than others. Each square represents a policy document.
– **Interaction:** Hovering over a square displays document information and highlights the square in orange. Filtered documents are highlighted in red.
– **Linkage:** Clicking on a square shows the full text in the text view, and selecting two files in the force-directed graph displays their comparison details in the text comparison view.

Vertical and horizontal scrollbars are provided to view the entire timeline when necessary.

Force-Directed Graph. The force-directed graph displays the relationships between the selected documents at the keyword level, illustrating the interconnections between documents from a keyword perspective.

- **Data Preparation:** For each document, the top 40 words with the highest numerical values are extracted as keywords using the TF-IDF algorithm after Jieba word segmentation.
- **Mapping:** Each orange node represents a document, and each blue node represents a keyword. A light gray line connects an orange node and a blue node if the keyword represented by the blue node appears in the document represented by the orange node. The radius of the blue node represents the number of files associated with the keyword in the current force map. If a keyword is only associated with one document, it is not displayed.
- **Interaction:** Hovering the mouse over a blue node enlarges its radius and displays the keyword represented by the node. Hovering the mouse over an orange node enlarges it and displays the document represented by the node. Double-clicking a node in the force map causes the line associated with that node to turn dark gray, making it easier to explore the details of a single document. Each node supports drag-and-drop functionality to update the force map layout and further mine information.
- **Linkage:** After selecting a document set in the topic river map and overview views, which have set selection functions, the force map displays information about the selected document set. Hovering the mouse over an orange node displays the document represented by the node and highlights the corresponding square in the time axis. Clicking an orange node displays the full text of the document in the text view. When two documents are selected in the time view, the comparison details of the two texts are displayed in the text comparison view.

Text Comparison View. The text comparison view is generated by selecting two policy documents from the force map and time view. It displays the comparison information of the two policy documents at the sentence level, enabling the assessment of the similarity between them from a sentence perspective.

- **Data preparation:** The two policy texts are sentence-separated, and the word frequency vectors of each sentence are obtained. The cosine similarity is calculated for all sentence combinations from the two different texts.
- **Mapping:** Sentence combinations with similarity greater than 0.7 are selected and arranged in descending order of similarity in the text comparison view. The color of the rectangle box becomes redder as the similarity between the two sentences increases. An asterisk (*) separates the two sentences in each combination. The sentence above the combination comes from the top text view, while the sentence below comes from the bottom text view.
- **Linkage:** The text comparison view is accessed from the force-directed graph and time view. When two texts are selected in both graphs, the comparison information of the two policy texts will be displayed in the text comparison view.

The text comparison view includes a vertical scrollbar for convenient viewing of all information.

4.2   System Visual Analysis Process

The operation of the system mainly includes selecting topics and filtering file sets, analyzing the main topics of the selected file set, studying the relationships between the selected file sets, and comparing two policy files, as follows:

1. Select the topic of interest from the timeline view by selecting the green river, then filter out the document cluster that meets the criteria in the overview view to display the spatiotemporal and semantic information of policy documents under the selected topic. This ensures the relevance between the selected document set and the topic being studied, improving the accuracy and effectiveness of subsequent analysis.
2. To analyze the main topics of the selected document set, filter out semantically similar titles in the overview view. This reveals the spatiotemporal and semantic information of the document set, presented through force-directed graphs, word clouds, and time views. This step facilitates a quick and convenient grasp of the main content and enables in-depth analysis in subsequent steps.
3. Studying document relationships: Clicking on circles or squares in the force-directed graph and time view that correspond to policy documents reveals their relationships. For instance, two orange dots representing documents that share many blue dots representing keywords in the force-directed graph, which is in a symmetrical state, indicate a high correlation between them. This step facilitates studying document correlation and understanding the inherent connections and influences of the selected document set.
4. Comparing policy documents: Selecting two documents allows for their display in both the text view and text comparison view, offering information on the sentence and document level of the selected documents. The color arrangement of rectangles in the text comparison view enables an assessment of the similarity of sentence pairs, while the quantity and color of rectangles allow for a judgement of semantic relevance between the two policy documents. This step enables a comparison of the similarities and differences between two documents, facilitating the identification of references and interrelationships between documents.
5. Inferencing references and forwarding relationships between documents can enhance the understanding of influences and transmission modes between them.

Through these steps, semantic and spatiotemporal information in policy texts can be deeply explored, and relationships between different policy documents can be inferred.

5 Case Study

Using the policy text multidimensional visualization analysis system introduced earlier, this chapter will conduct a case study by finding similar policy documents with different features, discovering the "many doors of policies" case, demonstrating the rationality and effectiveness of the system design, and further proving that the system can support government decision-making.

5.1 Case Data Preparation

Data Source. The case data in this chapter comes from the Zhejiang Province Policy Document Library website, which includes policy documents issued by various regions and departments in Zhejiang Province. The policy document set was obtained by using web scraping technology on the website.

Table 1. Description of Crawled Data Fields

Field	Description
Title	Each article has a different title
Document Number	100,000 missing values Each article has a different document number
Issuing Authority	20,000 missing values A total of 5,388 different authorities
Theme	27 categories including "commerce, customs, tourism", etc. 70,000 articles have themes
Time Information	Time Span: 1995–2023 Time Granularity: Day
Geographic Information	20,000 missing values A total of 115 different regions

Data Description. The total number of articles obtained by the crawler is 201,324, and the specific fields and detailed descriptions are shown in Table 1.

For this chapter, we selected a set of policy documents issued between April 12, 2013, and December 31, 2022. We cleaned out invalid documents and those with missing data, resulting in a total of 43,107 records for case analysis.

5.2 Data Processing for the Case Study

The main data processing procedures for this case study include two-dimensional mapping of title semantics and extraction of text keywords. The specific processing steps are as follows.

Two-Dimensional Mapping of Title Semantics. In this case study, we performed two-dimensional mapping of title semantics for the policy document set according to 27 categories of themes. The specific processing steps are as follows:

1. Generate a 768-dimensional title vector space for each title in the policy text set using the Chinese-BERT-wwm-ext model [31].
2. Use dimensionality reduction algorithms such as Principal Component Analysis (PCA) and t-Distributed Stochastic Neighbor Embedding (T-SNE) to project the title vectors onto a 2-dimensional plane. In this case, PCA is used to reduce the dimensionality while preserving 75% of the information, followed by T-SNE to further enhance the projection onto the 2D plane. The combination of these two methods results in a better overall reduction effect.

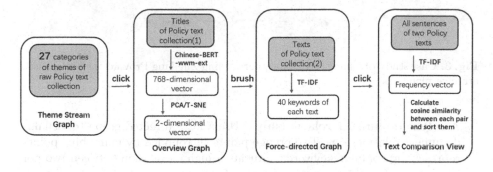

Fig. 2. Data Processing and visualization

Text Keyword Extraction. The original text data obtained by web crawlers was cleaned using regular expressions to remove irrelevant characters such as escape characters and HTML tags. The Python jieba segmentation tool was used to segment the original text, and the TF-IDF value of each word in the text collection was calculated. The top 40 words with the highest TF-IDF value were retained for each policy text as keywords (Figs. 2 and 3).

5.3 Case 1: Changxing County Forwards Zhejiang Province's Reservoir Governance Plan

1. **Choose a theme and filter a set of documents:** In the timeline, select the "Agriculture, Forestry, and Water Conservancy" theme represented by the green river and filter out a cluster of documents within the red box in the overview view.
2. **Analyze the main topics of the selected set of documents:** By presenting the selected set of documents' keywords in a word cloud, it is found that the main text of the selected policy documents revolves around water-related topics such as "rural" and "submerged".

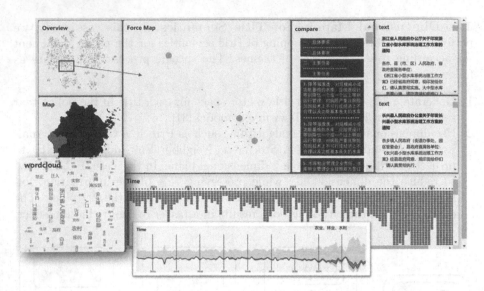

Fig. 3. Case study of Changxing County forwarding Zhejiang Province's reservoir governance plan

3. **Analyze document relationships:** Use a force-directed graph to visualize document relationships. Two orange points surrounded by many blue points, representing common keywords, indicate a high correlation between two policy documents. The symmetrical state of the entire graph shows consistency in connections to another orange point. Hovering the mouse reveals that the two documents are "Notice of the General Office of the People's Government of Zhejiang Province on Printing and Distributing the Work Plan for the Governance of Small Reservoir Systems in Zhejiang Province" and "Notice of the Office of the People's Government of Changxing County on Printing and Distributing the Work Plan for the Governance of Small Reservoir Systems in Changxing County".

4. **Document comparison and analysis:** Through a force-directed graph, the multidimensional visual analysis system reveals the strong correlation between two policy documents, namely "Notice of the General Office of the People's Government of Zhejiang Province on Printing and Distributing the Work Plan for the Governance of Small Reservoir Systems in Zhejiang Province" and "Notice of the Office of the People's Government of Changxing County on Printing and Distributing the Work Plan for the Governance of Small Reservoir Systems in Changxing County". Furthermore, a text comparison view shows that except for differences in the description of the notification recipients, all sentences describing specific work plans in the two documents are identical, indicating that the work plans in the latter document are identical to those in the former document.

5. **Infer borrowing and forwarding relationship:** Comparing the text view and timeline view, we find that the "Notice of the Office of the People's Government of Changxing County on Printing and Distributing the Work Plan for the Governance of Small Reservoir Systems in Changxing County" was issued after 2021, while the "Notice of the General Office of the People's Government of Zhejiang Province on Printing and Distributing the Work Plan for the Governance of Small Reservoir Systems in Zhejiang Province" was issued before 2021. It can be inferred that the work plan for reservoir governance issued by the Zhejiang Provincial Office before 2021 was transmitted to Changxing County, and the Changxing County People's Government evaluated the plan's suitability for the local situation and copied the original text as the work plan for the governance of the small reservoir system to the lower-level townships and villages.

This case of exploring policy texts in Zhejiang Province and Changxing County confirms that the "Small-Scale Reservoir System Governance Plan" issued by Changxing County People's Government completely borrowed from the relevant policy text in Zhejiang Province, representing a case of "multi-source policymaking" within a hierarchical departmental structure.

5.4   Case 2: Similar Policies Between Longquan City and Changxing County

1. **Theme selection and document set filtering:** Following the procedure in Case 1, the "Agriculture, Forestry, and Water Resources" theme represented

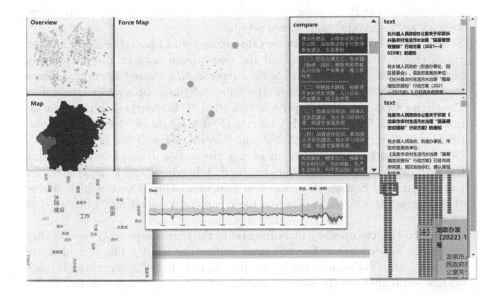

Fig. 4. Case 2: Similar policies between Longquan City and Changxing County

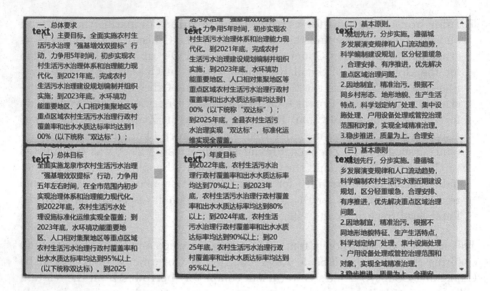

Fig. 5. Comparison of similar policy texts between Longquan City and Changxing County: the text above is from Changxing County; the text below is from Longquan City

by the green stream in the timeline is selected, and a cluster of document sets within the red box in the overview is filtered out.

2. **Analysis of the main topics in the selected document set:** Fig. 4 presents the word cloud representing the selected document set's keywords, which indicates that the policy documents mainly focus on water-related topics such as "reservoirs" and "construction."

3. **Study the relationship between documents:** In Fig. 4, the force-directed graph shows four documents, and the two orange dots at the bottom are highly correlated with many blue dots representing shared keywords. These two documents, titled "Notice of the Office of the People's Government of Changxing County on Issuing the Action Plan of "Strengthening the Foundation, Increasing Efficiency and Achieving Double Upgrades" for Rural Domestic Sewage Treatment (2021–2025)" and "Notice of the Office of the People's Government of Longquan City on Issuing the Action Plan of "Strengthening the Foundation, Increasing Efficiency and Achieving Double Upgrades" for Rural Domestic Sewage Treatment in Longquan City," have a high degree of correlation but do not belong to the completely copied mode observed in Case 1.

4. **Compare the two policy documents:** In the text comparison view, orange rectangles appear below the red ones, indicating similar but not identical sentence pairs. By comparing them, it is found that the sentences in each orange rectangle have the same meaning, but different sentence order. Therefore, it is determined that these are similar policy texts. Changxing County

and Longquan City are both at the same administrative level and have similar expressions in the "sewage treatment" policy. This is further explained in Fig. 5, where both start from the action plan of "strengthening the foundation, increasing efficiency and achieving double upgrades," with a goal to achieve "double compliance" within "5 years." Longquan City modified the timeline and compliance rate based on local conditions. The ideas for the "annual goals" and "basic principles" are also consistent between the two.

5. **Inference and Reference Relationship:** In Fig. 4, the time view in the lower right corner suggests that Changxing County's policy text predates that of Longquan City. Therefore, it can be inferred that Longquan City may have drawn inspiration from Changxing County's policy text while formulating its own "Rural Domestic Sewage Treatment Strong Foundation and Efficiency Dual-Indicator Action Plan." However, Longquan City made adjustments to its specific plan to suit its local situation, such as the overall goal. It is also possible that Zhejiang Province issued a policy on the "Rural Domestic Sewage Treatment Strong Foundation and Efficiency Dual-Indicator Action Plan," which was distributed to both Changxing County and Longquan City, as they are subordinate units under different cities. The two local units then formulated their own plans according to their local conditions. Unfortunately, due to the limitations of this system, it is not possible to explore Zhejiang Province's policy on the "Rural Domestic Sewage Treatment Strong Foundation and Efficiency Dual-Indicator Action Plan" and verify this hypothesis.

This case examines the similarity between policy texts in Longquan City and Changxing County, and infers that Longquan City borrowed policy ideas from Changxing County to create a policy suited for their local situation. This illustrates the "multi-departmental decision-making" of same-level departments in different regions.

6 Summary

In recent years, the Chinese government has actively promoted digital transformation, collecting massive amounts of data, and demanding more accurate and scientific decision-making. This article presents the design and development of a policy text multidimensional visual analysis system that has achieved the research task through two cases of "multi-departmental decision-making." The system's key components, including view mapping, interaction, linkage, and architecture design, are detailed. The multidimensional visual analysis system can assist government decision-making by facilitating interactive exploration of policy document sets. Future work involves exploring temporal, spatial, and semantic relationships among similar policy texts and summarizing the different manifestations of "multi-departmental decision-making."

Acknowledgment. This work is supported by the Natural Science Foundation of China (NSFC No. 62202105) and Shanghai Municipal Science and Technology Major Project (2021SHZDZX0103), General Program (No. 21ZR1403300), Sailing Program (No. 21YF1402900) and ZJLab.

References

1. Keim, D.A., Mansmann, F., Stoffel, A., Ziegler, H.: Visual analytics (2008)
2. Keim, D., Andrienko, G., Fekete, J.-D., Görg, C., Kohlhammer, J., Melançon, G.: Visual analytics: definition, process, and challenges. In: Kerren, A., Stasko, J.T., Fekete, J.-D., North, C. (eds.) Information Visualization. LNCS, vol. 4950, pp. 154–175. Springer, Heidelberg (2008). https://doi.org/10.1007/978-3-540-70956-5_7
3. Ruppert, T., et al.: Visual decision support for policy making: advancing policy analysis with visualization. Policy practice and digital science: integrating complex systems, social simulation and public administration in policy research, pp. 321–353 (2015)
4. Schiuma, G., Gavrilova, T., Carlucci, D.: Knowledge Visualisation for Strategic Decision Making in the Digital Age. Emerald (2022)
5. Park, S., Bekemeier, B., Flaxman, A., Schultz, M.: Impact of data visualization on decision-making and its implications for public health practice: a systematic literature review. Inform. Health Soc. Care **47**(2), 175–193 (2022)
6. Nash, K., Trott, V., Allen, W.: The politics of data visualisation and policy making. Convergence **28**(1), 3–12 (2022)
7. Ruppert, T., Bernard, J., Kohlhammer, J.: Bridging knowledge gaps in policy analysis with information visualization. Electronic Government and Electronic Participation-Joint Proceedings of Ongoing Research of IFIP EGOV and IFIP ePart 2022 (2013)
8. Ruppert, T.: Visual analytics to support evidence-based decision making. Ph.D. thesis, TU Darmstadt (TUPrints) (2018)
9. Howlett, M.P., Wellstead, A.M.: Re-visiting meltsner: policy advice systems and the multi-dimensional nature of professional policy analysis. Lee Kuan Yew School of Public Policy Research Paper No. LKYSPP10-001 (2009)
10. Raineri, P., Molinari, F.: Innovation in data visualisation for public policy making. The data shake: opportunities and obstacles for urban policy making, pp. 47–59 (2021)
11. Alharbi, M., Laramee, R.S.: Sos textvis: an extended survey of surveys on text visualization. Computers **8**(1), 17 (2019)
12. Kucher, K., et al.: An interdisciplinary perspective on evaluation and experimental design for visual text analytics: Position paper. In: 2022 IEEE Evaluation and Beyond-Methodological Approaches for Visualization (BELIV), pp. 28–37. IEEE (2022)
13. Weaver, C.: Multidimensional data dissection using attribute relationship graphs. In: 2010 IEEE Symposium on Visual Analytics Science and Technology, pp. 75–82. IEEE (2010)
14. Jänicke, S., Focht, J., Scheuermann, G.: Interactive visual profiling of musicians. IEEE Trans. Visual Comput. Graphics **22**(1), 200–209 (2015)
15. Zhang, Z., McDonnell, K.T., Zadok, E., Mueller, K.: Visual correlation analysis of numerical and categorical data on the correlation map. IEEE Trans. Visual Comput. Graphics **21**(2), 289–303 (2014)

16. Xia, J., Chen, W., Hou, Y., Hu, W., Huang, X., Ebertk, D.S.: Dimscanner: a relation-based visual exploration approach towards data dimension inspection. In: 2016 IEEE Conference on Visual Analytics Science and Technology (VAST), pp. 81–90. IEEE (2016)

17. Nana, Y., Qingnian, Z., Jiqiang, N.: Computational model of geospatial semantic similarity based on ontology structure. Sci. Surv. Mapp. **40**(3), 107–111 (2015)

18. Wang, X., Cui, Z., Jiang, L., Wenhuan, L., Li, J.: Wordlenet: a visualization approach for relationship exploration in document collection. Tsinghua Sci. Technol. **25**(3), 384–400 (2019)

19. Kang, H.B., Qian, X., Hope, T., Shahaf, D., Chan, J., Kittur, A.: Augmenting scientific creativity with an analogical search engine. ACM Trans. Comput-Hum. Interact. **29**(6), 1–36 (2022)

20. Han, H.L., Yu, J., Bournet, R., Ciorascu, A., Mackay, W.E., Beaudouin-Lafon, M.: Passages: interacting with text across documents. In: Proceedings of the 2022 CHI Conference on Human Factors in Computing Systems, pp. 1–17 (2022)

21. Fok, R., et al.: SCIM: intelligent skimming support for scientific papers. arXiv preprint arXiv:2205.04561 (2022)

22. Kavaz, E., Puig, A., Rodriguez, I., Taule, M., Nofre, M.: Data visualization for supporting linguists in the analysis of toxic messages (2021)

23. Handler, A., O'Connor, B.: Rookie: a unique approach for exploring news archives. arXiv preprint arXiv:1708.01944 (2017)

24. Knittel, J., et al.: Real-time visual analysis of high-volume social media posts. IEEE Trans. Visual Comput. Graphics **28**(1), 879–889 (2021)

25. Baumer, E.P.S., Jasim, M., Sarvghad, A., Mahyar, N.: Of course it's political! a critical inquiry into underemphasized dimensions in civic text visualization. In: Computer Graphics Forum, vol. 41, pp. 1–14. Wiley Online Library (2022)

26. Sondag, M., Turkay, C., Xu, K., Matthews, L., Mohr, S., Archambault, D.: Visual analytics of contact tracing policy simulations during an emergency response. In: Computer Graphics Forum, vol. 41, pp. 29–41. Wiley Online Library (2022)

27. Soufan, A., Ruthven, I., Azzopardi, L.: Searching the literature: an analysis of an exploratory search task. In: ACM SIGIR Conference on Human Information Interaction and Retrieval, pp. 146–157 (2022)

28. Kang, H., Chang, J.C., Kim, Y., Kittur, A.: Threddy: an interactive system for personalized thread-based exploration and organization of scientific literature. In: Proceedings of the 35th Annual ACM Symposium on User Interface Software and Technology, pp. 1–15 (2022)

29. Handler, A., Mahyar, N., O'Connor, B.: Clioquery: interactive query-oriented text analytics for comprehensive investigation of historical news archives. ACM Trans. Interact. Intell. Syst. (TiiS) **12**(3), 1–49 (2022)

30. Matejka, J., Grossman, T., Fitzmaurice, G.: Paper forager: supporting the rapid exploration of research document collections. In: Graphics Interface 2021 (2021)

31. Cui, Y., Che, W., Liu, T., Qin, B., Wang, S., Hu, G.: Revisiting pre-trained models for Chinese natural language processing. In: Proceedings of the 2020 Conference on Empirical Methods in Natural Language Processing: Findings, pp. 657–668, Online, Association for Computational Linguistics, November 2020

Heuristic Approach to Curate Disease Taxonomy Beyond Nosology-Based Standards

Zhiwen Hu[1,2(✉)] ⓘ and Ya Chen[1,2]

[1] School of Computer Science and Technology,
Zhejiang Gongshang University, Hangzhou 310018, China
huzhiwen@zjgsu.edu.cn
[2] Collaborative Innovation Center of Computational Social Science,
Zhejiang Gongshang University, Hangzhou 310018, China

Abstract. Understanding naming conventions for strengthening the integrity of naming human diseases remains nominal rather than substantial in the medical community. Since the current nosology-based criteria for human diseases cannot provide a one-size-fits-all corrective mechanism, numerous idiomatic but erroneous names frequently appear in scientific literature and news outlets, at the cost of sociocultural repercussions. To mitigate such impacts, we examine the ethical oversight of current naming practices and introduce some ethical principles for formulating an improved naming scheme. Relatedly, we organize rich metadata to unveil the nosological evolution of anachronistic names and demonstrate the heuristic approaches to curate exclusive substitutes for inopportune nosology based on deep learning models and *post-hoc* explanations. Our findings indicate that the nosological evolution of anachronistic names may have societal consequences in the absence of a corrective mechanism. Arguably, as an exemplar, *Rubella* could serve as a destigmatized replacement for *German measles*. The illustrated rationales and approaches could provide hallmark references to the ethical introspection of naming practices and pertinent credit allocations.

Keywords: Disease Taxonomy · ICD-11 · Health Communication · Credit Allocation · *German measles* · Long COVID · Monkeypox · Deep Learning

1 Introduction

On May 8, 2015, the World Health Organization (WHO) announced the initial optimal approaches for novel human contagious illnesses [1]. Nomenclature is the crystallization of human scientific and technological knowledge in natural language. In the medical community, appropriate names were deliberately invented for the designation of human diseases with pathological characteristics. However, underrepresented emphasis has been placed on the nomenclature of human diseases. The current wave of destigmatization calls for constant introspection of the offensive appellations of human diseases [1–3]. In the same week, the anachronistic usage of *German measles* in the leading journals *Nature* and *Science* without any caution implies that some strongly-held but

X. Meng et al. (Eds.): BDSC 2023, CCIS 1846, pp. 152–174, 2023.
https://doi.org/10.1007/978-981-99-3925-1_10

flawed names may brand social stigma and discrimination [4–6]. Still, the stigmatized nosology of the 'Long COVID' (also known as 'post-COVID syndrome' or 'chronic COVID-19' or 'chronic fatigue syndrome' (ME/CFS)) may discourage those affected by the condition to access care [7–10]. In the aftermath of the 2022 *Monkeypox* outbreak [11–15], the WHO is grappling with a patchwork of naming *Monkeypox* in order to reduce misconceptions, stigmatization, and discrimination [16].

As an exemplar, in the 19th century, the name *Rubella* was proposed as a substitute for the German term *Rötheln*, then the epidemic neologism *German measles* was gradually accepted as idiomatic usage [17–25]. However, anachronistic usages like that violate the latest naming protocols of the WHO – stigmatizing a specific country and its residents [1]. Arguably, the looming worry is to reignite the torch of discrimination and fuel the current infodemic unconsciously [3, 26–29].

Based on an extensive literature review, this study aims to punctuate heuristic introspection of naming practices for human diseases and address the following research issues: (1) Did the anachronistic names like *German measles* cost societal impacts? (2) What are the diachronic discourses of *German measles* and common synonyms? (3) What can we learn from the lexical evolution? (4) Should we hash out inopportune names like *German measles*? And How? (5) What are the pertinent principles of curating the exclusive substitute for an anachronistic nosology?

2 Materials and Methods

Rich collections of the printed or digital imprint of social individuals are formidable proxies to determine the dynamic pragmatics patterns of practical utterances and reveal the collective human behaviours from sociocultural preferences [30, 31]. Following the Preferred Reporting Items for Systematic Reviews and Meta-Analyses (PRISMA) guidelines [32], here we organize rich metadata available to unveil the scientific paradigms via the following experiments (Appendix 1).

2.1 Infodemiological Study

In the global online news coverage experiments, we aim to unveil the scientific paradigms of the diachronic discourse and emotional tone. Here, the metadata analysis aims to demonstrate the emotional polarity of the public in the context of global online news on *German measles*, *Middle Eastern Respiratory Syndrome*, *Spanish flu*, *Monkeypox*, and *Huntington's disease* over time, respectively.

First, the code scheme was curated following three main principles that we established before [33]. According to the code scheme, the search formulas are available in Appendix 2. Second, the unbiased and comprehensive metadata of global online news coverage and emotional tone retrieved through the open project GDELT Summary (https://api.gdeltproject.org/api/v2/summary/summary) between December 30, 2019 (the outbreak of COVID-19) and May 8, 2022, including the textual and visual narratives of different queries [34, 35]. Finally, by leveraging the capacity of GDELT's machine translation and neural network image recognition [35], the instant news portfolio in Fig. 1 summarizes the textual and visual narratives of different queries in 65 multilingual online news. The volume ratio is the total volume of matching articles divided by the total number of all articles monitored by GDELT. The emotional tone is the average tone of all matching documents, and the normalized score ranges from -10 (extremely negative) to $+10$ (extremely positive) based on the tonal algorithm.

2.2 Historiographical Study

The Google Books Ngram Corpus (GBNC) is a unique linguistic landscape that benefits from centuries of development of rich grammatical and lexical resources as well as its cultural context [36]. It contains n-grams from approximately 8 million books, or 6% of all books published in English, Hebrew, French, German, Spanish, Russian, Italian, and Chinese. The GBNC covers data logs from 1500 to 2019. A unigram (1-gram) is a string of characters uninterrupted by a space, and an n-gram (n consecutive words) is a sequence of a unigram, such as *Morbilli* (unigram), *Rubeola* (unigram), *Rubella* (unigram), *Rötheln* (unigram), and *German measles* (bigram). In this study, by retrieving the use frequency of a specific lexicon in historical development, we first obtain a glimpse of the nature of historical evolution.

Then, as we continue to stockpile seminal patterns, some have argued that correlation is threatening to unseat causation as the bedrock of scientific storytelling before. We must punctuate heuristic cautions of wrestling with in-depth information from retrospective sources, cross-validation, and the reassembly of the whole story. Finally, we provide compelling arguments to the extent of understanding the underneath nature of lexical dynamics and pathological differentials based on authentic materials and critical examination.

2.3 Semantic Similarity Experiment

Based on the epistemic results of the above historiographical study, as an exemplificative case, we could construct the initial candidates of *German measles*, which includes *morbilli, rubeola, rubella,* and *rötheln*. Relatedly, as prior knowledge, the term *rotheln* is ordinarily used as a translation of the German term *rötheln* in literature. From the outset, it's reasonable to expand the initial candidates to *morbilli, rubeola, rubella, rötheln,* and *rotheln*.

Directed at five expanded candidate words, we employed the BERT model and PubMedBERT model to quantify the semantic similarities between them, respectively. The cosine similarity formulas to calculate semantic relevance are as follows:

$$similarity = \frac{A \cdot B}{\|A\| \|B\|} = \frac{\sum_{i=1}^{n} A_i B_i}{\sqrt{\sum_{i=1}^{n} (A_i)^2} \times \sqrt{\sum_{i=1}^{n} (B_i)^2}}, \tag{1}$$

where A and B denote two vectors, A_i and $B_i (i = 1 \ldots n)$ represent the components of vector A and B.

The BERT model and PubMedBERT model have the same architecture with different corpora for preliminary training and pre-training. Coupling with a multi-layer bidirectional transformer encoder and bidirectional self-attention, the BERT and PubMedBERT models are more sensitive to semantics than the constrained self-attention used by GPT-2 model. The former uses the BookCorpus (800M words) and English Wikipedia (2,500M words) for training, its multilingual pre-training model can handle more than 100 languages [37]. The latter model uses the latest collection of PubMed abstracts (14M abstracts, 3.2B words, 21 GB), and its pre-training model can facilitate understanding the word semantics in the medical field [38]. The two models used the Wordpiece embeddings with their token vocabularies. The two models are capable to verify the homology between *rötheln*, and *rotheln*, and identify the target word with the closest similarity to *German measles* in the initial candidates. For *post-hoc* explanations, PubMedBERT-generated case studies available demystify the typical scenarios in pre-training narratives.

2.4 Semantic Drift Experiment

We analyzed the dynamic evolution of the five keywords *German measles, morbilli, rubeola, rubella*, and *rötheln*. In the experiments, the two-stage text corpora were retrieved from GBNC. Specifically, we choose two time periods: one or two hundred years after the word appeared and 1950 to 2020. Each keyword has two corpora, and each corpus has 1,000 targeted snippets published in two time periods with random sampling.

To accurately demonstrate the semantic evolution of each keyword, we coordinate their synchronic and diachronic semantic structures. Since a word's historical meaning can be inferred by its most semantically similar words in two time periods, we could track down how the semantics of words change over time [39, 40]. Firstly, we used the word co-occurrence matrix to build semantic representations in two time periods, in this way the meaning of the word could be approximated in the contexts over time. By the word co-occurrence matrix, we curated some semantic neighbors for the keywords *German measles, morbilli, rubeola, rubella*, and *rötheln*, respectively. Secondly, based on the word co-occurrence matrix, positive pointwise mutual information (PPMI) matrix entries are given by:

$$PPMI(x, y) = max\left(0, \log_2 \frac{C(x, y) \cdot N}{C(x)C(y)}\right), \tag{2}$$

where C represents word co-occurrence matrix, $C(x, y)$ refers to the number of co-occurrences of the words x and y, $C(x)$ represents the number of occurrences of the word x, $C(y)$ represents the number of occurrences of the word y, N represents the number of words in the corpus. Thirdly, we used singular value decomposition (SVD) to obtain a 4500×4500 matrix for the corpus of the two time periods. Finally, we employed principal component analysis (PCA) to reduce the dimensions of word embeddings from 4,500 to 2 and then projected the uncharted latent patterns in the five word-embeddings clusters.

3 Ethical Oversight of Naming Practices

In recent years, we have witnessed many outbreaks of human diseases, with proper names given by stakeholders. Sometimes, diseases are initially given interim names or common names. Then, the proper names are officially ratified by the International Classification of Diseases (ICD) of WHO. Even so, each round of naming practice is not always successful [1, 41, 42]. Of them, *Middle Eastern Respiratory Syndrome* (MERS)[43], *Spanish flu* [44, 45], *Monkeypox* [11, 13–15, 46], and *Huntington's disease* [47–50] have been accused of unnecessary societal impacts in previous studies (Fig. 1).

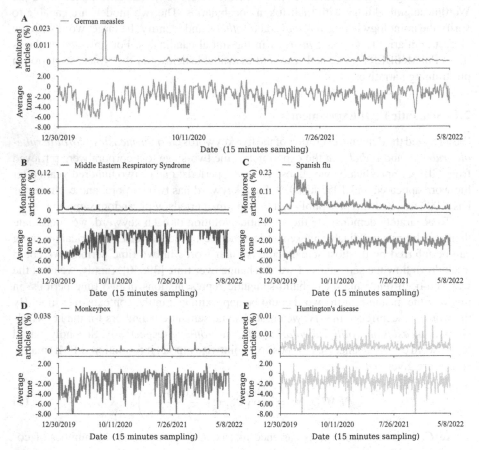

Fig. 1. Prevailing stereotypes of stigmatizing names with negative tones in wake of COVID-19 pandemic. The global instant news portfolio on GDELT Summary summarizes the textual and visual narratives of different queries in 65 multilingual online news: **A**, *German measles*; **B**, *Middle Eastern Respiratory Syndrome*; **C**, *Spanish flu*; **D**, *Monkeypox*; and **E**, *Huntington's disease*. The upper panels display the percent of all global online news coverage over time. The lower panels show the average emotional tone of all news coverage from extremely negative to extremely positive. The temporal resolution of sampling is 15 min per day.

Naming conventions are not merely for naming diseases but for the vitality of science and the promotion of social progress [2, 42, 51, 52]. Evidently, as shown in Fig. 1, the results of the infodemiological study show that the global news outlets (in 65 languages) enjoy long-standing but flawed naming conventions with extremely negative tones, such as *German measles*, *Middle Eastern Respiratory Syndrome*, *Spanish flu*, *Monkeypox*, and *Huntington's disease*. Admittedly, the coverage of effective tones is much more negative than the standard portrayal assumes on average [53]. This finding highlights that these controversial stereotypes confounded the generally accepted norms at the cost of social progress, such as worsening acute stress of patients, provoking the backlash against particular communities, triggering unjustified slaughtering of food animals, and creating needless travel barriers or trade barriers [1–3, 54, 55].

Understanding how naming conventions strengthen the integrity of naming practices remains nominal rather than substantial yet. In the COVID-19 infodemic, multifarious monikers have become explicit consideration in the COVID-19 paper tsunami, and the global profusion of tangled hashtags has found its way in daily communication [56]. Just as the remarks of the editorial of *Nature*, "As well as naming the illness, the WHO was implicitly sending a reminder to those who had erroneously been associating the virus with Wuhan and with China in their news coverage – including *Nature*. That we did so was an error on our part, for which we take responsibility and apologize."[57] Unfortunately, many more stigmatized names somewhat aggravate the collective perceptual biases and reignite recent backlash against Asians and diaspora [10, 33, 58]. Accordingly, scientists must verse themselves in naming conventions rather than feeding the trolls of stigma and discrimination.

4 Ethical Oversight of Naming Practices

Of similar concern, we witness that many anachronistic names, from *Spanish flu* to *Zika*, and from *Lyme* to *Ebola*, are named after geographic places in our daily communications. But they are stigmatized cases and plain inaccurate (Table 1).

Table 1. Many diseases' names have complained of both stigmatization and inaccurate.

Name	ICD-11 Code	Complains	References
Spanish Flu	1E30	The 1918–19 influenza outbreak now often referred to as the *Spanish flu* did not even originate in Spain	[59, 60]
Zika virus disease	1D48	A mosquito-borne disease caused by *Zika virus* was first identified in Uganda in 1947 in monkeys, and later identified in humans in 1952. *Zika virus disease* was named after the Zika forest of Uganda	[61]
Lyme disease	1C1G	*Lyme disease* was named after the "original location", the town of Old Lyme, Connecticut in 1975. More than 130 years ago, a German physician Alfred Buchwald first discovered the erythema migrans of what is now known to be *Lyme disease*	[60]

(*continued*)

Table 1. (*continued*)

Name	ICD-11 Code	Complains	References
Ebola disease	1D60.0	The hemorrhagic fever caused by the filovirus is named after the Ebola River at Legbala, Congo. Yambuku, a town situated 100 km away from Legbala, was the first epicenter in 1976	[60–62]

In retrospect, WHO released the latest naming protocols of newly identified infectious diseases in 2015, as a supplement to the Reference Guide on the Content Model of the ICD-11 alpha drafted by ICD in 2011 [1, 63, 64]. In May 2019, the World Health Assembly (WHA) formally adopted the 11th revision of the International Classification of Diseases (ICD-11). Specifically, we could crystallize the current recommendations into five protocols: (1) avoidance of geographic locations (e.g., countries, cities, regions); (2) avoidance of people's names; (3) avoidance of species/class of animal or food; (4) avoidance of cultural, population, industry, or occupational references; (5) avoidance of terms that incite undue fear.

In theory, all Member States should follow the nosology-based standard to name a newly identified human disease at a later stage. On the one hand, the global response has not always been smooth in practice. On the other hand, the international framework could not offer a one-size-fits-all surveillance mechanism for new designations and the pre-existed names. Currently, a cohort of inopportune names is widely professed in both scientific literature and news outlets without any caution, such as *Ebola disease*, *Rift Valley fever*, *Japanese encephalitis*, *Crimean Congo hemorrhagic fever*, *Chagas disease*, *Athlete's foot*, *Miner's asthma*, *Marburg disease*, *Legionnaire' disease*, *Creutzfeldt-Jakob disease*, *Hong Kong flu*, *Bird flu*, *Swine flu*, *Equine encephalitis*, *Paralytic shellfish poisoning*, *Monkeypox* (WHO is working on renaming *Monkeypox* to remove geographic stigma), and so on [1, 41, 42]. Accordingly, after the swine flu of 2009 outbreak, some countries still banned pork imports, although *Swine flu* cannot be transmitted from pigs at all. Moreover, they are scapegoating the resurgence of stigma in wake of geopolitical tensions and backlashes [10, 61].

Still, the most pressing challenges concerning the nomenclature of human diseases depend on well-posed questions, including but not limited to: (1) Who did coin a term to the designation of a specific disease? (2) Is it still an appropriate name today? (3) How many inopportune names garner in textbooks without any caution? (4) How to map out an exclusive substitute for a flawed name? To that end, as a supplement to the current nosology-based nomenclature standard, we propose the ethical principles for naming a new human disease or renaming pre-existed nosology, as well as pertinent credit allocation (Fig. 2).

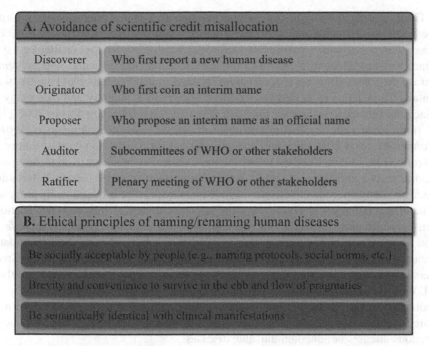

A. Avoidance of scientific credit misallocation

Discoverer	Who first report a new human disease
Originator	Who first coin an interim name
Proposer	Who propose an interim name as an official name
Auditor	Subcommittees of WHO or other stakeholders
Ratifier	Plenary meeting of WHO or other stakeholders

B. Ethical principles of naming/renaming human diseases

Be socially acceptable by people (e.g., naming protocols, social norms, etc.)

Brevity and convenience to survive in the ebb and flow of pragmatics

Be semantically identical with clinical manifestations

Fig. 2. Proposal of ethical principles for the latest naming protocols of human diseases.

First, as shown in Fig. 2, many contributors were involved in the general taxonomy and nomenclature process of human diseases, including the discover(s), originator(s), proposer(s), auditor(s), and ratifier(s). Without moral discernment, the Matthew effect of credit misallocations always discourages individual engagement in such practices [65]. Scientists, who preluded the accession of a particular disease, do not always earn their *bona fide* niches because of credit misallocation in the scientific accounts. Typically, the unsung originator Dick Thompson first coined the term "*Severe Acute Respiratory Syndrome*" (*SARS*) on 15 March 2003 [66]. His tour-de-force contribution is portrayed as a trivial anecdote. Similarly, Dr. Jean-Jacques Muyembe-Tamfum, one of the discoverers of *Ebola disease*, was unsung until 2015 [67–69]. Thus, figuring out the seminal motivations of nomenclatures in routine obscurity generally presupposed that we could track down the original records [70, 71]. To corroborate continuous introspection of previous multifarious findings, historians always find themselves buried in unending retrieval of tangled contingencies to pinpoint such inherent affiliations in pithy evidence.

Second, any proposed name for diseases should balance science, policy, and communication. Human diseases are often given names by stakeholders outside of the medical community. As a counterexample, *Pneumonoultramicroscopicsilicovolcanoconiosis*, referred to as pneumoconiosis or silicosis, was coined by Everett M. Smith in 1935 [72, 73]. Literally, the 45-letter neologism is "a form of a chronic lung disease caused by the inhalation of fine silicate or quartz dust", according to the *Oxford English Dictionary Online* (OED Online). Such a long disease entity does not roll off the tongue for efficient communication, and we should discard similar designations in scientific literature.

Third, erasing the stigmas of human diseases is a major public health priority. Whether a name change will ever destigmatize a human disease or not is a cliché. As a case in point, *Schizophrenia* (also known as Kraepelin's disease or Bleuler's syndrome) was first adopted in 1937 as a translation of the German name *Schizophrenie*. To erase the potential stigma of *Schizophrenia*, the National Federation of Families with Mentally III in Japan requested the Japanese Society of Psychiatry and Neurology to replace the official term *Seishin Bunretsu Byo* with *Togo-Shicchou-Sho* in 2002 [74–76]. In the same vein, South Korea changed its official term *Jeongshin-bunyeol-byung* to *Johyun-byung* in 2011 [77]. Subsequently, lexical harm reduction became a bone of contention [75, 78–82]. Keep the twists and turns of naming practices in mind, any novel proposal should go far beyond a mere semantic equivalent, as well as across cultures and languages. In practice, an alphanumeric code or a Greek letter is occasionally proposed for naming a pathogen or disease, but the opposers underline that such designations often introduce new confusion. For example, *Filovirus-associated haemorrhagic fever 1* and *Filovirus-associated haemorrhagic fever 2* were proposed as potential candidates instead of *Marburg disease* and *Ebola disease*, respectively [41]. Similarly, some Greek letters sound alike when they are translated into other languages, such as eta and theta [83]. With unreached consensus, some problematic notions are barning in our textbooks to educate generation after generation without any caution. Nonetheless, reassigning a curated standard name is the corrective approach to destigmatizing a flawed name of infectious diseases or noncommunicable diseases.

Last but not least, the sociocultural costs of inappropriate disease names receive little attention [60]. Scientists mostly work to reduce the physical toll and economic costs of diseases [84], although many of them endorse that disease names could be problematic [41]. Consistent with our findings, in most instances, inappropriate disease names remain in our blind spot, partially because the lasting damage they cause in affected communities is difficult to quantify. Just as the remarks of Dr. Keiji Fukuda, Assistant Director-General for Health Security of the WHO, "this may seem like a trivial issue to some, but disease names do matter to the people who are directly affected."[55] Previous work has revealed how the widespread use of inappropriate names could create a vicious circle in public communication, with institutional notions further reinforcing collective stigmatization, discrimination, and prejudice [10, 52, 79].

5   Looking Back and Looking Forward

Framed within the historical coevolution of scientific contexts, understanding the nosological continuity of diseases remains limited [70, 85–88]. As a case in point, the pathological associations between *German measles* (ICD-11 code, 1F02) and common synonyms (e.g., *Morbilli, Rubeola, Rubella, Rötheln*, etc.) are in the fog of confusion, although the debate has been going on over a century and a half earlier [17, 89–93]. These diachronic discourses and lexical dynamics also remain unclear [4, 17, 94–97].

Nowadays, the Google Books Ngram Corpus (GBNC) is a unique linguistic landscape that benefits from centuries of development of rich grammatical and lexical resources, as well as its cultural context [36, 98]. Arguably, the lexicographical and historiographical study promises to articulate the ins and outs of scientific narratives

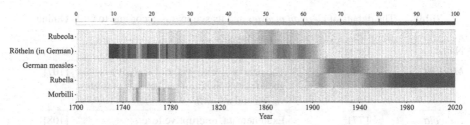

Fig. 3. Historiographical study. Google Books Ngram Corpus (GBNC) facsimiles the diachronic discourse of *Morbilli* (English corpus), *Rubeola* (English corpus), *Rubella* (English corpus), *Rötheln* (German corpus), and *German measles* (English corpus) from 1700 to 2019. The color of the heatmap represents the normalized frequency percentage of the five lexicons on that time. The higher the proportion, the darker the corresponding color, and the greater dominance of the lexicon.

by leveraging the capacity of these rich metadata corpora over four centuries (Fig. 3). Many miscellaneous disease names (e.g., *morbilli, morbilli scarlatinosi, rötheln, feuermasern, scarlatina morbillosa, rubeola notha, rosalia idiopathica, bastard measles* or *scarlatina, hybrid measles* or *scarlatina*, etc.) have sunk back into merited oblivion in the ups and downs of epic history. In contrast, German *measles* was destined to become an antiquated and anachronistic usage, and *rubella* initiated a herald wave of dominant place after 1944. An assessment of the correlation between German measles and common synonyms was carried out using a Spearman's rank correlation method. There was a strong, positive monotonic correlation between *German measles* and *rubella* ($r_s = 0.870, p < 0.001$).

The nosology of *German measles* and similar diseases is still far from being generally recognized, as well as their pathological differentials [71, 99]. *Measles* is an old English disease name that classical nosologists have vainly attempted to replace with such synonyms as *morbilli* and *rubeola* [100]. The English term *measles* was introduced by Dr. John of Gaddesden as an equivalent of the Latin term *morbilli* around the 14th century [70, 101, 102]. But such designation was generally criticized as "a product of semantic and nosographic confusion." [103] The term *rubeola* originally borrowed from the Latin word *Rubeus* (meaning *reddish*) in Avicenna of Bagdad's writings, is thought to have been used for the first time as a translation of the term *measles* [102, 104]. Indeed, the great majority of scientists recognize *German measles* to be an independent disease.

According to the OED Online, the earliest known references to *German measles* date back as far as 1856 (Table 2). Therefore, it is generally believed that the epidemic entity *German measles* was accepted growly after 1856 [17, 105, 106]. But this is not the case. The earliest usages could be stemmed back to about 1814 (Table 3).

Table 2. The debuts of *German measles* and its synonyms according to OED Online.

Name	Debut	Description	References
Morbilli	1526	The iuce of it with water of endyuye is good for the chyldren pockes and messeles varioli and *morbilli*	[107]
Rubeola	1771	Exanthemata, or eruptive fevers; comprehending 10 genera, *viz.* 1. Erysipelas; 2. Peftis; 3. Variola; 4. Varicella; 5. *Rubeola*; 6. Miliaria; 7. Scarlatina; 8. Urticaria; 9. Pemphigus; 10. Aphtha	[108]
Rötheln	1 January 1840	I shall therefore use the German word *Rötheln* to designate the mixed disease under consideration	[109]
German measles	12 July 1856	With regard to the name, '*German measles*' – its usual trite designation here – seems unexceptionable for common use	[17]
Rubella	1866	*Rötheln* is harsh and foreign to our ears…I therefore venture to propose *Rubella* as a substitute for *Rötheln*, or, at any rate, as a name for the disease which it has been my object in this paper to describe	[110]

The term *German measles* was established as a separate disease in 1814 and officially recognized by the International Congress of Medicine in 1881. The known clinical description came from German physicians Friedrich Hoffmann in 1740, De Bergen in 1752, and Orlow in 1758, respectively [105, 111, 112]. Before 1768, for more learned occasions, *Rötheln* and *morbilli* seem more decidedly to mark a distinct disease, than any other yet proposed [17, 97]. French physician Sauvages de Lacroix, who established the first methodical nosology for disease classification in 1763 [64, 113], first applied the term *rubeola* to what had been previously termed *morbilli* in 1768 [97]. And while almost immediately after him, the German physicians, Selle, Orlow, and Ziegler, clearly laid down the distinctive marks between *rubeola* and *morbilli*. On April 4, 1814, Dr. George de Maton read a paper entitled "*Some Account of a Rash Liable to be Mistaken for Scarlatina*" at the Royal College of Physicians in London [114–116], which results in the names *rubella* or *German measles* as a substitute for *Rötheln* [17, 94]. Then, the epidemic term *German measles* was accepted gradually as a synonym for *rubella*. *German measles*, *Rötheln* or *rubeola* per se, was officially ratified as a distinct disease at the 7th International Medical Congress, London, August 2 to 9, 1881 [96, 117–124]. A quarter-century later, the term *German measles* has ultimately become common usage.

Rubella has been "discovered – and named – multiple times" in the past centuries [127]. In modern literature, *rubella* has become a *de facto* synonym for *German measles* after 1944 [17–25]. In 1740, the English name *rubella* is derived from the Latin *rubellus*

Table 3. Historiographical records have provided extensive information about the coinages of *German measles* and common synonyms *Rubeola*, *Rötheln*, and *Rubella*.

Name	Debut	Credit	Evidence	References
Rubeola	1768	François Boissier de Sauvages de Lacroix (12 May 1706 –19 February 1767)	Shortly before (1768), the two diseases had been separated by Sauvages in his Nosology, and he was the first to call measles "*rubeola*," instead of "*morbilli*," by which name it had always been known before. This new name, "*rubeola*," was adopted by Cullen in his Nosology, published four years later (1772)	[97, 125]
Rötheln	1 January 1840	Robert Paterson (1814–1889)	I fear that the adoption of the word *rubeola* for this disease would produce confusion in medical nomenclature. I shall therefore use the German word *Rötheln* to designate the mixed disease under consideration, in preference to that of *rubeola*, or the use of a new term	[109, 126]
German measles	4 April 1814	William George Maton (1774–1835)	On April 4, 1814, Dr. George Maton… This first identification of *German measles* as a discrete illness was published one year later, an interval from presentation to publication not dissimilar to that in modern experience	[114–116]

(*continued*)

Table 3. (*continued*)

Name	Debut	Credit	Evidence	References
Rubella	1740	Friedrich Hoffmann (1660–1742)	Friedrich Hoffmann (1660–1742), …, Notable among his many clinical descriptions are those of *rubella* (called "German" measles as a consequence of his description,) chlorosis, and the diseases of the pancreas and liver	[111, 112]

reddish, and the clinical description of *rubella* was first described by Friedrich Hoffmann, the author of *Fundamenta Medicinae* [111, 112]. Then, *rubella* was considered by Dr. Maton to be a mere variant of measles or scarlet fever in 1814 [114, 115, 128]. Half a century later, English surgeon Henry Veale suggested the need to name the discrete disease, and formally proposed the name *rubella* as a substitute for *Rötheln* in 1866 [105]. As a major human infectious disease, *rubella* must have emerged only in the past 11,000 years for which some close relatives may still exist among animals [4, 71]. Indeed, consistent with the historiographical results (Fig. 3), *rubella* had been considered of "minor importance among the common communicable diseases" until 1940 [129]. Following the *rubella* epidemic of 1940, the occurrence of congenital rubella syndrome (CRS) was first recognized by Norman McAlister Gregg in 1941 [130, 131]. As of 2018, 81 countries were verified as having eliminated *rubella* via routine vaccination, and even today *rubella* remains endemic in other countries [132].

6 A Heuristic Roadmap of Exclusive Substitute

An exclusive substitution for an anachronistic usage could be a pre-existed synonym, a blend word, or a neologism. However, we should curate an exclusive substitute following the ethical principles (Fig. 2). Relatedly, as a heuristic case, we hash out the inappropriate name like *German measles* to quell confusion and avoid stigma. Here, we demonstrate an illustrational approach to determine an exclusive substitution for *German measles* without ambiguity.

First, the similarity coefficient between words is determined by deep learning models, and finally screen out an exclusive substitute for *German measles* according to the semantic similarity scores of word embeddings. In Fig. 4, the input example is first constructed by summing the corresponding token, segment, and position embeddings, and then word embeddings go through the BERT base model to obtain the vector representations with semantic information. As for the bigram like *German measles*, we averaged the individual word vector to get the final word vector. By quantifying the cosine similarity scores between the word vectors (Fig. 5), it turns out that the term *rotheln* is substantial equivalence to *rötheln* with the highest semantic fidelity, and the results of the BioBERT model and the PubMedBERT model shed light on each other. Most notably, as a model in the medical field, the PubMedBERT model maps out that *Rubella* should be the exclusive substitution for *German measles* with the highest semantic similarity.

Second, some case studies are given using the same function as the PubMedBERT model for *post-hoc* explanations (Table 4). According to syntactical function, in case #1, the qualifier 'this' refers to *rubella*, so the synonymous sentence of the original sentence was that *rubella* is another name for *German measles*. Semantically, *rubella* has an equivalence relationship with *German measles*, with a very high semantic relevance (0.954). In case #2, *rötheln* has a dependent relationship with *German measles* rather than an equivalence relationship. In cases #3 and #4, *morbilli* and *rubeola* tend to the appositions of *measles* rather than those of *German measles*. To sum up, the case studies further emphasize the high semantic similarity between *rubella* and *German measles*.

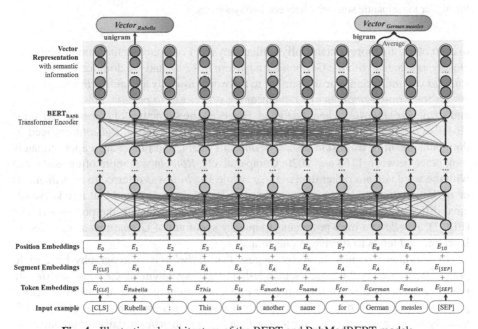

Fig. 4. Illustrational architecture of the BERT and PubMedBERT models.

Third, the purpose of the semantic drift experiments is to examine how and to what extent the meanings of *German measles*, *Morbilli*, *Rubeola*, *Rubella*, and *Rötheln* have changed over time. In the meantime, estimate the semantics of words from a particular period through historical synonyms. In Fig. 6, we projected the latent semantic drifts of *German measles*, *Morbilli*, *Rubeola*, *Rubella*, and *Rötheln* from their debuts to 2020 (Table 2 and Table 3). To highlight the cases of semantic drift, the five keywords (in colors) were shown with their historical synonyms (in gray). The closer two words are

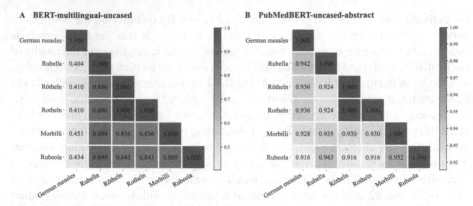

Fig. 5. Heatmaps of semantic similarity scores. **A,** the BERT model and **B,** the PubMedBERT model. The BERT semantic pretraining model is a pervasive pan-domain model. The PubMed-BERT model employed to cross-validate with the BERT model, along with a new medical vocabulary and improved lexical, syntactic and semantic learning. The higher scores in the heatmaps, the higher the semantic similarity between two synonyms.

to each other, the more semantically similar they are. For example, the term *Rubella* was closely associated with the German term *masern* in 1740, and the dominant meaning of *Rubella* was more semantically similar to the words *fowlpox* and *morbillivirus* in 2020. As for the term *German measles*, its meaning was closer to *pustula*, *flowered measles*, and *strawberry measles* when it debuted. However, the semantics of *German measles* is closer to those of *paramyxoviridae* and *three-day measles* today. *Rubeola* changed its dominant meaning from skin disease *scabies* to *röteln*, and this change approximately took place between 1768 and 2020. Comparatively, *Rötheln* was more often associated with the word *variola* rather than *anthrax*, while *Morbilli* was referred to as *pediculosis* or *rash* rather than *rosacea* or *red sandwort*. Therefore, it is found that five keywords have different degrees of semantic drift over time. Coupled with the previous results (Fig. 3), *rubella* is a high-pragmatic-frequency synonym of *German measles* in recent literature and tends to survive in due course.

In short, our results strongly suggest that *Rubella* is a geography-free, high-pragmatic-frequency, and high-semantic-homology synonym of *German measles*. In theory, *Rubella* is a pithy substitute for efficient communication according to Zipf's principle of least effort, compared with the blend-word *German measles* [133]. Additionally, it rolls much easier off the tongue than *German measles* in daily communication. In retrospect, some pioneers advocated the discarding of the offensive name *German measles* before [99, 134, 135], as the remarks, "it [*rubella*] is perhaps the best that has been used"[99] and "a better name for which [*German measles*] is *rubella*."[135] Such foresight is also consistent with our experimental results. Therefore, it should be an optimal substitute to fill in the niche of *German measles* in practice.

Table 4. Some case studies are retrieved using the same function as the PubMedBERT model.

No.	Examples	Semantic similarity scores
#1	*Rubella*: This is another name for *German measles*, it causes intellectual disability, deafness, and still birth	0.954
#2	All these physicians were German, and the disease was known as *Rötheln* (from the German name Röteln), hence the common name of "*German measles*"	0.903
#3	*Morbilli* sine catarrho has no doubt been described, but it is always held that in these cases our test for measles is awanting, and that it may be *German measles*, or something else equally non-protective against a similar attack	0.896
#4	By the way, *German measles* is not the same as regular measles (*rubeola*), and having immunity from one illness does not protect you from the other	0.892

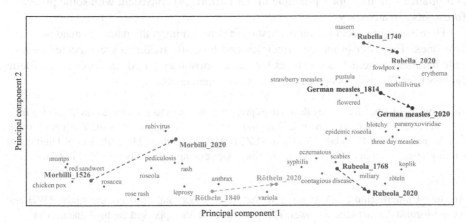

Fig. 6. The historical reconceptualization process of *German measles* and common synonyms. This sketch projected the latent semantic drifts of *German measles*, *Morbilli*, *Rubeola*, *Rubella*, and *Rötheln* from their debuts to 2020, and accurately demonstrated the dynamic semantic evolution.

7   Conclusion

On the 8th anniversary of *The best practices of new human infectious diseases* (WHO), we scrutinize the recommendations of the current naming schemes (e.g., the nosology-based standard WHA ICD-11) and discovered that they could not provide a one-size-fits-all remedial mechanism, particularly for the pre-existed names. There is still much to learn about the intricacies of naming conventions as they are framed within sociocultural variances. According to WHO best practices, curated names of human diseases should be scientifically pithy and socially acceptable, with the faith of minimizing marginal impacts on nations, economies, and people. However, without credit discernment, scientists who are participate in the routine nomenclature process do not necessarily receive their scientific credits. Thus, we emphasize the clarity of credit allocation to encourage individual participation in naming practices.

Relatedly, we explore how to eliminate the label paradox in due course and propose some ethical principles for existing naming schemes to fill the ethical void. To facilitate comprehension of the spirits of our proposal and heuristic roadmap, we orchestrate empirical study coupled with extensive metadata based on deep learning models and *post-hoc* explanations.

Concretely, our infodemiological study first demonstrates that long-standing but offensive names of human diseases continue to go viral in both the scientific community and news outlets, at the expense of social consequences, regardless of their seemingly innocuous origins. Our lexicographical and historiographical investigation could articulate the twists and turns of naming human diseases across multiple centuries, penetrate the essence of nosology, and finally bridge the gaps of contemporary considerations. As an exemplificative case, it is reasonable for *Rubella* to become an exclusive usage substitute for *German measles* because of the following reasons: (1) the same clinical manifestations and equivalent semantics; (2) without geographic stigmatization; (3) compliance with the Zipf's principle of least effort; (4) consistent with some pioneers' foresights and advocacy.

Heuristic introspection would assist us in determining pithy names instead of offensive ones. Thus, our proposed principles and heuristic roadmap are expected to provide hallmark remedial mechanisms for current nosology-based standards and reframe far-reaching discussions on human diseases nomenclature.

Acknowledgments. We hereby desire to express indebtedness to anonymous reviewers for their valuable and constructive comments. This study was partially supported by the Zhejiang Provincial Natural Science Foundation of China (LZ21F020004), and the Major Project of Digital and Cutting-edge Disciplines Construction, Zhejiang Gongshang University (SZJ2022B007).

Authors Contributions. ZWH was involved in the conceptual design of the study. ZWH and YC performed the metadata analyses. The authors wrote and approved the final manuscript.

Data Availability Statement. The synthetic data generated in this study and custom code supporting this study are available on GitHub (https://github.com/Computational-social-science/Naming_human_disease).

Ethics Approval and Consent to Participate. Not applicable.
Competing Interests. The authors declare no potential conflicts of interest.

References

1. World Health Organization: World Health Organization best practices for the naming of new human infectious diseases. https://apps.who.int/iris/bitstream/handle/10665/163636/WHO_HSE_FOS_15.1_eng.pdf
2. Fukuda, K., Wang, R., Vallat, B.: Naming diseases: first do no harm. Science **348**, 643 (2015). https://doi.org/10.1126/science.348.6235.643

3. Chandrashekhar, V.: The burden of stigma. Science **369**, 1419–1423 (2020). https://doi.org/ 10.1126/science.369.6510.1419

4. Bennett, A.J., et al.: Relatives of rubella virus in diverse mammals. Nature **586**, 424–428 (2020). https://doi.org/10.1038/s41586-020-2812-9

5. Gibbons, A.: Newly found viruses suggest rubella originated in animals. Science **370**, 157 (2020). https://doi.org/10.1126/science.370.6513.157

6. Gibbons, A.: Newly discovered viruses suggest 'German measles' jumped from animals to humans. Science (2020). https://doi.org/10.1126/science.abf1520

7. Editorial: Long COVID: let patients help define long-lasting COVID symptoms. Nature **586**, 170–170 (2020). https://doi.org/10.1038/d41586-020-02796-2

8. Alwan, N.A.: Lessons from Long COVID: working with patients to design better research. Nat. Rev. Immunol. **22**, 201–202 (2022). https://doi.org/10.1038/s41577-022-00692-6

9. Byrne, E.A.: Understanding long Covid: nosology, social attitudes and stigma. Brain. Behav. Immun. **99**, 17–24 (2022). https://doi.org/10.1016/j.bbi.2021.09.012

10. Sachs, J.D., et al.: The Lancet Commission on lessons for the future from the COVID-19 pandemic. Lancet **400**, 1224–1280 (2022). https://doi.org/10.1016/S0140-6736(22)01585-9

11. Cohen, J.: Monkeypox could establish new reservoirs in animals. Science **376**, 1258–1259 (2022). https://doi.org/10.1126/science.add4868

12. Kozlov, M.: Monkeypox goes global: why scientists are on alert. Nature **606**, 15–16 (2022). https://doi.org/10.1038/d41586-022-01421-8

13. Kozlov, M.: Monkeypox vaccination begins—can the global outbreaks be contained? Nature **606**, 444–445 (2022). https://doi.org/10.1038/d41586-022-01587-1

14. Burki, T.: Investigating monkeypox. Lancet **399**, 2254–2255 (2022). https://doi.org/10.1016/ S0140-6736(22)01096-0

15. Kraemer, M.U.G., et al.: Tracking the 2022 monkeypox outbreak with epidemiological data in real-time. Lancet Infect. Dis. **22**, 941–942 (2022). https://doi.org/10.1016/S1473-309 9(22)00359-0

16. Taylor, L.: Monkeypox: WHO to rename disease to prevent stigma. BMJ. o1489 (2022). https://doi.org/10.1136/bmj.o1489

17. Scotus, P.: The Rubeola epidemic. Lancet **68**, 57 (1856). https://doi.org/10.1016/S0140-673 6(02)76420-9

18. Wesselhoeft, C.: Rubella (German Measles). N. Engl. J. Med. **236**, 943–950 (1947). https:// doi.org/10.1056/NEJM194706192362506

19. Wesselhoeft, C.: Rubella (German Measles). N. Engl. J. Med. **236**, 978–988 (1947). https:// doi.org/10.1056/NEJM194706262362605

20. Wesselhoeft, C.: Rubella (German Measles) and congenital deformities. N. Engl. J. Med. **240**, 258–261 (1949). https://doi.org/10.1056/NEJM194902172400706

21. Dudgeon, J.A.: Immunization against Rubella. Nature **223**, 674–676 (1969). https://doi.org/ 10.1038/223674a0

22. Eichhorn, M.M.: Rubella: will vaccination prevent birth defects? Science **173**, 710–711 (1971). https://doi.org/10.1126/science.173.3998.710-a

23. Donald, M.W., Goff, W.R.: Attention-related increases in cortical responsivity dissociated from the contingent negative variation. Science **172**, 1163–1166 (1971). https://doi.org/10. 1126/science.172.3988.1163

24. Maugh, T.H.: Diabetes: epidemiology suggests a viral connection. Science **188**, 347–351 (1975). https://doi.org/10.1126/science.188.4186.347

25. Gordis, L., Gold, E.: Privacy, confidentiality, and the use of medical records in research. Science **207**, 153–156 (1980). https://doi.org/10.1126/science.7350648

26. Jardetzky, T.S., Lamb, R.A.: A class act. Nature **427**, 307–308 (2004). https://doi.org/10. 1038/427307a

27. Wadman, M.: The physician whose 1964 vaccine beat back rubella is working to defeat the new coronavirus. Science (2020). https://doi.org/10.1126/science.abb8290

28. Shimizu, K.: 2019-nCoV, fake news, and racism. Lancet **395**, 685–686 (2020). https://doi.org/10.1016/S0140-6736(20)30357-3

29. Editorial: COVID-19: fighting panic with information. Lancet. **395**, 537 (2020). https://doi.org/10.1016/S0140-6736(20)30379-2

30. Lazer, D., et al.: Computational social science. Science **323**, 721–723 (2009). https://doi.org/10.1126/science.1167742

31. Lazer, D.M.J., et al.: Computational social science: obstacles and opportunities. Science **369**, 1060–1062 (2020). https://doi.org/10.1126/science.aaz8170

32. Page, M.J., et al.: PRISMA 2020 explanation and elaboration: updated guidance and exemplars for reporting systematic reviews. BMJ **372**, n160 (2021). https://doi.org/10.1136/bmj.n160

33. Hu, Z., Yang, Z., Li, Q., Zhang, A.: The COVID-19 infodemic: infodemiology study analyzing stigmatizing search terms. J. Med. Internet Res. **22**, e22639 (2020). https://doi.org/10.2196/22639

34. Leetaru, K.H., Schrodt, P.A.: A 30-year georeferenced global event database: the global database of events, language, and tone (GDELT). In: The 54th Annual Convention of the International Studies Association. pp. 1–51, San Francisco, California, USA (2013)

35. Wang, W., Kennedy, R., Lazer, D., Ramakrishnan, N.: Growing pains for global monitoring of societal events. Science **353**, 1502–1503 (2016). https://doi.org/10.1126/science.aaf6758

36. Michel, J.-B., et al.: Quantitative analysis of culture using millions of digitized books. Science **331**, 176–182 (2011). https://doi.org/10.1126/science.1199644

37. Devlin, J., Chang, M.-W., Lee, K., Toutanova, K.: BERT: pre-training of deep bidirectional transformers for language understanding. In: Proceedings of the 2019 Conference of the North American, pp. 4171–4186. Association for Computational Linguistics, Stroudsburg, PA, USA (2019). https://doi.org/10.18653/v1/N19-1423

38. Gu, Y., et al.: Domain-specific language model pretraining for biomedical natural language processing (2020)

39. Li, Y., Engelthaler, T., Siew, C.S.Q., Hills, T.T.: The Macroscope: a tool for examining the historical structure of language. Behav. Res. Methods **51**(4), 1864–1877 (2019). https://doi.org/10.3758/s13428-018-1177-6

40. Li, Y., Hills, T., Hertwig, R.: A brief history of risk. Cognition **203**, 104344 (2020). https://doi.org/10.1016/j.cognition.2020.104344

41. Kupferschmidt, K.: Rules of the name. Science **348**, 745 (2015). https://doi.org/10.1126/science.348.6236.745

42. Kupferschmidt, K.: Discovered a disease? WHO has new rules for avoiding offensive names. Science (2015). https://doi.org/10.1126/science.aac4575

43. Enserink, M.: Amid heightened concerns, new name for novel coronavirus emerges. Science **340**, 673 (2013). https://doi.org/10.1126/science.340.6133.673

44. Dowell, S.F., Bresee, J.S.: Pandemic lessons from Iceland. Proc. Natl. Acad. Sci. **105**, 1109–1110 (2008). https://doi.org/10.1073/pnas.0711535105

45. Hoppe, T.: "Spanish Flu": when infectious disease names blur origins and stigmatize those infected. Am. J. Publ. Health. **108**, 1462–1464 (2018). https://doi.org/10.2105/AJPH.2018.304645

46. Spinney, L.: Smallpox and other viruses plagued humans much earlier than suspected. Nature **584**, 30–32 (2020). https://doi.org/10.1038/d41586-020-02083-0

47. Wexler, A.: Stigma, history, and Huntington's disease. Lancet **376**, 18–19 (2010). https://doi.org/10.1016/S0140-6736(10)60957-9

48. Rawlins, M.: Huntington's disease out of the closet? Lancet **376**, 1372–1373 (2010). https://doi.org/10.1016/S0140-6736(10)60974-9

49. Spinney, L.: Uncovering the true prevalence of Huntington's disease. Lancet Neurol. **9**, 760–761 (2010). https://doi.org/10.1016/S1474-4422(10)70160-5
50. Editorial: Dispelling the stigma of Huntington's disease. Lancet Neurol. **9**, 751 (2010). https://doi.org/10.1016/S1474-4422(10)70170-8
51. Hyman, S.E.: The unconscionable gap between what we know and what we do. Sci. Transl. Med. **6**, 1–4 (2014). https://doi.org/10.1126/scitranslmed.3010312
52. Gollwitzer, A., Marshall, J., Wang, Y., Bargh, J.A.: Relating pattern deviancy aversion to stigma and prejudice. Nat. Hum. Behav. **1**, 920–927 (2017). https://doi.org/10.1038/s41562-017-0243-x
53. Soroka, S., Fournier, P., Nir, L.: Cross-national evidence of a negativity bias in psychophysiological reactions to news. Proc. Natl. Acad. Sci. **116**, 18888–18892 (2019). https://doi.org/10.1073/pnas.1908369116
54. Pescosolido, B.A., Martin, J.K.: The stigma complex. Annu. Rev. Sociol. **41**, 87–116 (2015). https://doi.org/10.1146/annurev-soc-071312-145702
55. WHO: WHO issues best practices for naming new human infectious diseases (2015)
56. WHO: A guide to preventing and addressing social stigma. https://www.who.int/docs/default-source/coronaviruse/covid19-stigma-guide.pdf
57. Editorial: Stop the coronavirus stigma now. Nature **580**, 165–165 (2020). https://doi.org/10.1038/d41586-020-01009-0
58. London, A.J., Kimmelman, J.: Against pandemic research exceptionalism. Science **368**, 476–477 (2020). https://doi.org/10.1126/science.abc1731
59. Olson, D.R., Simonsen, L., Edelson, P.J., Morse, S.S.: Epidemiological evidence of an early wave of the 1918 influenza pandemic in New York City. Proc. Natl. Acad. Sci. **102**, 11059–11063 (2005). https://doi.org/10.1073/pnas.0408290102
60. Editorial: Calling it what it is. Nat. Genet. **52**, 355–355 (2020). https://doi.org/10.1038/s41588-020-0617-2
61. Fischer, L.S., Mansergh, G., Lynch, J., Santibanez, S.: Addressing disease-related stigma during infectious disease outbreaks. Disaster Med. Publ. Health Prep. **13**, 989–994 (2019). https://doi.org/10.1017/dmp.2018.157
62. WHO: Ebola haemorrhagic fever in Zaire, 1976. Bull. World Health Organ. **56**, 271–93 (1978)
63. WHO: Reference Guide on the Content Model of the ICD-11 alpha. https://www.who.int/classifications/icd/revision/Content_Model_Reference_Guide.January_2011.pdf
64. Kveim Lie, A., Greene, J.A.: From Ariadne's thread to the Labyrinth itself—nosology and the infrastructure of modern medicine. N. Engl. J. Med. **382**, 1273–1277 (2020). https://doi.org/10.1056/NEJMms1913140
65. Fortunato, S., et al.: Science of science. Science **359**, eaao0185 (2018). https://doi.org/10.1126/science.aao0185
66. Enserink, M.: War stories. Science **339**, 1264–1268 (2013). https://doi.org/10.1126/science.339.6125.1264
67. Honigsbaum, M.: Jean-Jacques Muyembe-Tamfum: Africa's veteran Ebola hunter. Lancet **385**, 2455 (2015). https://doi.org/10.1016/S0140-6736(15)61128-X
68. Anonymous: Jean-Jacques Muyembe Tamfum: a life's work on Ebola. Bull. World Health Organ. **96**, 804–805 (2018). https://doi.org/10.2471/BLT.18.031218
69. Kuhn, J.H., et al.: New filovirus disease classification and nomenclature. Nat. Rev. Microbiol. **17**, 261–263 (2019). https://doi.org/10.1038/s41579-019-0187-4
70. Sykes, W.: On the origin and history of some disease-names. Lancet **147**, 1007–1010 (1896). https://doi.org/10.1016/S0140-6736(01)39505-3
71. Wolfe, N.D., Dunavan, C.P., Diamond, J.: Origins of major human infectious diseases. Nature **447**, 279–283 (2007). https://doi.org/10.1038/nature05775

72. Trisnawati, I., Budiono, E., Sumardi, Setiadi, A.: Traumatic inhalation due to Merapi volcanic ash. Acta Med. Indones. **47**, 238–43 (2015)
73. Burhan, E., Mukminin, U.: A systematic review of respiratory infection due to air pollution during natural disasters. Med. J. Indones. **29**, 11–8 (2020). https://doi.org/10.13181/mji.oa.204390
74. Kim, Y.: Renaming the term schizophrenia in Japan. Lancet **360**, 879 (2002). https://doi.org/10.1016/S0140-6736(02)09987-7
75. Maruta, T., Volpe, U., Gaebel, W., Matsumoto, C., Iimori, M.: Should schizophrenia still be named so? Schizophr. Res. **152**, 305–306 (2014). https://doi.org/10.1016/j.schres.2013.11.005
76. Sartorius, N.: Stigma: what can psychiatrists do about it? Lancet **352**, 1058–1059 (1998). https://doi.org/10.1016/S0140-6736(98)08008-8
77. Park, J.-H., Choi, Y.-M., Kim, B., Lee, D.-W., Gim, M.-S.: Use of the terms "Schizophrenia" and "Schizophrenic" in the South Korean news media: a content analysis of newspapers and news programs in the last 10 years. Psychiatry Investig. **9**, 17 (2012). https://doi.org/10.4306/pi.2012.9.1.17
78. George, B., Klijn, A.: A modern name for schizophrenia (PSS) would diminish self-stigma. Psychol. Med. **43**, 1555–1557 (2013). https://doi.org/10.1017/S0033291713000895
79. Porter, R.: Can the stigma of mental illness be changed? Lancet **352**, 1049–1050 (1998). https://doi.org/10.1016/S0140-6736(98)07155-4
80. Corrigan, P.W.: Erasing stigma is much more than changing words. Psychiatr. Serv. **65**, 1263–1264 (2014). https://doi.org/10.1176/appi.ps.201400113
81. Koike, S., Yamaguchi, S., Ojio, Y., Ohta, K., Ando, S.: Effect of name change of schizophrenia on mass media between 1985 and 2013 in Japan: a text data mining analysis. Schizophr. Bull. **42**, 552–559 (2016). https://doi.org/10.1093/schbul/sbv159
82. Corrigan, P.W.: Beware the word police. Psychiatr. Serv. **70**, 234–236 (2019). https://doi.org/10.1176/appi.ps.201800369
83. Editorial: Embrace the WHO's new naming system for coronavirus variants. Nature **594**, 149–149 (2021). https://doi.org/10.1038/d41586-021-01508-8
84. Bedford, J., Farrar, J., Ihekweazu, C., Kang, G., Koopmans, M., Nkengasong, J.: A new twenty-first century science for effective epidemic response. Nature **575**, 130–136 (2019). https://doi.org/10.1038/s41586-019-1717-y
85. Anonymous: The nomenclature of diseases: I. BMJ. 2, 316–318 (1868)
86. Anonymous: The nomenclature of diseases: II. BMJ **2**, 396–397 (1869)
87. Anonymous: The nomenclature of diseases: III. BMJ. **1**, 55–57 (1869)
88. Philipson, G.H.: On the registration of diseases. BMJ **2**, 485–487 (1869). https://doi.org/10.1136/bmj.2.462.485
89. Willshire, W.H.: The epidemic of rubeola. Lancet **67**, 640 (1856). https://doi.org/10.1016/S0140-6736(02)55500-8
90. Kesteven, W.B.: The epidemic of rubeola. Lancet **67**, 671–672 (1856). https://doi.org/10.1016/S0140-6736(02)55536-7
91. Tripe, J.W.: The rubeola epidemic. Lancet **67**, 719–720 (1856). https://doi.org/10.1016/S0140-6736(02)59408-3
92. Scattergood, T.: Morbilli and rubeola. BMJ **1**, 121 (1870). https://doi.org/10.1136/bmj.1.474.121
93. Squire, W.: Remarks on epidemic roseola; rosella, rosalia, or rubeola. BMJ **1**, 99–100 (1870). https://doi.org/10.1136/bmj.1.474.99
94. Forbes, J.A.: Rubella: historical aspects. Arch. Pediatr. Adolesc. Med. **118**, 5–11 (1969). https://doi.org/10.1001/archpedi.1969.02100040007002
95. Ziring, P.R., Florman, A.L., Cooper, L.Z.: The diagnosis of rubella. Pediatr. Clin. North Am. **18**, 87–97 (1971). https://doi.org/10.1016/S0031-3955(16)32524-X

96. Banatvala, J.E., Brown, D.: Rubella. Lancet **363**, 1127–1137 (2004). https://doi.org/10.1016/S0140-6736(04)15897-2

97. Murchison, C.: Clinical lectures on medicine. Lancet **96**, 595–598 (1870). https://doi.org/10.1016/S0140-6736(02)79936-4

98. Lin, Y., Michel, J., Aiden, E.L., Orwant, J., Brockman, W., Petrov, S.: Syntactic annotations for the Google Books ngram corpus. In: Proceedings of the 50th Annual Meeting of the Association for Computational Linguistics, pp. 169–174. Association for Computational Linguistics,Stroudsburg, PA, USA, Jeju, Republic of Korea (2012)

99. Putnam, C.P.: Is German Measles (Rotheln or Rubella) an independent disease? Bost. Med. Surg. J. **129**, 30–33 (1893). https://doi.org/10.1056/NEJM189307131290202

100. Rota, P.A., Moss, W.J., Takeda, M., de Swart, R.L., Thompson, K.M., Goodson, J.L.: Measles. Nat. Rev. Dis. Prim. **2**, 16049 (2016). https://doi.org/10.1038/nrdp.2016.49

101. Gastel, B.: Measles: a potentially finite history. J. Hist. Med. Allied Sci. **28**, 34–44 (1973). https://doi.org/10.1093/jhmas/XXVIII.1.34

102. Drutz, J.E.: Measles: its history and its eventual eradication. Semin. Pediatr. Infect. Dis. **12**, 315–322 (2001). https://doi.org/10.1053/spid.2001.26640

103. Rosen, G.: A History of Public Health. M.D. Publications, New York (1958)

104. Panum, P.L.: Observations Made During the Epidemic of Measles on the Faroe Islands in the Year 1846. Bibliothek for Laeger, Copenhagen (1847)

105. Veale, H.: History of an epidemic of rötheln, with observations on its pathology. Edinb. Med. J. **12**, 404–414 (1866)

106. Tomkins, H.: The diagnosis of rötheln. BMJ **1**, 808 (1880). https://doi.org/10.1136/bmj.1.1013.808

107. Treveris, P.: The Grete Herball: a tendril of ancient herbal traditions reaching into 16th century England, London (1526)

108. Smellie, W.: Encyclopaedia Britannica. A. Bell and C. Macfarquhar, Edinburgh, Scotland (1771)

109. Paterson, R.: Observations on corpora Lutea: part I. Edinburgh Med. Surg. J. **53**, 49–67 (1840)

110. Veale, H.: On the etiology of stricture of the urethra. Edinb. Med. J. **12**, 602–606 (1867)

111. Ackerknecht, E.H.: A Short History of Medicine. Johns Hopkins University Press, Baltimore (1982)

112. Neuburger, M.: Some relations between British and German medicine in the first half of the eighteenth century. Bull. Hist. Med. **17**, 217–228 (1945)

113. Hess, V., Mendelsohn, J.A.: Sauvages' paperwork: how disease classification arose from scholarly note-taking. Early Sci. Med. **19**, 471–503 (2014). https://doi.org/10.1163/15733823-00195p05

114. Maton, W.G.: Some account of a rash liable to be mistaken for scarlatina. Med. Trans. Coll. Physicians. **5**, 149–165 (1815)

115. Cooper, L.Z.: The history and medical consequences of rubella. Rev. Infect. Dis. **7**, 2–10 (1985). https://doi.org/10.1093/clinids/7.supplement_1.s2

116. Grimwood, R.M., Holmes, E.C., Geoghegan, J.L.: A novel Rubi-like virus in the Pacific electric ray (Tetronarce californica) reveals the complex evolutionary history of the Matonaviridae. Viruses **13**, 585 (2021). https://doi.org/10.3390/v13040585

117. International Congress of Medicine: Transactions of the International Congress of Medicine, pp. 14–34, London (1881)

118. Anonymous: International Medical Congress. Lancet **117**, 392–393 (1881). https://doi.org/10.1016/S0140-6736(02)33362-2

119. Billings, J.S.: International medical congress, London, 1881. Bost. Med. Surg. J. **105**, 217–222 (1881). https://doi.org/10.1056/NEJM188109081051001

120. Anonymous: International Medical Congress. Lancet **117**, 478 (1881). https://doi.org/10.1016/S0140-6736(02)13222-3
121. Anonymous: The International Medical Congress. Nature **24**, 338–339 (1881). https://doi.org/10.1038/024338a0
122. Anonymous: The International Medical Congress. BMJ **2**, 300–305 (1881). https://doi.org/10.1136/bmj.2.1076.300
123. Anonymous: The International Medical Congress. BMJ **2**, 518–530 (1881). https://doi.org/10.1016/S0140-6736(01)93495-6
124. Anonymous: International Medical Congress. BMJ **2**, 545–566 (1881). https://doi.org/10.1136/bmj.2.1083.545
125. Shulman, S.T.: The history of pediatric infectious diseases. Pediatr. Res. **55**, 163–176 (2004). https://doi.org/10.1203/01.PDR.0000101756.93542.09
126. Paterson, R.: An account of the Rötheln of German authors, together with a few observations on the disease as it has been seen to Prevail in Leith and its neighbourhood. Edinburgh Med. Surg. J. **53**, 381–393 (1840)
127. Barnett, R.: Rubella. Lancet **389**, 1386 (2017). https://doi.org/10.1016/S0140-6736(17)30890-5
128. Warrack, J.S.: The differential diagnosis of scarlet fever, measles, and rubella. BMJ **2**, 486–488 (1918). https://doi.org/10.1136/bmj.2.3018.486
129. Editorial: Rubella in an isolated community. N. Engl. J. Med. **256**, 323–324 (1957). https://doi.org/10.1056/NEJM195702142560712
130. Gregg, N.M.: Congenital cataract following German measles in the mother. Epidemiol. Infect. **107**, 3–14 (1991). https://doi.org/10.1017/S0950268800048627
131. Lambert, N., Strebel, P., Orenstein, W., Icenogle, J., Poland, G.A.: Rubella. Lancet **385**, 2297–2307 (2015). https://doi.org/10.1016/S0140-6736(14)60539-0
132. WHO: The Measles & Rubella Initiative supports implementation of the Measles & Rubella Strategic Framework 2021–2030. https://s3.amazonaws.com/wp-agility2/measles/wp-content/uploads/2020/11/measles_rubella_initiative_final_print.pdf
133. Zipf, G.K.: Human Behavior and the Principle of Least Effort: An Introduction to Human Ecology. Addison-Wesley Press, Cambridge (1949)
134. Editorial: Reports of Meetings. N. Engl. J. Med. **224**, 216–217 (1941). https://doi.org/10.1056/NEJM194101302240517
135. Editorial: Miscellany. N. Engl. J. Med. **204**, 913–947 (1931). https://doi.org/10.1056/NEJM193104302041806

A Root Cause Localization Method of Base Station Cells with Poor Quality Using AI + SHAP

Shuxiang Ye[1], Mingshan Feng[2(✉)], Lei Xiang[3], and Lizhen Wang[1]

[1] Dianchi College of Yunnan University, Kunming 650228, China
[2] China Telecom Qujing Branch, QuJing 655000, China
13378848871@189.cn
[3] China Telecom Yunnan Branch, Kunming 650100, China

Abstract. For the transmission carrier of the digital and intelligent system, the transmission performance of the wireless base station directly affects the timeliness and stability of the data transmission. For base station cells with poor quality, if the root cause of poor quality can be found, the problem can be solved effectively and pertinently. Traditional methods rely on experts and require a large amount of on-site survey work in root cause analysis of poor quality cells in base stations, and at the county and township levels, there is a lack of experts and on-site survey is inconvenient. This paper innovatively proposes a method that uses AI + SHAP model interpretation to locate the root cause of base station cells with poor quality, which greatly improves the efficiency and accuracy of positioning, and the feasibility and effectiveness of the model are verified through extensive experiments.

Keywords: Data Wireless Transmission · AI + SHAP · Base Station Cells · Poor Quality

1 Introduction

With the development of technologies such as the Internet of Things (IOT), 5G and big data, relying on wireless transmission, data acquisition, upload and download are becoming more and more widely used. Performance requirements for wireless transmission are also increasing. The stability of wireless transmission performance directly affects the accuracy of data transmission and the stability of subsequent applications. In the process of wireless data transmission, the poor quality of the base station cell is the main factor affecting the wireless transmission performance. The Channel Quality Indication (CQI) is a key index to measure whether a base station cell is of poor quality. The root cause analysis of poor CQI index in base station cells is an important but tedious work for wireless network optimization.

In the traditional root cause analysis of the base station cells with poor quality, often using road test, data analysis, expert analysis and other methods. Guo et al. [1, 2] used the road test technology to optimize the network, but the traditional road test requires a

X. Meng et al. (Eds.): BDSC 2023, CCIS 1846, pp. 175–189, 2023.
https://doi.org/10.1007/978-981-99-3925-1_11

lot of manpower, material resources, time and energy, and the efficiency is low. With the completeness of base station data collection and data analysis tools, the method of data analysis + expert study and determine began to appear. Xu [3] studied the optimization of CQI index through the expert study and determine method. Shi et al. [4] proposed the "trace" method, but this method is too dependent on experts, and the number and vigour of experts limit the efficiency of the analysis. With the emergence of big data mining technology, the massive collection of base station data by major telecom operators, an analysis method of base station cells with poor quality based on big data mining technology has emerged. Tang, Guo, Wang, Yang et al. [5–8] carried out research on the root cause of base station cells with poor quality in the community from the big data mining method. With the development of artificial intelligence (AI) technology, some scholars began to use AI technology to analyze the quality of base station cells with poor quality. Shi et al. [4] studied using the mapping knowledge domain and XGboost. Wang et al. [9] studied using convolution Neural Network algorithms. Peng et al. [10] studied using the FP-growth algorithm. Shao et al. [11] studied using logical regression, decision tree, support vector machine, and k-neighborhood algorithms. Lei [12] summarized the advantages and disadvantages of various machine learning and deep learning algorithms in the application of base station fault processing. With the development of AI technology, more and more scholars begin to try to use AI algorithms to analyze base station cells with poor quality. However, the AI algorithm is good at dealing with classification and prediction problems. The above scholars solve the problem of locating the root cause of the fault alarm, that is, the problem of alarm convergence, but cannot solve the problem of root cause analysis that causes poor cell quality.

This paper is based on the Neural Network algorithm model in AI algorithms, using MR (Measurement Report) data, cell KPI (Key Performance Indicator) data, and cell TA (Timing Advance) distribution data as the model training data, and the SHAP (Shapley Additive ex-Planning) [13] is introduced to explain the model and find the root cause of poor quality. Some scholars in other fields. Dong, Han et al. [14–17] have carried out applied research in the field of environmental science and medical treatment, but in the field of communication, it is still the first.

2 Research Ideas.

2.1 General Idea of the Study

AI machine learning and Neural Network models widely used at present are mainly used for classification and prediction. Input features are classified through model training. It is a process from cause to result. The problem that needs to be solved in this study is the known results, in turn, analyze the cause of the results. That is to say, we need to analyze the influence factors of different cells with poor quality, and get the weight of influencing factors, this problem cannot be directly solved through machine learning methods. This study introduces SHAP to explain the model, combined with machine learning and Neural Network models, the model can be explained to achieve the purpose of analyzing the cause (see Fig. 1).

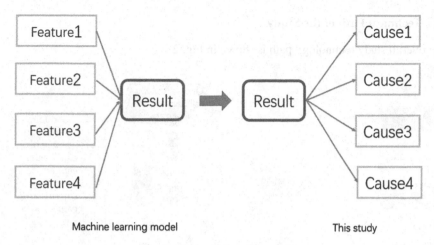

Fig. 1. General idea of research.

SHAP is a method to solve the interpretability of the model. SHAP is based on Shapley value, a game theory concept proposed by the economist Lloyd Shapley. "Game" refers to a situation where there are multiple features, each of which wanting to maximize its own results. The method is to determine the importance of a feature by calculating its contribution in the cooperation. For analysis of cell quality of base station, that is, among the many factors affecting CQI indicators, find out the poor quality factors for a certain cell and the contribution degree of these factors.

SHAP interprets the predicted value of the model as a linear function of the binary variables:

$$g(z') = \phi_0 + \sum_{j=1}^{M} \phi_j z_j' \tag{1}$$

where "g" is the interpretation model, "M" is the number of input features, "Z" is whether the corresponding feature exists (1 or 0), $\varnothing_0$ is the predicted mean value, $\varnothing_j$ is Shapley value of feature "j", which is the contribution degree of feature "j". For the linear model, such as Formula (2):

$$\hat{f}(x) = \beta_0 + \beta_1 x_1 + \ldots + \beta_p x_p \tag{2}$$

The sample has p features, β is the weight of the feature. The contribution of the jth feature prediction is:

$$\phi_j = \beta_j x_j - E(\beta_j X_j) = \beta_j x_j - \beta_j E(X_j) \tag{3}$$

SHAP theory has two methods of Shapley value estimation. KernelSHAP and tree-SHAP. TreeSHAP is fast, but it can only be used for tree-based algorithms. KernelSHAP is model-independent and can be used with any machine learning algorithm. In this study, we use KernelSHAP method.

2.2 Technical Path of the Study

The overall study technology path is shown in Fig. 2:

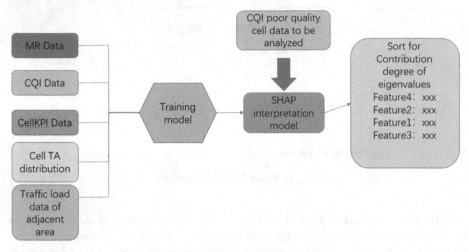

Fig. 2. Technology path of the study.

First select the features and data related to CQI indicators. This step requires business understanding, expert evaluation and literature evaluation. The second step is to use AI algorithm for model training. This study uses Neural Network algorithm. The third step uses the SHAP library to explain the model. The last step is to analyze the feature contribution according to the interpretation results, and verify the analysis results with the expert experience.

2.3 Model Process

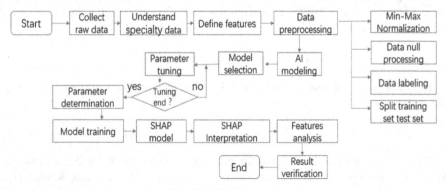

Fig. 3. Model process.

The model process is shown in Fig. 3. After collecting the base station data, the original collected data is specialty understood. Select data that meets the factors affecting the quality of the base station cell as the data and determine the features of the model. Through data normalization, outlier detection and other data preprocessing, data that can be used for model training are obtained. Determine the AI model through AI modeling as well as model parameter tuning. After the model training, introduce SHAP model explain the model, that is, open the black box parameters in the model to analyze the features in the model. For the specific cells, SHAP is used to explain the feature contribution, find out the factors that cause the large contribute of the poor quality of the cell. Selected some base station cells through on-site investigation and expert judgment to verify the feasibility and accuracy of this method.

3   Case Study

In this case study, the six-day operation data of China Telecom's wireless base station cell in a city were selected, involving 900thousands pieces of data in total, and the case study was carried out according to the model process in Fig. 3.

3.1 Data Collection and Specialty Understanding

Based on daily wireless network optimization experience, the main factors affecting CQI are network coverage and network load. Data related to network coverage and network load mainly include MR (Measurement Report) data, cell KPI (Key Performance Indicator) data, and cell TA (Timing Advance) distribution data. The average RSRP (Reference Signal Received Power) data and the number of RSRP sampling points in each segment were selected from the MR data. KPI data mainly includes Air interface downstream user area flow, Average downlink PRB (Physical resource block) occupancy, Average number of RRC (Radio Resource Control) connection users and Average number of downstream active users, and the TA distribution data are mainly TA reporting times.

3.2 Determination of Features

Through the understanding and analysis of the data, MR data include MR average RSRP, the number of RSPR ≥ -105 dBm sampling point, the number of RSPR ≥ -110 dBm sampling point, the number of RSPR ≥ -115 dBm sampling point, the number of RSPR ≥ -120 dBm sampling point and the number of RSPR < -120 dBm sampling point. For the TA distribution data, we mainly focus on the coverage range of base stations, so we converted the TA value into a distance range: below 0.5 km, 0.5 km–1 km, 1 km–1.5 km, 1.5 km–2.1 km, 2.1 km–3.1 km, 3.1 km–3.9 km, 3.9 km–6.3 km and above 6.3 km. Comprehensive analysis of the above data, 18 features were determined for the subsequent model training (see Table 1).

Table 1. Model feature selection.

MR data	TA distribution data	KPI data
The number of RSRP $\geq -$ 105 dBm sampling point	Below 0.5 km	Air interface downstream user area flow
The number of RSRP $\geq -$ 110 dBm sampling point	0.5 km–1 km	Average downlink PRB occupancy
The number of RSRP $\geq -$ 115 dBm sampling point	1.5 km–2.1 km	Average number of RRC connection users
The number of RSRP $\geq -$ 120 dBm sampling point	2.1 km–3.1 km	Average number of downstream active users
The number of RSRP $< -$ 120 dBm sampling point	3.1 km–3.9 km	
MR Average RSRP	3.9 km–6.3 km	
	above 6.3 km	

3.3 Data Preprocessing

In addition to conventional processing such as outlier processing and null processing for MR data and TA distribution data, the number of sampling points is converted into the percentage of sampling points to adapt subsequent model training. The characteristics of KPI data and MR average RSRP are specific data with significant differences in numerical dimensions. This will have a significant impact on the effectiveness of the model. Therefore, it must be normalized to 0–1. In this study, min/max normalization was used (see Table 2).

Table 2. Feature normalization table.

Average downlink PRB occupancy	Average number of RRC connection users	Average number of downstream active users	Air interface downstream user area flow	MR Average RSRP (dbm)
0.272	0.159753593	0.235525375	0.253422384	0.49887778
0.1966	0.213278576	0.188706219	0.1699441	0.447867782
0.0291	0.003422313	0.001429593	0.007156799	0.365435625
0.0465	0.014236824	0.015010722	0.026250448	0.316670067
0.4368	0.288158795	0.39421015	0.540544129	0.597633136

Finally, the label classification process is processed. The data are divided into two types according to whether the cell is poor quality, where the proportion of CQ1 > 7 is greater than 90, it is labeled as non-poor quality cell, and the proportion of CQI > 7 is less than 90, it is labeled as poor quality cell, 0.

In order to use SHAP library for interpretation after subsequent model training, all features are coded (see Table 3).

Table 3. Feature coding table.

feature	Coded
Average downlink PRB occupancy	PRB_use_ratio
Average number of RRC connection users	avg_RRC_users
Average number of downstream active users	avg_active_users
Air interface downstream user area flow	DL_Data
Below 0.5 km	TA_under_0.5
0.5 km–1 km	TA_0.5_to_1
1 km–1.5 km	TA_1_to_1.5
1.5 km–2.1 km	TA_1.5_to_2.1
2.1 km–3.1 km	TA_2.1_to_3.1
3.1 km–3.9 km	TA_3.1_to_3.9
3.9 km–6.3 km	TA_3.9_to_6.3
above 6.3 km	TA_above_6.3
MR Average RSRP	avg_RSRP
The number of RSPR ≥ -105 dBm sampling point	RSRP_above_105
The number of RSPR ≥ -110 dBm sampling point	RSRP_110_to_105
The number of RSPR ≥ -115 dBm sampling point	RSRP_115_to_110
The number of RSPR ≥ -120 dBm sampling point	RSRP_120_to_115
The number of RSPR < -120 dBm sampling point	RSRP_inf_to_120

3.4 AI Model Training

Multiple machine learning models were selected to train the data.

Firstly, the Random Forest model was used for training, and the parameters were selected as default. 900,000 data were divided into training set and test set according to 80% and 20% ratio. The model was evaluated after the training, the accuracy rate was 90%, the recall rate was 63.82%, and the f1-core was 0.8731. The classification report is shown in Table 4.

Table 4. The classification report of Random Forest

	Precision	Recall	F1-score	Support
0	0.81	0.29	0.42	45610
1	0.90	0.99	0.94	294963
Accuracy			0.90	340543
Macro avg	0.86	0.64	0.68	340573
Weighted avg	0.89	0.90	0.87	340573

Using Random Forest's own "feature_importances" method, you can see the importance of features (see Fig. 4).

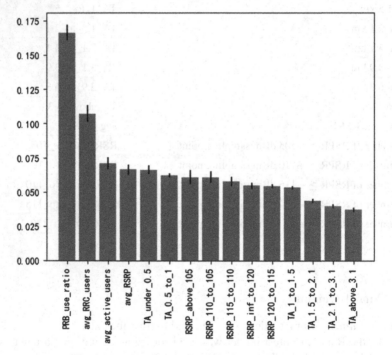

Fig. 4. Random Forest classifier feature importance.

The GBDT (Gradient Boosting Decision Tree) model was used to train the data. The accuracy rate was 89.88%, the recall rate was 66.48%, and the f1-core was 0.8817. The classification report is shown in Table 5.

Using GBDT 's own "feature_importances" method, you can see the importance of features (see Fig. 5).

From Figs. 4 and 5, it can be seen that the importance ranking of features is consistent. It can be seen that there are several important reasons for the poor quality of the

Table 5. The classification report of GBDT

	Precision	Recall	F1-score	Support
0	0.77	0.35	0.48	30245
1	0.91	0.98	0.94	196804
Accuracy			0.90	227049
Macro avg	0.84	0.66	0.71	227049
Weighted avg	0.89	0.90	0.87	227049

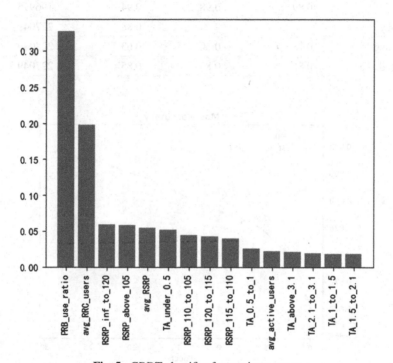

Fig. 5. GBDT classifier feature importance.

base station cell: "Average downlink PRB occupancy" and "Average number of RRC connection users". But these two models can't give the important reasons for the poor quality of a single base station cell.

The last training model used is the Neural Network model with three hidden layers is defined. The number of neurons is 256,128 and 64 respectively. The activation function of each layer uses "relu". There are 18 neurons in the input layer, corresponding to 18 features. There are 4 neurons in the output layer corresponding to 4 classification results. The output layer adopts "softmax" activation function. Because the classification label is a value of 0, 1, 2, or 3, so the loss function adopts "sparse_categorical_crossentropy".

In this study, 900000 data of all base stations in a city for two days were used to train the model. Split into training set and test set according to the ratio of 80% and 20%. The model is evaluated and the classification report is shown in the Table 6, and the accuracy of the model is shown in the Fig. 6.

Table 6. The classification report of Neural Network

	Precision	Recall	F1-score	Support
0	0.67	0.21	0.32	30134
1	0.89	0.98	0.94	196915
Accuracy			0.88	227049
Macro avg	0.78	0.60	0.63	227049
Weighted avg	0.86	0.88	0.85	227049

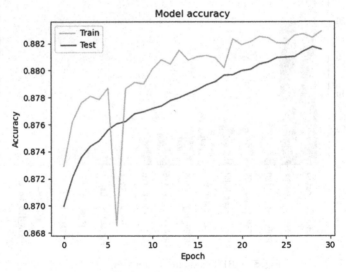

Fig. 6. Accuracy analysis.

Cross-validation using sklearn's "cross_val_score" method yielded the following accuracy rates:

[0.8764984, 0.87568726, 0.87612403, 0.87739028, 0.87665255].

The average accuracy of the Neural Network model is 87.65%, as shown in the Table 7:

Through cross-validation of training set data, the prediction accuracy of Neural Network model meets the requirements.

Table 7. The classification report

Model	Precision	Recall
RandomForestClassifier	89%	0.90
GradientBoostingClassifier	89%	0.90
Full Connect Neural Network	87.65%	0.88

3.5 SHAP Library Model Interpretation

Read the trained model using Neural Networks first, and the CQI poor quality cell data to be analyzed is processed into the same format as the training set according to the data preprocessing process. Use the SHAP library, import into the model for interpretation. Because it is used to analyze the influencing factors of poor quality cells, so we can filter out all non-poor cells and only retain the data of poor cells.

This study first introduces 100 poor quality cells for SHAP interpretation (see Fig. 7).

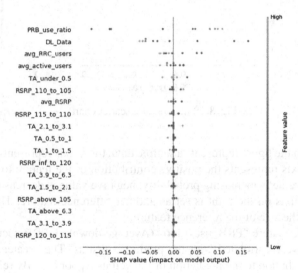

Fig. 7. Full sample scatter chart.

Each point in the figure represents a sample data, and the color of the point represents the size of the feature in a certain piece of data. The redder the color is, the larger the value is, and the bluer the color is, the smaller the value is. The x-axis represents the contribution of the feature to prediction results, positive values indicate increasing prediction probability and negative values indicate decreasing prediction probability. The y-axis represents the name of the feature.

It can be seen from the figure, the feature with "DL_Data" (Air interface downstream user area flow) have a great influence on whether the prediction result is a poor quality cell. The larger the volume of downlink data, the lower the probability of being predicted to be a poor quality cell. The feature with "TA_under_0.5" (Below 0.5 km) also has a great impact on whether the prediction result is a poor cell. The more sampling points with a distance less than 0.5 km, the smaller the probability that a cell will become a poor cell.

For the relationship analysis between single feature and other features, take "PRB_use_ratio" (Average downlink PRB occupancy) as an example as shown in Fig. 8.

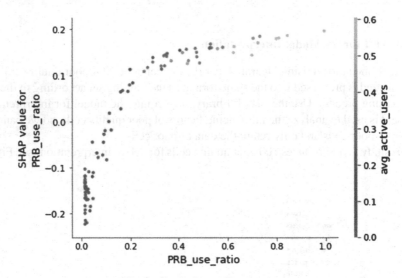

Fig. 8. Single feature scatter chart.

Each point in the figure represents a sample data, the x-axis represents the size of the feature. The y-axis represents the positive contribution of the feature to the prediction result. Positive value is increasing probability, negative value is decreasing probability. The coordinate axis on the right is set as another reference feature. The color of the sample point is the size of the reference feature.

It can see the feature "PRB_use_ratio" (Average downlink PRB occupancy) is significantly positively correlated with the predicted results. The greater the value, the greater the contribution to the prediction of the cell as a poor cell. By reference feature "avg_active_users" (Average number of downstream active users) can also see that the more the average number of active users, the higher the PRB utilization. It can intuitively observe the relationship between the features and the prediction results through the single feature scatter diagram. It can also observe the relationship between the two features. It is convenient to optimize the features of the model.

Finally, a single poor cell is selected for SHAP interpretation and analysis. The cell of 591298_177 is selected. The excellent rate of CQI in this cell is only 70.27%. It is a poor quality cell (see Fig. 9).

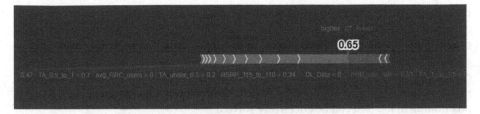

Fig. 9. SHAP analysis of single poor quality cell.

Figure 9 is one of the data of CQI cells with poor quality. The red color indicates that this feature increases the probability that the prediction result is positive, and the blue color indicates that the feature reduces the probability of a positive prediction result.

The features that can increase the probability include:

DL_Data (Air interface downstream user area flow) is 0.003, and the downlink data volume is very small. This feature increases the probability of predicting that the cell is of poor quality, and the degree of contribution is very high.

RSRP_115_to_110 (The number of RSPR $\geq$ −110 dBm sampling point) is 0.24, indicates that the proportion of RSRP between −110 dbm and −115 dbm is 24%. RSRP coverage is slightly poor, increasing the probability of poor quality cells.

TA_under_0.5 (Below 0.5 km) is 0.2, which indicates that only 20% of sampling points with coverage distance less than 0.5 km. Most users are distributed beyond 0.5 km, and this is also an increasing probability feature.

avg_RRC_users (Average number of RRC connection users) approximately equal to 0. The corresponding number of RRC connection users is 0.17. The number of active users is small, which increases the probability of poor quality cells.

The features of probability reduction include:

PRB_use_ratio (Average downlink PRB occupancy) is 0.01 indicates that the PRB utilization rate is very low, only 1.42%. This feature reduces the probability of predicting that the cell is of poor quality and has High contribution.

TA_1_to_1.5 (1 km–1.5 km) is 0, the proportion of users from 1 km to 1.5 km is 0. The network coverage of this cell is not far, reduce the probability of poor quality cells predicted.

Model analysis using AI + SHAP, It can not only analyze the contribution and impact of features on the results, but also analyze the impact features for a single sample. This has good effect in solving root cause analysis of single sample.

4   Result Analysis and Application.

The results of this study and analysis were verified by experts in wireless network optimization and maintenance. AI + SHAP analysis results are consistent with expert judgment. The accuracy of the analysis results is verified, the model can be implemented. Expert verification requires many years of experience, and also requires a large amount of on-site and background data comparison and analysis, which is inefficient. This model can be used to analyze the root cause of poor quality cells in batches, which promotes the evolution of traditional methods to social computing and improves the efficiency.

Especially provides strong support for the positioning of poor quality problems at the county and township levels with relatively backward technology. Under the situation of digital economy transformation and rural revitalization, a large number of digital applications have been extended to counties and townships. In the big data collection of Yunnan walnut industry, there are also a large number of collection points located in counties and townships. The problems of few technical personnel and slow problem positioning in the past can be effectively solved.

For 75 base stations in a county, the research team analyzed and optimized the CQI excellent rate index by this method.

According to the root cause of positioning, the following three optimization measures are mainly taken: Adjust the antenna feed to improve weak coverage or over-coverage, power parameter adjustment improves RSRP coverage and optimization of load balancing parameters to reduce cell load. Through the obvious optimization effect, the county's CQI excellent rate index increased from 93.5% to about 96%, which increased by nearly 3 percentage points.

Using traditional methods with remote diagnosis by experts to locate the root cause of a cell, which requires 2 h of time for an expert. By using the AI + SHAP model, it takes an expert 8 min to locate the root cause of a cell, which increases efficiency by 15 times. The root cause location of each cell saves 112 min. If some cells require on-site investigation, it can save more time.

The province had about 3,000 cells with poor quality a month, it requiring 25 experts to locate them for a month (750man-days). Using the method of this study requires approximately 10 experts to work for 5 working days to complete (50man-days). Save 100 man-days per month.

The achievement of this study has feasibility for implementation and generalizability.

Acknowledgments. This work is supported by the Foundation for Scientific Research Fund of Yunnan Provincial Department of Education (2023J1302).

References

1. Guo, G., Yu, L., Wei, R.: Road test of wireless network optimization. Telecommun. Technol. (01), 20–22 (2005)
2. Lin, S., Gao, Z., Gao, F., Huang, L.: TD-LTE network optimization analysis based on road test. Mod. Electron. Technol. (09),12–15 (2015)
3. Xu, Y.: Application research of 5G CQI index optimization scheme. J. Post Telecommun. Coll. **21**(03), 8–12 (2022)
4. Shi, W., Zhao, W., Meng, N., Guo, Y., Lu, W.: Research on root cause location algorithm of wireless network problems for digital operation. Des. Tech. Posts Telecommun. (01),67–72 (2022)
5. Tang, L., Feng, J., Xiao, X.: Cell location method for mobile communication network with poor stability based on big data. Des. Tech. Posts Telecommun. (05),37–41 (2016)
6. Guo, Z., Guo, N., Huang, Y.: Self-learning fault root cause location system based on multidimensional data mining. Electron. Technol. (15),146–149 (2021)
7. Wang, G., Ren, X.: Research on LTE service poor cell data processing method based on Python language. Ind. Control Comput. **35**(04), 115–116 (2022)

8. Yang, Z., Zhen, L., Meng, F., Jiao, J.: Evaluation of poor quality cell and root cause location analysis method for digital operation mobile network. Shandong Commun. Technol. **42**(02), 38–39+43 (2022)

9. Wang, Y., Teng, Z., Zhou, J., Xiao, B., Zhao, G.: Application of AI deep learning in mobile network abnormal cell detection and classification. Des. Tech. Posts Telecommun. (11),11–15 (2019)

10. Peng, D., Huang, H., Wang, Q.: 5G base station alarm convergence and root cause diagnosis based on AI technology. Secur. Inform. (09),106–109 (2021)

11. Shao, X., Xu, H., Li, X., Jiang, T.: Application of machine learning in the analysis of poor quality cells in network road test. Comput. Syst. Appl. (05),257–263 (2020)

12. Lei, Z., Shu, J., Guo, W.: A survey of cellular network fault management framework and methods based on machine learning. Appl. Res. Comput. **39**(12), 3521–3533 (2022)

13. Lundberg, S.M., LEE, S.I.: A unified approach to interpreting model predictions. In: Advances in Neural Information Processing Systems,pp. 4765–4774 (2017)

14. Dong, J., et al.: Urban O3 drivers based on interpretable machine learning. Environ. Sci. 1–12(2022)

15. Han, X.: Analysis of parameters related to low calorific value of coal based on machine learning. Autom. Appl. (10),78–82 (2020)

16. Zhang, S., Dou, Y.: Feature analysis based on XGBoost and SHAP model in PM_ (2.5) application in concentration prediction. J. Chifeng Univ. (Nat. Sci. Ed.) **38**(12), 10–17 (2022)

17. Li, J.: Prediction of diabetes based on machine learning and analysis of SHAP characteristics. Intell. Comput. Appl. **13**(01), 153–157 (2023)

Digital Society and Public Security

Does Internet Use Promote the Garbage Classification Behavior of Farmers? – Empirical Evidence from Rural China

Jie Ma[1], Yiming Song[1(✉)], and Liming Suo[2]

[1] School of Management and Economics, University of Electronic Science and Technology of China, Chengdu 611731, China
1339650460@qq.com
[2] School of Zhou Enlai Government, Nankai University, Tianjin 300350, China

Abstract. Garbage classification, as an environmental protection behavior carried out all over the world, has huge impact on the development of sustainability. Which means, it is particularly vital to study the methods how to make garbage classification works well. With the popularity of Internet use, its role in environmental remediation is increasingly apparent. Therefore, this paper is based on the garbage classification implementation of rural residents, trying to research whether the Internet can promote garbage sorting behavior. Using data from China Land Economic Survey (CLES), this study screens out 2573 rural household samples and adopts binary classic model of Probit to empirically examines the quantitative impact of the use of Internet on the garbage sorting behavior of rural residents. After completing the demonstration, the following conclusions are reached: (1) As rural residents use the Internet, their garbage sorting behavior has improved. For those who use the Internet often, they are 14.5% more possibly to comply with garbage classification than those who don't use the Internet very much. (2) Among individual characteristics, the differences in age, health status and education level have an obvious influence on the garbage classification behavior of farmers. (3) Farmers in areas where the government implements incentives and penalties are more likely, compared to areas without those interventions, to classify their garbage; farmers in areas with publicity reports are more likely to conduct garbage classification than those in areas without them. Therefore, this study is helpful to give play to the positive impact of Internet use and improve the garbage classification behavior to provide a reference.

Keywords: Internet use · Garbage classification behavior · Environmental pollution · Probit model · Rural China

1 Introduction

Various environmental challenges are threatening the global ecosystem and society. The problems of global unsustainability are becoming more prominent. Global warming is posing challenges to human health and individual species [1]. Marselle, et al. [2] showed that biodiversity is the basis of urban ecosystem function. Water pollution causes fundamental changes, which put people, plants, animals, soil, and the general environment in danger, causing 2 million deaths each year and creating the additional burden of chronic diseases [3]. With its rapid development, modern agriculture has produced an air pollution problem that is becoming more and more serious. Air pollutants such as $PM_{2.5}$ and PM_{10} pose a great threat to both human beings and natural environment, changing our lives forever [4]. Land degradation is advancing in an unstopped trend, which have been negatively affected the lives of millions of people. And it's also profoundly affecting biodiversity and ecosystems all the time [5]. In sum, global unsustainability poses huge challenges to human health, environmental security, and ecosystems.

At present, these environmental risks present complexity and uncertainty, but traditional environmental management can no longer meet the public's need for environmental governance. Along with the rise of the Internet use, many more people are realizing the environmental problems they face [6]. Zhang, et al. [7] researched the paths that increase awareness of individual's ability to perceive environmental risks through Internet use. At the same time, they also found the use of Internet services can help users reduce the loss and air pollution caused by climate disasters. The use of the Internet is affecting the lives of farmers and socio-economic outcomes in developing countries [8]. The Internet's effective communication technology helps to influence the reporting agenda of large print and electronic news media, and mass media can be used to reach the public and influence political decisions. Zhang, et al. [9] pointed out that nowadays, environmental pollution scandals have significant caught the attention of Chinese Internet users.

Every year, 2.01 billion tons of municipal household garbage is produced globally, and this is expected to rocket by 70% to 3.4 billion tons by 2050 without any action [10]. Wang, et al. [11] argued that growing populations and sustained economic growth will lead to an increase in household garbage in China year by year. The amount of garbage produced by Chinese residents is growing at an annual rate of 8–9%. Many cities already a garbage siege. The traditional landfill is mainly used to dispose of urban household garbage, accounting for 57% of China's total municipal solid garbage disposal volume in 2017. The increase of food garbage (50%–70%) and water content (40%–60%) leads to the rapid production of CH_4 and CO_2 after deposition in landfills [12]. Grishaeva, et al. [13] showed that landfills are major sources of soil and groundwater pollution and disease transmission. Incineration, another traditional garbage treatment method, produces heavy metals and CL in the process, resulting in hazardous substances such as particulate matter and dioxins, which have potential environmental risks. Chen, et al. [14] discussed the wide-spread attention focused on even the secondary pollution of the incineration process. Therefore, to reduce the sources of pollutants and to minimize the use of nonrenewable resources, garbage classification is of great significance for realizing sustainable management.

There exists a circular economy initiative, which offers a potential avenue to achieve a sustainable future by reintroducing the recycling of garbage materials or scrap products and rotten metals [15]. Cucchiella, et al. [16] suggested that sustainable garbage management can reduce the incidence of health problems, greenhouse gas emissions, and

environmental degradation caused by landfills. Rural areas often have relatively unde-
veloped economies and desperately lack the equipment and facilities to improve the
countryside's environment and public services. Farmers' environmental awareness are
also far less conscious than city dwellers, so there are serious environmental problems
in rural areas [17]. Zhao, et al. [18] revealed that rural areas in many developing countries haven't established extensive and effective garbage management systems, worse
environmental sanitation was then born. Garbage classification and recycling can help
increase the efficiency of rural environmental governance and thereby reduce the harms
currently being done to the rural environment.

China is the world's largest developing country. As the gradual development of urban-
rural integration, rural society has gradually become a "semi-acquaintance society",
but the gap between urban and rural areas is still necessary and feasible to improve
[19]. With the rise and popularity of the Internet, it has broken the reference group of
the neighborhood and community, providing an effective boost to the development of
education, health, social capital and other aspects of rural households [20]. In the field
of environmental governance, the new Internet media enables residents in rural areas to
obtain the promotion dynamics of urban garbage classification and the specific dynamics
of policy implementation based on more media channels. In developed rural areas, the
Internet supervision system has realized accurate supervision over the whole process of
garbage classification, delivery, collection, transportation, utilization and disposal [21].
From 2019 to 2022, China put forward the "Five-year Action Plan for Improvement
and Improvement of Rural Living Environment (2021–2025)", "Opinions of the CPC
Central Committee and The State Council on Comprehensively Promoting the Key Work
of Rural Revitalization in 2022" and other policies. Continuous improvement of rural
living environment has become an important measure to implement the national rural
revitalization strategy, which is regarded to play an crucial role in rural construction in
the new era. This article focused on rural China as a representative area to explore the
quantitative impact of Internet use on garbage classification behavior, which is conducive
to promoting rural revitalization in China and to providing a reference point for global
sustainable garbage management.

2   Theoretical Analysis

Wang, Lu and Liu [11] found the factors that drive household garbage classification
behavior have two types, psychological factors and external factors. The use of the Internet can promote garbage classification, directly (external) and indirectly (psychological). Internet use can indirectly promote garbage classification behavior by improving
the user's cognitive ability [22] and external cognitive ability. As for the direct approach,
Internet use can promote garbage classification behavior by improving information
access.

2.1   Internet Use Promotes Garbage Classification Through Self-cognitive Ability

(1) The use of the Internet improves a user's sense of public participation and thus
    improves the effectiveness of public environmental governance. Hebblewhite, et al.

[23] pointed out that the Internet creates active decision makers and strengthens social capital, supporting those young villagers who participated in local activities. Zhou, et al. [24] argued that high frequency Internet users pay more attention to the acquisition of a sense of leisure comparing with non-Internet users, that is, they have a stronger sense of participation.

(2) The Internet has been identified as a powerful cognitive-enhancing technology that contributes to human enhancement. Specifically, Tabuenca, et al. [25] found that the use of the Internet in new agronomic practices maybe becomes a momentous part of environment enhancement. For example, Google data is often used as an indicator of public awareness of water shortages and drought. Search histories reflect greater user awareness when the media reports on environmental crisis [26]. Xia, et al. [27] showed that perceived ease of use can directly promote the intention and behavior of garbage classification.

2.2 Internet Use Promotes Garbage Classification Through External Cognition

(1) Jiang, et al. [28] argued that online participation has potential as an important mechanism to improve governance. As an electronic consultation pathway, it is an important predictor of citizens' political participation. Wang and Mangmeechai [29] pointed out that residents' perception of policy effectiveness (perception of policy effectiveness) will promote pro-environment behaviors, and garbage classification is a pro-environment behavior.

(2) As its influence broadens, the Internet is increasingly impacting environmental quality, such that it can further enhance the inhibition effect of technological innovation on environmental pollution [30]. Deng, et al. [31] suggested that Internet use can improve the perception of pollution level of farmers. For example, the exposure of the public to Internet social media has a regulating effect on air quality perception.

2.3 Internet Use Promotes Garbage Classification Through Direct Contact

The Internet facilitates access to information and improves access to data as a powerful communication tool. Huxhold, et al. [32] showed that the Internet not only allows communication to be unrestricted by distance, but also helps people access information while ensuring intervention measures and various opportunities for social participation, making people aware that traditional media channels such as newspapers and announcements may cover up the truth. Zhang, et al. [33] argued that netizens are more concerned about the negative news related to environmental pollution than non-netizens. Therefore, Internet use can directly improve the public's ability to obtain information. Due to its decreasing satisfaction with environmental quality, the public is more likely to implement pro-environmental behaviors [22].

3   Data, Variable and Methods

3.1 Data

According to the 2020 census data from the National Bureau of Statistics, the rural population is about 507.97 million. Due to the significant achievements made in rural work in Jiangsu Province in improving the living environment of rural residents, the data

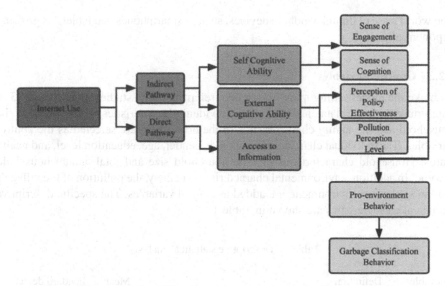

Fig. 1. The mechanism of Internet usage on garbage classification behavior

used in this paper are from the China Land Economic Survey (CLES), which is founded by Nanjing Agri-cultural University's Department of Humanities and Social Sciences, and is assisted by the Jin Shanbao Agricultural Modernization Research Institute.

The survey adopts the PPS sampling method and selects 26 survey districts and counties in 13 prefecture-level cities in Jiangsu Province. Two representative towns are selected in each district and county; one administrative village is selected in each of those towns; and 50 households are randomly selected in each of those villages. The original database contains 52 administrative villages and 2,628 households. Before using the samples, the study data are processed, removing those household samples that lack complete information. The final study sample contains 2,573 households.

3.2 Variable

3.2.1 Explained Variable

The explained variable is whether farmers conduct garbage classification behavior. In the garbage classification issue, garbage classification, household garbage, circular economy, influencing factors, classification, collection, and recycling are worthy of in-depth exploration garbage recycling, resources, and reduction pro-vide further discussion and practice direction for garbage classification.

3.2.2 Core Explanatory Variable

The core explanatory variable is whether farmers regularly use smartphones. The current research is particularly concerned with the way the Internet is used and how it affects economic, cultural, social and personal achievement, and satisfaction [34]. Due to the rapid development of modern technologies such as telecommunications technology.

The world's use of digital handheld devices, such as smartphones and tablets, is growing exponentially.

3.2.3   Control Variables

To make the model setting more reasonable, referring to the studies of Liu, et al. [35], combining with the data in CLES, the individual characteristics of the head of the household and the family characteristics in the house-hold are selected as the control variables. The individual characteristics include gender, age, education level, and health status. Household characteristics include household size and total annual household income. In addition, environmental characteristics, namely, the pollution of the village's human settlement environment, are added as control variables. The specific descriptive statistical characteristics are shown in Table 1:

Table 1. Descriptive statistical analysis

Variables	Definition	Mean	Standard deviation
WSB	Do farmers do household garbage classification? (1 = Yes; 0 = No)	0.482	0.500
phone	Do farmers often use smartphones? (1 = Yes; 0 = no)	0.487	0.500
gender	Farmer's gender (1 = Male; 0 = Female)	0.703	0.457
age	Farmer's age (one year old)	61.07	11.32
education	Farmer's education level (Years in school) (Number of years)	6.914	3.927
health	Farmer's health (1 = Incapacity to work; 2 = Poor; 3 = Medium; 4 = Good; 5 = Best)	3.914	1.105
size	Household total population (Num)	3.226	1.654
income	Total annual income of households (Yuan)	24,148	125,824
environment	The living environment of the village (1 = There is pollution; 0 = No pollution)	0.360	0.480

3.3   Methods

Since both the explained and the core explanatory variables are discrete binary variables, it is suitable to use the binary Probit model for this research. Based on the regression analysis method, the Probit regression model analyzed the influence of Internet use on the garbage classification behavior of the sampled farmers. The formula is as follows:

$$Y_i = \beta_0 + \beta_{1i}Int_i + \beta_{2i}Per_i + \beta_{3i}Fam_i + \delta_j + \mu_i$$

Subscripts i and j represent family i and sample village j, respectively. Y_i is the dependent variable, representing the garbage classification behavior of farmers. Int_i is the core variable that reflects whether farmers often use the Internet. Per_i and Fam_i represent the characteristics of the head of the household and the family respectively. β_0 represents the constant term. β_{1i} is the estimated Internet usage coefficient. β_{2i} and β_{3i} represent the estimated coefficients of individual and family characteristics of the control variables respectively. δ_j is a dummy variable, representing the environmental characteristics of each village. μ_i stands for random disturbance.

4 Results

4.1 Analysis of the Main Regression Results of Household Garbage Classification Behavior Caused by Internet Use

Table 2 shows the influence of Internet use on garbage classification behavior of farmers. As the results show in Table 2(1)-(4), the Probit model is used to estimate the garbage classification behavior of the sampled farmers. Meanwhile, considering that the Probit model is a nonlinear model, model (5) is used to determine the marginal effect estimation result based on model (4). In order to improve the accuracy of estimation, this study gradually increased variables. Using model (1) as the baseline, models (2)–(4) gradually control for personal characteristics, family characteristics, and environmental characteristics.

According to the estimation results in Table 2, in models (2)–(4), with the gradual increase of control variables, they are significant at the level of 10% and 5%, respectively, and the degree of significance and the estimation coefficient gradually in-creases. This indicates that the frequent use of smart phones can promote the garbage classification behavior of farmers, which further indicates that Internet use can improve their degree of participation in garbage classification.

According to the estimated results of model (5), farmers who frequently use smart phones are 14.5% more likely to participate in garbage classification than those who do not. In addition, the estimated results in Table 2 show that the variables of farmers' education level, health status and environmental pollution are significant at the levels of 5% and 1%, respectively, indicating that improving a farmer's education level and health status can also improve their degree of participation in garbage classification.

Table 2. Main regression results

	(1)	(2)	(3)	(4)	Marginal Effects
VARIABLES	WSB	WSB	WSB	WSB	WSB
phone	0.210***	0.087*	0.127**	0.132**	0.145**

(continued)

Table 2. (*continued*)

	(1)	(2)	(3)	(4)	Marginal Effects
	(4.23)	(1.67)	(2.25)	(2.34)	(2.34)
gender		0.032	0.033	0.031	0.010
		(0.55)	(0.57)	(0.52)	(0.16)
age		−0.012***	−0.012***	−0.013***	−0.012***
		(−4.50)	(−4.71)	(−4.78)	(−4.26)
education		0.031***	0.031***	0.032***	0.032***
		(4.28)	(4.19)	(4.30)	(4.03)
health		0.058**	0.059**	0.056**	0.054**
		(2.39)	(2.44)	(2.31)	(2.04)
size			−0.032*	−0.031*	−0.036**
			(−1.88)	(−1.86)	(−1.98)
income			0.000	0.000	0.000
			(1.08)	(1.08)	(0.99)
environment				−0.170***	−0.271***
				(−3.25)	(−4.75)
Constant	−0.148***	0.163	0.278	0.356	0.420*
	(−4.27)	(0.78)	(1.28)	(1.62)	(1.76)
Observations	2,573	2,573	2,573	2,573	2,164

z-statistics in parentheses
*** $p < 0.01$, ** $p < 0.05$, * $p < 0.1$

4.2 Robustness Test

In this study, the instrumental variable method is used to measure, and the changing explained variables and changing core variables are used to test, the robustness of the estimated results in Table 2. As shown in Table 3, Model (1) represents the regression analysis of farmers' willingness to conduct garbage classification as the instrumental variable. Model (2) shows that the core variable is "frequent use of a computer with Internet access". As the estimation results in Table 3 reveal, the coefficients of Internet use variables in model (1) and model (2) are significantly greater than zero (at least 5%), indicating that Internet use can improve the possibility of farmers participating in garbage classification, indicating that the estimation results in Table 2 are robust.

4.3 Test of Correlation

Correlation coefficients between variables are reported, as shown in Fig. 1. According to Pearson correlation analysis, it can be seen from Fig. 1 that age has a certain correlation with Internet use, gender, education, health status and family size, and there is a certain

Table 3. Estimation results of robustness test

	(1)		(2)
VARIABLES	WWB	VARIABLES	WSB
phone	0.201**	computer	0.216***
	(2.51)		(3.58)
gender	0.118	gender	0.011
	(1.46)		(0.18)
age	−0.007*	age	−0.012***
	(−1.71)		(−4.20)
education	0.057***	education	0.029***
	(5.66)		(3.55)
health	0.062*	health	0.047*
	(1.92)		(1.78)
size	−0.046**	size	−0.034**
	(−1.98)		(−2.00)
income	0.000	income	0.000
	(0.85)		(0.88)
environment	−0.005	environment	−0.255***
	(−0.07)		(−4.51)
Constant	1.080***	Constant	0.400*
	(3.52)		(1.69)
Observations	2,573	Observations	2,203

z-statistics in parentheses
*** p < 0.01, ** p < 0.05, * p < 0.1

correlation between health status and education, but there is no high correlation. Since there is no high correlation or exact correlation between the Internet and other independent variables, which means that the multicollinearity problem may seems unimportant (Fig. 2).

4.4 Heterogeneity Test

To test whether the Internet use variables have different influences on the garbage classification behavior of farmers due to individual differences, this study selects two typical external factors, namely, publicity reports and reward and punishment measures, and divides farmers in different regions into two groups:

In the Table 5, models (1) and (2) are based on whether t propaganda and reporting are conducted in the region: farmers in the region with propaganda and reporting have easier access to garbage classification policies and related knowledge, so they have a

Table 4. Results of heterogeneity test estimation

	(1)	(2)	(3)	(4)
VARIABLES	WSB	WSB	WSB	WSB
phone	0.072	0.163**	0.082	0.347**
	(0.37)	(2.40)	(1.18)	(2.18)
gender	−0.189	−0.023	−0.058	−0.106
	(−0.98)	(−0.32)	(−0.82)	(−0.61)
age	−0.012	−0.011***	−0.010***	−0.009
	(−1.25)	(−3.47)	(−2.98)	(−1.30)
education	0.030	0.021**	0.038***	0.038*
	(1.24)	(2.37)	(4.15)	(1.84)
health	0.331***	0.022	0.033	0.081
	(3.56)	(0.76)	(1.12)	(1.18)
size	0.002	−0.047**	−0.036*	−0.111**
	(0.04)	(−2.36)	(−1.75)	(−2.53)
income	0.000	0.000	0.000	0.000
	(0.71)	(0.83)	(0.63)	(0.94)
environment	−0.153	−0.250***	−0.274***	−0.145
	(−0.86)	(−3.99)	(−4.26)	(−0.98)
Constant	−1.681**	0.734***	0.216	1.059*
	(−2.07)	(2.82)	(0.80)	(1.74)
Observations	352	1,812	1,722	442
F test	0.000502	1.47e−10	0	0.000560
r2_a				
F				

z-statistics in parentheses
*** $p < 0.01$, ** $p < 0.05$, * $p < 0.1$

better understanding of that behavior. Therefore, that area have a greater impact on the garbage classification behavior of farmers.

Models (3) and (4) are based on whether the government implements reward and punishment measures: farmers in those areas are more likely to conduct garbage classification behavior compared to farmers in areas without those interventions. Because of the incentive mechanisms, the cost of garbage classification is comparatively lower for farmers in the area that implements reward and punishment measures. Therefore, the regions where the government implements reward and punishment measures has a greater impact on the garbage classification behavior of farmers (Table 4).

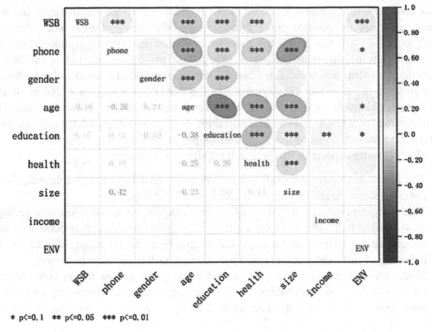

* p<=0.1   ** p<=0.05   *** p<=0.01

Fig. 2. The heat map for the matrix of Pearson's correlation coefficients.

5 Discussion

A large number of existing studies are highly relevant to this paper. On the one hand, Liu, Han and Teng [36] had shown the Internet's effect on protecting environment is significantly different from that of traditional approach like newspapers, broadcasts, periodicals and so on. On the other hand, Ma and Zhu [37] emphasized the Internet's ability to disseminate knowledge and information on garbage classification, especially the crucial role played by smartphones. Therefore, the major conclusion of the article can be summarized as the Internet will encourage farmers to engage in garbage classification behavior, which provides a practical basis and important reference for the positive effect of using the Internet to improve rural living environment.

This study also gets the result that the garbage classification behavior of farmers also occurred significantly in the younger, better educated, and healthy population. Besides, this study finds gender differences do not significantly affect rural households' waste classification behavior. This is vary from the research of Liu, et al. [38]. Liu, Xu, Shen, Chen and Esfahani [38] found that personal characteristics have a significant impact on garbage classification behavior, and women are more willing to implement garbage classification behavior. This may be a result of higher environmental concern among women.

The paper's heterogeneity results find that farmers in areas where the government conducts publicity reports are more likely to conduct garbage classification than those in areas where the government does not conduct publicity reports. This is similar to the conclusions of Liu, et al. [39]. Apart from this, the heterogeneity consequences of this study also show that farmers are more likely to conduct garbage classification in areas where incentives and punishments are implemented than those in areas where they are not. Yang, et al. [40] showed that the government should promote environmental protection related rewards and punishments to guide enterprises to transition to low-carbon and green development, which indicates that the implementation of reward and punishment measures can promote the transformation of the market economy such that obtaining environmental benefits is incentivized. However, few studies have shown the impact of environmental protection rewards and punishments on promoting garbage classification behavior, so the outcomes of this study can supply proof for policy formulation.

The following aspects of this research require further study:

(1) The penetration rate of broadband access in Jiangsu Province is relatively high. Future studies should include rural areas from other regions.
(2) This study concentrates on exploring Internet usage's impact on household garbage classification behavior. With the explosive development of internet popularity and dissemination forms, the future research direction can be more focused on the influence of different Internet using methods on garbage sorting behavior.
(3) Since rural living environment also includes sewage treatment, the toilet revolution, and other environmental problems, in the near future, research should pay attention to the Internet technology's influence on other environmental behaviors among farmers.

6 Conclusions and Implications

This paper adopts the binary Probit model to figure out farmers in the Jiangsu Province of China by using CLES data to study Internet usage impact on their waste classification behavior. Three conclusions are as follow:

(1) The use of the Internet can promote the garbage classification behavior of farmers. For those who use the Internet often, they are 14.5% more likely to conduct garbage classification than those who do not often use the Internet.
(2) Among individual characteristics, the differences in age, health status and educational level have a deep influence on the garbage classification behavior of farmers.
(3) As participating in political affairs can positively affect farmers' garbage classification behavior [41], farmers in areas where the government implements incentives and penalties are more likely, compared to areas without those interventions, to classify their garbage. As network communication plays multiple positive roles in building citizens' environmental literacy, farmers in areas with publicity reports are more likely to conduct garbage classification than those in areas without them.

Given this study's conclusions, the following policy recommendations are worthy of further consideration:

(1) It is indispensable to rebuild or to improve rural Internet infrastructure's construction and public finance should be appropriately tilted to rural areas.
(2) It is necessary to increase publicity and establish a network of relationships, so that more rural residents are aware of the positive externalities of garbage classification behavior.

(3) Establish local incentive mechanisms and implement reasonable reward and punishment measures.

References

1. Millington, R., Cox, P.M., Moore, J.R., Yvon-Durocher, G.: Modelling ecosystem adaptation and dangerous rates of global warming. Emerg. Top. Life Sci. **3**, 221–231 (2019). https://doi.org/10.1042/ETLS20180113
2. Marselle, M.R., Lindley, S.J., Cook, P.A., Bonn, A.: Biodiversity and health in the urban environment. Curr. Environ. Health Rep. **8**(2), 146–156 (2021). https://doi.org/10.1007/s40572-021-00313-9
3. Hassan Al-Taai, S.H.: Water pollution Its causes and effects. IOP Conf. Ser. Earth Environ. Sci. **790** (2021). https://doi.org/10.1088/1755-1315/790/1/012026
4. Zhai, H., Yao, J., Wang, G., Tang, X.: Study of the effect of vegetation on reducing atmospheric pollution particles. Remote Sens. **14** (2022). https://doi.org/10.3390/rs14051255
5. Arroyo, I., Cervantes, V., Tamaríz-Flores, V., Castelán, R.: Land degradation neutrality: state and trend of degradation at the subnational level in Mexico. Land **11** (2022). https://doi.org/10.3390/land11040562
6. Dong, H.: "Internet Plus" environmental risk management: background, concept and prospect. J. Nanjing Univ. Technol. (Soc. Sci. Ed.) **2019**(5), 57–66 (2019)
7. Zhang, J., Gong, X., Zhu, Z., Zhang, Z.: Trust cost of environmental risk to government: the impact of Internet use. Environ. Dev. Sustain. 1–30 (2022). https://doi.org/10.1007/s10668-022-02270-1
8. Yuan, F., Tang, K., Shi, Q.: Does internet use reduce chemical fertilizer use? Evidence from rural households in China. Environ. Sci. Pollut. Res. **28**(5), 6005–6017 (2020). https://doi.org/10.1007/s11356-020-10944-4
9. Zhang, J., Cheng, M., Wei, X., Gong, X., Zhang, S.: Internet use and the satisfaction with governmental environmental protection: evidence from China. J. Clean. Prod. **212**, 1025–1035 (2019). https://doi.org/10.1016/j.jclepro.2018.12.100
10. Kaza, S., Yao, L., Bhada-Tata, P., Woerden, F.V.: What a Waste 2.0: a global snapshot of solid waste management to 2050. International Bank for Reconstruction and Development/The World Bank (2018)
11. Wang, K., Lu, J., Liu, H.: Residents' waste source separation behaviours in Shanghai, China. J. Mater. Cycles Waste Manag. **23**(3), 937–949 (2021). https://doi.org/10.1007/s10163-021-01179-7
12. Lou, Z., Luochun, W., Nanwen, Z., Youcai, Z.: Martial recycling from renewable landfill and associated risks: a review. Chemosphere **131**, 91–103 (2015). https://doi.org/10.1016/j.chemosphere.2015.02.036
13. Grishaeva, Y.M., Spirin, I.V., Kiseleva, S.P., Napolov, O.B., Matantseva, O.Y.: Solid municipal waste management for sustainable development. IOP Conf. Ser. Earth Environ. Sci. **988** (2022). https://doi.org/10.1088/1755-1315/988/2/022085
14. Chen, H., et al.: Immobilisation of heavy metals in hazardous waste incineration residue using SiO_2-Al_2O_3-Fe_2O_3-CaO glass-ceramic. Ceram. Int. **47**, 8468–8477 (2021). https://doi.org/10.1016/j.ceramint.2020.11.213
15. Jacobs, C., Soulliere, K., Sawyer-Beaulieu, S., Sabzwari, A., Tam, E.: Challenges to the circular economy: recovering wastes from simple versus complex products. Sustainability **14** (2022). https://doi.org/10.3390/su14052576

16. Cucchiella, F., D'Adamo, I., Gastaldi, M., Koh, S.C.L., Rosa, P.: A comparison of environmental and energetic performance of European countries: a sustainability index. Renew. Sustain. Energy Rev. **78**, 401–413 (2017). https://doi.org/10.1016/j.rser.2017.04.077

17. Lu, S., Zhou, Z., Lu, Y.: Rural residents' perceptions, attitudes, and environmentally responsible behaviors towards garbage exchange supermarkets: an example from Huangshan City in China. Sustainability **14** (2022). https://doi.org/10.3390/su14148577

18. Zhao, A., Zhang, L., Ma, X., Gao, F., Zhu, H.: Effectiveness of extrinsic incentives for promoting rural waste sorting in developing countries: evidence from China. https://search.ebscoh ost.com/login.aspx?direct=true&db=buh&AN=158286904&lang=zh-cn&site=ehost-live

19. Zuo, X., Kang, M., Lu, J.: The impact of social interaction and Internet use on rural residents' willingness to sort domestic waste. 资源科学 **44**, 47–58 (2022). https://doi.org/10.18402/resci.2022.01.04

20. Zuo, X.F., Lu, J.: Internet use and relative poverty of farmers: micro-evidence and influence mechanism. E-Government (4), 13–24 (2020). https://doi.org/10.16582/j.cnki.dzzw.2020.04.002

21. Y., S.X. Rural practice of "Internet+"garbage classification: a case study of X town in Zhejiang Province. J. Nanjing Tech Univ. (Soc. Sci. Ed.) **19**(2), 37–44 (2020)

22. Wang, W.: Research on the impact of internet use on public environmental governance sense of efficacy. Stat. Inf. Forum **37**(3), 108–117 (2022)

23. Hebblewhite, G., Hutchinson, N., Galvin, K.: Adults with intellectual disabilities' lived experiences of wellbeing and the internet: a descriptive phenomenological study. Disab. Soc. **37**, 567–590 (2020). https://doi.org/10.1080/09687599.2020.1829554

24. Zhou, R., Fong, P.S., Tan, P.: Internet use and its impact on engagement in leisure activities in China. PLoS ONE **9**, e89598 (2014). https://doi.org/10.1371/journal.pone.0089598

25. Tabuenca, B., Garcia-Alcantara, V., Gilarranz-Casado, C., Barrado-Aguirre, S.: Fostering environmental awareness with smart IoT planters in campuses. Sensors (Basel) **20** (2020). https://doi.org/10.3390/s20082227

26. Pretorius, A., Kruger, E., Bezuidenhout, S.: Google trends and water conservation awareness: the internet's contribution in South Africa. S. Afr. Geogr. J. **104**, 53–69 (2021). https://doi.org/10.1080/03736245.2021.1901239

27. Xia, Z., Zhang, S., Tian, X., Liu, Y.: Understanding waste sorting behavior and key influencing factors through internet of things: evidence from college student community. Resourc. Conserv. Recycling **174** (2021). https://doi.org/10.1016/j.resconrec.2021.105775

28. Jiang, J., Meng, T., Zhang, Q.: From internet to social safety net: the policy consequences of online participation in China. Governance **32**, 531–546 (2019). https://doi.org/10.1111/gove.12391

29. Wang, H., Mangmeechai, A.: Understanding the gap between environmental intention and pro-environmental behavior towards the waste sorting and management policy of China. Int. J. Environ. Res. Publ. Health **18** (2021). https://doi.org/10.3390/ijerph18020757

30. Wu, J.: Research on the impact of technological innovation on environmental pollution – based on the moderating effect of internet development. In: E3S Web of Conferences, vol. 143 (2020). https://doi.org/10.1051/e3sconf/202014302054

31. Deng, X., Song, Y., He, Q., Xu, D., Qi, Y.: Does Internet use improve farmers' perception of environmental pollution? Evidence from rural China. Environ. Sci. Pollut. Res. Int. **29**, 44832–44844 (2022). https://doi.org/10.1007/s11356-022-19076-3

32. Huxhold, O., Hees, E., Webster, N.J.: Towards bridging the grey digital divide: changes in internet access and its predictors from 2002 to 2014 in Germany. Eur. J. Ageing **17**(3), 271–280 (2020). https://doi.org/10.1007/s10433-020-00552-z

33. Zhang, J., Cheng, M., Mei, R., Wang, F.: Internet use and individuals' environmental quality evaluation: evidence from China. Sci. Total. Environ. **710**, 136290 (2020). https://doi.org/10.1016/j.scitotenv.2019.136290

34. Van Deursen, A.J., Helsper, E.J.: Collateral benefits of Internet use: explaining the diverse outcomes of engaging with the Internet. New Media Soc. **20**, 2333–2351 (2018). https://doi. org/10.1177/1461444817715282
35. Zhou, Y.H., Yang, Z.Z.: Does internet use promote rural residents' consumption: based on the survey of 739 farmers in Jiangxi Province. Econ. Geogr. **41**(10), 224–232 (2021). https:// doi.org/10.15957/j.cnki.jjdl.2021.10.025
36. Liu, P., Han, C., Teng, M.: The influence of Internet use on pro-environmental behaviors: an integrated theoretical framework. Resourc. Conserv. Recycling **164** (2021). https://doi.org/ 10.1016/j.resconrec.2020.105162
37. Ma, W., Zhu, Z.: Internet use and willingness to participate in garbage classification: an investigation of Chinese residents. Appl. Econ. Lett. **28**(9), 788–793 (2021). https://doi.org/ 10.1080/13504851.2020.1781766
38. Liu, Q., Xu, Q., Shen, X., Chen, B., Esfahani, S.S.: The mechanism of household waste sorting behaviour-a study of Jiaxing, China. Int. J. Environ. Res. Publ. Health **19** (2022). https://doi. org/10.3390/ijerph19042447
39. Liu, J., Chen, Y., Wang, X.: Factors driving waste sorting in construction projects in China. J. Clean. Product. **336** (2022). https://doi.org/10.1016/j.jclepro.2022.130397
40. Yang, Y., Dai, J., Zeng, Y., Liu, Y.: Analysis on the stochastic evolution process of low-carbon transformation for supplier groups in construction supply chain. PLoS ONE **17**, e0264579 (2022). https://doi.org/10.1371/journal.pone.0264579
41. Song, Y., Zhan, Y., Qi, Y., Xu, D., Deng, X.: Does political participation influence the waste classification behavior of rural residents? Empirical evidence from rural China. Agriculture **12** (2022). https://doi.org/10.3390/agriculture12050625

Traffic State Propagation Prediction Based on SAE-LSTM-SAD Under the SCATS

Shenjun Zheng[1], Yun Lu[1], Tian Tian[1], Junqing Shen[1], Beilun Shen[1], Yun Sun[1], Liang Zhang[1], and Dongwei Xu[2(✉)]

[1] ChinaOly Technology, Hangzhou, China
[2] Zhejiang University of Technology, Hangzhou, China
dongweixu@zjut.edu.cn

Abstract. In many metropolitan areas, traffic congestion has become increasingly severe. Traffic state propagation prediction is a key component of Intelligent Transportation Systems (ITS). In this paper, a hybrid deep learning framework is developed that incorporates the stacked auto encoder (SAE) model, the long short-term memory model and the stacked auto decoder (SAD) model to learn the traffic state propagation mechanism and realize the prediction of traffic state propagation. Our experimental results, based on real traffic data under the Sydney Coordinated Adaptive Traffic System (SCATS) in Hangzhou, show that the proposed hybrid architecture for traffic state propagation prediction is superior to that of other state-of-the-art models.

Keywords: Traffic state propagation prediction · Stacked auto encoder

1 Introduction

Due to the modernization of cities, urban roadway networks are becoming complicated, and the number of cars on the road has rapidly increased in recent years. Because of this, road traffic congestion has become a growing problem, and traffic jams occur every day. Traffic congestion causes many social and economic problems, such as increased travel time, inefficient fuel usage, excessive exhaust gas emission [1], and poor productivity [2]. It is intuitively clear that traffic state forecasting [3–9] can help the administration department to prevent traffic accidents and provide better traffic guidance for road users, which can in turn reduce travel times and carbon emissions in metropolitan areas.

Traffic state propagation prediction is very challenging because it has nonlinear characteristics and spatiotemporal dependencies with external factors (e.g., morning rush hour, rain, holidays or entertainment activities). During the early stage of research in this area, various kinds of traffic prediction models were developed because many researchers viewed the traffic congestion prediction as type of time series prediction. Classical statistical parametric methods includes Bayesian networks [10], Kalman filters [5, 11] and autoregressive integrated moving averages (AMIMAs) [12–14]. Nonparametric models have also been employed to solve traffic prediction problems [15, 17].

X. Meng et al. (Eds.): BDSC 2023, CCIS 1846, pp. 208–220, 2023.
https://doi.org/10.1007/978-981-99-3925-1_13

NN approaches, such as artificial NN (ANN) [18], have been used to predict traffic conditions. Furthermore, powerful deep learning approaches have been widely and successfully adopted in traffic prediction [3, 19–23] have been widely and successfully adopted in traffic prediction. In the SCATS, traffic flow can be obtained at the entrance to each roadway and in intersections, but not on road segments, making conventional traffic prediction difficult to achieve.

We propose a traffic state propagation prediction approach called the "stacked autoencoder – long short-term memory – stacked auto decoder" (SAE-LSTM-SAD) model. The contributions of this paper are four-fold:

(1) The road traffic state network under the SCATS is constructed based on the critical threshold for each roadway, which can be obtained using MFD (Macroscopic Fundamental Diagram) theory.
(2) Based on the SAE model, the adjacent matrix of the road traffic state network is encoded as the input of the LSTM model, which is used to extract the temporal features of the road traffic state network.
(3) From the temporal features of the road traffic state network, the future encoding can be predicted and used as the input of the SAD model. The decoder process can realize the propagation prediction of the road traffic state network.
(4) Our experiments on a road traffic network in Hangzhou show that the proposed framework outperforms other baseline methods.

2 Related Work

2.1 Urban-Scale Macroscopic Fundamental Diagrams

In an early study, Daganzo [24] proposed an adaptive control method to manage and alleviate traffic congestion. Since then, many experiments [25–28] have focused on urban-scale macroscopic fundamental diagrams. We view urban traffic roadways as traffic networks when making traffic predictions.

2.2 SAE-SAD

Rumelhart et al. [29] first proposed a stack autoencoder, which is an unsupervised learning algorithm. An autoencoder includes an encoding part and a decoding part. An SAE uses an encoder to realize data compression and a decoder to realize data decompression. In 2006, Hinto et al. [30] used the SAE as a descending dimension method. Then, Bengio et al. [31] added the sparsity to the autoencoder, which can extract useful features while using few neurons. Moreover, Vincent et al. [32] added noise to the input data to form a denoising autoencoder (DAE).

2.3 Recurrent Neural Network-Based Traffic Forecasting

Recently, deep learning approaches have proven to be an extremely useful component of traffic forecasting [3]. SAEs have performed better than classical statistical methods and machine learning models. Futuremore, recurrent NNs can easily obtain the nonlinear temporal dependencies of time series data. As representative variants of recurrent

NNs, LSTM [33] and GRU [34] were first introduced in traffic forecasting, where they demonstrated superior capabilities. In particular, LSTM, a successful RNN architecture, incorporates memory mechanisms that address the problem of vanishing gradients.

3 The Road Traffic State Propagation Prediction Based on SAE-LSTM-SAD

The SAE-LSTM-SAD structure is shown in Fig. 1. There are four main steps for road traffic state propagation prediction. First, the road traffic state network is constructed by MFD. Second, the encoding of the road traffic state network is realized based on the SAE. Third, the time features are effectively extracted by LSTM. Finally, the road traffic state propagation is predicted by SAD.

3.1 The Construction of Road Traffic State Network Under the SCATS Based on MFD

The road traffic state data include the volume and occupancy on the entrance of each roadway in an intersection. A diagram based on the MFD of the relationship between volume and occupancy is shown in Fig. 2.

Then we can obtain the volume(q)-occupancy(o) model:

$$q = ov_f\left(1 - \frac{o}{o_j}\right) \tag{1}$$

where v_f means free flow; o_j means occupancy density; q_m is the critical volume threshold; and o_m is the critical occupancy threshold. From Eq. 1, we can see that the volume(q)-occupancy(o) model is a quadratic function relation. By means of parabolic

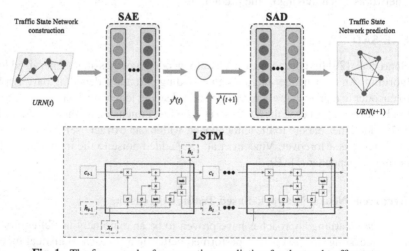

Fig. 1. The framework of propagation prediction for the road traffic state

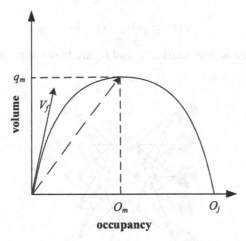

Fig. 2. A diagram of the relationship between volume and occupancy

fitting with the real values of the volume and occupancy data, the critical traffic state threshold of each roadway can be gained.

An urban road network model with intersections at time t can be described as in Eq. 2:

$$URN(t) = (N, E, ES(t)) \tag{2}$$

where, $N = \{n_1, n_2, \ldots, n_n\}$ is the set of nodes; n is the number of links; $E = \{e_{ij}|i,j \in N\}$ is the set of edges, with $e_{ij} \neq e_{ji}$; and $ES(t)$ is as in Eq. 3:

$$ES(t) = \begin{cases} 0 \ (q(t) > q_m \ or \ o(t) > o_m) \\ 1 \ else \end{cases} \tag{3}$$

which implies that the roadway is invalid when congestion on the roadway occurs.

3.2 Stacked AutoEncoder Model

The road traffic state network has strong correlation and redundancy characteristics. To extract features from the road traffic state network, an autoencoder is used to build a neural network. The purpose of an autoencoder is to reproduce its input and make it close to the input. The illustration of an autoencoder is shown in Fig. 3. An autoencoder first encodes the traffic data. Then, an autoencoder decodes the feature vector. Decoding aims to identify the useful extracted features. Through encoding and decoding, the original input data can be reconstructed, thus the feature extraction is completed. Given a set of traffic input data $\left\{x_1^{(l)}, x_2^{(l)}, \ldots, x_n^{(l)}\right\}$, where $x_i^{(l)} \in R^d$, denotes the hidden unit i in lth layer. $y\left(x_i^{(l)}\right)$ represents the encoder vector and $z(x_i^{(l)})$ represents the decoder vector of the output layer. The formulas are as shown in Eqs. 4–5:

$$y(x) = f(W_1x + b_1) \tag{4}$$

$$z(x) = g(W_2 y(x) + b_2) \tag{5}$$

where W_1 and W_2 are weight matrix, b_1 and b_2 are bias vector. We take the sigmoid function.

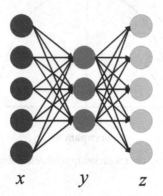

$$x \qquad y \qquad z$$

Fig. 3. The structure of autoencoder

The reconstruction error $L(X, Z)$, as shown in Eq. 6:

$$L(X, Z) = \frac{1}{2} \sum_{i=1}^{n} \left\| x_i^{(l)} - z\left(x_i^{(l)}\right) \right\|^2 \tag{6}$$

As shown in Fig. 4, the stacked autoencoder model stacks multiple autoencoders. The SAE model trains the first autoencoder by the input data and miniminzing the reconstruction error. After the training of all the layers is completed, the backpropagation algorithm (BP) can be used to minimize the cost function and achieve the optimized the parameters of the SAE model.

In order to prevent overfitting from the training of the SAE model, we use the dropout method to solve this problem. This problem could copy the input data as output and make the extracted features useless. Dropout can randomly remove some hidden units from the hidden layers as shown in Fig. 5, the network become thinner.

Dropout can enhance the feature extraction ability and achieve a high accuracy. The processes of dropout are shown in Eqs. 7–10:

$$r_j^{(l)} \sim Bernoulli(p) \tag{7}$$

$$\tilde{y}^{(l)}(x) = r^{(l)} * y^{(l)}(x) \tag{8}$$

$$y^{(l+1)}(x) = f\left(W_1^{(l+1)} \tilde{y}^{(l)}(x) + b_1^{(l+1)}\right) \tag{9}$$

$$z^{(l+1)}(x) = g\left(W_2^{(l+1)} y^{(l+1)}(x) + b_2^{(l+1)}\right) \tag{10}$$

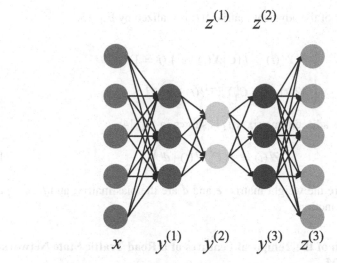

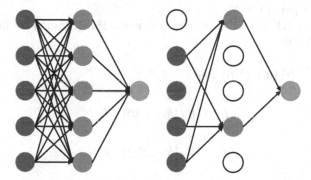

Fig. 4. The structure of SAE

Fig. 5. An example of dropout method. The left network is fully connected, and the thinned network with dropout method, where the hidden units (white) have been dropped in the right. The output layer does not have dropout.

Based on the $URN(t)$, the adjacent matrix $A(t)$, which is an $n \times n$ matrix, can be obtained. By splicing the line vector of $A(t)$, an $n^2 \times 1$ vector, denoted $X(t)$, can be obtained as the input of the SAE.

The output of the j_{th} hidden layer is shown in Eq. 11:

$$Y^j(t) = \left\{ y_1^j(t), y_2^j(t), \ldots \right\} \tag{11}$$

and the corresponding decoder output is realized by Eq. 12:

$$Z^j(t) = \left\{ z_1^j(t), z_2^j(t), \ldots \right\} \tag{12}$$

Then, the encode of the adjacent matrix $A(t)$ is realized by Eq. 13:

$$\begin{cases} Y^1(t) = f\left(C_1^1 X(t) + e^1\right) (j = 1) \\ Y^j(t) = f\left(C_1^j Y^{(j-1)}(t) + e^j\right) (j > 1) \end{cases} \tag{13}$$

and the decode of the adjacent matrix $A(t)$ is shown in Eq. 14:

$$Z^j(t) = g\left(C_2^j Y^j(t) + d^j\right) \tag{14}$$

where, C_1 and C_2 are the weight matrix; e and d are the bias matrix; and f and g are nonlinear mapping functions.

3.3 The Extraction of the Temporal Features of a Road Traffic State Network Based on LSTM

By using the SAE, the effective encode of the road traffic state network, $y^h(t)$, can be obtained as the input of LSTM.

Each memory cell in LSTM involves four units. The definitions of these units are given in Eqs. 15–18:

$$f_t = f(W_f [h_{t-1}, y^h(t)] + b_f) \tag{15}$$

$$i_t = f(W_i [h_{t-1}, y^h(t)] + b_i) \tag{16}$$

$$o_t = f(W_o [h_{t-1}, y^h(t)] + b_o) \tag{17}$$

$$\tilde{C}_t = tanh (W_c [h_{t-1}, y^h(t)] + b_c) \tag{18}$$

where W_f, W_i, W_o, and W_c are the weight vectors and b_f, b_i, b_o, and b_c are the bias vectors in each cell, and f () and $tanh$ () represent the activation function.

The output of the forget unit f_t in a cell controls how much historical information is retained, and the outputs of the input unit, output unit, and cell state unit (i_t, o_t, and $\tilde{C}_t$) control the amount of newly entered information retained in the cell.

The update of the cell and the output are calculated as in Eqs. 19–20:

$$C_t = f_t * C_{t-1} + i_t * \tilde{C}_t \tag{19}$$

$$h_t = o_t * tanh (C_t) \tag{20}$$

where C_t, h_t represent the value of the cell state and the output of the cell, respectively, at time of t, and $*$ represents multiplication.

3.4 The Prediction of Road Traffic State Propagation Based on SAD

Based on the temporal feature, the effective encode of the network at time $t + 1$ is shown in Eq. 21:

$$\overline{y^h\left(t+1\right)} = W_{fc} \cdot h_t + b_{fc} \tag{21}$$

where W_{fc} is the weight matrix and b_{fc} is the bias matrix.

Based on the SAE model, we can also defined the stacked auto decoder (SAD) process as in Eq. 22:

$$\overline{Z^j(t+1)} = g\left(C_2^j \overline{Y^j(t+1)} + d^j\right) \tag{22}$$

Finally, the decoder vector $\overline{Z^1(t+1)}$ can be obtained.

The loss function is shown in Eq. 23:

$$Loss = \frac{1}{n^2} \sum_{i=1}^{n^2} (\overline{Z^1(t+1)}(1, i) - X(t+1)(1, i)) \tag{23}$$

where $\overline{Z^1(t+1)}(1, i)$ represents the i_{th} entry in the vector $\overline{Z^1(t+1)}$ and $X(t+1)(1, i)$ represents the i_{th} entry in the vector $X(t+1)$.

The vector $\overline{Z^1(t+1)}$ is an $n^2 \times 1$ vector, which can be transformed into an $n \times n$ matrix and denoted $\overline{X(t+1)}$.

4 Experiment

4.1 Data Description

The dataset used for our experiment contains two kinds of traffic state data (traffic volume and occupancy) from Hangzhou under the SCATS from 1st Jun. 2017–30th Jun. 2017. There are 52 roadways selected for our experiment. The traffic state data are aggregated every 15 min. Thus, every roadway contains 96 data points per day. The volume(q)-occupancy(o) method is used to preprocess traffic state data. In addition, seven tenths data in the dataset are set as training set, and three tenths data are set as test set.

4.2 Index of Performance

We choose four performance indexes to evaluate model. They are defined as follows, in Eqs. 24–25:

$$Accuracy = \frac{n_{tp} + n_{tn}}{n_{tp} + n_{tn} + n_{fp} + n_{fn}} \tag{24}$$

$$Precision = \frac{n_{tp}}{n_{tp} + n_{fp}} \tag{25}$$

where n_{tp} is the number of values correctly identified as uncongested, n_{tn} is the number of values correctly identified as congested, n_{fp} and n_{fn} are the numbers of values failed to be identified as uncongested and congested.

4.3 Baselines

The comparison model we choose is as follows: (1) ARIMA (Autoregressive integrated moving average) is a famous method for forecasting future; (2) KNN (k-nearest neighbor) is a classic algorithm; (3) SVM (support vector machine) is usually used in regression tasks; (4) LSTM is a well-known model for traffic forecasting. All tests use a historical time window of 180 min (with 12 observed data points) to predict traffic state over the next 15, 30, 45 and 60 min.

4.4 Experimental Settings

In our experiment, in the SAE and SAD network, the hidden layers is 2. There are 2 LSTM layers, and each has 64 hidden units. Moreover,we add the dropout layer and choose 0.2 as the value of dropout rate. The activation functions are the sigmoid function in the SAE and SAD blocks, hyperbolic tangent in the LSTM layer, and sigmoid in the fully connected layer. We train our models by minimizing the MAE using Adam for 100 epochs with batch size 256.

The hidden units in SAE-LSTM-SAD is from [100, 200, 300, 400, 500] and analyze prediction accuracy, which is shown in Fig. 6. From the results, the prediction accuracy and precision are best when the value is [400,400]. When there are too many hidden units, the architectures are generally more complex.

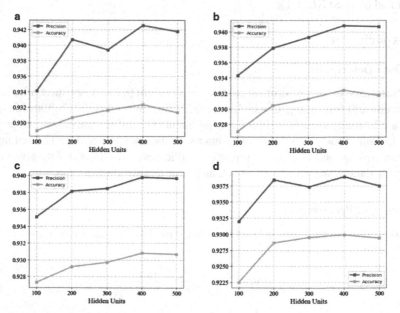

Fig. 6. Comparison result of setting different hidden units. (a) 15 min. (b) 30 min. (c) 45 min. (d) 60 min.

4.5 Results of Experiments

The results of the models are listed in Table 1.

Table 1. The Predciton Results of the SAE-LSTM-SAD Model and Other Benchmark Methods

Metric	Model	15-min	30-min	45-min	60-min
Accuracy	ARIMA	0.84622	0.84787	0.84842	0.84840
	KNN	0.85288	0.86286	0.86017	0.86513
	SVM	0.86172	0.86394	0.86612	0.86758
	LSTM	0.93073	0.92834	0.92410	0.90484
	SAE-LSTM-SAD	**0.93236**	**0.93242**	**0.93080**	**0.92991**
Precision	ARIMA	0.89999	0.90025	0.89998	0.89979
	KNN	0.90006	0.89991	0.90009	0.90011
	SVM	0.89995	0.89985	0.90011	0.90001
	LSTM	0.93688	0.93470	0.92995	0.91854
	SAE-LSTM-SAD	**0.94255**	**0.94081**	**0.93979**	**0.93892**

As shown in Table 1, the SAE-LSTM-SAD model and the LSTM model consistently achieve better performance than other baselines. The reason is that these models fail to capture the temporal feature. Which indicates that SAE-LSTM-SAD and LSTM generate less bias in prediction. For example, For predicting 15 min of traffic, both SAE-LSTM-SAD and LSTM have higher accuracy and precision than ARIMA, KNN and SVM. The main reason is that the ARIMA, KNN and SVM can not effectively handle time series data. In addition, long-term traffic state prediction (60-min) is more challenging than short-term one. Furthermore, SAE-LSTM-SAD surpasses LSTM model in terms of accuracy and precision, contributing 2.507% and 2.038% improved in accuracy and precision. The slightly lower prediction result of the LSTM model is because LSTM only considers the temporal features. SAE-LSTM-SAD can obtain the spatial features, and then learn the spatial and temporal corrlations between the roadways under the SCATS. The results determined that our proposed method yields the best capacity of identify smooth congested roadways based on accuracy and precision. Also as shown in Fig. 7, SAE-LSTM-SAD is superior to other methods based on the Receiver Operating Characteristic (ROC) metrics.

ROC curve represents the fraction of true positive rate (TPR) versus the fraction of false positive rate (FPR). They are defined as in Eqs. 26–27:

$$TPR = \frac{n_{tp}}{n_{tp} + n_{fn}} \tag{26}$$

$$FPR = \frac{n_{fp}}{n_{fp} + n_{tn}} \tag{27}$$

Specifically, TPR is used to measure the prediction precision of correctly identifying when the true data is smooth. FPR is used to measure the prediction precision of incorrectly identifying when the true data is uncongestion: the small value is, the better the result is. Thus, the more the ROC deviates from the 45-degree diagonal, the closer it gets to (0, 1), the better the prediction result is.

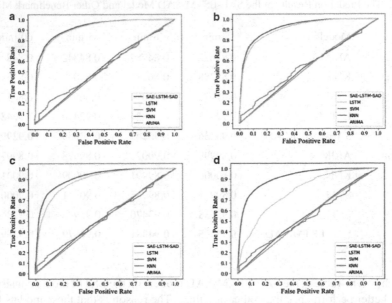

Fig. 7. ROC of the Proposed Method and Other Benchmark Methods with Different Prediction Pattern. (a) 15 min. (b) 30 min. (c) 45 min. (d) 60 min.

The evaluation results of ORC quality are shown in Table 2.

Table 2. AUC of the Proposed Method and Other Benchmark Methods with Different Prediction Pattern

Model	15-min	30-min	45-min	60-min
ARIMA	0.52106	0.52607	0.52103	0.52300
KNN	0.53431	0.52950	0.53039	0.54132
SVM	0.54203	0.55091	0.53705	0.53204
LSTM	0.91623	0.90780	0.88819	0.77913
SAE-LSTM-SAD	**0.92543**	**0.92190**	**0.91762**	**0.91459**

As expected, it is clear to see that our proposed model exceeds the best rocords of other models. SAE-LSTM-SAD mdeol displays a reliability in traffic state propagation prediction.

5 Conclusions

In this study, an SAE-LSTM-SAD model is proposed to address traffic state propagation prediction in the SCATS. We employ the SAE model to transform the adjacent matrices of the road traffic state network into low-dimensional vector representations and employ the LSTM model to learn the temporal properties of the road traffic state network. Then, the SAD model realizes the traffic state propagation prediction of road traffic state networks. The experimental results demonstrate that the SAE-LSTM-SAD model has good performance.

Acknowledgments. This work was supported by the Key R&D Programs of Zhejiang under Grant (2022C01121).

References

1. Barth, M., Boriboonsomsin, K.: Real-world carbon dioxide impacts of traffic congestion. Transp. Res. Rec. **2058**(1), 163–171 (2008)
2. Hartgen, D.T., Gregory Fields, M., Moore, A.T.: Gridlock and Growth: The Effect of Traffic Congestion on Regional Economic Performance. Reason Foundation, Los Angeles (2009)
3. Lv, Y., Duan, Y., Kang, W., Li, Z., Wang, F.Y.: Traffic flow prediction with big data: a deep learning approach. IEEE Trans. Intell. Transp. Syst. **16**(2), 865–873 (2014)
4. Wu, Y., Tan, H.: Short-term traffic flow forecasting with spatial-temporal correlation in a hybrid deep learning framework. arXiv preprint arXiv:1612.01022 (2016)
5. Xu, D.-W., Wang, Y.-D., Jia, L.-M., Qin, Y., Dong, H.-H.: Real-time road traffic state prediction based on ARIMA and Kalman filter. Front. Inf. Technol. Electron. Eng. **18**(2), 287–302 (2017). https://doi.org/10.1631/FITEE.1500381
6. Asif, M.T., et al.: Spatiotemporal patterns in large-scale traffic speed prediction. IEEE Trans. Intell. Transp. Syst. **15**(2), 794–804 (2013)
7. Lopez-Garcia, P., Onieva, E., Osaba, E., Masegosa, A.D., Perallos, A.: A hybrid method for short-term traffic congestion forecasting using genetic algorithms and cross entropy. IEEE Trans. Intell. Transp. Syst. **17**(2), 557–569 (2015)
8. Ma, X., Yu, H., Wang, Y., Wang, Y.: Large-scale transportation network congestion evolution prediction using deep learning theory. PLoS ONE **10**(3), e0119044 (2015)
9. Zhang, S., Yao, Y., Hu, J., Zhao, Y., Li, S., Hu, J.: Deep autoencoder neural networks for short-term traffic congestion prediction of transportation networks. Sensors **19**(10), 2229 (2019)
10. Huang, W., Song, G., Hong, H., Xie, K.: Deep architecture for traffic flow prediction: deep belief networks with multitask learning. IEEE Trans. Intell. Transp. Syst. **15**(5), 2191–2201 (2014)
11. Okutani, I., Stephanedes, Y.J.: Dynamic prediction of traffic volume through Kalman filtering theory. Transp. Res. Part B Methodol. **18**(1), 1–11 (1984)
12. Ahmed, M.S., Cook, A.R.: Analysis of freeway traffic time-series data by using Box-Jenkins techniques. Transp. Res. Board **722**, 1–9 (1979)
13. Hamed, M.M., Al-Masaeid, H.R., Said, Z.M.B.: Short-term prediction of traffic volume in urban arterials. J. Transp. Eng. **121**(3), 249–254 (1995)
14. Williams, B.M., Hoel, L.A.: Modeling and forecasting vehicular traffic flow as a seasonal ARIMA process: theoretical basis and empirical results. J. Transp. Eng. **129**(6), 664–672 (2003)

15. Xu, D.-W., Wang, Y.-D., Jia, L.-M., Zhang, G.-J., Guo, H.-F.: Real-time road traffic states estimation based on kernel-KNN matching of road traffic spatial characteristics. J. Central South Univ. **23**(9), 2453–2464 (2016). https://doi.org/10.1007/s11771-016-3304-9
16. Xu, D.W., Wang, Y.D., Jia, L.M., Li, H.J., Zhang, G.J.: Real-time road traffic states measurement based on Kernel-KNN matching of regional traffic attractors. Measurement **94**, 862–872 (2016)
17. Hong, W.C.: Traffic flow forecasting by seasonal SVR with chaotic simulated annealing algorithm. Neurocomputing **74**(12–13), 2096–2107 (2011)
18. Huang, S.H., Ran, B.: An application of neural network on traffic speed prediction under adverse weather condition. In: Transportation Research Board Annual Meeting (2006)
19. Jia, Y., Wu, J., Du, Y.: Traffic speed prediction using deep learning method. In: 2016 IEEE 19th International Conference on Intelligent Transportation Systems (ITSC), pp. 1217–1222. IEEE (2016)
20. Ma, X., Dai, Z., He, Z., Ma, J., Wang, Y., Wang, Y.: Learning traffic as images: a deep convolutional neural network for large-scale transportation network speed prediction. Sensors **17**(4), 818 (2017)
21. Ma, X., Tao, Z., Wang, Y., Yu, H., Wang, Y.: Long short-term memory neural network for traffic speed prediction using remote microwave sensor data. Transp. Res. Part C Emerg. Technol. **54**, 187–197 (2015)
22. Zhao, Z., Chen, W., Wu, X., Chen, P.C., Liu, J.: LSTM network: a deep learning approach for short-term traffic forecast. IET Intel. Transp. Syst. **11**(2), 68–75 (2017)
23. Duan, Y., Lv, Y., Wang, F.Y.: Travel time prediction with LSTM neural network. In: 2016 IEEE 19th International Conference on Intelligent Transportation Systems (ITSC), pp. 1053–1058. IEEE (2016)
24. Daganzo, C.F.: Urban gridlock: macroscopic modeling and mitigation approaches. Transp. Res. Part B Methodol. **41**(1), 49–62 (2007)
25. Daganzo, C.F., Geroliminis, N.: An analytical approximation for the macroscopic fundamental diagram of urban traffic. Transp. Res. Part B Methodol. **42**(9), 771–781 (2008)
26. Geroliminis, N., Daganzo, C.F.: Macroscopic modeling of traffic in cities. In: Transportation Research Board 86th Annual Meeting, No. 07-0413 (2007)
27. Geroliminis, N., Daganzo, C.F.: Existence of urban-scale macroscopic fundamental diagrams: some experimental findings. Transp. Res. Part B Methodol. **42**(9), 759–770 (2008)
28. Herrey, E.M., Herrey, H.: Principles of physics applied to traffic movements and road conditions. Am. J. Phys. **13**(1), 1–14 (1945)
29. Rumelhart, D.E., Hinton, G.E., Williams, R.J.: Learning representations by back-propagating errors. Cogn. Model. **5**(3), 1 (1988)
30. Hinton, G.E., Osindero, S., Teh, Y.W.: A fast learning algorithm for deep belief nets. Neural Comput. **18**(7), 1527–1554 (2006)
31. Bengio, Y., Lamblin, P., Popovici, D., Larochelle, H.: Greedy layer-wise training of deep networks. In: Advances in Neural Information Processing Systems, pp. 153–160 (2007)
32. Vincent, P., Larochelle, H., Bengio, Y., Manzagol, P.A.: Extracting and composing robust features with denoising autoencoders. In: Proceedings of the 25th International Conference on Machine Learning, pp. 1096–1103. ACM (2008)
33. Hochreiter, S., Schmidhuber, J.: Long short-term memory. Neural Comput. **9**(8), 1735–1780 (1997)
34. Cho, K., Van Merriënboer, B., Gulcehre, C., Bahdanau, D., Bougares, F., Schwenk, H., Bengio, Y.: Learning phrase representations using RNN encoder-decoder for statistical machine translation. arXiv preprint arXiv:1406.1078 (2014)

Citation Prediction via Influence Representation Using Temporal Graphs

Chang Zong⬩, Yueting Zhuang(✉)⬩, Jian Shao⬩, and Weiming Lu⬩

Zhejiang University, Hangzhou 310007, China
{zongchang,yzhuang,jshao,luwm}@zju.edu.cn

Abstract. Predicting the impact of publications has become an important research area, which is useful in various scenarios such as technology investment, research direction selection, and technology policymaking. Citation trajectory prediction is one of the most popular tasks in this area. One major challenge of this task is to quantify the influence of publications with integrated structural and temporal features from evolutionary citation graphs. Recent machine learning approaches are based on the aggregation of metadata features from citation graphs. However, richer information on the handling of temporal and attributes remains to be explored. In this paper, we propose CPIR, a new citation trajectory prediction framework that is able to represent the influence (the momentum of citation) of new or existing publications using the history information of all their attributes. Our framework consists of three modules: difference-preserved graph embedding, fine-grained influence representation, and learning-based trajectory calculation. To test the effectiveness of our framework in more situations, we collect and construct a new temporal graph dataset from the real world, named AIPatent, which stems from global patents in the field of artificial intelligence. Experiments are conducted on both the APS academic dataset and our contributed AIPatent dataset. The results demonstrate the strengths of our approach in the citation trajectory prediction task.

Keywords: Citation prediction · Temporal graph · Time series · Network analysis

1 Introduction

Distinguishing high-impact publications is crucial to making decisions in business and research activities, such as investment in technology fields, selecting research topics, and policymaking. Citations of a publication are usually applied to evaluate its potential impact. The question of how to predict citations has attracted more attention in recent years than before. With the development of graph technologies, the task can be described as predicting a publication's future citation trajectory with the graph and time-series information. One major challenge of this task is to quantify the influence of a publication with integrated structural and temporal features from evolutionary graphs.

X. Meng et al. (Eds.): BDSC 2023, CCIS 1846, pp. 221–237, 2023.
https://doi.org/10.1007/978-981-99-3925-1_14

Existing methods on this problem can be summarized in three ways. The first approach [1,2] tries to make use of prior knowledge and network techniques by assuming that citation trajectories obey the Power Law or log-normal functions. Then, traditional statistical methods are applied directly to sequences to make predictions. Another way [3,4] focuses on taking advantage of text features of abstracts and reviews. Features are fed into recurrent neural network (RNN) models for time-series predictions. With the increasing popularity of graph neural networks (GNNs), recent works attempt to apply various structural learning models to exploit information from attributes of publications [5–9].

However, citations are affected by many potential factors, and there is a lot of implicit information that should be considered in practice. For example, attributes of a publication, such as authors and keywords, should be treated significantly. The reputation of a scholar and the popularity of a field can greatly affect future citations of a publication. In addition, each attribute contributes to a publication at different levels (Fig. 1). The approaches in previous works simply apply GNNs to aggregate attribute features, which leads to a lack of fine-grained influence representation. Based on the above knowledge, a more powerful framework is needed to predict citation trajectories with the influence of publications derived from a temporal graph to handle the problem: **How to quantify the influence of a publication using all the historical information from its attributes?**

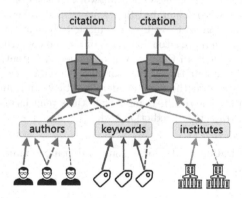

Fig. 1. A diagram illustrating that citations of publications can be affected by their attributes and relation types in different levels.

Current studies on temporal graphs try to manage changes in two adjacent snapshots, assuming that nodes should update smoothly or evolve dramatically [10,11]. However, these assumptions require one to manually set a change rate to limit the evolution, which is not flexible. Existing methods still mainly focus on handling structural and temporal features in separate steps, which leads to a lack of expressiveness to treat dynamic graphs as a whole. Furthermore, accumulative citations are usually modeled as log-normal or cumulative distribution functions

[7,12]. It is still worth trying some alternatives to perform a further analysis. The potential enhancement mentioned above should be studied to handle another problem: **How can we improve the expressiveness of the framework for prediction tasks using temporal graphs?**

With the observations above, we propose CPIR (Citation Prediction via Influence Representation), a new framework to predict citation trajectories with influence representation using temporal graphs. First, we extend the R-GCN mechanism [13] to temporal heterogeneous graphs to automatically learn the evolutionary gaps between two adjacent snapshots. Second, we implement a fine-grained influence (citation momentum) representation module to make use of all historical information from a publication's attributes to obtain integrated structural and temporal features. Third, a learnable general logistic function is applied for the first time to fit the citation trajectories using the influence representation from the previous module.

We experiment our framework with two real world datasets. One is APS[1], a public dataset of academic articles. Another, named AIPatent, is a new dataset that we construct with global patents in the field of artificial intelligence. Compared to some baselines, the results show that CPIR outperforms those methods in all cases.

Our key contributions are summarized as the following points:

- **Novel framework for the citation prediction problem.** We propose a new framework, named CPIR, which implements a structural-temporal integrated feature learning process to obtain fine-grained influence representation of a publication.
- **Improved evaluation strategy for the task.** We construct a new temporal graph dataset named AIPatent for the task and design three rational subtasks to evaluate our method and baselines from a comprehensive perspective.
- **Multifaceted analysis for further studies.** We analyze the experimental performance from multiple points of view, including baseline comparison, ablation study, time distance analysis, and prediction result analysis to explain how CPIR works. The significance and further efforts of our work are also mentioned to guide future studies.

2   Related Work

2.1   Citation and Popularity Prediction

Modern approaches to citation count prediction (CCP) aim to combine attribute information with temporal features. GNNs are commonly used to capture topological features of citation networks. The encoded nodes are sent to RNNs or attention models for time-series forecasting. A previous work [9] follows this simple encoder-decoder architecture. Some previous studies [8,14–16] put emphasis on cascade graphs for popularity prediction, using a kernel method to estimate

---

[1] https://journals.aps.org/datasets.

structural similarities. These works are based on simply combining graph embedding with time-series methods. In contrast, we introduce a method to fully utilize all past characteristics of the attributes of a publication. A recent work called HINTS [7] adds an imputation module to aggregate the information from each snapshot of graphs. Another work proposes a heterogeneous dynamical graph neural network (HDGNN) [17] to predict the cumulative impact of articles and authors. The latest work [18] uses an attention mechanism to represent the sequence of content from citation relations. Although these works can take advantage of richer information, their lack of fine-grained design to represent the influence of a publication with integrated structural and temporal information is not conducive to achieving good prediction performance.

2.2 Temporal Graph Embedding

We focus on deep learning-based temporal graph embedding approaches. Several previous works implement a straightforward way to combine GCN and RNN models to extract structural and temporal features [19–21]. RNN variants are applied as the temporal module to perform downstream tasks such as anomaly detection. Meanwhile, temporal attention models can be a substitute for GCN to extract topological features [22–24]. A recent paper [25] tries to represent global structural information of graphs at each timestamp, rather than focus solely on nodes. Another article [26] concerns the granularity of the timestamp and attempts to take into account the precision of arbitrary times. Tensor decomposition is also a useful approach to represent evolution patterns in graphs [27]. The work [28] further extends the architecture of a static GNN to dynamic graphs by updating hierarchical node embeddings. Some modern approaches [29,30] apply contrast learning or the transformer model to the traditional GCN framework for additional information. Instead of extracting temporal features after encoding structural information, we find that applying the RNN method to the history information of each attribute can capture better integrated structural and temporal information for downstream tasks.

3   Problem Statement

3.1   Preliminaries

Following [31], we define a graph that contains timestamps as $G = (V, E, A, T)$, where V, E, A, and T are sets of nodes, edges, attributes, and timestamps. We denote a temporal graph as a sequence of snapshots over time, denoted by $G_{tmp}^T = \{G^1, G^2, ..., G^T\}$, where $G^t = (E^t, R^t, A^t, F^t)$ $(1 \leq t \leq T)$ is a snapshot with its entities and relations at time t.

3.2   Problem Definition

For a publication p in the year of T, the sequence of citation counts of p in the next N years can be noted as $\hat{C}_p = \{C_p^{T+1}, C_p^{T+2}, ..., C_p^{T+N}\}$, where C_p^{T+N} is the citation count in the year $T + N$. Then, Given a temporal graph G_{tmp}^T with snapshots from year 1 to T, our goal is to learn a function $f(\cdot)$, which maps the publication p to its sequence of citation counts $\hat{C}_p$ in the next N years. The problem is described in the following.

$$\hat{C}_p = f(G_{tmp}^T, p) = \{C_p^{T+1}, C_p^{T+2}, ..., C_p^{T+N}\}, G_{tmp}^T = \{G^1, G^2, ..., G^T\} \tag{1}$$

4 Proposed Framework: CPIR

We now introduce our proposed CPIR. The framework of our proposed method is described in Fig. 2. Three motivations of our method are listed as follows:

– Evolutionary differences between two adjacent snapshots should be dynamically preserved, as different networks may have entirely different behaviors [32].
– Citations of a publication can be affected by all historical information on its attributes, which can be denoted as **influence**. Our approach should quantify the influence of all entities and their different contributions to a publication for feature aggregation.
– The growth of citations can be viewed as the prevalence of publications. The general logistic function, a widely used function to model disease prevalence [33], may fit well with the citation trajectories.

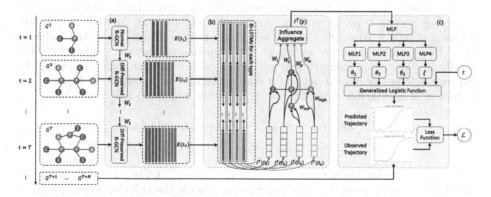

Fig. 2. Framework of **CPIR**, which takes previous graph snapshots as input, and successively executes through three steps: **(a)** difference-preserved graph embedding, **(b)** fine-grained influence representation, **(c)** learning-based trajectory calculation, and finally gets a learnable loss as output.

4.1   Difference-Preserved Graph Embedding

Given a temporal graph generated from publications. Our framework first realizes an embedding method to extract node features from these graph snapshots. We employ a relational graph convolution network (R-GCN) [13] and modify it to preserve the evolutionary difference for the same nodes between adjacent snapshots, using a learnable parameter. The hidden-layer embeddings can be updated as:

$$
\begin{aligned}
h_{i,t}^{l+1} = \sigma(&\sum_{r\in R}\sum_{j\in N_{i,t}^r} W_r^{(l)} h_{j,t}^{(l)} + W_0^{(l)} h_{i,t}^{(l)} \\
&+ \sum_{r\in R}\sum_{k\in N_{i,t-1}^r} W_t^{(l)} W_r^{(l)} h_{k,t-1}^{(l)} + W_t^{(l)} W_0^{(l)} h_{i,t-1}^{(l)}) \,,
\end{aligned}
\tag{2}
$$

where $h_{i,t}^{(l+1)}$ denotes the feature vector of the node i in layer $l+1$ at the time t, r represents a relation type in the set R, $N_{i,t}^r$ is the set of neighbors of the node i with the relation type r at the time t, $W_0^{(l)}$ is the aggregation weight for the node i in layer l. $W_r^{(l)}$ is the aggregation weight for neighbors with relation r in layer l, $W_t^{(l)}$ is a feature transformation weight from the time $t-1$ to the time t, σ is an activation function. For $t = 0$, as there is no previous adjacent feature can be transformed, the model is degenerated to a normal R-GCN layer.

4.2   Fine-Grained Influence Representation

In this module, we first try to quantify the influence of each attribute of a publication using sequential past features generated from the previous module.

    We assume that the influence of a publication is aggregated from its attributes according to the type of relation. And each attribute can further accumulate its own influence from its history. We then apply a Bi-LSTM model followed by a fully connected layer to digest the sequence of feature vectors for each attribute. We set an independent Bi-LSTM model for each type of relation to capture different temporal behaviors among them. The equation to calculate the influence of an attribute related to a publication is defined below.

$$
\begin{aligned}
I^T(O_e(p,r)) &= FC_r(\overrightarrow{LSTM}_r(seq)\| \overleftarrow{LSTM}_r(seq)) \\
seq &= \{V_e^1(p,r), V_e^2(p,r), ...V_e^T(p,r)\} \,,
\end{aligned}
\tag{3}
$$

where $I^T(\cdot)$ is the value of influence at the time T, $O_e^r(p,r)$ is the object of attribute entity e related to the publication p with the relation type r, $FC_r(\cdot)$ is a fully connected operation for the type r, $\overrightarrow{LSTM}_r(seq)$ and $\overleftarrow{LSTM}_r(seq)$ represents LSTM layers of two directions, the notation $\|$ means a concatenate operation, seq is the past feature sequence of an entity, $V_e^T(p,r)$ is the feature vector of entity e at the time T output from the last layer using Eq. 2.

    The influence of attributes should be aggregated to represent the overall influence of a publication, which is treated as a momentum to be cited in the future. We assume that attributes can affect publications at different levels, considering their positions and types. For example, the first author of a publication plays a more significant role than the others. We define two parameters W_{high} and W_{low} as proxies of higher-level and lower-level effects, respectively. Furthermore, different relationships may affect a publication to different degrees. We then set another parameter W_r to represent the contribution according to each relationship. The influence of a publication is computed as follows:

$$I^T(p) = \sum_{r \in R} W_r \sum_{e \in E_r} (I^T(O_e(p,r))W_{high} + I^T(O_e(p,r)W_{low}) , \qquad (4)$$

where $I^T(p)$ represents the overall influence of the publication p at the time T, $I^T(O_e(p,r))$ is the influence of p's attribute from Eq. 3, R is the set of relation types and E_r is the set of entities with relation type r. W_{high} and W_{low} are the higher-level and lower-level effects, W_r is the relational contribution to the publication p.

4.3   Learning-Based Trajectory Calculation

Treating citations as the prevalence of publications, we employ a generalized logistic function, an extension of the sigmoid function widely used in simulating the prevalence of pandemics [33], to fit citation trajectories. One frequently used form of generalized logistic function is denoted as below.

$$f(t; \theta_1, \theta_2, \theta_3, \xi) = \frac{\theta_1}{[1 + \xi exp(-\theta_2(t - \theta_3))]^{1/\xi}} , \qquad (5)$$

where θ_1, θ_2, θ_3 represent final size, increasing rate, and lag phase, respectively, and ξ controls the smoothness of the curve's shape.

In our task, all those four parameters are effected by the influence representation calculated from the previous module. So, given the representation as the input, all four parameters of the function can be automatically updated from the framework. We set four distinct MLP (multilayer perceptron) models to indicate these learnable parameters, as each parameter may behave totally different depending on the input. The future sequence of cumulative citation counts can be predicted using the following equation.

$$C(\mathcal{M}, t) = \frac{\theta_1(\mathcal{M})}{1 + \xi(\mathcal{M})exp[-\theta_2(\mathcal{M})(t - \theta_3(\mathcal{M}))]^{1/\xi(\mathcal{M})}}, \mathcal{M} = I^T(p) , \qquad (6)$$

where $\mathcal{M}$ is the momentum of citation, which is equal to the influence representation of the publication p at the time T, $C(\mathcal{M}, t)$ donates the mapping function to calculate the citation count at the time t using the influence of p, $\theta_1(\mathcal{M})$ can be treated as the peak of citation counts, $\theta_2(\mathcal{M})$ shows the rising rate of being cited, $\theta_3(\mathcal{M})$ can denote the lag phase before the publication is firstly cited, and $\xi(\mathcal{M})$ indicates the smoothness of the curve.

4.4   Loss Function

Following previous studies, we apply MALE (mean absolute logarithmic error) and RMSLE (square root mean logarithmic error) as our loss functions to evaluate our CPIR framework and baselines. They are log-scaled versions of MAE and

RMSE, which are commonly used in prediction tasks but are sensitive to outliers. The loss is the average value for all prediction years and target publications. Two functions are presented in the following.

$$L_{MALE} = \frac{1}{M} \sum_{j=0}^{M-1} \frac{1}{N} \sum_{i=0}^{N-1} |log\hat{C}_{i,j} - logC_{i,j}|$$

$$L_{RMSLE} = \sqrt{\frac{1}{M} \sum_{j=0}^{M-1} \frac{1}{N} \sum_{i=0}^{N-1} (log\hat{C}_{i,j} - logC_{i,j})^2} \,,$$

(7)

where $\hat{C}_{i,j}$ is our predicted citation counts for the j_{th} publication in the i_{th} year, $C_{i,j}$ is the corresponding observed citation counts, M is the total number of publications, N is the number of years we desire to predict in the future.

5   AIPatent Dataset

We provide a new temporal graph dataset named **AIPatent**. We notice that the quality and industry relevance of a dataset is important when studying temporal graphs in real situations. Existing public datasets usually suffer from inaccuracy and are used only for academic scenarios. AIPatent is collected and constructed from a global patent commercial platform filtered by tags related to artificial intelligence.

5.1   Dataset Construction

For extracting patents related to fields of artificial intelligence, we first collect CPC codes (Cooperative Patent Classification) that refer to the PATENTSCOPE Artificial Intelligence Index[2]. Then, patents published between the year 2002 and 2021 are filtered using these CPC codes from the platform. Patents are downloaded and processed to generate our temporal graphs with Python scripts. We finally get 20 heterogeneous snapshots divided by year, and each one is saved in an individual file along with randomly initialized feature vectors for each node. A snippet of the original data and the processed snapshots is shown in Fig. 3.

5.2   Dataset Analysis

Each snapshot in AIPatent is divided into four subgraphs according to the relationships. Some network analysis is performed, and three graph properties are shown in Table 1, including the number of entities indicated as $|E|$, the number of relations indicated as $|R|$, and the average degree indicated as $\bar{D}$. Furthermore, Fig. 4 shows the citation trajectories and the citation distribution of some randomly selected nodes in AIPatent. It tells us that the more citations accumulate, the fewer patents we can observe. We notice that the average degrees shown in the *citedBy* subgraph are around 7, which is close to the number stated by the existing citation networks.

---

[2] https://www.wipo.int/tech_trends/en/artificial_intelligence/patentscope.html.

The original patent data

Publication ID	Country	Inventors	Citation Patents	CPC	Publication Date	...
US111739****	US	Person1; Person2	US201403304****; CN107499****; CN107564****	B60W2050/007; B60W2050/0072	2021/11/16	...
...	...	...	...	...	...	...
CN107499****	CN	Person4; Person5	CN104769****; CN105517****; CN103223****	B60W30/182	2017/12/22	...

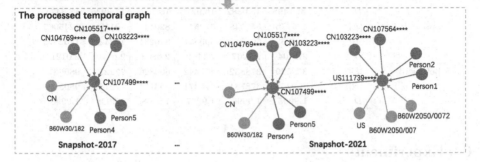

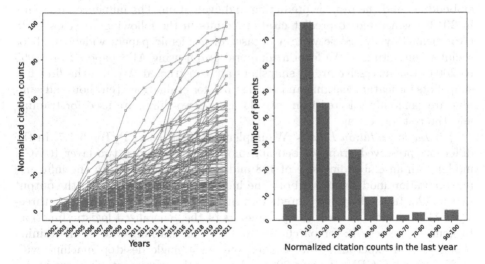

Fig. 3. A snippet of dataset that we use in CPIR and baselines. Some data is obfuscated. **Above**: The form of the original data we collect. **Below**: The processed temporal graph we use for the task.

Fig. 4. Citation statistics in **AIPatent**. **Left**: Citation trajectories of 200 randomly selected patents over 20 years. Red lines reflect citations above the average. Purple lines are for citations below the average. **Right**: The distribution of accumulative citation counts in the last year.

Table 1. Dataset statistics of a segment of **AIPatent** from the year 2015 to 2020.

Relation Types	Properties	2015	2016	2017	2018	2019	2020
citedBy	$|E|$	156684	197290	254438	332312	430199	521963
	$|R|$	560958	715101	937972	1211852	1592095	1993470
	$\bar{D}$	7.1603	7.2462	7.3729	7.2934	7.4016	7.6383
relatedTo	$|E|$	346023	419615	521160	654882	830763	1044713
	$|R|$	2448072	3155158	4150369	5469801	7224994	9322740
	$\bar{D}$	14.1498	15.0382	15.9273	16.7046	17.3936	17.8474
appliedBy	$|E|$	476775	559548	672545	820147	1011069	1245065
	$|R|$	510239	591512	699531	840231	1024256	1252572
	$\bar{D}$	2.1404	2.1267	2.1142	2.0802	2.0490	2.0121
belongTo	$|E|$	309520	378852	475442	603826	772219	980661
	$|R|$	309451	378781	475371	603754	772147	980589
	$\bar{D}$	1.9995	1.9996	1.9997	1.9998	1.9998	1.9998

6   Experiments

6.1   Experimental Settings

(1) Datasets. For AIPatent, we use the first ten snapshots for temporal graph embedding, and the rest for prediction and evaluation. The influence of patents in 2012 is generated to predict citation counts in the following 10 years. APS (American Physical Society) is a dataset of academic papers widely used for social science studies. We form a temporal graph using APS papers from 1995 to 2004. Ten successive graph snapshots are constructed. We use the first five snapshots for feature learning and the last five for evaluation. Ten thousand samples are randomly selected from two datasets. Two-thirds are used for training and the rest for testing.

(2) Implementation Details. We implement CPIR using PyTorch 1.7. In the difference-preserved graph embedding module, we set up a two-layer R-GCN model with an embedding size of 128 and a hidden size of 64. In the influence representation module, we set both the hidden size of Bi-LSTM and the output size to 128. In the trajectory prediction module, we set up four separate three-layer MLP models to learn the parameters of the generalized logistic function. In general, we set 512 for batch size and 0.05 for learning rate in all training processes. All experiments are carried out on a single desktop machine with an Nvidia A100 GPU. We run 20 epochs for each experiment, since we notice that the performance can hardly improve after it. We keep the best result of 5 attempts for each experiment.

6.2   Performance Comparison

(1) Baselines. We examine the performance of CPIR compared to a variety of baselines.

- **GRU+MLP** is a basic but widely used framework for time-series prediction problems. Without any graph embedding method, history citation counts are directly used for predicting following sequences.
- **TGNN** [9] uses a straightforward encoder-decoder framework for citation count prediction, which contains a GCN model for embedding and a LSTM model for sequence generation.
- **HINTS** [7] is another framework for predicting citation counts consisting of three modules: graph encoder, weighted metadata imputation, and a citation curve generator.
- **HDGNN** [17] is a more recent framework that can extract the feature of a publication by aggregating both attributes and neighboring nodes with RNN and attention models.
- **DeepCCP** [16] is another latest approach to model the citation network in a cascade graph and implement an end-to-end deep learning framework to encode both structural and time-series information.
- **CPIR+GCN** and **CPIR+MLP** are two modified versions based on our CPIR, which are generated by replacing the graph embedding and count prediction modules with simple GCN and MLP models, respectively, to verify our primary contribution.

(2) Subtask design. Three subtasks are performed in our work. The first task, denoted **NT**, is to predict citation counts in new publications that are rarely cited, with citation counts less than 5 (for AIPatent) and 2 (for APS). The second task is to predict publications that have grown up and been cited many times in previous years, with citations greater than 30 (for APS) and 12 (for AIPatent), denoted **GT**. The third task is for samples randomly derived from graphs without citation count limit, denoted **RT**. These three subtasks are trained with the same hyperparameters.

(3) Results. The results of the three subtasks are shown in Table 2. We observe that CPIR can greatly reduce errors on all subtasks compared to baselines (33.27%, 47.76%, 36.44% on APS and 38.14%, 7.11%, 24.01% on AIPatent, demonstrating that our attempt to quantify the fine-grained influence of publications is encouraging. Considering most cases of Newborn Task, our CPIR variants achieve the best in predicting newly published patents, showing that a simple sequence model is adequate when there is a lack of citation information.

6.3   Ablation Study

We denote "CPIR-X" as the variant of CPIR to replace the module "X" with a similar or simpler one. The charts in Fig. 5 show the performance of these variants.

CPIR-Influence is a framework that directly aggregates attribute features, rather than using all the history information from each entity. The tremendous degeneration in two datasets (54.51% on APS and 61.38% on AIPatent) demonstrates that the influence representation module dominates performance. Furthermore, a smaller reduction (13.74% on APS and 15.78% on AIPatent) occurs

Table 2. Performance results using APS (**Above**) and AIPatent (**Below**) to predict citation counts. Experiments are performed on three subtasks with our CPIR and baselines.

Methods	RMLSE			MALE		
	RT	NT	GT	RT	NT	GT
GRU+MLP	0.9233	0.5846	0.4755	0.7893	0.5024	0.3179
TGNN	0.8964	0.5446	0.4325	0.7661	0.4759	0.2972
HINTS	0.8973	0.5539	0.3588	0.7723	0.4901	0.2950
DeepCCP	0.9013	0.5426	0.4342	0.7661	0.4747	0.2956
HDGNN	0.8988	0.5419	0.3786	0.7652	0.4716	0.2471
CPIR+GCN	0.6671	0.2912	0.3234	0.5133	**0.1943**	0.2280
CPIR+MLP	0.7078	0.3541	0.3296	0.5506	0.2702	0.2451
CPIR	**0.5864**	**0.2883**	**0.2641**	**0.4005**	0.2050	**0.1916**
Methods	RMSLE			MALE		
	RT	NT	GT	RT	NT	GT
GRU+MLP	0.9858	0.5843	0.5261	0.7901	0.4385	0.5143
TGNN	0.9644	0.5647	0.5060	0.7745	0.4101	0.5029
HINTS	0.9783	0.5780	0.4826	0.7852	0.4379	0.4912
DeepCCP	0.9685	0.5695	0.5083	0.7814	0.4363	0.4028
HDGNN	0.9640	0.5651	0.4989	0.7734	0.4171	0.3970
CPIR+GCN	0.6941	0.5564	0.3920	0.5279	0.4042	0.2946
CPIR+MLP	0.7195	**0.5329**	0.5007	0.5544	**0.3741**	0.3833
CPIR	**0.5995**	0.5338	**0.3855**	**0.4156**	0.3801	**0.2787**

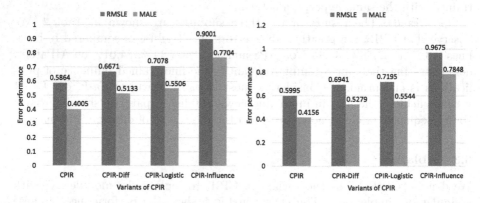

Fig. 5. An ablation analysis with variants of CPIR on APS (**Left**) and AIPatent (**Right**) datasets. The influence representation module is the primary factor driving the performance.

in **CPIR-Diff**, which simply replaces our difference-preserved module with a normal R-GCN. Moreover, **CPIR-Logistic** applies a commonly used log-normal function instead of our generalized logistic function. A decrease (20.70% on APS and 20.02% on AIPatent) shows that our hypothesis of treating citations as the prevalence of publications is close to real world situations.

6.4   Time Distance Analysis

We make further analysis on the performance of CPIR considering different time distances. For target publications, we use snapshots before time T (including T) for feature extraction, to predict their cumulative citation counts in the N_{th} year after T, denoted $T + N$. The maximum value of N is 5 for APS and 10 for AIPatent. The results are shown in Fig. 6. The precision gradually declines with distance increases, which indicates that a publication's potential impact is much easier to predict in its near future than in the long term. The long-term prediction is based not only on the current influence of the past behavior, but also on some undiscovered changes in the near future. Meanwhile, CPIR outperforms the average of baselines in all years, particularly in the near future.

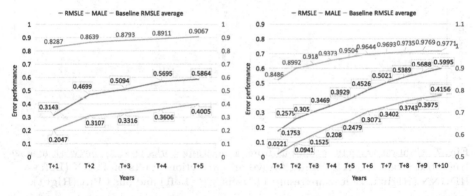

Fig. 6. Prediction performance depending on year distances after the current time T. CPIR and baselines are evaluated for 5 years on APS (**Left**) and for 10 years on AIPatent (**Right**).

6.5   Prediction Result Analysis

To understand why our CPIR can make such a close prediction to the true observations, we randomly select a number of samples from AIPatent and plot their citation trajectories generated from our proposed framework and some baselines. Figure 7 shows that CPIR can greatly squeeze curves to fit observation lines much better than others. As CPIR is the only approach to extract temporal features at the attribute level, our proposed influence representation model pays more attention to fine-grained history variations and finally produces citation numbers closer to real ones. Meanwhile, restricting citation curves to a slow increasing range is helpful to identify outliers in this situation, leading to social significance in applications. However, some striking citation changes still cannot be captured with CPIR, which needs to be further studied.

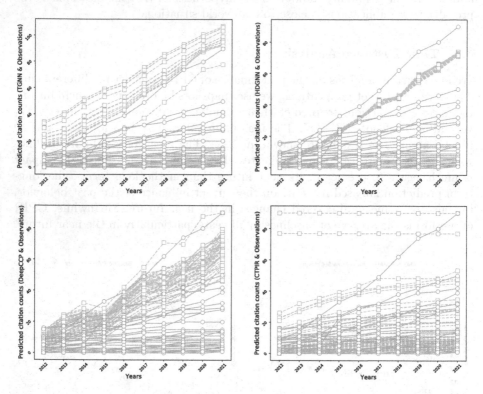

Fig. 7. Citation trajectories output from some frameworks used in our work against true observations on **AIPatent**. **Above** are prediction results of TGNN (**Left**) and HDGNN (**Right**). **Below** are results of DeepCCP (**Left**) and our CPIR (**Right**).

7   Conclusion

In this paper, we propose **CPIR**, a framework for predicting citation trajectory with influence representation using temporal graphs. Motivated by three hypotheses mentioned in Sect. 4, our proposed framework can represent the influence of publications from a fine-grained perspective using a more expressive temporal graph learning approach than baselines. We also provide a new dataset named **AIPatent** to facilitate further temporal graph studies. With a comprehensive task design, an improved evaluation strategy and multifaceted analysis are performed to verify the effectiveness of our framework. The ability to capture outlier citation changes can be studied in future work.

Supplemental Material Statement: Source code for our CPIR is available from our GitHub repository[3]. The APS and AIPatent datasets are available from our Google Drive[4]

Acknowledgment. This work is supported by the Key Research and Development Program of Zhejiang Province, China (No. 2021C01013).

References

1. Zhu, X.P., Ban, Z.: Citation count prediction based on academic network features. In: 2018 IEEE 32nd International Conference on Advanced Information Networking and Applications (AINA), pp. 534–541. IEEE (2018)
2. Xiao, S., et al.: On modeling and predicting individual paper citation count over time. In: Ijcai, pp. 2676–2682 (2016)
3. Li, S., Zhao, W.X., Yin, E.J., Wen, J.-R.: A neural citation count prediction model based on peer review text. In: Proceedings of the 2019 Conference on Empirical Methods in Natural Language Processing and the 9th International Joint Conference on Natural Language Processing (EMNLP-IJCNLP), pp. 4914–4924 (2019)
4. Abrishami, A., Aliakbary, S.: Predicting citation counts based on deep neural network learning techniques. J. Informet. **13**, 485–499 (2019)
5. Cummings, D., Nassar, M.: Structured citation trend prediction using graph neural networks. In: ICASSP 2020–2020 IEEE International Conference on Acoustics, Speech and Signal Processing (ICASSP), pp. 3897–3901. IEEE (2020)
6. Yu, X., Gu, Q., Zhou, M., Han, J.: Citation prediction in heterogeneous bibliographic networks. In: Proceedings of the 2012 SIAM International Conference on Data Mining, SIAM, pp. 1119–1130 (2012)
7. Jiang, S., Koch, B., Sun, Y.: Hints: citation time series prediction for new publications via dynamic heterogeneous information network embedding. In: Proceedings of the Web Conference 2021, pp. 3158–3167 (2021)
8. Li, C., Zhou, F., Luo, X., Trajcevski, G.: Kernel-based structural-temporal cascade learning for popularity prediction. In: 2021 IEEE Global Communications Conference (GLOBECOM), pp. 1–6. IEEE (2021)
9. Holm, A.N., Plank, B., Wright, D., Augenstein, I.: Longitudinal citation prediction using temporal graph neural networks (2020)
10. Gracious, T., Gupta, S., Kanthali, A., Castro, R.M., Dukkipati, A.: Neural latent space model for dynamic networks and temporal knowledge graphs. In: Proceedings of the Thirty-Fifth AAAI Conference on Artificial Intelligence (2021)
11. Trivedi, R., Farajtabar, M., Wang, Y., Dai, H., Zha, H., Song, L.: Know-evolve: Deep reasoning in temporal knowledge graphs (2017)
12. Bai, X., Zhang, F., Lee, I.: Predicting the citations of scholarly paper. J. Informet. **13**, 407–418 (2019)
13. Schlichtkrull, M., Kipf, T.N., Bloem, P., van den Berg, R., Titov, I., Welling, M.: Modeling relational data with graph convolutional networks. In: Gangemi, A., Navigli, R., Vidal, M.-E., Hitzler, P., Troncy, R., Hollink, L., Tordai, A., Alam, M. (eds.) ESWC 2018. LNCS, vol. 10843, pp. 593–607. Springer, Cham (2018). https://doi.org/10.1007/978-3-319-93417-4_38

---

[3] https://github.com/changzong/CPIR.
[4] https://drive.google.com/drive/folders/1EXybj3N36XUwUonfgtoVbSSDtRCxBEo i?usp=sharing.

14. Xu, Z., Qian, M., Huang, X., Meng, J.: Casgcn: predicting future cascade growth based on information diffusion graph (2020)

15. Tang, X., Liao, D., Huang, W., Xu, J., Zhu, L., Shen, M.: Fully exploiting cascade graphs for real-time forwarding prediction. In: Proceedings of the AAAI Conference on Artificial Intelligence, vol. 35, pp. 582–590 (2021)

16. Zhao, Q., Feng, X.: Utilizing citation network structure to predict paper citation counts: a deep learning approach. J. Informet. **16**, 101235 (2022)

17. X. Xu, T. Zhong, C. Li, G. Trajcevski, and F. Zhou, Heterogeneous dynamical academic network for learning scientific impact propagation, Knowledge-Based Systems, (2022), p. 107839

18. Huang, S., Huang, Y., Bu, Y., Lu, W., Qian, J., Wang, D.: Fine-grained citation count prediction via a transformer-based model with among-attention mechanism. Inf. Process. Manage. **59**, 102799 (2022)

19. Park, H., Neville, J.: Exploiting interaction links for node classification with deep graph neural networks. In: IJCAI, pp. 3223–3230 (2019)

20. P. Shrestha, S. Maharjan, D. Arendt, and S. Volkova, Learning from dynamic user interaction graphs to forecast diverse social behavior, in Proceedings of the 28th ACM International Conference on Information and Knowledge Management, 2019, pp. 2033–2042

21. Cai, L., et al.: Structural temporal graph neural networks for anomaly detection in dynamic graphs. In: Proceedings of the 30th ACM International Conference on Information & Knowledge Management, pp. 3747–3756 (2021)

22. Xu, D., Cheng, W., Luo, D., Liu, X., Zhang, X.: Spatio-temporal attentive rnn for node classification in temporal attributed graphs. In: IJCAI, pp. 3947–3953 (2019)

23. Li, Y., Zhu, Z., Kong, D., Xu, M., Zhao, Y.: Learning heterogeneous spatial-temporal representation for bike-sharing demand prediction. In: Proceedings of the AAAI Conference on Artificial Intelligence, vol. 33, pp. 1004–1011 (2019)

24. Park, C., et al.: St-grat: a novel spatio-temporal graph attention networks for accurately forecasting dynamically changing road speed, in Proceedings of the 29th ACM International Conference on Information & Knowledge Management, pp. 1215–1224 (2020)

25. Beladev, M., Rokach, L., Katz, G., Guy, I., Radinsky, K.: tdgraphembed: Temporal dynamic graph-level embedding. In: Proceedings of the 29th ACM International Conference on Information & Knowledge Management, pp. 55–64 (2020)

26. Leblay, J., Chekol, M.W., Liu, X.: Towards temporal knowledge graph embeddings with arbitrary time precision. In: Proceedings of the 29th ACM International Conference on Information & Knowledge Management, pp. 685–694 (2020)

27. Ma, J., Zhang, Q., Lou, J., Xiong, L., Ho, J.C.: Temporal network embedding via tensor factorization. In: Proceedings of the 30th ACM International Conference on Information & Knowledge Management, pp. 3313–3317 (2021)

28. You, J., Du, T., Leskovec, J.: Roland: graph learning framework for dynamic graphs. In: Proceedings of the 28th ACM SIGKDD Conference on Knowledge Discovery and Data Mining, pp. 2358–2366 (2022)

29. Gao, C., Zhu, J., Zhang, F., Wang, Z., Li, X.: A novel representation learning for dynamic graphs based on graph convolutional networks. IEEE Trans. Cybern. (2022)

30. Zhong, Y., Huang, C.: A dynamic graph representation learning based on temporal graph transformer. Alexandria Eng. J. (2022)

31. Cai, B., Xiang, Y., Gao, L., Zhang, H., Li, Y., Li, J.: Temporal knowledge graph completion: A survey (2022)
32. Kashtan, N., Noor, E., Alon, U.: Varying environments can speed up evolution. Proc. Natl. Acad. Sci. **104**, 13711–13716 (2007)
33. Lee, S.Y., Lei, B., Mallick, B.: Estimation of covid-19 spread curves integrating global data and borrowing information. PLoS ONE **15**, e0236860 (2020)

Enhancing Time Series Anomaly Detection with Graph Learning Techniques

Yiping Chen[1,2], Yuqian Lv[1,2], Zhongyuan Ruan[1,2], and Songtao Peng[1,2(✉)]

[1] Institute of Cyberspace Security, Zhejiang University of Technology,
Hangzhou 310023, China
[2] College of Information Engineering, Zhejiang University of Technology,
Hangzhou 310023, China
`pengst.aiing@gmail.com`

Abstract. As a frontier area of digital technology development, security in cyberspace is a major concern to ensure sustainable development. The time series technique, a data structure that describes phenomena over time, has been widely used in anomaly detection tasks in cyberspace. Further, we introduce graph learning techniques to focus on the relationships between nearby time series. Firstly, we utilize Dynamic Time Warping (DTW) to obtain the similarity between different moments of data. Then, we construct a variant of the adjacency matrix to capture the global information and local relationships of time series and improve the loading efficiency of the Graph Convolutional Network (GCN). Finally, generate graph embedding features for anomaly detection after passing the variant k-means. Our proposed method shows excellent performance on numerous realistic datasets and explores the implied feature relationships between time series using graphs. With its efficiency and interpretability, our model provides some theoretical support and experimental validation for cyberspace security techniques.

Keywords: Time series · Similarity analysis · Graph learning · Anomaly detection · Cyber security

1 Introduction

With the rapid development of technologies such as digitalization and the Internet of Things, various security events are arising. Compared with traditional data focusing on the variability of discrete samples, time series data preserves more trend change information for event analysis. Time series are the extraction, statistics, and mapping of different time-varying events in the real world. Generally, physical entities are converted into digital data using monitoring equipment at a fixed sampling time, and then, these data are arranged in the sampling order to finally obtain a set of time series. In the application of practical scenarios, time series are studied to classify three tasks: prediction, classification, and anomaly detection. Among them, time series anomaly detection is the target of our research, i.e., to mine the data for outliers or anomalous patterns.

© The Author(s), under exclusive license to Springer Nature Singapore Pte Ltd. 2023
X. Meng et al. (Eds.): BDSC 2023, CCIS 1846, pp. 238–250, 2023.
https://doi.org/10.1007/978-981-99-3925-1_15

By identifying the anomalous intervals of the time series, a number of anomalous states in real-world situations such as industrial failures, network attacks, and road congestion can be distinguished.

However, the existing anomaly detection research on time series relies too much on pre-known labels. To cope with the problem of difficult sample labeling, we focus on the improvement and design of unsupervised learning models. Meanwhile, the existing time series analysis methods focus only on the historicity and variability among the series, while ignoring the stability and interpretability brought by the correlation among the series. Unlike existing studies that complicate the detection model, we aim to use the GCN model to learn the spatial relationships of time series graphs and understand the nature of matrix composition analysis graphs. And then we use the clustering method to determine time series anomalies. In summary, the contributions of our work are listed below.

- We utilize DTW to obtain the similarity between different time series and convert the similarity matrix into an adjacency matrix.
- We construct a graph for describing the similarity of strongly correlated moments and load the graph to a GCN with the implementation of the variant k-means for anomaly detection.
- The superiority of our proposed method over multiple baseline models on numerous real-world datasets is demonstrated.
- Exploring the implied correlation among time series through graph analysis and revealing the relationships and dependencies between different variables.

This paper is structured as follows. In Sect. 2, we present the existing related work. In Sect. 3, the theoretical approach is presented. In Sect. 4, we present the data set, evaluation metrics, experimental content, and experimental results. Our summary is in Sect. 5.

2   Related Work

We first review the main tasks of existing time series studies, and the specific use of similarity or graphs to deal with time series anomaly detection. Finally, a brief summary of where methodological improvements can still be made nowadays is presented.

Time Series Tasks. Existing time series analysis tasks could be divided into the following categories: prediction, classification, and anomaly detection. First, Gooijer et al. [6] surveyed related studies on prediction from earlier years. Some articles [1,14,16] synthesize time series forecasting problems from recent years. Then, some articles [8,10,15,17] examined the classification model of time series. Finally, there are several studies [3,4,20] showing background applications of time series anomaly detection tasks. Nowadays, Li et al. [13] found that time series anomalies can also be classified into three states: time series point anomalies, time series interval anomalies, and time series overall anomalies, for which various methods exist to detect anomalies respectively.

Time Series Analysis. Dai et al. [5] compared various similarity measures and applied them to stock forecasting. Deng et al. [7] designed a novel clustering method to calculate the Frechet distance as the similarity weight composition. Langfu et al. [12] designed a time series prediction model based on graph attention and calculated the cosine similarity of the time series as the adjacency matrix component. Romanova et al. [18] performed anomaly detection on time series using FastDTW and KNN. Zhang et al. [21] used CNN and graph mining techniques to study the time series and calculated the cosine similarity of the time series as one of the inputs to the model.

Difficulties and Solutions. The precious works mainly focused on complex machine learning methods, which leads to the inexplicability and high cost of proposed algorithms. Meanwhile, existing works ignored the temporal and spatial interpretability among time series when they exploited graphs for analysis. Therefore, based on graph learning and clustering techniques, we propose an efficient and interpretable model for time series anomaly detection.

3   Framework

In this section, the statement of our target problem will be provided. Then we will introduce the framework of our proposed algorithm, which consists of three components, the similarity of time series, graph learning, and k-means variants.

3.1   Research Subjects and Problem Statement

Our study is on multivariate time series, which are specifically studied and classified in the paper [13]. Multivariate time series record observations of multiple variables over time, with each variable (i.e., feature) being a dimension. We use $X = (x_1, x_2, \cdots, x_i, \cdots, x_n)$ to represent multivariate time series, where n is the number of time series and $x_i = (f_1^i, f_2^i, \cdots, f_c^i, \cdots, f_m^i)$ is a single time series. f_c^i denotes the c-th feature of a time series x_i and m denotes the number of features of a time series.

Our aim is to screen out abnormal time periods in multivariate time series by graph and machine learning. The graph learning approach analyzes the graph features to get the implied relationships of the time series. Unsupervised clustering is used to simplify the process of anomaly detection and improve efficiency. The abnormal state of the time series is different from normal, so the graph and clustering approach is convenient and effective.

3.2   Overall Framework

This subsection briefly describes the overall framework of the model, and our model is divided into three parts together.

The first part is the similarity calculation, the distance algorithm is used to obtain the time series similarity values, and then the similarity matrix is composed after our processing. The second part is graph learning, where the similarity matrix is converted into an adjacency matrix by using the ranking selection principle to feed into the GCN along with the node features. Finally, a modified version of clustering is used to detect anomalies in the time series. Detailed step details are shown in Fig. 1.

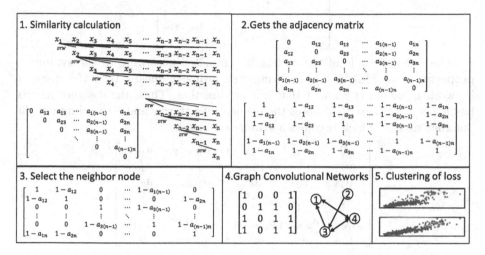

Fig. 1. The picture depicts the overall framework of our model, which consists of three parts, the first part being points 1 and 2, the second part being points 3 and 4, and the third part being point 5.

3.3 Similarity of Time Series

DTW is usually used to construct matching relationships between two different time series. Due to the complexity and redundancy, Salvador et al. [19] proposed an approximate DTW algorithm, FastDTW, that provides optimal or near-optimal alignments with an O(N) time and memory complexity. We use Fast DTW to compute temporal similarity, which is an improvement in computation time and resources compared to DTW. Since FastDTW still conforms to the rules of DTW, we mainly focus on the distance calculation of DTW, i.e., similarity calculation, in the following contents.

Given a time series $x_i = (f_1^i, f_2^i, \cdots, f_c^i, \cdots, f_m^i)$ and another time series $x_j = (f_1^j, f_2^j, \cdots, f_q^j, \cdots, f_m^j)$, the DTW distance between these two-time series could be calculated as the following formulation.

$$r(f_c^i, f_q^j) = d(f_c^i, f_q^j) + min\{d(f_{c-1}^i, f_q^j), d(f_c^i, f_{q-1}^j), d(f_{c-1}^i, f_{q-1}^j)\} \quad (1)$$

where $d(f_c^i, f_q^j)$ represents the wrapped distance between features f_c^i and f_q^j. We use d_{ij} to represent the accumulation of $r(f^i, f^j)$ among various features.

As illustrated in Matrix 2, the distance between the current time series x_i and all following moments $(x_{i+1}, x_{i+2}, \cdots, x_n)$ are normalized as elements of an upper triangular matrix, where $a_{ij} = \frac{d_{ij} - min(d_{i\cdot})}{max(d_{i\cdot}) - min(d_{i\cdot})}$.

$$\begin{bmatrix} 0 & a_{12} & a_{13} & \cdots & a_{1(n-1)} & a_{1n} \\ & 0 & a_{23} & \cdots & a_{2(n-1)} & a_{2n} \\ & & 0 & \cdots & a_{3(n-1)} & a_{3n} \\ & & & \ddots & \vdots & \vdots \\ & & & & 0 & a_{(n-1)n} \\ & & & & & 0 \end{bmatrix} \quad (2)$$

The lower triangle of the matrix is completed according to the symmetry property, as in Matrix 3. The symmetry property means that the distance between moments is a scalar that has no direction. Thus, the distance matrix has $a_{ij} = a_{ji}$, where a_{ij} denotes the element of i-th row and j-th column of the distance matrix, which becomes a symmetric matrix.

$$\begin{bmatrix} 0 & a_{12} & a_{13} & \cdots & a_{1(n-1)} & a_{1n} \\ a_{12} & 0 & a_{23} & \cdots & a_{2(n-1)} & a_{2n} \\ a_{13} & a_{23} & 0 & \cdots & a_{3(n-1)} & a_{3n} \\ \vdots & \vdots & \vdots & \ddots & \vdots & \vdots \\ a_{1(n-1)} & a_{2(n-1)} & a_{3(n-1)} & \cdots & 0 & a_{(n-1)n} \\ a_{1n} & a_{2n} & a_{3n} & \cdots & a_{(n-1)n} & 0 \end{bmatrix} \quad (3)$$

Finally, the similarity matrix is transformed from the distance matrix, which is formulated in Matrix 4.

$$\begin{bmatrix} 1 & 1-a_{12} & 1-a_{13} & \cdots & 1-a_{1(n-1)} & 1-a_{1n} \\ 1-a_{12} & 1 & 1-a_{23} & \cdots & 1-a_{2(n-1)} & 1-a_{2n} \\ 1-a_{13} & 1-a_{23} & 1 & \cdots & 1-a_{3(n-1)} & 1-a_{3n} \\ \vdots & \vdots & \vdots & \ddots & \vdots & \vdots \\ 1-a_{1(n-1)} & 1-a_{2(n-1)} & 1-a_{3(n-1)} & \cdots & 1 & 1-a_{(n-1)n} \\ 1-a_{1n} & 1-a_{2n} & 1-a_{3n} & \cdots & 1-a_{(n-1)n} & 1 \end{bmatrix} \quad (4)$$

3.4 Graph Learning

Towards considering the correlation of different moments in the similarity matrix, we include graph learning for information aggregating. This part can be divided into two steps. First, we convert the similarity into the adjacency matrix. Next, we input the graph generated by the adjacency matrix into a GCN model.

In order to obtain the adjacency matrix, we retain the top-k elements in each row of the similarity matrix and set the others to zeros. An example adjacency matrix is given as Matrix 5.

$$\begin{bmatrix} 1 & 1-a_{12} & 0 & \cdots & 1-a_{1(n-1)} & 0 \\ 1-a_{12} & 1 & 0 & \cdots & 1-a_{2(n-1)} & 1-a_{2n} \\ 0 & 0 & 1 & \cdots & 1-a_{3(n-1)} & 0 \\ \vdots & \vdots & \vdots & \ddots & \vdots & \vdots \\ 0 & 0 & 1-a_{3(n-1)} & \cdots & 1 & 1-a_{(n-1)n} \\ 1-a_{1n} & 1-a_{2n} & 1-a_{3n} & \cdots & 0 & 1 \end{bmatrix} \quad (5)$$

At this time, the similar sequences are treated as neighbor nodes of the current sequence (node), and the similarity values are treated as connection weights. The similarity matrix becomes the adjacency matrix, which can form a directed weighted network. The graph information will be input into the GCN model [11] for the next step of feature extraction.

3.5   K-means Variant

Since the time series anomaly detection task is concerned with both normal and abnormal states of each sequence, we use the variant k-means with $k = 2$. The main difference between traditional k-means and our modification is the selection of the initial clustering centers and the updates of centers. In the first step, the k-means variant initially selects the first time series and the point farthest from it as the two clustering centers, respectively. In the second step, the Euclidean distances from the cluster centers are calculated separately for the time series, and the attribution categories are classified. In the third step, the distance from the first time series is recalculated to update the centers of the clusters. Repeat the above operation, stop updating the clustering centers when the position change of the updated centers is less than the set threshold, and output the clustering results.

The loss function used to update the GCN parameters is given by the clustering, and the purpose of the update is to minimize the intra-class distance and maximize the inter-class distance of the clustering results.

4   Experiment

The anomalous event dataset is simply processed to retain more information. The labels of the dataset are extracted separately and used for the final model evaluation, not for model training. This section follows the datasets introduction, metric introduction, result comparison, and visualization analysis.

4.1   Datasets

We use the BGP dataset, which contains multiple Internet anomalous events with fluctuating changes in data, and different events have different effects on the features. The following Table 1 lists the basic information of the BGP dataset. Model comparisons and visualizations are performed using 5min and 10min once sampled data, respectively, with the aim of using a large amount of data to evaluate the model and a small amount of data to do an analytical summary.

4.2   Metrics

The metrics we use are divided into two parts: model evaluation metrics and graph evaluation metrics.

Table 1. A brief introduction to the datasets

Dataset	Total	Anomaly	Rate	Features	Time or Field
Code Red	7136	472	6.61%	48	2001.07.17-2001.07.21
Nimda	10336	353	34.2%	48	2001.09.15-2001.09.23
Slammer	7200	1130	15.69%	48	2003.01.23-2003.01.27
Moscow	7200	171	2.38%	48	2005.05.23-2005.05.27
Malaysian	7200	185	2.57%	48	2015.06.10-2015.06.14

Model Evaluation Metrics. Model evaluation metrics measure the performance of the training model and are an assessment of how well the model performs overall. Based on the true and predicted labels, the model results can be represented as true positive (TP), true negative (TN), false positive (FP), and false negative (FN), respectively. Further, it can be used to calculate the following accuracy, precision, recall, and F1-score metrics.

$$Accuracy = \frac{TP + TN}{TP + FN + FP + TN} \tag{6}$$

$$Precision = \frac{TP}{TP + FP} \tag{7}$$

$$Recall = \frac{TP}{TP + FN} \tag{8}$$

$$F1 - score = \frac{2 \times Rcall \times Precision}{Recall + Precision} \tag{9}$$

Faced with the situation that the proportion of normal data in the anomaly detection dataset is much larger than the anomaly data, we use macro-averaging to obtain each metric.

Graph Evaluation Metrics. We experimentally transform the time series on the time domain to a graph on the spatial domain consisting of time series as nodes and similarity as edge weights. Our graph learning focuses on analyzing the distribution, aggregation, and degree values of the nodes in the graph.

We use an adjacency matrix $\Phi = (\phi_{ij})_{n \times n}$, where ϕ_{ij} is the element of the adjacency matrix, to construct a directed network, which has nodes including in-degree and out-degree. The degree of a node i in a directed network consists of the in-degree k_i^{in} and the out-degree k_i^{out}.

$$k_i^{out} = \sum_{j=1}^{N} \phi_{ij}, \quad k_i^{in} = \sum_{j=1}^{N} \phi_{ji} \tag{10}$$

Some points need to be noted. First, since the presence or absence of edge weights has no effect on our anomaly detection model, we set the weights of all edges in the directed weight graph to a consistent 1 to facilitate calculating the degree of the analyzed nodes. The second point is that the neighboring nodes pick the ten most similar time series, so the out-degree of all nodes is 10.

The third point is that the in-degree of a node is variable, and the larger the in-degree value of a node, the more edges are associated with that node, i.e., the more connections to other nodes in the graph.

4.3 Results Comparison

Model Comparison. We performed the results on the BGP datasets (Code red, Nimda, Slammer, Moscow, and Malaysia) to compare with the baselines, which include LOF, COF, CBLOF, HBOS, IForest, and OCSVM. Notably, the statistical distribution-based (HBOS) and tree-structure-based (iForest) approaches generally outperformed the clustering-based (LOF, COF, CBLOF) approaches. Meanwhile, our proposed model has a significant performance improvement over all baselines for all datasets, and most notably a 21% improvement in the F1 metric on the Malaysian dataset. See Table 2 for details.

Table 2. Baseline Model Comparison

Dataset	Index	LOF	COF	CBLOF	HBOS	iForest	OCSVM	Ours
Code Red	Acc	85.76	85.76	86.32	87.99	87.71	86.04	94.44
	Pre	52.89	52.89	53.86	59.07	58.29	53.67	77.95
	Rec	54.23	54.23	55.50	63.24	62.12	55.35	77.41
	F1	53.23	53.23	54.36	60.53	59.62	54.14	**77.68**
Nimda	Acc	62.79	63.38	66.70	71.29	70.41	66.89	78.42
	Pre	51.15	52.77	61.99	74.73	72.29	62.53	68.74
	Rec	50.46	51.11	54.78	59.85	58.88	54.99	87.61
	F1	46.26	47.10	51.90	58.53	57.26	52.18	**70.19**
Slammer	Acc	77.36	77.92	81.81	87.50	87.36	83.75	93.61
	Pre	49.77	51.31	62.11	77.93	77.55	67.52	79.65
	Rec	49.84	50.89	58.24	69.00	68.74	61.91	96.48
	F1	49.45	50.69	59.38	72.09	71.78	63.72	**85.4**
Moscow	Acc	88.82	88.82	92.15	92.15	92.15	92.15	99.03
	Pre	52.12	52.12	61.38	61.38	61.38	61.38	80.00
	Rec	58.05	58.05	93.19	93.19	93.19	93.19	99.51
	F1	52.05	52.05	66.34	66.34	66.34	66.34	**87.25**
Malaysian	Acc	88.54	88.68	92.01	92.43	92.43	92.43	98.96
	Pre	51.66	52.04	61.30	62.46	62.46	62.46	79.73
	Rec	55.96	57.35	90.64	94.80	94.80	94.80	99.47
	F1	51.36	51.95	66.10	67.87	67.87	67.87	**89.02**

Module Comparison. We have conducted ablation experiments to compare the effectiveness of our module with other methods. Specifically, we compared the Graph Convolutional Network (GCN) approach for extracting graph features with Principal Component Analysis (PCA), as the module's purpose is to reduce the final output dimension. We also compared our k-means variant with K-Nearest Neighbor (KNN), as the module's role is to perform clustering for anomaly detection. Our experimental results demonstrate that our module is more effective than any single method alone. Please see Table 3 for detail.

Table 3. Ablation experiments: module comparison

Model	Index	Code Red	Nimda	Slammer	Moscow	Malaysian
KNN	Acc	86.32	67.09	84.17	92.15	92.43
	Pre	54.44	63.07	68.67	61.38	62.46
	Rec	56.48	55.21	62.70	93.19	94.80
	F1	55.06	52.46	64.65	66.34	67.87
PCA	Acc	86.88	68.07	84.44	92.15	92.43
	Pre	55.98	65.78	69.44	61.38	62.46
	Rec	58.73	56.29	63.23	93.19	94.80
	F1	56.88	53.87	65.27	66.34	67.87
Ours	Acc	94.44	78.40	93.61	99.03	98.96
	Pre	77.95	68.74	79.65	80.00	79.73
	Rec	77.41	87.61	96.48	99.51	99.47
	F1	**77.68**	**70.19**	**85.40**	**87.25**	**89.02**

4.4 Visual Analysis

Matrix Conversion Visualization. The visualization of matrix conversion from similarity matrix to adjacency matrix takes advantages for better understanding our proposed methods to handle time series. And the results show that computing the time series similarity is efficient and the conversion to an adjacency matrix can still represent the features and states of the time series.

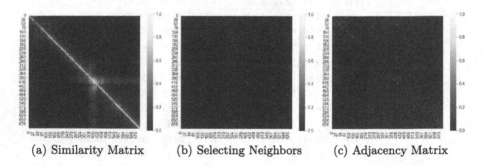

(a) Similarity Matrix   (b) Selecting Neighbors   (c) Adjacency Matrix

Fig. 2. Matrix conversion visualization. (a) shows the similarity between each pair of time series; (b) sets the similarity value to 0 for all non-neighboring nodes; (c) assigns the neighboring nodes to 1 and finally obtains the adjacency matrix.

The dataset used in Fig. 2 is the Code Red dataset sampled at 10 min intervals, and the figure shows the values after calculating correlations for different time series pairs.

Figure 2a shows there is a clear region of the larger correlation coefficient between 378 and 420, while the anomaly interval for this dataset ranges from 375 to 427. It indicates that the differentiation of normal anomaly states using DTW to calculate similarity is effective. After that, we remain the top-k similarity for each node and assign the others to 0 in Fig. 2b. Finally, in Fig. 2c, we assign all remaining similarity in Fig. 2b to 1 and obtain the adjacency matrix. The converted adjacency matrix transforms from a weighted directed graph to an unweighted directed graph.

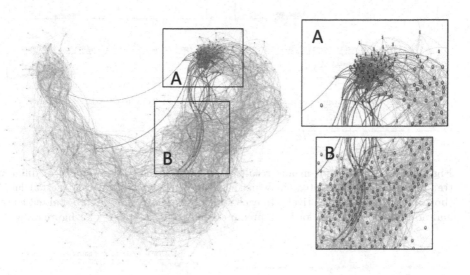

Fig. 3. Case visualization. Time series are represented as nodes. Normal data are marked as red and labeled with 0, abnormal data are marked as blue and labeled with 1. The edge width represents the similarity of the node pair, the wider, the higher. And the edge color denotes the category of its source node, where normal nodes output red edges and abnormal nodes output blue edges. (Color figure online)

Case Visualization. Figure 3 is the directed weighted network obtained from the adjacency matrix induced from Fig. 2b. Each time node was chosen to be connected to the 10 most similar time nodes and the node positions are automatically generated through Gephi [2] following ForceAtlas2 [9].

As shown in Fig. 3(A), anomalous nodes (blue) mostly connect with each other intimately due to their high similarity and small proportion. In contrast, the connectivity of normal nodes (red), which are illustrated in Fig. 3(B) as an example, is much sparser than that of anomalies since the huge weight of their proportion. Reviewing Fig. 2a, we can find that the similarity between different node pairs is also different. Thus, the weights, i.e. line width, of edges shown in Fig. 3 are significantly different. From the viewpoint of graph theory, time series can be converted from the temporal domain to the spatial domain to observe graph features, and the graphical method is effective.

K-means Results. After the GCN module, each node is transformed into a two-dimensional vector, which could be represented as a coordinate. Then, we feed those nodes as well as their resulting vectors into our variant k-means cluster.

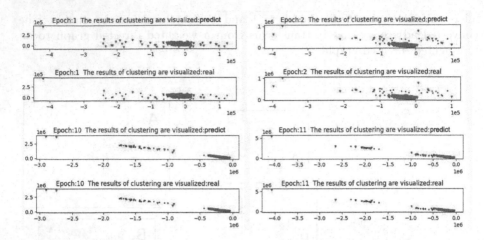

Fig. 4. Visualization of k-means results. The performance of the model in different training epochs is illustrated, in which the predicted labels (top) and actual labels (bottom) are shown respectively. In each subfigure, abnormal nodes are marked as red and normal nodes as blue for both predicted and actual labels. (Color figure online)

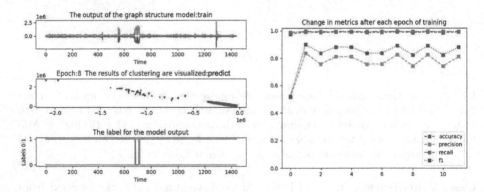

Fig. 5. Results Show. The left figure shows the GCN output, k-means output, and final label prediction; the right figure shows the variation of four metrics in each epoch.

In Fig. 4, the variation of clustering results under various training epochs is visualized, where nodes are marked with two kinds of colors (blue and red) according to their ground-true labels. In the first epoch, the distribution of these nodes shows elliptical clusters which means that our model could not distinguish them well. Then, in the second epoch, the overall positions of these nodes elongate from left to right, and the distribution changes from a dense group to a scattered bar. It can be observed that the anomalies detected by the model starts to emerge from the surroundings of the normal points and get close to the actual labels. After that, in the following epochs, e.g., epoch 10 and epoch 11, we can easily find that the training of the model causes the distribution of anomalies to move in the upper left corner of the window. Based on the results, our proposed k-means variant exert a good discriminative effect on the anomalous time series.

Final Results. Figure 5 shows the final results. Our model achieves appreciative results after a short training period, the output of the GCN model eliminates the temporal disturbances in the first step, and the clustering divides the dataset into abnormal and normal quickly. The combination of GCN and k-means is well suited for the anomaly detection task.

5 Conclusion

Taking Internet security events as the research background, this paper proposes a multivariate time series anomaly detection method based on graphs and clustering. We analyze the similarity of time series to form the structural relationship between the time series and implement a new research idea of combining time series analysis with graph analysis. We realize the aggregation of structural information with the GCN technique and unsupervised anomaly detection with a k-means variant of our own design. We validate the good performance of the model using multiple anomalous event datasets and explain the superiority of our model in depth in visual analysis. In our future work, we will add more strategic considerations to the composition, explore the relationship between time series features, and even derive the relationship between times to finally achieve the improvement of anomaly detection performance.

Acknowledgements. This work was partially supported by the National Key R&D Program of China under Grant 2020YFB1006104. The authors would like to thank all the members of the IVSN Research Group, Zhejiang University of Technology for the valuable discussions about the ideas and technical details presented in this paper.

References

1. Bandara, K., Bergmeir, C., Smyl, S.: Forecasting across time series databases using recurrent neural networks on groups of similar series: a clustering approach. Expert Syst. Appl. **140**, 112896 (2020)
2. Bastian, M., Heymann, S., Jacomy, M.: Gephi: an open source software for exploring and manipulating networks. In: Proceedings of the International AAAI Conference on Web and Social Media, pp. 361–362 (2009)
3. Blázquez-García, A., Conde, A., Mori, U., Lozano, J.A.: A review on outlier/anomaly detection in time series data. ACM Comput. Surv. (CSUR) **54**(3), 1–33 (2021)
4. Choi, K., Yi, J., Park, C., Yoon, S.: Deep learning for anomaly detection in time-series data: review, analysis, and guidelines. IEEE Access **9**, 120043–120065 (2021)
5. Dai, C., Wu, J., Pi, D., Becker, S.I., Cui, L., Zhang, Q., Johnson, B.: Brain EEG time-series clustering using maximum-weight clique. IEEE Trans. Cybern. **52**(1), 357–371 (2020)
6. De Gooijer, J.G., Hyndman, R.J.: 25 years of time series forecasting. Int. J. Forecasting **22**(3), 443–473 (2006)

7. Deng, A., Hooi, B.: Graph neural network-based anomaly detection in multivariate time series. In: Proceedings of the AAAI Conference on Artificial Intelligence, pp. 4027–4035 (2021)
8. Deng, H., Runger, G., Tuv, E., Vladimir, M.: A time series forest for classification and feature extraction. Inf. Sci. **239**, 142–153 (2013)
9. Jacomy, M., Venturini, T., Heymann, S., Bastian, M.: Forceatlas2, a continuous graph layout algorithm for handy network visualization designed for the gephi software. PloS One **9**(6), e98679 (2014)
10. Karim, F., Majumdar, S., Darabi, H., Harford, S.: Multivariate lstm-fcns for time series classification. Neural Networks **116**, 237–245 (2019)
11. Kipf, T.N., Welling, M.: Semi-supervised classification with graph convolutional networks. arXiv preprint arXiv:1609.02907 (2016)
12. Langfu, C., et al.: A method for satellite time series anomaly detection based on fast-dtw and improved-knn. Chinese J. Aeronautics **36**(2), 149–159 (2023)
13. Li, G., Jung, J.J.: Deep learning for anomaly detection in multivariate time series: Approaches, applications, and challenges. Information Fusion (2022)
14. Lim, B., Zohren, S.: Time-series forecasting with deep learning: a survey. Philosophical Trans. Roy. Soc. A **379**(2194), 20200209 (2021)
15. Liu, P., Sun, X., Han, Y., He, Z., Zhang, W., Wu, C.: Arrhythmia classification of lstm autoencoder based on time series anomaly detection. Biomed. Signal Process. Control **71**, 103228 (2022)
16. Masini, R.P., Medeiros, M.C., Mendes, E.F.: Machine learning advances for time series forecasting. J. Econ. Surv. **37**(1), 76–111 (2023)
17. Peng, S., Nie, J., Shu, X., Ruan, Z., Wang, L., Sheng, Y., Xuan, Q.: A multi-view framework for bgp anomaly detection via graph attention network. Comput. Networks **214**, 109129 (2022)
18. Romanova, A.: Time series pattern discovery by deep learning and graph mining. In: Kotsis, G., Tjoa, A.M., Khalil, I., Moser, B., Mashkoor, A., Sametinger, J., Fensel, A., Martinez-Gil, J., Fischer, L., Czech, G., Sobieczky, F., Khan, S. (eds.) DEXA 2021. CCIS, vol. 1479, pp. 192–201. Springer, Cham (2021). https://doi.org/10.1007/978-3-030-87101-7_19
19. Salvador, S., Chan, P.: Toward accurate dynamic time warping in linear time and space. Intell. Data Anal. **11**(5), 561–580 (2007)
20. Sgueglia, A., Di Sorbo, A., Visaggio, C.A., Canfora, G.: A systematic literature review of iot time series anomaly detection solutions. Future Generation Computer Systems (2022)
21. Zhao, F., Gao, Y., Li, X., An, Z., Ge, S., Zhang, C.: A similarity measurement for time series and its application to the stock market. Expert Syst. Appl. **182**, 115217 (2021)

Image Dehazing Based on CycleGAN with an Enhanced Generator and a Multiscale Discriminator

Yun Lu[1], Shenjun Zheng[1], Yun Sun[1], Liang Zhang[1], Yi Jiang[1], Hongru Wang[1], Jun Ni[1], and Dongwei Xu[2]([⊠])

[1] ChinaOly Technology, Zhejiang, China
[2] Zhejiang University of Technology, Zhejiang, China
dongweixu@zjut.edu.cn

Abstract. Haze is a major issue that influences the image quality and impacts accuracy of computer vision tasks. We propose a novel algorithm for single image dehazing based on CycleGAN with an enhanced generator and a multiscale discriminator (DCEM). The proposed method generates dehazed images without relying on physical scattering models. The DCEM is based on CycleGAN and incorporates a pyramid pooling network in the enhanced generator that utilizes multiresolution inputs. The multiscale discriminator assists the generator in paying attention to details in the generated images with different scales. The proposed CycleGAN is evaluated on the NYU-Depth dataset and the RESIDE dataset. The results demonstrate that the proposed DCEM outperforms current methods.

Keywords: Image dehazing · Cycle-GAN · Computer vision tasks First Section

1 Introduction

Generally, outdoor images are extensively used. Nevertheless, the presence of water vapor and suspended particles in the atmosphere often leads to the acquisition of hazy and low-quality images. Therefore, image dehazing has become a crucial technology for enhancing the quality of such images.

Prior-based methods have been used in image dehazing [2]. Learning-based methods [12], on the other hand, employ CNN to learn the transmission maps. Some of these methods attempt to directly translate hazy images into dehazed images without using the atmospheric scattering model but through the model construction.

GANs [7] have frequent applications in the field of image generation. They are designed to generate realistic images and can be trained using both genuine and fake images [13]. GANs have also shown promising results in completing image-to-image translation tasks, where they are trained with source images and corresponding images from the target domain in a paired manner [5]. More recently, the CycleGAN [18] was introduced as an approach to unpaired image-to-image translation. The CycleGAN can ensure that the image produced by passing through two generators remains faithful to the original source image.

© The Author(s), under exclusive license to Springer Nature Singapore Pte Ltd. 2023
X. Meng et al. (Eds.): BDSC 2023, CCIS 1846, pp. 251–258, 2023.
https://doi.org/10.1007/978-981-99-3925-1_16

Tan et al. [15] figured out a model that the higher contrast of haze-free images in comparison to hazy images. Zhu et al. [17] leveraged the different depth statistics of hazy images. Li et al. [10] proposed a lightweight CNN that can be easily combined with other strategies. Additionally, Chen et al. [4] proposed GCAN model that employs a smoothed dilated convolution and a gated fusion subnetwork to improve dehazing performance.

Prior-based and learning-based methods have been proven effective. We propose a approach for image dehazing through the use of an enhanced CycleGAN. The objective of our approach is to generate high-quality dehazed images by employing a CycleGAN with an enhanced generator and a multiscale discriminator. In comparison to the conventional CycleGAN, the enhanced generator of our approach extracts features from multiresolution images and includes a pyramid pooling network [16] at its end. Furthermore, we have replaced the discriminator with a multiscale discriminator.

The contributions are listed as follows.

The DCEM is an enhanced CycleGAN architecture with an improved generator and a multiscale discriminator.

DCEM is capable of generating images that are more realistic and closer to their real counterparts.

DCEM does not rely on the atmospheric scattering model and can be trained with unpaired image data.

The experiments results indicate that the DCEM outperforms the compared methods.

2   Proposed Method

CycleGAN is a SOTA architecture for image-to-image translation, but it is often criticized for producing images with insufficient details. To address this, we propose the DCEM architecture, which is based on cyclegan but incorporates an enhanced generator and a multiscale discriminator. Specifically, the enhanced generator includes a pyramid pooling network to extract features from multi-resolution inputs, while the multiscale discriminator provides feedback on image details at different scales. please refer to Fig. 1 for the CycleGAN architecture, and Fig. 2 and Fig. 3 for the enhanced generator and multiscale discriminator architectures, respectively.

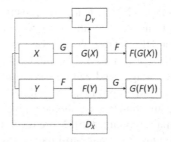

Fig. 1. The architecture of the CycleGAN. X and Y represent images from different domains.

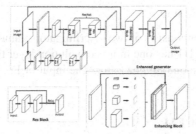

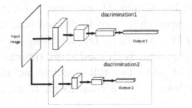

Fig. 2. The structure of the enhanced generator. It includes the architectures A1 and A2 and the pyramid pooling network.

Fig. 3. The structure of the multiscale discriminator.

2.1 Enhanced Generator

The enhanced generator consists of the architectures G1, G2 and a pyramid pooling network, as shown in Fig. 2. G1 and G2 have similar architectures including convolutions, a residual network and a transposed convolution. The inputs of G1 and G2 are the original image and its 2 × downsampled image, respectively. G2 is embedded in G1 by concatenating the output of G2 and the feature maps of the convolutions of G1. Then, the concatenated result is fed into the residual network of G1. The output of G1 is obtained by upsampling the feature map of the residual network to its original size. The residual networks of G1 and G2 have 9 and 6 ResBlocks, respectively. The multiresolution structure can help to create an image on a fine scale.

It is not enough to create realistic details; thus, a pyramid pooling network consisting of two pyramid pooling blocks is added after G1. The architecture of the pyramid pooling block is shown in Fig. 2. To preserve more details of the original images, the output of G1 and the original image are fed into the pyramid pooling network. Additionally, the network needs to embed the details of the features from different scale images in the final image. In the pyramid pooling block, there exists a four-scale pyramid built by downsampling the input by 4 ×, 8 ×, 16 ×, and 32 ×. Then, a 1 × 1 convolution is implemented for dimension reduction. The four-scale feature maps are upsampled to the original size and concatenated together with the input of the pyramid pooling block. Then, a 3 × 3 convolution is implemented on the concatenation of the feature maps and the output of the pyramid pooling block is obtained. After two pyramid pooling blocks and another 3 × 3 convolution, the result of the enhanced generator is obtained.

2.2 Multiscale Discriminator

A multiscale discriminator consists of two discriminators named D1 and D2. They have similar architectures, and D1 has one more convolution layer than D2. The input of D1 is the output of the corresponding generator. The input of D2 is the $2 \times$ downsampled input of D1.

2.3 Full Objective of DCEM

There are hazy and haze-free images from domains X and Y that are the inputs of the DCEM. Similar to the CycleGAN, the DCEM includes two enhanced generators G and F and two multiscale discriminators Dx and Dy. Our goal is to learn two mappings $G: X \rightarrow Y$ and $F: Y \rightarrow X$. In addition, Dx contains two discriminators D_{x1} and D_{X2}, where D_{x1} and D_{X2} are respectively used to discriminate the images $F(Y)$ the $2 \times$ downsampled images of $F(Y)$. Similarly, D_{Y1} contains two discriminators, D_{Y1} and D_{Y2}, where D_{Y1} and D_{Y1} are respectively used to discriminate the images $G(X)$ and the $2 \times$ downsampled images of $G(X)$. Our full objective includes two adversarial losses and one cycle consistency loss, where λ controls the relative importance of the cycle consistency loss:

$$
\begin{aligned}
L(G, F, D_X, D_Y) &= L_{GAN}(G, D_Y, X, Y) \\
&+ L_{GAN}(F, D_X, Y, X) \\
&+ \lambda L_{cyc}(G, F)
\end{aligned}
\tag{1}
$$

$$
G^*, F^* = \arg \min_{G,F} \max_{D_X,D_Y} L(G, F, D_X, D_Y)
\tag{2}
$$

Adversarial Loss

Referring to the GANs, the adversarial loss $G: X \rightarrow Y$ and two-scale discriminators D_Y is formulated as:

$$
\begin{aligned}
L_{GAN}(G, D_Y, X, Y) &= E(y)[\log D_{Y1}(y)] \\
&+ E(x)[\log(1 - D_{Y1}(G(x)))] \\
&+ E(y')[\log D_{Y2}(y')] \\
&+ E(x')[\log(1 - D_{Y2}(G(x')))]
\end{aligned}
\tag{3}
$$

where $x \in X$, $y \in Y$, and x and y denote the $2 \times$ downsampled images from X and Y, respectively. G tries to reduce the difference between the images $G(x)$ and the images from domain Y and then minimizes this objective. Conversely, D_{Y1} and D_{Y2} try to maximize the objective. That is, the adversarial loss is calculated as:

$$
\min_G \max_{D_Y} L_{GAN}(G, D_Y, X, Y)
\tag{4}
$$

Another similar adversarial loss $F: Y \rightarrow X$ and the two-scale discriminators Dx is calculated as

$$
\min_F \max_{D_X} L_{GAN}(G, D_X, X, Y)
\tag{5}
$$

Table 1. Average PSNRs and SSIMs for the NYU-Depth dataset

	DCP	CAP	Berman et al	Ren et al	DehazeNet	CycleGAN	Cycle-Dehaze	ours
PSNR	10.98	12.78	12.26	13.04	12.84	13.38	15.41	**15.44**
SSIM	0.64	0.70	0.70	0.66	0.71	0.52	0.66	**0.76**

Table 2. Average PSNRs and SSIMs for the OTS dataset

	DCP	CAP	GCAN	CycleGAN	Cycle-Dehaze	ours
PSNR	15.74	21.65	20.58	23.10	23.55	**24.74**
SSIM	0.814	0.887	0.859	0.851	0.865	**0.890**

Cycle Consistency Loss

Actually, the adversarial losses can guide the generated images $G(x)$ and $F(Y)$ to match the distributions of the images, respectively. However, $G(x)$ and $F(Y)$ can be any images that match the corresponding distribution but may be quite different from the original images. Thus, it is necessary for another constraint to make sure that the generated images are as expected. Image x should match x by mapping G and F: $x \rightarrow G(x) \rightarrow F(G(x)) \approx x$. It is similar for image y. We introduce the cycle consistency loss from the CycleGAN, which is formulated as:

$$L_{cyc}(G, F) = E_{(x)}[||F(G(x)) - x||_1]$$
$$+E_{(y)}[||G(F(y)) - y||_1] \tag{6}$$

3 Experiments

3.1 Datasets

The experiments are implemented on the NYU-Depth14 dataset and the Outdoor Training Set (OTS) of RESIDE11. The NYU-Depth dataset includes 1449 pairs of clean and synthesized images with labels and depths. It is divided into 1300 image pairs for training and 149 image pairs for testing. RESIDE is a hazy image dataset consisting of five subsets. The images in the OTS are real outdoor images and the corresponding synthesized images from Beijing. A total of 2500 and 98 images with a resolution of approximately 550 × 412 are as the training and test sets from the OST, respectively.

3.2 Results on the NYU-Depth Dataset

Table 1 shows the testing results of CycleGAN and other SOAT approaches on the NYU-Depth data. Most of the results are taken from a previous paper6. Compared with the

CycleGAN-based methods, the DCEM achieves a significant improvement in both the PSNR and SSIM. Although Cycle-Dehaze has a similar PSNR, its SSIM is 0.1 lower than that of DCEM. Other methods23 achieve the second-best SSIMs, but their PSNRs are quite lower than that of the DCEM.

3.3 Results on the OTS

We choose five models shown in Table 2 as2. It illustrates that the DCEM also has the best results. Moreover, all of the CycleGAN-based methods achieve high performance, especially with respect to the PSNR.

Figure 4 shows the dehazed images of the different models. It is observed that the DCP will result in color distortions in the images with sky and the colors of the images are darker. The problem of darkness also appears in the CAP and GCAN results. Some of the images dehazed by the GCAN are distorted, especially the images with sky. The CycleGAN, Cycle-Dehaze and DCEM basically retain the overall color information, but the first two are not as good as the DCEM in detail recovery, and neither are the others. Furthermore, the DCEM can dehaze more while retaining more original image information.

To prove the effectiveness of each modified structure, we implement an ablation study by designing experiments for each structure. The following architectures based on the CycleGAN are assessed: 1) Cycle-GAN: only the CycleGAN is used; 2) Cycle-GAN + R: only the multiresolution structure is added; 3) Cycle-GAN + D: only the multiscale discriminator is utilized; and 4) Cycle-GAN + P: only one pyramid pooling network is embedded in the generators.

Table 3. The PSNRs and SSIMs of models with different components using the OST

	Cycle-GAN	Cycle-GAN	Cycle-GAN	Cycle-GAN	Ours
PSNR	23.04	23.83	24.58	24.25	**24.74**
SSIM	0.848	0.852	0.878	0.877	**0.890**

3.4 Ablation Study

Table 3 is quantitative results of each contrast models. The models are trained in OTS. The average PSNRs and SSIMs of the test results are shown in Table architecture. It illustrates that all of the modified structures are effective at improving the evaluation indexes. Figure 5 shows the images dehazed by different architectures in the ablation study. Compared with the Cycle-GAN, the other three architectures effectively improve the quality of the dehazed images.

4 Conclusion

We propose an image dehazing method based on CycleGAN with an enhanced generator and a multiscale discriminator. The DCEM is based on CycleGAN does not rely on a physical model or paired data. The DCEM utilizes the enhanced generator and multiscale discriminator to improve the details and colors in dehazed images. The experiential results show that the CycleGAN gets the best PSNRs and SSIMs. Moreover, we have implemented an ablation experiment to prove the effectiveness of each structure of the DCEM.

Acknowledgment. This work was supported by the Key R&D Programs of Zhejiang under Grant(2022C01121).

References

1. Ancuti, C., Ancuti, C.O., De Vleeschouwer, C., et al.: Night-time dehazing by fusion. In: 2016 IEEE International Conference on Image Processing (ICIP), pp. 2256–2260. IEEE (2016)
2. Berman, D., Treibitz, T., Avidan, S.: Air-light estimation using haze-lines. In: 2017 IEEE International Conference on Computational Photography (ICCP), pp. 1–9. IEEE (2017)
3. Cai, B., Xu, X., Jia, K., et al.: Dehazenet: an end-to-end system for single image haze removal. IEEE Trans. Image Process. 25(11), 5187–5198 (2016)
4. Chen, D., He, M., Fan, Q., et al.: Gated context aggregation network for image dehazing and deraining. In: 2019 IEEE Winter Conference on Applications of Computer Vision (WACV). IEEE (2019)
5. Choi, Y., Choi, M., Kim, M., et al.: Stargan: unified generative adversarial networks for multi-domain image-to-image translation. In: Proceedings of the IEEE Conference on Computer Vision
6. Engin, D., Genç, A., Kemal Ekenel, H.: Cycle-dehaze: enhanced cyclegan for single image dehazing. In: Proceedings of the IEEE Conference on Computer Vision and Pattern Recognition Worksho
7. Goodfellow, I., Pouget-Abadie, J., Mirza, M., et al.: Generative adversarial nets. In: Advances in Neural Information Processing Systems, pp. 2672–2680 (2014)
8. He, K., Sun, J., Tang, X.: Single image haze removal using dark channel prior. IEEE transactions on pattern analysis and machine intelligence 33(12), 2341–2353 (2010). And Pattern Recognition. 2018: 8789–8797
9. Isola, P., Zhu, J.Y., Zhou, T., et al.: Image-to-image translation with conditional adversarial networks. In: Proceedings of the IEEE Conference on Computer Vision and Pattern Recognition, pp. 1125–1134 (2017)
10. Li, B., Peng, X., Wang, Z., et al.: Aod-net: all-in-one dehazing network. In: Proceedings of the IEEE International Conference on Computer Vision, pp. 4770–4778 (2017)
11. Li, B., Ren, W., Fu, D., et al.: Benchmarking single-image dehazing and beyond. IEEE Trans. Image Process. 28(1), 492–505 (2018)
12. Liao, Y., Su, Z., Liang, X., et al.: HDP-net: haze density prediction network for nighttime dehazing. In: Pacific Rim Conference on Multimedia, pp. 469–480. Springer, Cham (2018). https://doi.org/10.1007/978-3-030-00776-8_43
13. Radford, A., Metz, L., Chintala, S.: Unsupervised representation learning with deep convolutional generative adversarial networks. arXiv preprint arXiv:1511.06434, 2015

14. Silberman, N., Hoiem, D., Kohli, P., et al.: Indoor segmentation and support inference from rgbd images. In: European Conference on Computer Vision, pp. 746–1375–1383. Springer, Heidelberg (2012) https://doi.org/10.1007/978-3-642-33715-4_54
15. Tan, R.T.: Visibility in bad weather from a single image. In: 2008 IEEE Conference on Computer Vision and Pattern Recognition, 1–8. pp. 825–833. IEEE (2008)
16. Zhang, H., Patel, V.M.: Densely connected pyramid dehazing network. In: Proceedings of the IEEE Conference on Computer Vision and Pattern Recognition, 3194–3203.760 (2018)
17. Zhu, Q., Mai, J., Shao, L.: A fast single image haze removal algorithm using color attenuation prior. IEEE Trans. Image Process. 24(11), 3522–3533 (2015)
18. Zhu, J.Y., Park, T., Isola, P., et al.: Unpaired image-to-image translation using cycle-consistent adversarial networks. In: Proceedings of the IEEE International Conference on Computer Vision, pp. 2223–223 (2017)

Artificial Intelligence and Cognitive Science

Accurate and Rapid Localization of Tea Bud Leaf Picking Point Based on YOLOv8

Fengru Xu[1], Bohan Li[1], and Shuai Xu[1,2(✉)]

[1] Nanjing University of Aeronautics and Astronautics, Nanjing 211106, China
xushuai7@nuaa.edu.cn
[2] State Key Laboratory for Novel Software Technology,
Nanjing University, Nanjing 211106, China

Abstract. Aiming at the problem that agricultural tea picking robots cannot efficiently identify and locate tea bud picking points in complex environments, this paper applies YOLOv8 and OpenCV for accurate and rapid localization of tea bud picking points. Firstly, based on the collected tea tree dataset, bud and leaf target detection is performed using YOLOv8; Secondly, OpenCV was used to perform RGB-HSV color conversion in order to get the contours of tea bud leaves, then the selection of points is determined using morphological algorithms to locate them; Finally, experiment on the picking point localization method is carried out, where the results of multiple methods are compared. Empirical results show that: 1) For the improved YOLOv8 algorithm in bud leaf target detection, the accuracy is 92.65%, the recall rate is 70.13%, the AP value is 88.62%, and the F1 score is 0.80; 2) In terms of tea bud leaves under natural conditions, the precision of locating the picking point using OpenCV image processing method is 83.6%, and the recall rate was 86.0%, both outperforming comparison methods. These findings suggest that the proposed approach has practical utility for identifying the locations of tea bud leaf picking points.

Keywords: Object Detection · Picking Point Localization · Tea Bud Leaf · Image Processing · Deep Learning

1 Introduction

Accurate identification and localization of tea bud leaves picking points are the key links for the efficient operation of tea picking robots. Using artificial intelligence technology to carry out research of positioning method for picking tea bud leaves, changing the traditional method of manual picking, is of great significance to improving the efficiency of tea picking and alleviating labor shortages.

Existing studies have proposed corresponding analysis methods for the identification of tea tree buds and leaves: 1) traditional methods [1-3]; 2) deep learning methods [5-7]. For the traditional method, Yang et al. [1] first isolated the G1 component of the tea image within the RGB color space. They then utilized the distinctive shape characteristics of the tea tree buds and leaves to detect their edges. Wang et al. [2] divided the pixels in the color space, and then combined the color distance and edge distance for region growth and merging to segment tea tree buds and leaves. Zhang et al. [3] based on the RGB-D color space, relying on the difference in color and size between the buds and the background (old leaves, stems, soil) to identify on the color image. However, the method adopted in the above literature has high requirements for color discrimination and is easily affected by natural environments such as weather. For the deep learning method [4], Xu et al. [5] employed the Faster R-CNN model to detect tea tree buds and leaves, and the outcomes indicated that the algorithm exhibited a remarkable level of precision and recall. Wang et al. [6] extracted the features of tea image based on SSD algorithm, so as to realize the accurate and adaptive detection of tea buds and leaves. Xu et al. [7] proposed a two-level fusion network classification and detection method, combining YOLOv3 and DenseNet201 to achieve accurate detection of tea bud leaves. The methods described previously are effective in correctly distinguishing between tea tree buds and leaves in the image, but the recognition speed is slow and cannot meet the real-time requirements of automatic tea picking. YOLOv8 is currently the latest algorithm framework of the YOLO series. It integrates many current SOTA technologies, has high scalability, and has improved performance and flexibility.

Tea tree buds and leaves are small in size, so even a slight deviation in the picking location can negatively impact the quality of the buds and leaves. Therefore, after detecting the tea tree buds and leaves area, it is necessary to further determine the location of the picking point within the area. Chen et al. [8] utilized the FCN model [9] and the "moment" function in OpenCV to identify the precise locations where tea tree buds and leaves should be picked. FCN is a fully convolutional deep neural network, which classifies images at the pixel level and solves the semantic level image segmentation problem. Pei et al. [10] processed the outline of the tea tree buds and leaves to obtain a rectangle that tightly surrounds them, and then selected the center point of that rectangle as the picking point. Chen et al. [11] fed the picking point labeling information into the convolutional neural network and trained a good picking point recognition model, but using the convolutional neural network to identify the picking point area of tea tree buds and leaves cannot obtain specific and accurate features. It is prone to multiple misidentifications.

The aim of this research is to employ the YOLOv8 algorithm for the detection of tea tree bud leaves, followed by extracting the contour of these buds and leaves within the designated region using the HSV color threshold segmentation technique, and use the OpenCV morphological algorithm to find the feature points that meet the conditions, in order to provide accurate information for picking points. Positioning provides useful reference.

2   Materials and Methods

2.1   Image Acquisition

The bud leaf data of Taiping monkey head in this study were collected in the tea garden base of Taiping District, Huangshan City. The collection equipment was a Nikon digital camera, and the corresponding two-dimensional image resolution was 6 000 pixels × 4 000 pixels. In order to prevent the model from overfitting and increase its robustness, more than 5,000 pictures of tea trees in multi-climate environments and with different bud and leaf densities were collected. Figure 1 is a set of image datasets of tea tree buds and leaves.

Fig. 1. Some samples of the dataset

2.2 Labeling and Partitioning of Datasets

Typically, premium-grade tea is composed of either one leaf and one bud or two leaves and one bud, and the research object of this paper, Taiping Monkey Kui tea, is a typical representative of two leaves and one bud, which is highly sought after by tea lovers. In order to obtain better detection effect, the two leaves and one bud part of the enhanced tea tree bud leaf dataset are labeled with LabelImg software, as shown in Fig. 2, the target area to be detected is framed with a closed rectangular wireframe, and the type of target is marked. 70% of the labeled dataset was randomly selected as the training set, while the remaining 30% was designated as the test set.

Fig. 2. The labeling for the dataset

2.3 YOLOv8 Object Detection Algorithm Model

The YOLO series object detection algorithm converts the detection problem into a regression problem, which is a typical end-to-end algorithm model [12], and only one basic convolutional network operation is required to obtain the value of the marquee area, position information and confidence of the target detection object, which greatly enhances the efficiency of detection.

YOLOv8 is the latest algorithm framework in the YOLO series, and its network characteristics make it superior to other known deep learning methods in real-time and accuracy of object detection. YOLOv8 outperformed YOLOv5 on the official COCO Val 2017 dataset. The diagram depicting the architecture of YOLOv8 can be observed in Fig. 3.

The YOLOv8 network is composed of three main components: the Backbone network for feature extraction, the Neck network for feature fusion, and the Head network for output prediction. The YOLOv8 network first preprocesses the image, resizes it to $640 \times 640 \times 3$, and then enters it into the Backbone network. The Convolutional (Conv) module and the Channel-to-Feature (C2f) module both perform downsampling on the input feature map by halving its length and width, while also doubling the number of output channels compared to the number of input channels. The Conv module comprises a convolutional layer (Conv), a batch normalization layer (BN), and a SiLU activation function[13]. The C2f module is a new structure proposed by YOLOv8 based on the original YOLO idea, which is composed of different convolutions, and the convolution group operation is employed to ensure that the number of channels in each set of feature maps matches the number of channels in the original architecture. There are also more hopping layer connections and additional Split operations in the structure, which realizes the multiplexing of features and continuously improves the learning ability of the network, thereby improving the accuracy of target detection. Finally, Backbone network introduces the SPPF (Spatial Pyramid Pooling with Factorized Convolutions) structure, which involves processing the input through multiple layers of MaxPooling and extracting features by pooling kernels of different sizes, thus increasing the receptive field of the network[14].

The Neck network, which follows the backbone network, will generate feature maps of varying sizes, consisting of three layers each, based on the output of the three-layered backbone network. The Neck network consists of a series of Conv modules and C2f modules, and includes Upsample and Concat operations. Upsampling is a technical means of sampling low-resolution images into high-resolution images[15], and Concat is a channel-level connection operation[16]. The Neck network realizes multi-scale feature fusion by passing features in both directions, so that feature maps of different sizes can finally be output at the same size.

The three-layer output of the feature fusion network Neck is input to the final prediction network Head, following the adjustment of the channel number in the final output by the Conv module, a convolution operation with a kernel size of 1x1 is utilized to accomplish the tasks of prediction and classification, thereby obtaining the ultimate results for target detection.

2.4   Tea Bud Leaf Picking Point Positioning Method

After the model identifies the tea plant bud leaf area in the detected image, it needs to separate the target bud leaf area for further processing, Fig. 4(a) is the detected tea tree bud leaf image, and the value on the detection box is the confidence level. To

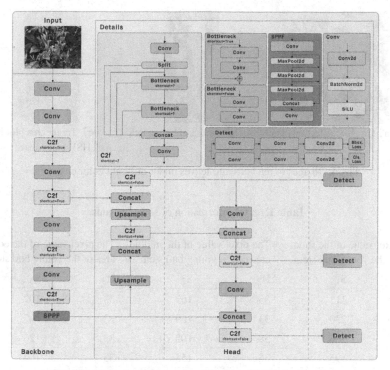

Fig. 3. The network structure diagram of YOLOv8 model

precisely determine the position of the point where the object is to be picked up, the outline of the tea bud leaves also needs to be extracted. Figure 4(b) and Fig. 4(c) are respectively pictures of tea bud and leaf areas under the RGB color channel and HSV color channel, respectively, due to the variable change of external light and shooting angle, so the sample map of buds in bright places and stems in dark places will be generated under RGB channels, and the threshold range of the target part is difficult to determine. However, under the HSV channel, it is not affected by this factor, and the threshold information has a great deal of certainty. Through comparative analysis, it can be obtained that the color transition of the background part of tea tree bud leaves and old leaves under the H and S color channels is obvious, so the outline of the bud leaves is extracted under the H and S channels.

A common method of contour extraction is threshold segmentation, which separates the target from the background based on color characteristics. Under the HSV color model, the values of the H and S channels determine the hue and saturation of the pixel, and the value of V determines the brightness of the pixel under the corresponding color characteristics. Since the brightness information cannot distinguish the bud leaves from the background, the value ranges of H and S in the threshold segmentation are determined by randomly selecting several points according to three specific parts of the bud leaves from 100 HSV images containing tea tree bud leaves, and some of the data are shown in Table 1.

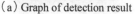

（a）Graph of detection result 　（b）Graph of target area 　（c）Target area plot in HSV color space

Fig. 4. Images of tea buds and leaves under different color channels

Table 1. Pixel information of some tea buds.

The pixel value of the shoot area of the young bud stem		The pixel value of the middle area of the young bud stem		The pixel value of the edge area of the young bud stem	
H_1	S_1	H_2	S_2	H_3	S_3
41	213	33	161	33	102
39	230	33	169	33	107
41	160	38	103	33	123
39	195	36	155	33	104
44	171	35	240	37	184

The average values of H and S in the above three specific regions are calculated, and the value ranges of H and S in the overall tea bud and leaf regions can be obtained after comparative analysis, and the relevant formulas are as follows:

$$\overline{H}_j = \frac{\sum_1^n H_i}{n}, n = 100, j = 1, 2, 3 \tag{1}$$

$$\overline{S}_j = \frac{\sum_1^n S_i}{n}, n = 100, j = 1, 2, 3 \tag{2}$$

$$H \in (\min(\overline{H}_j), \max(\overline{H}_j)), j = 1, 2, 3 \tag{3}$$

$$S \in (\min(\overline{S}_j), \max(\overline{S}_j)), j = 1, 2, 3 \tag{4}$$

where: i is a randomly selected pixel; j = 1, 2, 3 represent three specific regions of tea bud leaves, respectively, from Eqs. (1) and (2) can obtain the mean information of pixels H and S of different parts of the young bud, substituting Eqs. (3) and (4) to obtain:

$$H \in (33, 47) \tag{5}$$

$$S \in (90, 240) \tag{6}$$

According to the threshold information obtained in Eqs. (5) and (6), the outline of tea plant shoots was binarized and extracted, Set the values of the pixels that satisfy H ∈ (33,47) and S ∈ (90,240) respectively to 255, and vice versa to 0, as shown in (7):

$$g(x, y) \begin{cases} 255 & (H \in (33, 47) \text{ and } S \in (90, 240)) \\ 0 & (\text{other}) \end{cases} \tag{7}$$

where g(x,y) is the pixel value at x pixels abscissa and y pixels in ordinate for the binary image after segmentation.

The median filtering of the binary image to remove the salt and pepper noise generated during the threshold segmentation process shows the effect shown in Fig. 5(a). Then the image is corroded to separate the bud leaves from the bud stem, and the leaf stem melt line appears. Since the corrosion operation will scatter the target bud leaf area, it is necessary to find its maximum communication area after the morphological operation, and obtain part of the young shoots profile as shown in Fig. 5(b), and the dotted line is the location of the fuse line. At this point, the intersection of the circuit breaker line and the target picking area is the ideal picking point, and the pixels at this location are

(a) Binary contour extraction of tea young bud   (b) Picking point localization

Fig. 5. The process of locating the picking point of tea buds

(a) Horizontal path of single young bud picking point   (b) Picking point positioning

Fig. 6. Location of tea plant shoots picking point

expanded into rectangular bars 30 pixels long and 10 pixels wide, defining them as the lateral path of the picking point. As shown in Fig. 6(a), the red area is the horizontal path of the picking point, and the two-dimensional pixel coordinates of the picking point can be obtained by restoring it to the original figure, and the final effect is shown in Fig. 6(b).

3 Experiment and Discussion

3.1 Operating Conditions and Training Process

This study uses the YOLOv8 model. The experiment runs on the Windows 10 operating system, the processor is Intel Xeon E5, the main frequency is 2.3 GHz, the running memory is 32 GB, and the GPU used for training is RTX 3090. The program runs in a virtual Python environment built by Anaconda, where Pytorch version is 1.13.0.

The model was optimized using the SGD optimizer, the optimizer momentum parameter was 0.937, the total training generation of the model was 100, the basic learning rate was 0.001, the weight decay coefficient was 0.0005, the number of batch samples was 8, and the EMA decay coefficient was 0.9999.

The graphs in Fig. 7 indicate that the training and test sets' loss curves have converged, suggesting that the detection model's final version has reached a stable state.

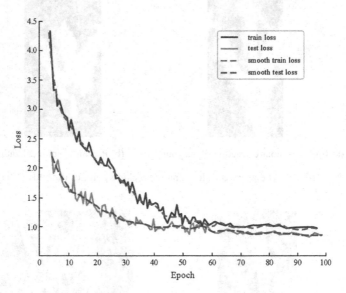

Fig. 7. Loss curve of training set and verification set

3.2 Detection Results and Comparative Analysis

Figure 8 demonstrates the effectiveness of the detection model in identifying tea bud leaves under natural circumstances, as most of the leaves are accurately detected using the methodology employed in this study.

Fig. 8. Tea bud leaves detection results

To conduct a more thorough analysis of the efficacy of the YOLOv8 detection model in identifying tea bud leaves, it was compared with YOLOv4 [17] and YOLOv3 [18]. The comparison experiments of the models are all trained and tested on the same dataset. Figure 9 shows the comparison of the detection results of the three methods under natural conditions, and it can be seen that for the same tea plant dataset, the YOLOv8 model detected 17 bud leaf regions, the YOLOv4 model detected 12 bud leaf regions, and the YOLOv3 model detected 8 bud leaf regions. For the part of the bud leaf that is obscured by the leaf in the picture, YOLOv8 shows better performance.

(a) YOLOv8   (b) YOLOv4   (c) YOLOv3

Fig. 9. Comparison of detection results

The commonly used evaluation indicators of detection models are mAP and FPS, the former representing average accuracy and the latter representing deduction speed. The mAP value is calculated from the Precision and Recall of the predictive model. In this study, for single object detection, the average accuracy can be expressed by the AP (average precision) value, which is the area enclosed by the precision-recall curve, and the F_1 score is used to represent the harmonic mean of precision and recall. Precision, Recall, and F1score are calculated in formulas such as (8), (9), and (10).

$$\text{Precision} = \frac{TP}{TP + FP} \times 100\% \tag{13}$$

$$\text{Recall} = \frac{TP}{TP + FN} \times 100\% \tag{14}$$

$$\text{F1score} = 2\frac{\text{Precision} \times \text{Recall}}{\text{Precision} + \text{Recall}} \tag{15}$$

If the target to be detected is positive class and the others are negative class, then: TP is positive class prediction is positive class, FN is positive class prediction is negative class, FP is negative class prediction is positive class, TN is negative class prediction is negative class.

Figure 10 displays the precision-recall curves for the three models. Through comparison, it can be found that the closed area of the YOLOv8 curve is larger than the area before the improvement, that is, the AP value is higher, the average accuracy is higher, and the detection effect of the convolutional neural network is better.

Table 2 shows the Precision, Recall, Average precision, F1 score, and FPS that can be processed for different models. The results show that the network complexity and network density of the YOLOv8 model are higher, which makes the detection accuracy higher than that of other models. The Precision value of the YOLOv8 model is 92.65%, which is 5.23% higher than YOLOv4 and 8.49% higher than YOLOv3. The Recall value of the YOLOv8 model is 70.13%, which is 4.35% higher than YOLOv4 and 18.71% higher than YOLOv3. The AP value of the YOLOv8 model is 88.62%, which is 5.02% higher than YOLOv4 and 12.29% higher than YOLOv3. The YOLOv8 model has an F1 score of 0.80, which is 0.05 higher than that of YOLOv4 and 0.16 higher than that of YOLOv3. It can be obtained that the YOLOv8 model used in this study can improve the accuracy of tea tree bud leaf detection and achieve the purpose of real-time detection, which is the most suitable for the application requirements of the three detection models.

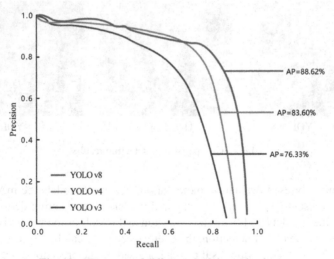

Fig. 10. PR curves of different models on the data set

Table 3 presents a comparison between this approach's accuracy and that of other methods for detecting tea bud leaves. In Table 3, Lv et al. trained and learned tea buds and leaves of different open shapes based on the AlexNet recognition model, and the recognition accuracy was 88%. The tea tree bud leaves were identified by Chen et al. using the Faster R-CNN model with an accuracy of 79%. Zhou et al. segmented tea buds and leaves based on the K-means method of high chromatic separation pretreatment, and the recognition accuracy was above 80%. Zhang et al. built a deep learning model

Table 2. Model performance index evaluation and comparison

Evaluation indicators	Precision/%	Recall/%	AP/%	F1score	FPS
YOLOv8	92.65	70.13	88.62	0.80	9.30
YOLOv4	87.42	65.78	83.60	0.75	8.70
YOLOv3	84.16	51.42	76.33	0.64	7.30

Table 3. Comparison of YOLOv8 and other tea bud leaves recognition methods

The source of the method	Method	The precision of the identification %
Lv et al. 2019 [19]	AlexNet recognition model	88
Chen et al. 2020 [8]	Faster R-CNN recognition model	79
Zhou et al. 2020 [20]	K-means method for high chromatic separation pretreatment	>80
Zhang et al. 2021 [21]	ResNet recognition model	90.99
Methods for this article	YOLOv8 recognition model	92.65

for green tea based on ResNet CNN, and the recognition accuracy was 90.99%. The YOLOv8 model was utilized in this study to detect tea bud leaves, and the recognition accuracy achieved was 92.65%.

3.3 Picking Point Positioning Results and Comparative Analysis

The tea tree bud leaf test set was passed into the picking point positioning model for testing, and the results ar e shown in Fig. 11. Among them, P(w,h) on the positioning box is the pixel coordinate position corresponding to the picking point, with the vertex in the upper left corner of the picture as the origin, w is the number of abscissa pixels corresponding to the picking point, and h is the number of ordinate pixels corresponding to the picking point.

In this study, a number of evaluation indicators were obtained for the proposed circuit breaker intersection point method, where TP is the number of correctly positioned picking points, FP is the number of erroneously positioned picking points, and FN is the number of unlocated picking points. It is compared with the moment function method, the least circumscribed rectangle center point method, and the convolutional network training method, and the results are shown in Table 4. As can be seen, the fusing line intersection method achieves 83.6% accuracy and 86.0% recall in locating tea plant bud picking points. Compared with the moment function method, the precision is improved by 6.3% and the recall is improved by 4.3%. Compared with the smallest bounded rectangle center point method, the precision rate is improved by 9.9%, and the recall

Fig. 11. Location results of picking points for multiple plants

rate is improved by 8.9%. Compared with the convolutional network training method, the accuracy is improved by 7.2%, and the recall rate is slightly insufficient. In addition, the average time of locating a picking point in this study is 0.136 s, so it can meet the accuracy and speed requirements required for picking point localization.

Table 4. Comparison of evaluation indicators

Method of positioning	TP	FP	FN	Precision/%	Recall/ %
Fusing line intersection method	1003	197	168	83.6	86.0
Moment function method	908	266	202	77.3	81.8
The smallest bounded rectangle center point method	856	305	254	73.7	77.1
Convolutional network training method	928	287	142	76.4	86.7

4   Conclusion

A new approach for identifying the locations where tea bud leaves should be picked using the YOLOv8 algorithm was introduced in this research. On the one hand, the backbone network and feature fusion network of the YOLOv8 model have introduced a new module C2f, which alleviates the phenomenon of gradient disappearance by enhancing the density between network layers, strengthens the propagation and reuse of features, and improves the detection accuracy of tea bud leaves. In other words, using the OpenCV image processing method to identify picking points within the target area results in an precision rate of 83.6% and a recall rate of 86.0%, compared to other positioning methods, this approach demonstrates an improvement of at least 6.3% and 4.3%, respectively.

The experimental results show that for the tea buds and leaves in the natural environment, this research method can achieve good results in locating picking points, which provides useful reference for tea picking robots. In order to further improve the small target detection capability of the model and expand the application scenarios, the attention mechanism will continue to be improved in the next step.

Acknowledgments. This work was supported in part by the Natural Science Foundation of Jiangsu Province under Grant No. BK20210280, in part by the Fundamental Research Funds for the Central Universities under Grant No. NS2022089, and in part by the Jiangsu Provincial Innovation and Entrepreneurship Doctor Program under Grant No. JSSCBS20210185.

References

1. Yang, F.Z., Yang, L.L., Tian, Y.N., et al.: Identification method of tea shoots based on color and shape characteristics. Trans. Chin. Soc. Agricult. Mach. **40**(S1), 119–123 (2009)
2. Wang, J.: Research on tea image segmentation algorithm combining color and regional growth. Tea Science **31**(1), 72–77 (2011)
3. Zhang, B.: Research on tea identification and localization technology based on RGB-D: [Master's thesis]. Shenyang University of Technology, Shenyang (2020)
4. Zhao, Z.Q., Zheng, P., Xu, S.: Object detection with deep learning: a review. IEEE Trans. Neural Networks Learn. Syst. **30**(11), 3212–3232 (2019)
5. Xu, G.J., Zhang, Y., Lai, X.Y.: Image recognition method of tea shoots based on Faster R-CNN deep network. Optoelectron. Laser **31**(11), 1131–1139 (2020)
6. Wang, Z.Y.: Research on Tea Bud Detection Technology Based on Image. Shenyang University of Technology, Shenyang (2020)
7. Xu, W., Zhao, L., Li, J., et al.: Detection and classification of tea buds based on deep learning. Comput. Electron. Agric. **192**, 106547 (2022)
8. Chen, Y.T., Chen, S.F.: Localizing plucking points of tea leaves using deep convolutional neural networks. Comput. Electron. Agricult. **171**(C): 105298–105298 (2020)
9. Long, J., Shelhamer, E., Darrell, T.: Fully Convolutional Networks for Semantic Segmentation. IEEE Trans. Pattern Anal. Mach. Intell. **39**(4), 640–651 (2015)
10. Pei, W., Wang, X.L.: Extraction of two-dimensional picking coordinates of tea leaves based on image information. Zhejiang J. Agricult. Sci. **28**(3), 522–527 (2016)
11. Chen, M.T.: Identification and localization of famous tea shoots based on computer vision. Qingdao University of Science and Technology (2019)
12. Redmon, J., Divvala, S., Girshick, R.: You only look once: Unified, real-time object detection. In: Conference on Computer Vision and Pattern Recognition. Las Vegas, USA, pp. 779–788. IEEE (2016)
13. Elfwing, S., Uchibe, E., Doya, K.: Sigmoid-weighted linear units for neural network function approximation in reinforcement learning. Neural Netw. **107**, 3–11 (2018)
14. Wu, W., Liu, H., Li, L., et al.: Application of local fully Convolutional Neural Network combined with YOLO v5 algorithm in small target detection of remote sensing image. PLoS ONE **16**(10), e0259283 (2021)
15. Nie, X., Ding, H., Qi, M., et al.: Urca-gan: Upsample residual channel-wise attention generative adversarial network for image-to-image translation. Neurocomputing **443**, 75–84 (2021)
16. Zeng, Q., Li, X., Lin, H.: Concat Convolutional Neural Network for pulsar candidate selection. Mon. Not. R. Astron. Soc. **494**(3), 3110–3119 (2020)
17. Bochkovskiy, A., Wang, C.Y., Liao, H.Y.M.: Yolov4: Optimal speed and accuracy of object detection. arXiv preprint arXiv:2004.10934 (2020)

18. Redmon, J., Farhadi, A.: YOLOv3: an incremental improvement. arXiv preprint arXiv:1804. 02767 (2018)
19. Lv, J., Xia, H.L., Fang, M.R., et al.: Research on intelligent identification of tea bud state based on AlexNet. J. Heilongjiang Bayi Agricultural Reclamation Univ. **31**(2), 72–78 (2019)
20. Zhou, Z.: Study on identification of young K-means tea leaves based on high color difference separation pretreatment. Guangdong Sericult. **54**(11), 74–75 (2020)
21. Zhang, Y., Zhao, Z.M., Wang, X.C., et al.: Construction of green tea variety recognition model based on ResNet convolutional neural network. Tea Sci. **41**(2), 261–271 (2021)

Compressor Fault Diagnosis Based on Graph Attention Network

Junqing Shen[1], Shenjun Zheng[1], Tian Tian[1], Yun Sun[1], Hongru Wang[1],
Jun Ni[1], Ronghu Chang[1], and Dongwei Xu[2(✉)]

[1] ChinaOly Technology, Hangzhou, China
[2] Zhejiang University of Technology, Hangzhou, China
dongweixu@zjut.edu.cn

Abstract. This paper presents a novel method for diagnosing compressor faults using the Graph Attention Network (GAT). Specifically, we address the challenge of analyzing multivariate time series data generated by compressors. Our proposed method consists of three main steps. Firstly, we construct a temporal graph for each variable of the multivariate time series using the Limited Penetrable Visibility Graph (LPVG) to capture the temporal dependencies within each variable. Subsequently, we feed these temporal graphs into the GAT to obtain a representation of each variable. Secondly, we leverage the inter-variable dependencies by constructing an adaptive inter-variable graph, where each node represents a variable, and the node feature is the previously obtained variable representation. We then input this inter-variable graph into another GAT to further capture the dependencies between variables. Finally, we use the output from the GAT to train a classifier for fault diagnosis, resulting in an end-to-end model. Our proposed method outperforms existing techniques in diagnosing faults in a real dataset.

Keywords: Compressor Fault Diagnosis · Multivariate Time Series · Limited Penetrable Visibility Graph · Graph Attention Network

1 Introduction

Compressors are a type of driven fluid machinery that serves a crucial role in industrial equipment and modern machinery by elevating low-pressure gas to high-pressure gas. They are also considered as the core component of refrigeration systems. However, faults often occur during the operation of compressors due to several factors, including insufficient exhaust capacity, overheating, abnormal temperature and pressure, corrosion erosion, bearing wear, and shell cracks. When a compressor malfunctions, it can result in a chain of adverse effects that may lead to the failure of the compressor or other associated parts, or even to the complete shutdown of the entire refrigeration system, resulting in significant

Supported by the Key R&D Programs of Zhejiang under Grant (2022C01121).

economic losses, and potentially endangering lives. As a result, it is impera-tive to diagnose any potential faults in the compressor to prevent these adverse outcomes.

When compressor working, we can collect the monitoring data of the com-pressor through a variety of sensors, and the compressor fault diagnosis is gen-erally based on those data. Monitoring data, which are multivariate time series, consist of variables such as current, voltage and vibration data. When using mul-tivariate time series for compressor fault diagnosis, we need to assume a priori that there is a correlation between different variables. The value of a variable at a certain time depends not only on the historical values, but also on other variables. This makes us capture not only the dynamic relationship of data in time, but also the relationship between variables in space when we do fault diag-nosis. But the relationship between variables is often complex and nonlinear. This brings the problem that when a possible fault occurs, the values of some fault-sensitive variables change, while other variables are the same as the normal values. Or no fault occurred, but some variables changed abnormally. Therefore, it is necessary to construct the relationship between variables efficiently. How-ever, traditional methods emphasize the temporal relationship, but ignore the relationship between variables, but our method focuses on this.

Graphs provide an effective tool for depicting relationships between multiple variables. Graph Neural Networks (GNNs), which operate on graph structures, have achieved remarkable results owing to their superior characteristics such as permutation-invariance and local connectivity. The core of GNNs lies in message passing, which facilitates the perception of changes in neighbor nodes. Among the various GNN architectures, the Graph Convolutional Network (GCN) and the Graph Attention Network (GAT) are commonly used. GAT, unlike other GNNs, allows for adaptive attention allocation, enabling it to determine the importance of neighbor nodes.

In the context of multivariate time series analysis, we can represent the data as a graph structure, where each node represents a single variable, and the edge between nodes represents the correlation between variables. We can extract the representation of the univariate time series as the feature of the corresponding node. Given the sensitivity of the relationship between variables, we consider GAT to be a suitable option for modeling the graph structure of the multivariate time series.

In this study, we propose a novel method for compressor fault diagnosis utiliz-ing Graph Attention Network. The monitoring data generated during compressor operation comprises multivariate time series. Our proposed method employs two different graphs that correspond to two distinct graph construction approaches. Firstly, we utilize the Limited Penetrable Visibility Graph (LPVG) to transform univariate time series into a temporal graph. The nodes of this graph correspond to the data points in the time series, and the edge relationships between nodes are established based on the LPVG method. Secondly, we construct an inter-variable graph that reflects the relationships between variables. In this graph, each node represents a variable, and we adaptively establish the edge relationships between nodes. The main contributions of our study are as follows:

- In our proposed method, we first utilize the LPVG method to construct a temporal graph for each univariate time series, thereby capturing the relationship between data points. Subsequently, the graph attention network is employed to extract features of the temporal graph, resulting in a representation of each univariate time series.
- We then utilize an adaptive approach to construct an inter-variable graph that captures the relationship between variables. Before training, we initialize the relationship between variables randomly and then update the relationship automatically during the training process.
- The feature extracted in the first step serves as the node feature in the inter-variable graph in the second step. Another graph attention network is then utilized to extract the representation of the inter-variable graph. Finally, the resulting representation is employed in fault diagnosis.
- Our proposed method has achieved promising results on real-world compressor data, demonstrating its effectiveness in compressor fault diagnosis.

The rest of this paper is organized as follows. In Sect. 2, an overview of the related work is provided. The proposed method is described in Sect. 3. The experimental results are presented in Sect. 4. Section 5 concludes the paper.

2   Related Work

Fourier Transform (FT) is a mathematical technique that enables the conversion of a signal from time domain to frequency domain. The analysis of the time domain signal is accomplished by studying the characteristics of the frequency domain signal [1,2]. The FT method transforms the relatively complex time and space signals into the frequency domain, and then the characteristics of the original signals are analyzed by analyzing the frequency spectrum. In practical applications, the Fast Fourier Transform (FFT) algorithm is commonly used. For fault detection of induction motor, Pandarakone et al. [3] proposed a deep learning-based approach that uses FFT to analyze the load current of the stator, and then extract features of selected frequency components with Convolutional Neural Network (CNN). Yoo et al. [4] noted that FFT has difficulties in finding the fault characteristic frequency component, and proposed to use Principal Component Analysis (PCA) to extract features from the FFT signal, and then employ Hotelling's T^2 to measure the fault. However, the global nature of the frequency spectrum produced by the Fourier transform prevents it from effectively describing the local characteristics of signals in the temporal dimension. Although the Fourier transform can clearly identify the frequency components contained in a signal, it is difficult to associate different time signals with the corresponding frequency components, thereby rendering the Fourier analysis less useful for more sophisticated analysis. To overcome this limitation, Short-time Fourier Transform (STFT) has been developed as an improved method [5]. STFT divides the entire time-domain signal into small time-domain signals and performs Fourier transform on each of them to obtain the characteristics of the local region in the time dimension. Many methods based on STFT have been proposed [6–9]. BENKEDJOUH et al. [10] developed a deep learning-based method for fault diagnosis using STFT. Their approach analyzed data obtained under different speed and load conditions, and constructed a multi-fault classifier based on STFT to diagnose various faults.

The Wavelet transform is a transform analysis method similar to Fourier transform, which builds on and extends the principles of Fourier transform, and resolves the limitation of the window size not changing with frequency. It is a highly suitable method for analyzing and processing signals in the time-frequency domain [11,12]. Deng et al. [13] proposed a fault diagnosis method that integrates empirical wavelet transform, fuzzy entropy, and support vector machine (SVM) to demonstrate the superiority of empirical wavelet transform in signal decomposition through experiments. Chen et al. [14] proposed a fault diagnosis method that combines resonance sparse signal decomposition and wavelet transform to prove the effectiveness and applicability of their approach. Yu et al. [15] developed a technique for analyzing non-stationary signals of rotating machinery, utilizing a polynomial chirplet transform (PCT) with a synchro extracting transform (SET) to complete the analysis and demonstrate its superiority. Ali et al. [16] employed discrete wavelet transform (DWT) to analyze Induction Motor faults. They evaluated the threshold and energy values of each decomposition level for the DWT analysis and used the threshold as a criterion for fault diagnosis.

Empirical Mode Decomposition (EMD) is a signal decomposition method that separates a signal into its intrinsic mode functions (IMFs) based on the signal's own temporal characteristics without using any predefined basis functions [17]. This feature gives EMD a distinct advantage in handling nonlinear and non-stationary data. Wang et al. [18] proposed a fault diagnosis method based on EMD which combines the fault correlation patterns with different noises in a nonlinear and adaptive manner using multiple learning algorithms. This method extracts features corresponding to the fault and completes bearing fault diagnosis.

Fault diagnosis methods based on machine learning are widely used in many applications. The commonly used methods include Principal Component Analysis (PCA) [19], Support Vector Machine (SVM) [20], and K-Nearest Neighbor (KNN) [21]. Wang et al. [22] proposed a network based on Stacked Sparse Autoencoder, which mainly consists of SVM and PCA, and used this network to improve the accuracy of fault diagnosis. Sanchez et al. [23] proposed a fault diagnosis method based on KNN and random forest. They calculated 30 features in the time domain, 24 features commonly used in fault diagnosis of rotating machinery, and 6 features in the electrogram field from vibration signals. Fault diagnosis was carried out according to KNN and random forest, and good results were obtained in five datasets. Long et al. [24] proposed a motor fault diagnosis method using an attention mechanism, improved AdaBoost for multi-sensor information, Hilbert transform, and Fourier transform.

With the rapid growth and expansion of Artificial Neural Networks (ANNs), research in the field has permeated all areas of life and has become the primary direction for the development of artificial intelligence. Owing to their superior learning capability for nonlinear data, neural networks have found numerous applications across different domains, including fault diagnosis [25–28]. Commonly employed neural network models for fault diagnosis include Convolutional Neural Networks (CNNs) [29,30], Autoencoders (AEs) [31,32], Recurrent Neural Networks (RNNs) [32], Long Short Term Memory (LSTM) networks [29,33,34], among others. Zhong et al. [35] proposed a functional mapping method based on CNNs, which can extract fault dataset features and apply them to fault diagnosis by reusing the CNNs trained on normal datasets. Shao et al. [36] proposed a novel method for feature learning based on deep Autoencoders for fault diagnosis. Firstly, they designed a new loss function using maximum entropy for the depth Autoencoder to improve its ability to learn from vibration signals. Secondly, they optimized key parameters of the depth Autoencoder using an artificial fish-swarm algorithm to extract signal features and achieve accurate fault diagnosis. Huang et al. [37] proposed a variational auto-encoder model based on RNN for fault diagnosis. The model first extracts time-series data features using the variational auto-encoder based on RNN, followed by further feature extraction using PCA and linear difference analysis, resulting in improved fault diagnosis accuracy. Han et al. [38] proposed a CNN-based deep learning algorithm for diagnosing motor faults. They treated the vibration signal as an image and processed it using CNN, while also considering the motor driving speed in the processing. Cabrera et al. [39] proposed a fault diagnosis method based on LSTM, which combines the Bayesian search algorithm with LSTM to optimize hyperparameters. They also employed an efficient time-series dimensionality reduction method to reduce the computing time required for LSTM to capture fault modes.

3   Compressor Fault Diagnosis Based on Graph Attention Network

The framework of our model is shown in Fig. 1. The input of the model is multivariate time series. For each univariate time series, the temporal graph corresponding to the time series is constructed by LPVG, and then the features of the temporal graph are extracted by GAT, and the output node features are concatenated to get the representation of this time series. At the same time, we adaptively construct an inter-variable graph that reflects the relationship between variables. Each node represents a variable in this inter-variable graph, and the node feature is the representation of the variable. In Sect. 3.1, we introduce the process of building a graph using LPVG, and in Sect. 3.2, we introduce the process of using GAT to extract the features of a graph. The process of adaptive construction of inter-variable graph is introduced in Sect. 3.3. The process of using GAT to extract features of the inter-variable graph and fault diagnosis is introduced in Sect. 3.4.

3.1   Construction of Temporal Graph

For a time series data $X = \{X_i\}(i = 1, 2, ..., n)$, we can transform it into a temporal graph using the method LPVG, i.e., Limited Penetrable Visibility Graph [40].

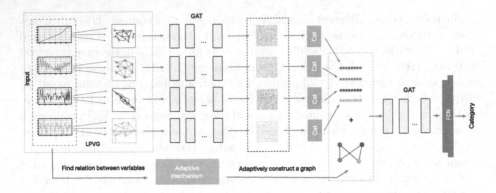

Fig. 1. The framework of our proposed method

Specifically, we define N as limited penetrable line-of-sight, which means we can penetrate at most N obstacles and see objects obscured by these obstacles. For any two data points in a time series, if and only if the number of times n that the visual line between the two data points is truncated by the data points between them satisfies $n \leq N$, we think that after constructing the graph, the corresponding nodes of the two data points are connected. Figure 2 shows the connection of limited penetrable visibility graph when N is set to 1. The solid line in Fig. 2 indicates that the visual line between the two data points is not truncated by other data points, and the dotted line indicates that the visual line between the two data points is truncated by other data points. Whether the connection line between the two data points is solid or dashed, we all think that the two data points are connected to each other as long as they meet the above conditions. Different temporal graphs can be obtained for the same time series with different N.

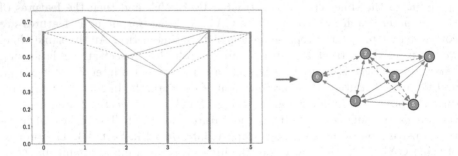

Fig. 2. The schematic diagram of LPVG

3.2   Feature Extraction of Temporal Graph

Given a temporal graph G built in 3.1, the input of the attention layer in a GAT is a set of node features in G, $h^l = \{h_1^l, h_2^l, ..., h_N^l\}$, $h_i^l \in \mathbb{R}^{d_l}$. Where N is the number of nodes, l is the l-th layer in GAT and d^l is the dimension of feature vectors in layer l. GAT first carries out a linear transformation for the input node features, and then uses a shared feature linear transformation weight $W^l \in \mathbb{R}^{d^{l+1} \times d^l}$ to transform low-dimensional features into higher-dimensional features. Then the attention mechanism is implemented for the high-dimensional features of each node itself (The purpose of implementing the self-attention mechanism for the node itself is to consider the influence of its own) and its first-order neighbor nodes, and get the attention matrix e^l. Each element in the attention matrix represents the attention coefficient between the two nodes, and the calculation formula is as follows:

$$e_{ij}^l = \delta \left(W^l h_i^l, W^l h_j^l \right) \tag{1}$$

where $W^l h_i^l$ represents linear transformation, $\delta(\cdot)$ represents attention mechanism, which is equivalent to a single-layer feedforward neural network, and e_{ij}^l represents the importance of node j to node i. Because the GAT only considers the attention between the node i itself and its first-order neighbor node set $N_i (j \in N_i)$. Elements in the attention matrix without edge relationships are assigned to be zero. In order to make the attention coefficient more standardized and easy to calculate, we first use the LeakyReLU function for the elements in the attention matrix $\mathbf{e}$, and then normalize all the neighbor nodes and themselves of node i to obtain the standardized attention matrix α^l. The calculation formula of its elements is as follows:

$$\alpha_{ij}^l = \frac{\exp \left(\text{LeakyReLU} \left(e_{ij}^l \right) \right)}{\sum_{k \in N_i} \exp \left(\text{LeakyReLU} \left(e_{ik}^l \right) \right)} \tag{2}$$

The normalized attention coefficient is combined with the high-dimensional features of node i and its neighbors to update the node features, and the node output of the next layer is obtained as follows:

$$h_i^{l+1} = \sigma \left(\sum_{j \in N_i} \alpha_{ij}^l W^l h_j^l \right) \in \mathbb{R}^{d^{l+1}} \tag{3}$$

where $\sigma(\cdot)$ is the activation function. In order to ensure the stability of the self-attention mechanism, the multi-head attention mechanism is usually added to the Graph Attention Network. The graph attention layer repeats the above steps K times and concatenates the K outputs as follows:

$$h_i^{l+1} = \overset{K}{\underset{k=1}{\|}} \sigma \left(\sum_{j \in N_i} \alpha_{ij}^l W^l h_j^l \right) \tag{4}$$

Finally, the updated node features are obtained as $H = \{h_1, h_2, ..., h_N\}$

3.3 Construction of Inter-variable Graph

For different types of compressor faults, faults are generally reflected in some variables (vibration, current, etc.). Therefore, we build an inter-variable graph to reflect the hidden relationship between them. Specifically, the nodes of the inter-variable graph are variables, and the edge relationship between nodes reflects the relationship between variables. Because we do not know the relationship between variables in advance, we use neural network to find out the relationship between variables adaptively. Here we use the method proposed by Wu et al. [41] to build this graph. The build process is shown in the following formula:

$$M_1 = \tanh(\alpha E_1 \theta_1) \tag{5}$$

$$M_2 = \tanh(\alpha E_2 \theta_2) \tag{6}$$

$$A = \text{ReLU}(\tanh(\alpha(M_1 M_2^\mathsf{T} - M_2 M_1^\mathsf{T}))) \tag{7}$$

$$idx = \text{argtopk}(A[i :]) \tag{8}$$

$$A[i, -idx] = 0 \tag{9}$$

where E_1 and E_2 in formulas (5) and (6) are randomly initialized node features(These node features are not used to fault diagnosis), respectively, and can be updated in model training. θ_1 and θ_2 in formulas (5) and (6) are the parameters, α is the hyperparameter of the activation function tanh, the return value of the argtopk function in formula (8) is the index of the top-k largest values in the vector, and the A in formula (7) and (9) is the corresponding adjacency matrix of the inter-variable graph.

3.4 Feature Extraction of Inter-variable Graph and Fault Diagnosis

Given o variables, after extracting the features for each variable according to the description in Sect. 3.1, we can get the o node feature set $H_1, H_2, ..., H_o$. As shown in the Fig. 1, we perform a Flatten operation on the node feature set corresponding to each variable, i.e., all the node features in the node feature set corresponding to the variable are concatenated, and the resulting one-dimensional representation is used as the feature of the variable in the inter-variable graph. For a built inter-variable graph G_v, the node feature set in the G_v is $H_v = \{H_1, H_2, ..., H_o\}$. We put them into a Graph Attention Network to extract the features between variables. Finally the features are input into the full connection layer to get the category output. The specific process is as follows. Firstly, the attention coefficient between nodes is calculated according to the feature set $H_v = \{H_1, H_2, ..., H_o\}$:

$$E_{ij} = \delta(W_v H_i, W_v H_j) \tag{10}$$

where E_{ij} is the attention coefficient of node j to node i in the inter-variable graph, $\delta(\cdot)$ represents the attention mechanism, W_v is linear transformation matrix and H_i and H_j represent the features of node i and the features of node j, respectively. Secondly the attention matrix A_v between nodes is calculated, and the calculation formula of each element in the matrix is as follows:

$$a_{v_{ij}} = \frac{\exp \text{LeakyReLU}(E_{ij})}{\sum_{k \in N_i} \exp \text{LeakyReLU}(E_{ik})} \quad (11)$$

Then the attention matrix and node features are put into the Graph Attention Network for calculation, and the output feature of node i in the inter-variable graph are obtained:

$$H_i = \sigma \left(\sum_{j \in N_i} a_{v_{ij}} W_v H_j \right) \quad (12)$$

Finally, the output features of the inter-variable graph are passed through a Softmax layer to get the final fault category.

4   Experiments

4.1   Dataset

In order to verify the effectiveness of our model, we take the real data collected from a fully enclosed refrigeration compressor as our dataset. The current data and three-dimensional vibration data of the refrigeration compressor are collected when the refrigeration compressor is in the normal state, the inner calandria touching the stator, the crank hitting the inner calandria, the support spring falling off, the suction muffling loosening and the suction valve piece foreign body. When collecting, the sampling is carried out at seven different sampling points on the refrigeration compressor, the sampling time of each point is 20 s, and the sampling frequency is 25.6 kHz, so the amount of data of the refrigeration compressor in each state is 14025.6k. The speed of the compressor is 3000 rpm, so the speed cycle of the compressor is 512. The collected data include normal data of one kind of compressor and fault data of five types of compressors. Because the original collected multivariate time series is very long, we need to split it and take the segmented multivariate time series as the data of our model.

4.2   Hyperparameters

When splitting the total multivariate time series, because the vibration period of the compressor is 512, we take 512 as the length of each sub-series, so the size of the adjacency matrix of the temporal graph is 512×512; when constructing the inter-variable graph, because the number of variables used in this experiment is 4, the size of the adjacency matrix of the inter-variable graph is 4×4. When extracting the features of the temporal graph, the number of multi-heads set by the Graph Attention Network is 6, and the number of units in the hidden layer is 128 and 64 respectively. When extracting the features of the inter-variable graph, the number of multi-heads set by the Graph Attention Network is 8, and the number of units in the hidden layer is 128 and 64 respectively. In the model training, we set the ratio of the training set and the test set to 8 : 2 respectively. For each variable of different fault categories, the sample data of training set and test set are 5600 and 1400 respectively. The sample numbers of the five types of fault compressors selected in the test set are 232 and the normal compressor samples are 240.

4.3   Comparison Models

In order to verify the effectiveness of our proposed method. We take the Graph Convolutional Network (GCN) and the Graph Attention Network (GAT) which only consider the temporal dimension characteristics but do not consider the relationship between variables as the comparison models. At the same time, we add some classical machine learning classification methods as comparison models: Classification and Regression Tree (CART), Random Forest (RF), Boosting Tree (BT) and KNN.

4.4   Results

We present a visualization of the three-dimensional vibration data of each kind of compressor fault, as illustrated in Fig. 3, which demonstrates the characteristic diagrams of the three-dimensional vibration data of the compressor in normal state and in different fault states, respectively. It can be observed that significant differences exist between different types of compressor faults in Fig. 3 when we examine the vibration data from the X-axis and Y-axis. However, when we combine the three-dimensional vibration data, we find that the vibration conditions of different types of compressors are very similar. Figure 4 depicts the three-dimensional spatial diagram of the vibration data of compressors under different types of faults, comprising a category of normal compressor samples and five types of compressor samples with different faults. The figure reveals that the vibration modes between different categories are highly similar, and the classification of compressor faults based on a section of three-dimensional vibration data is inaccurate. Due to the large volume of data and the irregularity of data changes, identifying the types of faults becomes even more challenging.   To demonstrate the effectiveness of constructing a graph for feature extraction from time series data, we conducted experiments to compare our proposed method with machine learning algorithms. These algorithms are proficient in capturing the characteristics of time series data and mining hidden features to classify the data. The results of these experiments are presented in Table 1. From the table, it can be observed that the classification accuracy of the CART decision tree algorithm is poor, only reaching 70.74%. This algorithm uses the Gini index to measure the purity of the dataset. However, due to its ineffective preprocessing of time series data, its sensitivity is low, resulting in poor performance. The prediction accuracy of KNN is also relatively low, as it relies on capturing the changing patterns of historical data to predict the closest data point. However, due to the irregular vibration of compressor faults, KNN does not achieve good results. On the other hand, the BT algorithm achieves an accuracy that is nearly

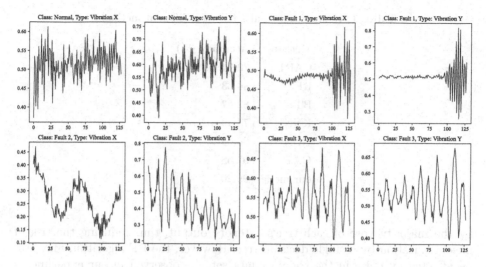

Fig. 3. Vibration data under different fault conditions

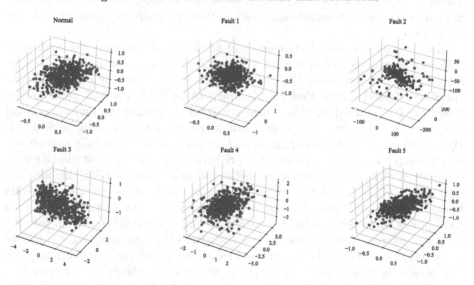

Fig. 4. Three-dimensional map of vibration data under different types of faults

14% higher than that of the CART algorithm. This is because the BT algorithm introduces the concept of residual to each base classifier. During training, it constantly changes the weight of training samples according to the training results, learns multiple base classifiers, and linearly combines the classifiers with different weights to improve the performance of the final classification. RF achieved the highest prediction accuracy, reaching 86.33%, compared to other machine learning algorithms. The success of RF can be attributed to its ability to contain multiple sub-decision trees, where the category of its output is determined

Table 1. Comparison results between different methods

Method	Accuracy (%)
CART	70.74
RF	86.33
BT	82.67
KNN	74.49
GCN	96.03
GAT	97.58
our model	99.20

by the majority vote of each tree's category output, thus reducing the risk of misclassification by a single decision tree. However, the RF algorithm may still be affected by noise in the training data sets, as observed in our experiments where there was a certain amount of noise in the compressor vibration data. Such noise can lead to overfitting, which in turn can result in reduced prediction accuracy.

To demonstrate the effectiveness and feasibility of the proposed method in this section, we compared it with Graph Convolutional Network (GCN) and Graph Attention Network (GAT) which do not consider the relationship between variables. Table 1 shows that the accuracy of GCN, GAT, and multivariate-based GAT is more than 95%. These results demonstrate the significance and efficacy of constructing a temporal graph based on timing data in Sect. 3.1. By constructing the temporal graph and utilizing the GAT to fully extract the relationship between data points, the prediction accuracy of fault classification is improved. The GAT shows a prediction accuracy that is 1.53% higher than that of the GCN. The GCN assigns the same weight when assigning weights between nodes, even though it can also extract the feature correlation between data points. However, the GCN does not account for the differences in features between different data points. In contrast, the GAT can adaptively calculate an attention coefficient based on the characteristics of the neighboring nodes and assign the weight between the nodes accordingly. Therefore, it can update the node features adaptively during training and achieve higher classification accuracy.

Furthermore, the proposed method constructs not only the temporal graph but also the inter-variable graph, which can fully extract the temporal features and the relationship between variables. In model training, the inter-variable graph is trained adaptively, enabling the final extracted features to include not only the temporal features of different variables but also the relationship between variables, which greatly improves the final prediction accuracy.

5   Conclusion

In this paper, a novel approach is proposed for compressor fault diagnosis using Graph Attention Network (GAT). This method introduces a new idea for diagnosing faults in multivariate time series data, which takes into account the spatio-temporal characteristics of the data, especially the importance of spatial correlation to fault diagnosis. The proposed approach employs graph neural networks as a powerful tool for fault diagnosis. The results of our experiments on real data collected from a compressor demonstrate that the proposed method achieves better accuracy in fault diagnosis compared to existing methods. It is worth noting that the proposed approach can also be applied to motor fault diagnosis, which is also related to the analysis and diagnosis of multivariate time series data.

Acknowledgements. This work was supported by the Key R&D Programs of Zhejiang under Grant (2022C01121).

References

1. Bracewell, R.: The Fourier Transform and its Applications, 2nd edn. McGraw-Hill Kogakusha Ltd., Tokyo (1978)
2. Bracewell, R.N.: The fourier transform. Sci. Am. **260**(6), 86–9, 92–5 (1989
3. Pandarakone, S.E., Masuko, M., Mizuno, Y., Nakamura, H.: Deep neural network based bearing fault diagnosis of induction motor using fast fourier transform analysis. In: 2018 IEEE Energy Conversion Congress and Exposition (ECCE), pp. 3214–3221. IEEE (2018)
4. Yoo, Y.-J.: Fault detection of induction motor using fast fourier transform with feature selection via principal component analysis. Int. J. Precis. Eng. Manuf. **20**(9), 1543–1552 (2019)
5. Griffin, D.W., Lim, J.S.: Signal estimation from modified short-time fourier transform. In: ICASSP (1983)
6. De Santiago-Perez, J.J., Rivera-Guillen, J.R., Amezquita-Sanchez, J.P., Valtierra-Rodriguez, M., Romero-Troncoso, R.J., Dominguez-Gonzalez, A.: Fourier transform and image processing for automatic detection of broken rotor bars in induction motors. Meas. Sci. Technol. **29**(9), 095008 (2018)
7. Aimer, A.F., Boudinar, A.H., Benouzza, N., Bendiabdellah, A., et al.: Bearing fault diagnosis of a PWM inverter fed-induction motor using an improved short time fourier transform. J. Electr. Eng. Technol. **14**(3), 1201–1210 (2019)
8. Wang, L.-H., Zhao, X.-P., Wu, J.-X., Xie, Y.-Y., Zhang, Y.-H.: Motor fault diagnosis based on short-time fourier transform and convolutional neural network. Chinese J. Mech. Eng. **30**(6), 1357–1368 (2017)
9. Vippala, S.R., Bhat, S., Reddy, A.A.: Condition monitoring of bldc motor using short time fourier transform. In: 2021 IEEE Second International Conference on Control, Measurement and Instrumentation (CMI), pp. 110–115. IEEE (2021)
10. Benkedjouh, T., Zerhouni, N., Rechak, S.: Deep learning for fault diagnosis based on short-time fourier transform. In: 2018 International Conference on Smart Communications in Network Technologies (SaCoNeT), pp. 288–293(2018)

11. Zhang, D.: Wavelet transform. In: Fundamentals of Image Data Mining, pp. 35–44, Springer (2019)
12. Pathak, R.: The Wavelet Transform. Atlantis Studies in Mathematic, Atlantis Press/World Scientific (2009)
13. Deng, W., Zhang, S., Zhao, H., Yang, X.: A novel fault diagnosis method based on integrating empirical wavelet transform and fuzzy entropy for motor bearing. IEEE Access **6**, 35042–35056 (2018)
14. Chen, B., Shen, B., Chen, F., Tian, H., Xiao, W., Zhang, F., Zhao, C.: Fault diagnosis method based on integration of RSSD and wavelet transform to rolling bearing. Measurement **131**, 400–411 (2019)
15. Yu, K., Lin, T.R., Ma, H., Li, H., Zeng, J.: A combined polynomial chirplet transform and synchro extracting technique for analyzing nonstationary signals of rotating machinery. IEEE Trans. Instrum. Meas. **69**(4), 1505–1518 (2019)
16. Ali, M.Z., Liang, X.: Induction motor fault diagnosis using discrete wavelet transform. In: 2019 IEEE Canadian Conference of Electrical and Computer Engineering (CCECE), pp. 1–4. IEEE (2019)
17. Asr, M.Y., Ettefagh, M.M., Hassannejad, R., Razavi, S.N.: Diagnosis of combined faults in rotary machinery by non-naive bayesian approach. Mech. Syst. Signal Process. **85**, 56–70 (2017)
18. Wang, J., Du, G., Zhu, Z., Shen, C., He, Q.: Fault diagnosis of rotating machines based on the EMD manifold. Mech. Syst. Signal Process. **135**, 106443 (2020)
19. Lachouri, A., Baiche, K., Djeghader, R., Doghmane, N., Ouhtati, S.: Analyze and fault diagnosis by multi-scale PCA. In: 2008 3rd International Conference on Information and Communication Technologies: From Theory to Applications, pp. 1–6. IEEE (2008)
20. Widodo, A., Yang, B.-S.: Application of nonlinear feature extraction and support vector machines for fault diagnosis of induction motors. Expert Syst. Appl. **33**(1), 241–250 (2007)
21. Samanta, S., Bera, J., Sarkar, G.: Knn based fault diagnosis system for induction motor. In: 2016 2nd International Conference on Control, Instrumentation, Energy & Communication (CIEC), pp. 304–308. IEEE (2016)
22. Wang, Y., Liu, M., Bao, Z., Zhang, S.: Stacked sparse autoencoder with pca and svm for data-based line trip fault diagnosis in power systems. Neural Comput. Appl. **31**(10), 6719–6731 (2019)
23. Sanchez, R.-V., Lucero, P., Vásquez, R.E., Cerrada, M., Macancela, J.-C., Cabrera, D.: Feature ranking for multi-fault diagnosis of rotating machinery by using random forest and KNN. J. Intell. Fuzzy Syst. **34**(6), 3463–3473 (2018)
24. Long, Z., et al.: Motor fault diagnosis using attention mechanism and improved adaboost driven by multi-sensor information. Measurement **170**, 108718 (2021)
25. Xu, X., Cao, D., Zhou, Y., Gao, J.: Application of neural network algorithm in fault diagnosis of mechanical intelligence. Mech. Syst. Signal Process. **141**, 106625 (2020)
26. Sheikholeslami, M., Gerdroodbary, M.B., Moradi, R., Shafee, A., Li, Z.: Application of neural network for estimation of heat transfer treatment of al2o3-h2o nanofluid through a channel. Comput. Methods Appl. Mech. Eng. **344**, 1–12 (2019)
27. Smyrnis, G., Maragos, P., Retsinas, G.: Maxpolynomial division with application to neural network simplification. In: ICASSP 2020–2020 IEEE International Conference on Acoustics, Speech and Signal Processing (ICASSP), pp. 4192–4196. IEEE (2020)
28. Tang, S., Yuan, S., Zhu, Y.: Convolutional neural network in intelligent fault diagnosis toward rotatory machinery. IEEE Access **8**, 86510–86519 (2020)

29. Pan, H., He, X., Tang, S., Meng, F.: An improved bearing fault diagnosis method using one-dimensional CNN and LSTM. Strojniski Vestnik/J. Mech. Eng. **64** (2018)

30. Peng, D., Liu, Z., Wang, H., Qin, Y., Jia, L.: A novel deeper one-dimensional CNN with residual learning for fault diagnosis of wheelset bearings in high-speed trains. IEEE Access **7**, 10278–10293 (2018)

31. Kingma, D.P., Welling, M.: An introduction to variational autoencoders. arXiv preprint arXiv:1906.02691 (2019)

32. Liu, H., Zhou, J., Zheng, Y., Jiang, W., Zhang, Y.: Fault diagnosis of rolling bearings with recurrent neural network-based autoencoders. ISA Trans. **77**, 167–178 (2018)

33. Zhao, H., Sun, S., Jin, B.: Sequential fault diagnosis based on lstm neural network. Ieee Access **6**, 12929–12939 (2018)

34. Qiao, M., Yan, S., Tang, X., Xu, C.: Deep convolutional and LSTM recurrent neural networks for rolling bearing fault diagnosis under strong noises and variable loads. IEEE Access **8**, 66257–66269 (2020)

35. Zhong, S.-S., Fu, S., Lin, L.: A novel gas turbine fault diagnosis method based on transfer learning with CNN. Measurement **137**, 435–453 (2019)

36. Shao, H., Jiang, H., Zhao, H., Wang, F.: A novel deep autoencoder feature learning method for rotating machinery fault diagnosis. Mech. Syst. Signal Process. **95**, 187–204 (2017)

37. Huang, Y., Chen, C.-H., Huang, C.-J.: Motor fault detection and feature extraction using RNN-based variational autoencoder. IEEE Access **7**, 139086–139096 (2019)

38. Han, J.-H., Choi, D.-J., Hong, S.-K., Kim, H.-S.: Motor fault diagnosis using CNN based deep learning algorithm considering motor rotating speed. In: 2019 IEEE 6th International Conference on Industrial Engineering and Applications (ICIEA), pp. 440–445. IEEE (2019)

39. Cabrera, D., et al.: Bayesian approach and time series dimensionality reduction to LSTM-based model-building for fault diagnosis of a reciprocating compressor. Neurocomputing **380**, 51–66 (2020)

40. Gao, Z.-K., Cai, Q., Yang, Y.-X., Dang, W.-D., Zhang, S.-S.: Multiscale limited penetrable horizontal visibility graph for analyzing nonlinear time series. Sci. Rep. **6**(1), 1–7 (2016)

41. Wu, Z., Pan, S., Long, G., Jiang, J., Chang, X., Zhang, C.: Connecting the dots: multivariate time series forecasting with graph neural networks. In: Proceedings of the 26th ACM SIGKDD International Conference on Knowledge Discovery & Data Mining, pp. 753–763 (2020)

Conductance-Threshold Dual Adaptive Spiking Neural Networks for Speech Recognition

Shasha Zhou and Xianghong Lin[✉]

College of Computer Science and Engineering, Northwest Normal University, Lanzhou 730070, China
linxh@nwnu.edu.cn

Abstract. Spiking neural networks (SNNs) have become popular in brain-like computing due to their biological plausibility and computational power. SNNs use spike coding to integrate temporal and frequency characteristics of information, making them advantageous for processing dynamic time-series signal-related problems such as speech signals. However, to effectively simulate the neural system and solve practical problems, it is crucial to construct a suitable spiking neuron model with realistic physiological properties and computational efficiency. In this work, we proposed a dual adaptive Integrate-and-Fire neuron model (DAIF) with dynamic conductance and threshold, which has more biologically realistic dynamics and is relatively simple to compute. Based on this model, a recurrent neural net-work for speech recognition was constructed using different spiking neuron models, leading to the establishment of a complete speech recognition model. We also conducted simulation experiments on the DAIF model and tested it on the Spike Heidelberg Digits (SHD) dataset, yielding good experimental results. Our work highlights the potential value of constructing efficient spiking neuron models for speech recognition tasks.

Keywords: Spiking Neuron Model · Recurrent Spiking Neural Network · Surrogate Gradient · Speech Recognition · Neuromorphic Computing

1 Introduction

Speech recognition is an important technology in artificial intelligence technology, a human-computer interaction technique that enables efficient text entry. In recent years, it has been discovered by researchers that artificial neural networks (ANNs), particularly deep neural networks (DNNs), are extremely efficient in performing au-tomatic speech recognition (ASR) tasks. This is primarily due to their capacity to handle large amounts of training data and their high computational resources. Compared to traditional Gaussian mixture models (GMM) and other techniques, DNNs have demonstrated superior performance on different speech datasets, and have consequently emerged as the dominant method in speech recognition [1]. Speech recog-nition technology has also started to move from the laboratory to the market, with applications in multiple scenarios such as smart homes and mobile devices, becoming necessary for these applications to be able to be implemented.

SNNs have received much attention as an important model of brain-like neural computation [2, 3]. In SNNs, neurons transmit information through precisely timed spike trains [4], which is a beneficial tool for processing complex spatio-temporal information. Many researchers have conducted studies on SNNs for speech recogni-tion tasks, resulting in some promising results. Wu et al. [5] proposed using MFCC as the front-end and combining with self-organizing mapping (SOM) to extract the features of speech, so that the input information is converted into spike trains; Zhang et al. [6] used a Liquid State Machine (LSM) to extract information from input patterns and combined it with an online learning algorithm. Dong et al. [7] proposed the mechanism of unsupervised con-volutional spiking neural network (CSNN) and linear support vector machine (SVM). Wu et al. [8] proposed a speech recognition network based on ANN-SNN weight sharing. Yao et al. [9] extended the concept of attention to temporal input and proposed a Temporal-Wise Attention SNN (TA-SNN) model with temporal attention mechanism. Sun P et al. [10] introduced a learnable axonal delay during training. However, most of the researches on speech recognition based on spiking neural networks focus on feature extraction, coding and learning algorithms of speech signals, but ignore the importance of spiking neuron model (SNM) for solving practical problems.

In this paper, we firstly summarize the existing spiking neuron models, integrate the requirements of neurodynamic characteristics and computational efficiency of neuron models, and make a compromise between physiological realism and compu-tational cost to propose a dual adaptive Integrate-and-Fire neuron model, which takes into account both the change of firing threshold and the change of conductance during the process of neuron information transmission. Secondly, different spiking neuron models are used to construct recurrent neural networks and complete speech recognition models are established to explore the performance of different spiking neuron models in speech recognition tasks. Finally, we do simulation experiments on the proposed DAIF neuron model, and perform several experiments on SHD speech dataset. Our experiments demonstrate that the accuracy of speech recognition can be enhanced by constructing reasonable neuron models.

2   Dual Adaptive Integrate-and-Fire Model

Research shows that neuron is the basic unit of nervous system [11, 12], and is the basis for nervous system to deal with complex problems. Based on the different cog-nition and understanding of biological neurons and the need of different computa-tional functions, researchers have proposed many spiking neuron computational models. In 1907, Lapicque[13] simulated the neurophysiological phenomena of neu-rons with electronic circuits and constructed the earliest neuron model Integrate-and-Fire (IF) neuron model. In 1952, biologists Hodgkin and Huxley carried out a large number of experiments and analysis on squid axons, and proposed Hodgkin-Huxley (H-H) model [14]. This neuron model carries out mathematical modeling according to the electrodynamic mechanism of action potential, uses four nonlinear differential equations to express the electrody-namic characteristics of neuron, lays the theoretical foundation for nervous impulse and conduction experiments, and is considered as the neuron model with the most biolog-ical plausibility. Leaky Integrate-and-Fire (LIF) neuron model [15] is simplified from

H-H model, only considering the leakage current in H-H model, expressed by first-order differential equation, which intuitively de-scribes the relationship between the membrane potential of neuron and its input cur-rent. It is the most commonly used neuron model in spiking neural networks because of its computational simplicity. Because LIF neuron model contains only one varia-ble and cannot express the complex neurodynamic characteristics of neurons, re-searchers have successively proposed many variant of the models, such as: the time-dependent Spike Response Model (SRM) [16], the adaptive Leaky Integrate-and-Fire Model (ALIF) with adaptive threshold [17], Double Exponential Adaptive Threshold Model (DEXAT) with double exponential decay threshold [18], Adaptive Exponential Integrate-and-Fire Model (AELIF) with exponential adaption [19], the Conductance-based Adaptive Exponential Integrate-and-Fire Model (CadEx) [20], etc. However, their improvements are one-sided.

A large number of experimental analyses have shown that the conductance of ion channels in the neuronal axonal membrane is not constant and they strongly depend on the membrane potential. During the formation of action potentials, the refractory period is characterized by an increase in firing threshold and conductance after the spike-firing. We combine the advantages of more realistic physiological properties of the H-H model and higher computational efficiency of the LIF model, and consider the changes of conductance and threshold: On the one hand, the change of conduct-ance takes into account the temporal asymptotic characteristics of input current, on the other hand, the change of threshold controls the firing rate of action potential. In this paper, a dual adaptive Integrate-and-Fire neuron model (DAIF) with dynamic conductance and threshold is proposed, which simulates richer neurodynamic char-acteristics while possessing high computational efficiency, expressed by the following equation:

$$\tau_m \frac{dV}{dt} = -g_L(V - V_L) + I - g_A(V - V_A) \tag{1}$$

$$\tau_a \frac{dg_A}{dt} = -g_A \tag{2}$$

$$\tau_{th} \frac{dV_{th}}{dt} = -V_{th} \tag{3}$$

where τ_m is membrane time constant, g_A is time-dependent adaptive conductance, V_L and V_A is an associated reversal potential, V_{th} is dynamic threshold potential for spike-firing, when the membrane potential V is greater than or equal to the threshold potential, the neuron immediately generates excitation, i.e., fire spikes, accompanied by action potential conduction, and resetting the membrane potential.

After the neuronal membrane potential accumulates to reach the threshold and fire a spike, the membrane potential and the dynamic changes of conductance and threshold are according to the following auxiliary reset mechanism:

$$if\ V \geq V_{th}\ then \begin{cases} V \leftarrow V_{reset} \\ V_{th} \leftarrow V_{th} + \Delta V_{th} \\ if\ g_A \leq \bar{g}_A\ then\ if\ g_A \leftarrow g_A + \Delta g_A\ else\ g_A \leftarrow \bar{g}_A \end{cases} \tag{4}$$

where $\overline{g}_A$ is the maximal subthreshold adaptation conductance, V_{reset} is the reset value. Combining Eqs. (1), (2) and (3): each output spike increases the conductance g_A and threshold V_{th} by a fixed amount, when $g_A \geq \overline{g}_A$, the conductance no longer increases and between spikes the conductance g_A and threshold V_{th} decays with the adaptation time constant.

In general, the differential equations are solved numerically by approximating the model equations with finite differences, using Euler equation discretization to obtain the expression for the dual adaptive Integrate-and-Fire neuron model as follows:

$$V(t+1) = \alpha V(t) + (1-\alpha)\big[I - g_A(t)\,(V(t) - V_A)\big] \tag{5}$$

$$g_A(t+1) = \beta g_A(t) + \Delta g_A \cdot S(t) \; if \; g_A(t) \leq \overline{g}_A \; else \; g_A(t+1) = \overline{g}_A \tag{6}$$

$$V_{th}(t+1) = \rho V_{th}(t) + \Delta V_{th} \cdot S(t) \tag{7}$$

where $\alpha = \exp(-\Delta t / \tau_m)$, $\beta = \exp(-\Delta t / \tau_a)$, $\rho = \exp(-\Delta t / \tau_{th})$.

3   Recurrent Spiking Neural Networks

A spiking neural network model consists of a large number of interconnected neurons that transmit information in the form of spikes. However, in living organisms, the layer connection of neurons is not limited to feed-forward connections. Instead, neu-rons receive feed-back signals from themselves and other neurons in addition to sig-nals from previous neurons. Recurrent spiking neural network (RSNN) is a model of spiking neural network with feed-forward connections and feed-back connection loops. Compared with Feed-Forward Spiking Neural Network (FSNN), the feedback connection of Recurrent Spiking Neural Network (RSNN) makes it more realistic in biology. Additionally, this structure can represent more complex time-varying information and has certain memory characteristics.

For the application of this research, we construct a dual adaptive spiking neural network model with recurrent structure. As shown in the right side of Fig. 1, it includes one or more hidden recursion layers, which are jointly composed of the dual adaptive Integration-and-fire neuron model and the LIF neuron model. Among them, the dual adaptive Integration-and-Fire neuron model is used for the input layer and the hidden recursion layer of the network model. The LIF neuron model is only used in the output layer. In Fig. 1, we show the speech recognition model. Firstly, the speech signal is converted into spike trains, and the spike trains is used as the income of SNN. At this time, the SNN based on DAIF is used for learning, and finally the speech recognition result is output.

It can be found that the speech recognition model, no matter in the input data module or the network structure module, is developed around the spike trains, which makes the model very similar to the biological neural activity in the speech recognition process.

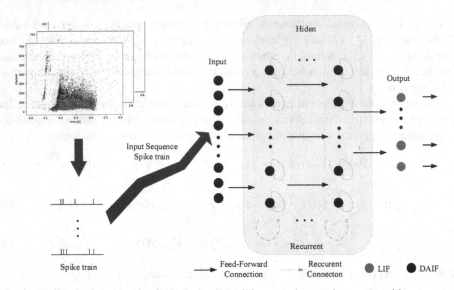

Fig. 1. An illustrative example of a dual adaptive spiking neural network structure with a recurrent structure is shown. First, we show a sample speech data set, followed by the input spike trains, and finally the recurrent spiking neural network model.

4 Surrogate Gradient Methods

In a spiking neural network, Whether the spike is emitted is determined by the mem-brane potential and threshold,

$$S(t) = \Theta(V(t) - V_{th}) \tag{8}$$

where S is spike, V is membrane potential, V_{th} is the fixed threshold, Θ is the Heavyside step function, expressed as:

$$\Theta(x) = \begin{cases} 1, & x \geq 0 \\ 0, & x < 0 \end{cases} \tag{9}$$

when the membrane potential reaches the threshold potential, the spike is fired, and the spike state is recorded as 1; otherwise, the spike is not fired, and is recorded as 0.

The learning algorithms of traditional artificial neural network, such as error-based back propagation algorithm, need to differentiate the Heavyside step function when using the chain rule for error back propagation. From Eq. (9), we can easily find that the value of the function only jumps at the instant of spike-firing, and its deriva-tive with respect to time is infinite at the instant of spike-firing, and is zero at other positions. That is, a gradient burst condition occurs at the time of pulse emission, and a gradient collapse condition occurs at other times. Therefore, the traditional super-vised learning algorithm of artificial neural network can not be used directly for spik-ing neural network.

In the study of supervised learning algorithm for spiking neural networks, researchers propose a method to replace gradient called surrogate gradient [25, 26], that is, to replace the derivative of the spiking function Θ with a continuous smooth function: $d\Theta/dV$. The problem of non-differentiability of spike firing function Θ is avoided. It is experimentally shown that the surrogate gradient method achieves an accuracy comparable to or even higher than the existing algorithms on several datasets [27, 28]. It is experimentally shown that the surrogate gradient method achieves an accuracy comparable to or even higher than the existing algorithms on several data sets. In fact, the surrogate gradient is not unique, and it can be replaced by a variety of approximation functions, such as sigmoid function, gaussian function, and boxcar function. In this paper, we choose to use the boxcar function, whose expression is

$$\frac{d\Theta}{dV} = \frac{\partial S[t]}{\partial V[t]} = \begin{cases} 0.5 & \text{if} \quad |V[t] - V_{th}| \leq 0.5 \\ 0 & \text{otherwise} \end{cases} \tag{10}$$

The boxcar function is simple to compute and has values only in a certain time range before and after the moment of spike-firing, which can avoid the gradient ex-plosion caused by the derivative becoming infinite at the moment of pulse issuance, and the gradient is available in a certain time range before and after the moment of spike-firing, preserving the temporal relationship of the spiking neural network.

5 Experiment and Result

5.1 DAIF Neuron Simulation Experiment

Brian2 is a simulator of neuroscience, which can accurately simulate the principle of neurons. With Brian2, researchers can model and simulate the behavior of individual neurons and study the interactions between neurons in neural networks. This enables them to gain insights into how the brain processes information and how it can be emulated using artificial neural networks.

In order to fully understand the working principle of our proposed DAIF neuron model, Brain2 was used to conduct neuron simulation experiments on a single neuron based on the differential equation of the DAIF neuron model described in Sect. 2. As shown in Fig. 2, we simulated the changes of membrane potential (Fig. 2 (b)), conductance and threshold adaptation (Fig. 2 (c) - (d)) of a single DAIF neuron model with constant current (Fig. 2 (a)). The following parameter values were used during the simulation: $\Delta V_{th} = 2$ mV, $\Delta g_A = 0.5$ nS, $I = 1.0$ nA.

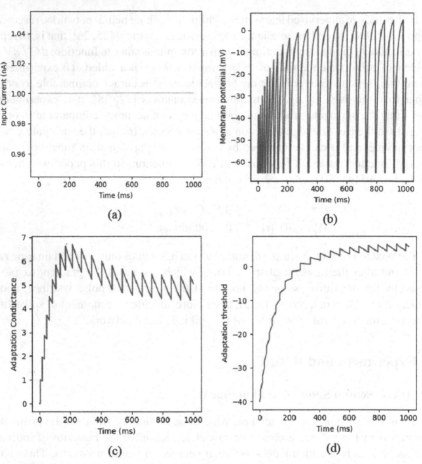

Fig. 2. Simulation results for single neuron. (a) The input constant current of a neuron. (b) Neuron membrane potential changes. (c) The adaptation conductance in response to the inputs. (d) The adaptation threshold in response to the inputs.

5.2 Speech Recognition Experiment

Datasets. To verify the effectiveness of our proposed dual adaptive Integrate-and-Fire neuron model (DAIF) with conductance and threshold, we evaluated our proposed model on the recently published Spiking Heidelberg Digits (SHD) dataset by Cramer et al. [21]. This dataset was developed specifically for benchmarking of spiking neural networks, using the cochlear implant model Lauscher to process raw audio signals to generate spike trains of 700 input channels with high time complexity. The SHD dataset contains 10420 samples from 12 different speakers, ranging from 0.24 s to 1.17 s, for 20 digit classes from "0" to "9" in English and German, with 8,332 samples in the training set and 2,088 samples in the test set. It shows a sample from the SHD dataset in Fig. 3.

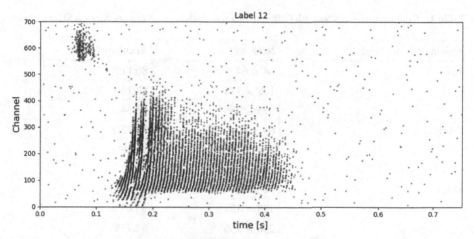

Fig. 3. A sample labeled 12 of SHD dataset.

Results and Analysis. This experiment uses our proposed dual adaptive Integrate-and-Fire neuron model with conductance and threshold to construct the spiking neural network, and also uses LIF and ALIF neuron models to construct the spiking neural network with the same structure. Generally speaking, the accuracy of the neural network model will be improved with the increase of the network size, but it also means that more computing resources need to be consumed, which is more prone to overfitting. Therefore, we did multiple experiments. For the spiking neural network composed of each neuron model, the number of hidden layers is 2, and different numbers of hidden layer neurons are set, which are 64, 128 and 256 respectively. The detailed comparison is shown in Table 1.

As can be seen from Table 1, for the SHD dataset, the recognition accuracy of our proposed model is higher than that of speech recognition based on other neuron models under three network sizes. At the same time, with the increase of the number of hidden layer neurons, the accuracy of speech recognition is improved to some extent. Our experimental results show that our proposed neuron model achieves the highest accuracy of 93.67% when the network size is 128 × 128. That is, our model can achieve better results in smaller network sizes, showing certain advantages of the model.

Figure 4 shows the effect of the number of iterations on the accuracy of the validation set for a network size of 128 × 128.It can be seen from the Fig. 3., with the progress of training, the speech recognition accuracy gradually converges, and the accuracy fluctuation also gradually decreases with the increase of iteration times. It should be noted that the accuracy has reached a high level when the number of iterations is less than 20, but the accuracy of the experiment fluctuates greatly at this time, indicating that the network does not converge at this time, and further training is needed to provide the stability of the model performance.

Table 1. Comparison of SNNs with Different Neuron Models and Network Size on SHD Dataset.

Spiking Neuron Model	Network	Accuracy (%)
LIF	64×64	80.11%
	128×128	82.16%
	256×256	85.34%
ALIF	64×64	88.12%
	128×128	92.19%
	256×256	92.20%
DAIF	64×64	90.79%
	128×128	93.67%
	256×256	92.77%

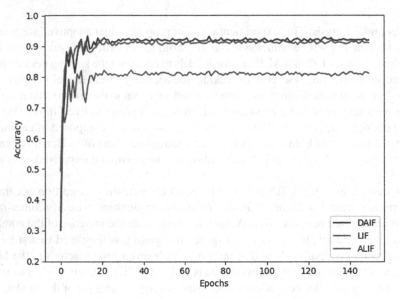

Fig. 4. Accuracy variation on validation set.

In Table 2, we give the speech recognition performance of RSNN with heterogeneous time constants, RSNN with adaptation, RSNN with temporal attention, RSNN with spatio-temporal filter and attention, SNN with feed-forward structure and our proposed dual adaptive spiking neural network on SHD dataset. The results in Table 2 show that our method also has an advantage over the state-of-the-art methods in terms of speech recognition accuracy.

Table 2. Accuracy Comparison of Studies on SHD Datasets.

Publication	Method (Network)	Accuracy (%)
Perez-Nieves et al. [22]	RSNN with heterogeneous time constants	82.7
Yin et al. [23]	RSNN with adaption	84.4
Yao et al. [9]	RSNN with temporal attention	91.1
Yu et al. [24]	RSNN with spatio-temporal filters and attention	92.4
Sun et al. [10]	FSNN with adaptive axonal delays	92.45
This work	**RSNN with dual adaption**	**93.67**

6 Conclusion

This paper presents a dual adaptive spiking neuron model with dynamic conductance and threshold, and at the same time, we complete the simulation experiments of DAIF neuron model in Brian2 neural simulator under PyCharm. We use the dual adaptive spiking neuron model and its commonly used spiking neuron model to construct recurrent neural network, and build a complete speech recognition model, and carry out several groups of experiments on SHD speech dataset. Compared with other neurons, the dual adaptive spiking neuron model has a higher accuracy, which further verifies the validity of it. Therefore, we come to conclusion that constructing a reasonable neuron model can effectively improve the accuracy of speech recognition, and further confirm the importance of constructing a spiking neuron model with more realistic physiological characteristics and higher computational efficiency.

References

1. Mohamed, A., Dahl, G.E., Hinton, G.: Acoustic modeling using deep belief networks. IEEE Trans. Audio Speech Lang. Process. **20**(1), 14–22 (2011)
2. Ghosh-Dastidar, S., Adeli, H.: Spiking neural networks. Int. J. Neural Syst. **19**(04), 295–308 (2009)
3. Wang, X., Lin, X., Dang, X.: Supervised learning in spiking neural networks: a review of algorithms and evaluations. Neural Netw. **125**, 258–280 (2020)
4. Seth, A.K.: Neural Coding: rate and time codes work together. Curr. Biol. **25**(3), R110–R113 (2015)
5. Wu, J., Chua, Y., Li H.: A biologically plausible speech recognition framework based on spiking neural networks. In: 2018 International Joint Conference on Neural Networks, pp. 1–8. IEEE, Rio de Janeiro Brazil (2018)
6. Zhang, Y., Li, P., Jin, Y., et al.: A digital liquid state machine with biologically inspired learning and its application to speech recognition. IEEE Trans. neural networks Learn. Syst. **26**(11), 2635–2649 (2015)
7. Dong, M., Huang, X., Xu, B.: Unsupervised speech recognition through spike-timing-dependent plasticity in a convolutional spiking neural network. PLoS ONE **13**(11), e0204596 (2018)
8. Wu, J., Yılmaz, E., Zhang, M., et al.: Deep spiking neural networks for large vocabulary automatic speech recognition. Front. Neurosci. **14**, 199 (2020)

9. Yao, M., Gao, H., Zhao, G., et al.: Temporal-wise attention spiking neural networks for event streams classification. In: IEEE/CVF International Conference on Computer Vision, pp. 10221–10230. IEEE, Montreal Canada (2021)
10. Sun, P., Eqlimi, E., Chua, Y., et al.: Adaptive axonal delays in feedforward spiking neural networks for accurate spoken word recognition. arXiv preprint **23**(02), 08607 (2023)
11. Koch, C., Segev, I.: The role of single neurons in information processing. Nat. Neurosci. **3**(11), 1171–1177 (2000)
12. Cash, S.S., Hochberg, L.R.: The emergence of single neurons in clinical neurology. Neuron **86**(1), 79–91 (2015)
13. Lapique, L.: Recherches quantitatives sur l'excitation electrique des nerfs traitee comme une polarization. J. Physiol. Pathol **9**, 620–635 (1907)
14. Hodgkin, A.L., Huxley, A.F.: A quantitative description of membrane current and its application to conduction and excitation in nerve. J. Physiol. **117**(4), 500 (1952)
15. Koch, C., Segev, I.: Methods in Neuronal Modeling: From Lons to Networks, 2nd edn. MIT Press, Cambridge (1998)
16. Gerstner, W.: Spike-response model. Scholarpedia **3**(12), 1343 (2008)
17. Bellec, G., Scherr, F., Subramoney, A., et al.: A solution to the learning dilemma for recurrent networks of spiking neurons. Nat. Commun. **11**(1), 1–15 (2020)
18. Shaban, A., Bezugam, S.S., Suri, M.: An adaptive threshold neuron for recurrent spiking neural networks with nanodevice hardware implementation. Nat. Commun. **12**(1), 1–11 (2021)
19. Hertäg, L., Hass, J., Golovko, T., et al.: An approximation to the adaptive exponential integrate-and-fire neuron model allows fast and predictive fitting to physiological data. Front. Comput. Neurosci. **6**, 62 (2012)
20. Górski, T., Depannemaecker, D., Destexhe, A.: Conductance-based adaptive exponential integrate-and-fire model. Neural Comput. **33**(1), 41–66 (2021)
21. Cramer, B., Stradmann, Y., Schemmel, J., et al.: The heidelberg spiking data sets for the systematic evaluation of spiking neural networks. IEEE Trans. Neural Networks Learn. Syst. **33**(7), 2744–2757 (2020)
22. Perez-Nieves, N., Leung, V.C.H., Dragotti, P.L., et al.: Neural heterogeneity promotes robust learning. Nat. Commun. **12**(1), 5791 (2021)
23. Yin, B., Corradi, F., Bohté, S M.: Effective and efficient computation with multiple-timescale spiking recurrent neural networks. In: International Conference on Neuromorphic Systems, pp. 1–8. ACM (2020)
24. Yu, C., Gu, Z., Li, D., et al.: STSC-SNN: spatio-temporal synaptic connection with temporal convolution and attention for spiking neural networks. arXiv preprint **22**(10), 05241 (2022)
25. Neftci, E.O., Mostafa, H., Zenke, F.: Surrogate gradient learning in spiking neural networks: bringing the power of gradient-based optimization to spiking neural networks. IEEE Signal Process. Mag. **36**(6), 51–63 (2019)
26. Wu, J., Chua, Y., Zhang, M., et al.: A tandem learning rule for effective training and rapid inference of deep spiking neural networks. IEEE Trans. Neural Networks Learn. Syst. **34**(1), 446–460 (2021)
27. Kaiser, J., Mostafa, H., Neftci, E.: Synaptic plasticity dynamics for deep continuous local learning (DECOLLE). Front. Neurosci. **14**, 424 (2020)
28. Wu, Y., Deng, L., Li, G., et al.: Spatio-temporal backpropagation for training high-performance spiking neural networks. Front. Neurosci. **12**, 331 (2018)

Mitigating Backdoor Attacks Using Prediction of Model Update Trends

Shaocong Xu[1,2], Shibo Jin[1,2], Panpan Li[1,2], Shanqing Yu[1,2(✉)], Jinyin Chen[1,2], and Dongwei Xu[1,2]

[1] Institute of Cyberspace Security, Zhejiang University of Technology, Hangzhou 310023, China
[2] College of Information Engineering, Zhejiang University of Technology, Hangzhou 310023, China
yushanqing@zjut.edu.cn

Abstract. Federated Learning (FL) is a novel distributed machine learning technique that enables multiple data owners to train a superior model without sharing the original data. Nevertheless, FL is susceptible to attacks from malevolent clients due to distributed training and looser censorship of client data. Backdoor attacks are one of the attack methods against FL, in which a malicious client embeds a backdoor in the uploaded model updates through local training to compromise the global model. In order to counter backdoor attacks, we propose a defense method that uses Recurrent Neural Networks(RNN) to anticipate model update vectors to screen out malicious clients. Through experiments on three datasets, the results indicate that our approach effectively safeguards the global model by detecting and eliminating malicious clients.

Keywords: Federated Learning · Backdoor Attack · Recurrent Neural Networks · Convolutional Neural Network · Distributed Machine Learning

1 Introduction

In light of the emergence of privacy protection regulations across various countries in recent years, centralized model training has faced significant constraints. In response, Google has put forth a novel distributed machine learning technique named Federated Learning (FL). In contrast to the traditional centralized model training method, FL solely utilizes model updates transmitted by clients and refrains from gathering private data, effectively alleviating the impact of privacy legislation. FL differs from a traditional distributed machine learning scenario where data is first collected in a centralized location and subsequently distributed to individual clients [9,11].

Nonetheless, It has been discovered that FL is vulnerable to backdoors, in which malevolent clients frequently introduce backdoors through model poisoning [1,3,16]. For instance, in a classification task, the malicious clients corrupt

Supported by Zhejiang University of Technology.

one class of data by appending trigger and altering its label to a different class. By training on this compromised data, the attacker obtain model updates that incorporates a backdoor. When these malicious updates are aggregated with the update vectors of other clients, the global model will be implanted with a backdoor.

In this work, we propose a method named PMT to mitigate backdoors by predicting model update trends. Our defense process involves pre-training a global model on the server and subsequently training a RNN model using the update vector obtained during global model training. This approach enables the prediction of model update trends, which can distinguish between malicious and benign updates. Experiments confirm our approach effectively mitigates backdoors in FL.

The rest of this paper is structured as follows. In Sect. 2, we briefly describe the background information. In Sect. 3, we introduce our proposed approach. In Sect. 4, we demonstrate the efficacy of our defense approach across various experimental configurations. In Sect. 5, we offer several concluding observations.

2   Background and Related Work

2.1   Federated Learning

FL is a machine learning technique that trains a global model by distributing data across multiple clients [13]. The objective of the clients is to minimize their training losses, which can be expressed as:

$$\arg \min_{w \in R^d} f(w) = \frac{1}{K} \sum_{k=1}^{K} f_k(w) \tag{1}$$

where $f_k(\theta)$ is the local loss function of client k and w is the global model parameter.

The FL training process is as follows: at round t, the server randomly selects a subset S_t, and transmits the model parameters w_t for the current round to these clients. Upon receiving the global model, the clients train locally for multiple rounds via stochastic gradient descent (SGD), and acquiring locally optimized models. Each client computes its local update $\Delta_t^k = w_t^k - w_t$ and transmits it to the server. The server aggregates updates from selected clients by aggregation functions, such as FedAvg function which is widely used by various papers [5, 10, 15], to update the global model.

The FedAvg function is given by:

$$w_{t+1} = w_t + \eta \times \sum_{k=1}^{K} \frac{n_k}{n} \Delta_{k,t} \tag{2}$$

where n_k represents the number of samples from the k-th client and $n = \sum_{k \in S_t} n_k$ denotes the total number of samples in the chosen clients at round t. Prior to aggregation, the local updates are weighted by the number of samples to account for variations in the size of data sets across clients.

2.2   Backdoor Attacks

Backdoor attacks are a significant category of target attacks. In contrast to untargeted attacks [2,4], Malicious clients aim to cause the model to misclassify the source class as the target class and to minimize the impact on other classes. In FL setting, the data is distributed among the clients, and the server does not elicit data directly from individual clients, but the global model is exposed to the training process. The malicious clients can build wicked updates to plant backdoor into the global model [1,12,19,21]

The malicious clients poison their own datasets by adding the specific trigger to the source class and changing its label to the target class. Then, train the model through their poisoned datasets to build malicious updates and embed backdoor by aggregating their updates into the global model [6,14]. Backdoor attacks are dangerous because they can cause the model to generate manipulated outputs that go undetected. Once the backdoor is implanted in the global model, the backdoor can be activated by the attacker when input data containing a specific trigger is present, and the model output will be changed to the target class.

3   Our Approach

We assume that the server has a certain amount of training data which can be completely different from the individual client's data before the training starts, and the server's training data can be used to pre-train a global model and save each model update during this process. This allows the global model to have a high initial accuracy. The recorded model updates are flattened and utilized to train the RNN model, which is capable of predicting the subsequent model updates based on the updates accumulated in previous rounds of global model training. In this work, we employ GRU [7] as the predictive model.

To reduce computational burden, the high-dimensional vector obtained after flattening the model update needs to be dimensionally reduced. Given a small batch input $x_t \in R^{n \times d}$, n is the number of input samples, and d is the flattened update vector length, dimensionality reduction to l-dimensions is achieved by multiplying the input with a trainable weight matrix $w_{trans} \in R^{d \times l}$ prior to inputting it into the GRU model. The output vector of the GRU model is also l-dimensional, i.e., $O_{t+1} \in R^l$. Subsequently, $x_{t+1} \in R^d$ is multiplied by w_{trans} to obtain x'_{t+1}. The MSE loss function updates the GRU model with x'_{t+1} and O_{t+1} . The training method is depicted in the Fig. 1.

After pre-training the global model and GRU model, we commence the process of federated model training. During the Federated Learning process, the server leverages the pre-trained RNN model and the recorded updates to predict the update trend for each round. Following this, the server computes the L2 norm to determine the proximity between the predicted update and other updates. The proximity is calculated using the following formula:

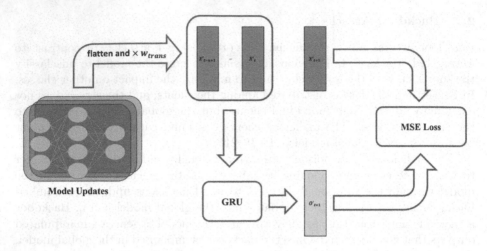

Fig. 1. The process of training GRU model

$$p_i = \sqrt{\sum_{j=1}^{l}(u_{p,j} - u_{i,j})^2} \tag{3}$$

where p_i represents the proximity between the predicted update and update from client i, u_p, j denotes the value of prediction vector u_p in dimension j, and u_i denotes the update from client i. A lower proximity indicates that the update is more likely to be malicious. The server eliminates updates with low proximity, records and aggregates the remaining updates to obtain a new global model.

4　Experiments

4.1　Setup

In this paper, Consider a scenario where K clients participate in the federated learning process, among which $K-1$ clients are malicious. Malicious clients aim to inject their own updates with a backdoor that causes the global model to misclassify base class with a specific trigger as the target class. The backdoor attack approach assumes that the malicious client injects a trigger into all the data labeled as the base class in their own dataset, subsequently changing their labels to the target class, and utilizes these poisoned data to train and obtain malicious updates. In addition, malicious clients have no impact on the server or other clients, aside from their attempt to inject malicious updates into the federated learning process.

Our approach was evaluated on three datasets: MNIST, Fashion MNIST [17], KMNIST [8]. The dataset is partitioned into $K+1$ non-overlapping copies, with one copy residing on the server and the remaining copies distributed among K clients. The server utilizes its own dataset to pre-train the global model until it reaches convergence, and records the model updates for each round. These model updates are subsequently employed as time-series data to train the GRU model. Following the pre-training phase, the standard federated learning process is initiated, in which a random set of C clients is selected from the pool of K clients in each round, and these selected clients perform local training for several epochs before uploading their updates to the server. It should be noted that $C \leq K$.

We measure the performance of the following four aggregation methods:(i) FedAvg (Eqation 2), (ii) coordinate-wise median(comed) [20], (iii) sign aggregation(sign) [2], (iv) FedAvg with PMT. The performance metrics utilized include the precision of the validation set, precision of the base class, and precision of the backdoor attack. Specifically, the precision of the backdoor attack is evaluated on a validation dataset with a trigger added to the base class and the label changed to the target class.

Fig. 2. Conventional Backdoor Attack.

4.2 Conventional Backdoor Attacks

We conducted systematic experiments on the kmnist and mnist datasets. For instance, a trigger can be a plus sign with a size of 5 by 5, which is placed at the top-left corner of an image. The label of the image is then changed to 2 (see Fig. 2). We visualized the corresponding metrics for FedAvg and FedAvg with PMT in Fig. 3 and Fig. 4, reported the ultimate accuracy in Table 1. Our results show that the proposed method significantly improves the system's resilience against conventional backdoor attacks.

4.3 Distributed Backdoor Attack

We conducted a distributed backdoor attack (DBA) [18] on the Fashion MNIST dataset. In contrast to standard backdoor attacks, DBA often involve multiple malicious clients attacking simultaneously. These malicious clients partition the pixel map of the trigger into multiple copies, with each client using a portion of it to corrupt its own dataset, making the malicious updates more closely resemble

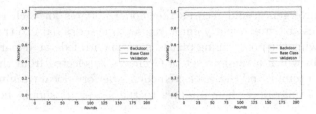

Fig. 3. Training curves for FedAvg and FedAvg with PMT on MNIST. The left figure only uses FedAvg, while the right figure employs PMT.

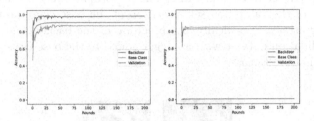

Fig. 4. Training curves for FedAvg and FedAvg with PMT on KMNIST. The left figure only uses FedAvg, while the right figure employs PMT.

honest updates. For instance, the plus trigger can be divided into four parts, with each client using one of them to contaminate the dataset as illustrated in Fig. 5. We visualized the metrics for FedAvg and FedAvg with our proposed method in the DBA scenario in the Fig. 6 and reported the final accuracy in Table 2. Our results indicate that our method significantly enhances the system's resistance to distributed backdoor attacks.

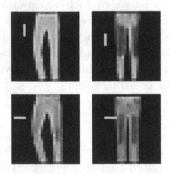

Fig. 5. Distributed Backdoor Attack.

Table 1. The final accuracies of backdoor, validation, and base classes were evaluated for various aggregations on MNIST (top) and KMNIST (bottom).

Aggregation	Backdoor(%)	Validation(%)	Base Class(%)
FedAvg - No Attack	0.102	98.2	**99.3**
FedAvg	99.9	**98.3**	98.7
Comed	99.9	98.1	98.3
Sign	99.9	97.2	98.2
FedAvg with PMT	**0**	96.2	98.7

Aggregation	Backdoor(%)	Validation(%)	Base Class(%)
FedAvg - No Attack	0.700	**91.4**	**92.1**
FedAvg	98.1	90.8	86.9
Comed	97.6	90.9	85.4
Sign	93.5	90.8	87.4
FedAvg with PMT	**0**	82.8	84.8

Table 2. The final accuracies of backdoor, validation, and base classes in DBA setting.

Aggregation	Backdoor(%)	Validation(%)	Base Class(%)
FedAvg - No Attack	0.503	**93.4**	**88.8**
FedAvg	99.8	92.9	81.6
Comed	96.7	92.2	77.1
Sign	99.1	92.4	82.8
FedAvg with PMT	**0**	90.2	87.4

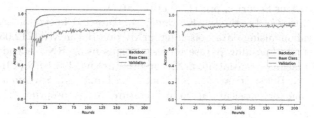

Fig. 6. Training curves for FedAvg and FedAvg with PMT on Fashion-MNIST in DBA setting. The left figure only uses FedAvg, while the right figure employs PMT.

5   Conclusion

The present study examines Federated Learning (FL) through the lens of defending against attacks and proposes a novel defense approach named PMT. The key idea behind PMT is to pre-train a global model on a subset of the server-collected data. The model update vector generated during this pre-training phase is then utilized to train an RNN model that can predict the trend of future model updates. In the subsequent iterations of the traditional federated learning model, the RNN model helps to detect malicious clients by comparing its own prediction vector with the update vectors uploaded by the clients. Section 4 outlines our experimental results, which demonstrate the efficacy of PMT in countering backdoor attacks. In our future endeavors, we aspire to enhance the performance of PMT from a non-iid perspective

Acknowledgements. This work was supported in part by the National Natural Science Foundation of China under Grant No. 62103374, by Key R&D Projects in Zhejiang Province under Grant No. 2021C01117, and by the National Key Research and Development Program of China under Grant No. 2018AAA0100800.

References

1. Bagdasaryan, E., Veit, A., Hua, Y., Estrin, D., Shmatikov, V.: How to backdoor federated learning. In: International Conference on Artificial Intelligence and Statistics, pp. 2938–2948. PMLR (2020)
2. Bernstein, J., Zhao, J., Azizzadenesheli, K., Anandkumar, A.: Signsgd with majority vote is communication efficient and fault tolerant. arXiv preprint arXiv:1810.05291 (2018)
3. Bhagoji, A.N., Chakraborty, S., Mittal, P., Calo, S.: Analyzing federated learning through an adversarial lens. In: International Conference on Machine Learning, pp. 634–643. PMLR (2019)
4. Blanchard, P., El Mhamdi, E.M., Guerraoui, R., Stainer, J.: Machine learning with adversaries: byzantine tolerant gradient descent. In: Advances in Neural Information Processing Systems, vol. 30 (2017)
5. Bonawitz, K., et al.: Practical secure aggregation for privacy-preserving machine learning. In: Proceedings of the 2017 ACM SIGSAC Conference on Computer and Communications Security, pp. 1175–1191 (2017)
6. Chen, X., Liu, C., Li, B., Lu, K., Song, D.: Targeted backdoor attacks on deep learning systems using data poisoning. arXiv preprint arXiv:1712.05526 (2017)
7. Cho, K., et al.: Learning phrase representations using RNN encoder-decoder for statistical machine translation. arXiv preprint arXiv:1406.1078 (2014)
8. Clanuwat, T., Bober-Irizar, M., Kitamoto, A., Lamb, A., Yamamoto, K., Ha, D.: Deep learning for classical Japanese literature. arXiv preprint arXiv:1812.01718 (2018)
9. Dean, J., et al.: Large scale distributed deep networks. In: Advances in Neural Information Processing Systems, vol. 25 (2012)
10. Geyer, R.C., Klein, T., Nabi, M.: Differentially private federated learning: a client level perspective. arXiv preprint arXiv:1712.07557 (2017)
11. Li, M., et al.: Scaling distributed machine learning with the parameter server. In: 11th {USENIX} Symposium on Operating Systems Design and Implementation ({OSDI} 14), pp. 583–598 (2014)
12. Liu, Y., et al.: Trojaning attack on neural networks (2017)
13. McMahan, B., Moore, E., Ramage, D., Hampson, S., y Arcas, B.A.: Communication-efficient learning of deep networks from decentralized data. In: Artificial Intelligence and Statistics, pp. 1273–1282. PMLR (2017)

14. Shafahi, A., Huang, W.R., Najibi, M., Suciu, O., Studer, C., Dumitras, T., Goldstein, T.: Poison frogs! targeted clean-label poisoning attacks on neural networks. In: Advances in Neural Information Processing Systems, vol. 31 (2018)
15. Sun, Z., Kairouz, P., Suresh, A.T., McMahan, H.B.: Can you really backdoor federated learning? arXiv preprint arXiv:1911.07963 (2019)
16. Wang, H., et al.: Attack of the tails: yes, you really can backdoor federated learning. Adv. Neural. Inf. Process. Syst. **33**, 16070–16084 (2020)
17. Xiao, H., Rasul, K., Vollgraf, R.: Fashion-mnist: a novel image dataset for benchmarking machine learning algorithms. arXiv preprint arXiv:1708.07747 (2017)
18. Xie, C., Huang, K., Chen, P.Y., Li, B.: DBA: distributed backdoor attacks against federated learning. In: International Conference on Learning Representations (2020)
19. Xu, J., Wang, R., Liang, K., Picek, S.: More is better (mostly): on the backdoor attacks in federated graph neural networks. arXiv preprint arXiv:2202.03195 (2022)
20. Yin, D., Chen, Y., Kannan, R., Bartlett, P.: Byzantine-robust distributed learning: towards optimal statistical rates. In: International Conference on Machine Learning, pp. 5650–5659. PMLR (2018)
21. Zhang, Z., et al.: Neurotoxin: durable backdoors in federated learning. In: International Conference on Machine Learning, pp. 26429–26446. PMLR (2022)

The Motor Fault Diagnosis Based on Current Signal with Graph Attention Network

Liang Zhang[1], Yi Jiang[1], Long Zhou[1], Yun Sun[1], Hongru Wang[1], Jun Ni[1], Jinhua Wu[1], and Dongwei Xu[2(✉)]

[1] ChinaOly Technology, Hangzhou, China
[2] Zhejiang University of Technology, Hangzhou, China
dongweixu@zjut.edu.cn

Abstract. Motor fault diagnosis is a very important task for ensuring normal motor operation. Motor vibration sensors can be effectively used for fault diagnosis but is expensive for installation. Therefore, motor current signals have attracted considerable attentions from researchers. This paper proposes a fault diagnosis method for motor current signals based on a graph attention network. The graph network is constructed by the extreme points of the filtered current signal. The graph attention networks (GATs) are used to extract current signal features for motor fault diagnosis. The experimental results demonstrate that the proposed model outperforms other current-based fault diagnosis methods.

Keywords: Motor Fault Diagnosis · Motor Current Signal · Graph Attention Network

1 Introduction

Currently, with rapid economic development, motors are widely used in daily life and industrial production. However, motors are susceptible to environmental influences and wear during operation, which causes motors to malfunction, which may cause economic losses and affect the efficiency of mechanical production and even threaten personal safety.

Any component of the motor may be damaged due to failures such as overload, wear, and external force. It can be classified into four main categories: bearing faults, stator faults, rotor faults and other faults [1]. Bearing faults account for 40% of failures in large mechanical systems and 90% in small mechanical systems, respectively [2]. The data currently being studied for motor fault diagnosis include vibration signals [3–5], current signals [1,6], and acoustic signals [7]. The vibration sensor has certain requirements on the installation location. By contrast, the acquisition of current signals is more convenient. Many motors already have current monitoring function, so they do not need additional sensors, which reduces the cost. Even if some motors do not have the above function, the phase current of the motor can be easily measured by installing a current sensor.

supported by the Key R&D Programs of Zhejiang under Grant(2022C01121).

In addition, traditional feature extraction methods usually rely on certain techniques, and fault diagnosis is based on the statistical learning method [8–12]. There are still some problems with these traditional methods. The traditional feature extraction method is unstable because the motor fault mechanism is complex and the signal is nonlinear and nonstationary.

Deep learning can effectively train the deep network and express the deep abstract features of the data. The above problems in fault diagnosis can be effectively overcome by deep learning. The stacked sparse autoencoder [13], sparse autoencoder [14], deep belief network (DBN) [15], denoising autoencoder [16], sparse filtering [17], and convolutional neural network (CNN) [18,19] are used in motor fault diagnosis.

In this paper, our method mainly studies the phase current of the motor to diagnose the motor bearing fault. The original current signal is filtered by a filter to obtain the fault characteristic signal. Then, we propose a method to construct a graph network from the extreme points of the signal and convert the electrical signal into graph network data. Finally, the graph attention network and CNN are used to extract features to realize the fault diagnosis.

The main contributions of this paper are as follows:

- A method of constructing a graph network based on extreme points of the motor current signal sequence is proposed;
- The graph attention network (GAT) is used to extract motor current signal features for motor fault diagnosis;
- The proposed method shows good results on public datasets for motor fault diagnosis.

2   Related Work

The time-frequency domain method based on nonstationary signals such as motor vibration signals is the most effective. Lei et al. [9] proposed a kurtosis-based method for fault diagnosis. Lin et al. [20] obtained the optimal envelope mean. He et al. [21] took a new machine learning approach to diagnosing bearing failures. Sun et al. [22] introduced data mining technology to the fault diagnosis field. Yang et al. [11] proposed an effective fault feature extraction method. Pandya et al. [12] used the KNN classifier method for diagnosis. Ma et al. [23] proposed an ensemble EMD (CEEMD) method for diagnosing. Ge et al. [24] proposed a submodal diagnostic technique. Deep learning overcomes some shortcomings of traditional methods. Many CNN-based motor fault diagnosis methods were proposed [25–28]. Jia et al. [29] proposed a self-encoded diagnostic technique with a significant improvement. Cho et al. [30] and Shao et al. [31] et al. respectively proposed methods to significantly improve the diagnostic effect. Sun et al. [32] realized automatic feature extraction. The image classification method can also be used for fault diagnosis. Lu et al. [33] transformed the vibration signal into a bispectrum contour map utilizing bispectrum technology and introduced a probabilistic neural network for diagnostic. Kang et al. [34] proposed an induction motor fault diagnosis method using 2-D gray-level images created by Shannon wavelets. Ding et al. [35] proposed a multi-scale diagnostic technique with significant effects G. Karatzinis et al. [36] proposed a current-based method using fuzzy cognitive networks (FCNs). Hoang et al. [6] proposed a current-based method using deep learning and information fusion.

3   The Construction of Graph Network Based on Motor Current Signal

In this article, the main research is to diagnose motor faults caused by bearing defects. Bearing defects not only cause abnormal vibration of the motor but also cause abnormal phase currents. Traditional motor fault diagnosis is generally realized based on motor vibration data. But the cost of installing vibration sensors is relatively high. The cost of obtaining phase current data is small, while it is difficult to be directly used for motor fault diagnosis. The examples of original motor phase current are shown in Fig. 1.

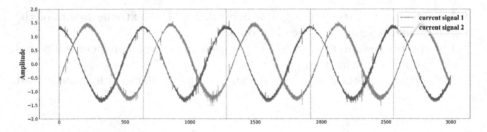

Fig. 1. Schematic diagram of motor current signal division

Based on the peaks in the first phase current signal, the multi-phase current signal can be divided into equal small samples $c_n^{(p)}$, $n = 1, 2, \cdots, M$, $p = 1, 2, \cdots, P$, where p represents the current phase, as shown in Fig. 1. The small sample's length is the minimum period length, which is denoted as N. We found that in the current signal samples that have the same phase are similar. Therefore, the low-frequency components in the signal need to be removed first; then a high-pass filter is used to remove noise to obtain the fault characteristic signal (FCS) of each category. In the experiment, a bandpass filter is designed based on the Fourier transform. The allowable pass frequency is $0.01f$–$0.3f$, where f represents the sampling frequency of the original current signal:

$$fc_n^{(p)} = FFT(c_n^{(p)}) \tag{1}$$

$$fc_n^{(p)} = \begin{cases} fc_n^{(p)}, & 0.01f < \omega < 0.3f \\ 0, & else \end{cases} \tag{2}$$

$$ifc_n^{(p)} = IFFT(fc_n^{(p)}) \tag{3}$$

where, FFT is fast Fourier transform; $IFFT$ is inverse fast Fourier transform. ω is the signal frequency; the amplitudes corresponding to the remaining frequencies in the spectrum $fc_n^{(p)}$ obtained by the fast Fourier transform are set to zero. Then, the fault characteristic signal $ifc_n^{(p)}$ is obtained through transforming the $fc_n^{(p)}$ by inverse fast Fourier transform. The processing results of the phase current in a single small sample are shown in Fig. 2.

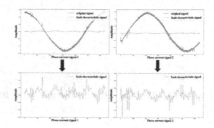

Fig. 2. Examples of phase current filtered by bandpass

Then, the extreme points of the fault characteristic signals are taken as the nodes to construct the graph networks:

$$f_n^{(p)}(x) = ifc_n^{(p)}, x \in 1, 2, \cdots, N \tag{4}$$

$$Exmax_n^{(p)} = \{x|x \in 2, 3, \cdots, N-1 : f_n^{(p)}(x) > f_n^{(p)}(x-1) \\ \wedge f_n^{(p)}(x) > f_n^{(p)}(x+1)\} \tag{5}$$

$$Exmax_n^{(p)} = \{x|x \in 2, 3, \cdots, N-1 : f_n^{(p)}(x) < f_n^{(p)}(x-1) \\ \wedge f_n^{(p)}(x) < f_n^{(p)}(x+1)\} \tag{6}$$

$$V_n^{(p)} = Exmax_n^{(p)} \cup Exmin_n^{(p)} \tag{7}$$

$$E_n^{(p)} = \{e_m^{(i)}|u, v \in Exmax_n^{(p)} \vee u, v \in Exmin_n^{(p)} : |u - v| \leq d \\ \wedge f_n^{(p)}(u)f_n^{(p)}(v) \geq 0\} \tag{8}$$

$$G_n^{(p)} = (V_n^{(p)}, E_n^{(p)}) \tag{9}$$

where, $Exmax_n^{(p)}$ and $Exmix_n^{(p)}$ are the set of maximum and minimum points in the fault characteristic signal $ifc_n^{(p)}$, respectively. The points in these two sets are the nodes in the graph network $G_n^{(p)}$. Two points are found in these two sets whose adjacent distance does not exceed d and whose characteristic signal value is the same. These two points are defined to have a connected edge relationship.

And obtaining the set of all connected edge relationships $E_n^{(p)}$, which is the set of connected edges in the graph network, as shown in Fig. 3. Each small sample can construct P graph networks.

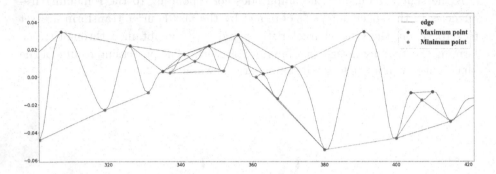

Fig. 3. Partial graph network structure diagram based on motor current signal

The graph network constructed from a single small sample has personality problem, so we merge 10 graph networks corresponding to the same phase current in continuous small samples as a new graph network to enhance its generalization ability:

$$\tilde{G}_n^{(p)} = (\tilde{V}_n^{(p)}, \tilde{E}_n^{(p)}) = \{G_n^{(p)}, G_{n+1}^{(p)}, \cdots, G_{n+9}^{(p)}\}$$
$$= \begin{cases} \tilde{V}_n^{(p)} = V_n^{(p)} \cup V_{n+1}^{(p)} \cup \cdots \cup V_{n+9}^{(p)} \\ \tilde{E}_n^{(p)} = E_n^{(p)} \cup E_{n+1}^{(p)} \cup \cdots \cup E_{n+9}^{(p)} \end{cases} \quad (10)$$

$$\tilde{X}_n^{(p)} = [ifc_n^{(p)}, ifc_{n+1}^{(p)}, \cdots, ifc_{n+9}^{(p)}]^{\mathrm{T}} = [x_{n,1}^{(p)}, x_{n,2}^{(p)}, \cdots, x_{n,N}^{(p)}] \quad (11)$$

$$X_n = \{\tilde{G}_n^{(p)}, \tilde{X}_n^{(p)}, \quad p = 1, 2, \cdots, P\} \quad (12)$$

where $\tilde{V}_n^{(p)}$ and $\tilde{E}_n^{(p)}$ are the nodes and edges of the fusion graph network $\tilde{G}_n^{(p)}$, respectively. When the graph networks are fused, the nodes and edge sets of the graph network corresponding to the same phase current are merged separately. The experimental data used in this article contain two-phase current data. After fusion, there are two graph networks, and the node characteristics in each graph network are the 10 characteristics corresponding to the current node among the 10 fault signal characteristics. To facilitate calculation, our input feature $\tilde{X}_n^{(p)}$ contains the features of all nodes and actually only uses the features corresponding to the nodes in the graph network $\tilde{G}_n^{(p)}$.

The pseudo code is as follows £Q

The construction of current graph network

1. sample ← original current signal
2. for CS in sample.currents

3. FCS ← filter CS by bandpass filter
4. *Exmax* ← maximum points in FCS
5. *Exmin* ← minimum points in FCS
6. edges ← find edges from *Exmax* and *Exmin*
7. current graph ← construct graph according to *Exmax*, *Exmin*, and edge
8. G ← fuse every 10 graphs

4   The Motor Fault Diagnosis Model

4.1   The Motor Fault Category

There are many forms of damage to motor bearings. In the proposed method, the faults are divided into three categories: health, inner ring fault, and outer ring fault according to the location of bearing damage. And one-hot encoding is used to describe the fault categories, as shown in Table 1.

Table 1. Fault categories encoding

Fault categories	Health	Inner ring fault	Outer ring fault
One-hot encoding	100	010	001

4.2   Graph Attention Network (GAT)

The graph convolutional network (GCN) is widely used in many fields as the representative graph neural network. However, GCN has two disadvantages: the weights of different neighbor nodes in the same neighborhood are exactly the same, which limits the model's ability to capture spatial information correlation. Therefore, we adopt GAT to extract the features in the data. For graph data $G=(V, E)$, V is a set of nodes and E is a set of edges. GAT introduces self-attention to replace the propagation method in GCN. Figure 4 shows the feature extraction process of a single node feature in the graph attention layer. The input of the graph attention layer is a series of node features, $h^l = \{h_1^l, h_2^l, \cdots, h_N^l\}$, $h_i^l \in \mathbb{R}^{F^l}$, where N is the number of nodes and F^l is the number of features of each node in the current layer. This layer generates a new set of node features $h^{l+1} = \{h_1^{l+1}, h_2^{l+1}, \cdots, h_N^{l+1}\}$, $h_i^{l+1} \in \mathbb{R}^{F^{l+1}}$. To obtain more advanced features, a shared weight matrix $W^l \in \mathbb{R}^{F^{l+1} \times F^l}$ is used to transform the input features into a feature space of dimension F^{l+1}, which is the number of new features. Then, the attention mechanism is executed on all connected edges $a : \mathbb{R}^{F^{l+1}} \times \mathbb{R}^{F^{l+1}} \to \mathbb{R}$. The attention factor can be calculated through the following equation:

$$e_{ij}^l = a(W^l h_i^l, W^l h_j^l) \tag{13}$$

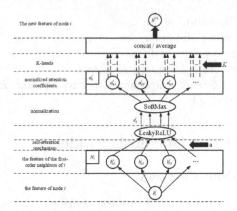

Fig. 4. A graph attentional layer with K-head attention mechanism

where e_{ij}^l represents the importance of node j of the l-th layer to node i. Usually, we only calculate the attention coefficient between node i and its first-order neighbor node, which is denoted as $N_i(j \in N_i)$. In the experiment, the attention mechanism a is a single-layer feedforward neural network, which can be calculated by the weight vector $a^l \in \mathbb{R}^{2F^{l+1}}$. To standardize the attention coefficient more, we first use the LeakyReLU activation function (with negative input slope $\alpha = 0.2$), then we use the softmax function to normalize the attention coefficients related to all node i, and finally obtain the normalized attention coefficient α_{ij}^l:

$$\alpha_{ij}^l = \underset{j \in N_i}{softmax}(LeakyRelu((a^l)^T[W^l h_i^l || W^l h_j^l])) \qquad (14)$$

where $.^T$ represents matrix transpose and $||$ represents a fusion operation.

Finally, the normalized attention coefficient is used in the node feature update process, and through the nonlinear activation function σ, the new node feature is obtained:

$$h_i^{l+1} = \sigma(\sum_{j \in N_i} \alpha_{ij}^l W^l h_j^l) \qquad (15)$$

To make the learning process of self-attention more robust, we usually use a K-head attention mechanisms to carry out formula (15) and connect the results, finally obtaining the following output feature representation:

$$h_i^{l+1} = \prod_{k=1}^{K} \sigma(\sum_{j \in N_i} \alpha_{ij}^{lk} W^{lk} h_j^l) \qquad (16)$$

where $\prod$ denotes that fusion operation, α_{ij}^{lk} is the normalized attention coefficient calculated by the k-th attention mechanism in the l-th layer; W^{lk} is the corresponding weight matrix; the feature number of the new node h_i^{l+1} is KF^{l+1}.

Specifically, when multi-head attention is used for classification task, the above fusion operation may no longer be suitable, which should be replaced by the average value:

$$h_i^{l+1} = \sigma\left(\frac{1}{K}\sum_{k=1}^{K}\sum_{j\in N_i}\alpha_{ij}^{lk}W^{lk}h_j^l\right) \tag{17}$$

4.3 The Motor Fault Diagnosis Based on Current Signal with Graph Attention Network

The structure diagram of the proposed motor fault diagnosis method is shown in Fig. 5. First, according to the multi-phase current signal of the motor, the graph networks can be constructed. Second, fusing the features extracted from multi-current graph networks via two GATs. Then, 3 layers of convolution are used to extracted features. Finally, the multidimensional feature map is expanded into 1 dimension and implementing fault classification by fully connected neural network.

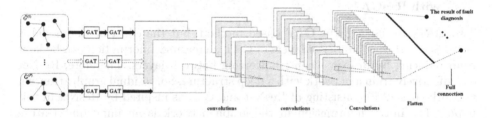

Fig. 5. Motor Fault Diagnosis Model

Two GATs are used to extract the network features of the fusion graph of the each-phase current. The two GATs for each phase current have the same structure, and both contain two graph attention layers. The multi-head attention mechanism in the first layer takes the method in formula (16) for feature fusion, and the second layer uses the method in formula (17) to average the features. The output feature matrix of the graph network corresponding to each phase current extracted by two GATs is:

$$\text{first } GAT \qquad Z_{\mathrm{I}}^{(p)} = h_{\mathrm{I}}^{(2)(p)} \tag{18}$$

$$\text{second } GAT \qquad Z_{\mathrm{II}}^{(p)} = h_{\mathrm{II}}^{(2)(p)} \tag{19}$$

where $Z_{\mathrm{I}}^{(2),(p)}$ and $Z_{\mathrm{II}}^{(2),(p)}$ represent the features of the fault characteristic signal of the p-th phase current in the n-th sample extracted by the two GATs, respectively. And the feature matrix size is $N \times F_{\mathrm{II}}^{(2)}$. These feature matrices of multi-current are fused in a new dimension to obtain fusion features Z_0 the size is $N \times F_{\mathrm{II}}^{(2)} \times P$:

$$Z_0 = Z_{\mathrm{II}}^{(1)} ||| Z_{\mathrm{II}}^{(2)} \cdots ||| Z_{\mathrm{II}}^{(p)}, p = 1, 2, \cdots, P \tag{20}$$

Then, multiple two-dimensional convolutions are used to extract features:

$$Z_r = ReLu(\phi_r * Z_{r-1} + b_r), r \geq 1 \tag{21}$$

where (*) represents the convolution operation, ϕ_r and b_r represent the convolution kernel and bias, respectively, in the r-th layer convolution operation, Z_r represents the feature matrix after the r-th layer convolution operation, ReLU is the activation function, and then, the multidimensional features obtained by the convolution operations are expanded to a 1-dimensional feature matrix. Finally, a fully connected neural network layer and the softmax activation function are used for fault classification.

4.4   The Motor Fault Diagnosis Based on Current Signal with ResGAT

Two GATs are used in the GAT based method, but the effect of the model is decreased with the number of layers of GAT increasing. Information can be kept from reducing by ResNet when transferring between layers. Therefore, ResNet can effectively train a network with a deep structure. So, residual graph attention network (ResGAT) consisting of ResNet and GAT is inspired by ResNet in this paper. The initial information in the graph network is an important feature and multi-layer GAT can extract the multi-order neighbor features of nodes. ResGAT ensures that these initial information will not be "forgotten" through identity mapping. The structure of the residual graph attention block is shown in Fig. 6. It contains two layers of GAT and the features are fused through formula 17. So the size of output is the same as the input. The model structure based on ResGAT is shown in Fig. 7. The first GAT in the GAT based model is replaced by ResGAT. The integrity of graph information is maintained by ResGAT when extracting graph features.

5   Experiment

5.1   Experimental Test-Bed and Data Preparation

The dataset [37] used in this work are collected from the test-bed shown in Fig. 8.

To make the experimental data more reliable, many kinds of artificial and real damaged bearings are tested in the experiment, in which the real damaged bearings are obtained by an accelerated life test. A total of 32 kinds of bearings were tested, including 6 healthy, 12 artificially damaged and 14 naturally damaged bearings. ISO 15243 divides bearing damage into six modes. However, it only considers the general damage modes, so a new classification method to describe

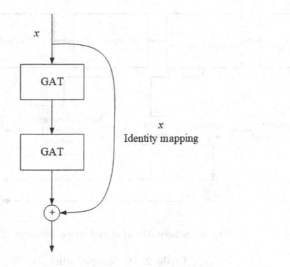

Fig. 6. The structure diagram of residual graph attention block

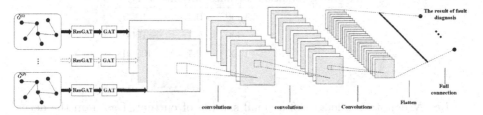

Fig. 7. The structure diagram of the motor fault diagnosis model based on ResGAT

bearing information and damage information in detail is proposed. Among them, the first three describe the bearing-related information, and the fourth describes the bearing damage details according to ISO 15243. According to the healthy state, the bearing includes healthy bearing, inner ring fault bearing and outer ring fault bearing.

In experiments, different motor working conditions can be provided by changing the rotational speed of the motor (S), load torque (M), and radius force (F), as shown in Table 2. This study mainly uses real damaged bearing data. Table 3 shows the bearing codes contained in the three bearing health conditions.

The phase current of the motor is measured over two phases by a current sensor (LEM CKSR 15-NP), current signal 1 (CS1) and current signal 2 (CS2). When measuring the motor current, a 25 kHz low pass filter is used to filter the current signal, and the sampling frequency is 64 kHz. Each bearing is measured 20 times for 4 s each time. Figure 9 shows the two-phase current signals in the three healthy states of the bearings, which show that the difference between the signals is very slight.

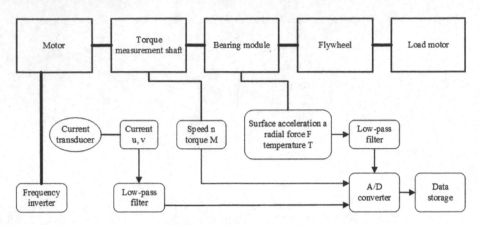

Fig. 8. Schematic of signal measurement [37]

Table 2. Working conditions

Working condition	S(rpm)	M(Nm)	F(N)
A	1500	0.1	1000
B	900	0.7	1000
C	1500	0.7	40000

Let N denote the length of a small sample of current. Based on the actual current data, under working conditions A and C, N=640; under working condition B, N=1067. Therefore, in each measurement, approximately 400 small samples can be obtained under working conditions A and C, and 240 small samples can be obtained under working condition B. After building a network with small samples, the graph network that fuses 10 small samples continuously is used as an inputting sample. The training and testing datasets are divided by 9:1, as shown in Table 4.

Because the current analysis under different motor working conditions is similar, we choose working condition A for analysis. According to our proposed method, the phase current of the motor is first processed to obtain the fault characteristic signal (FCS) of the current, as shown in Fig. 10, 11. Figure 10 shows the two-phase current FCS of a small bearing sample under different fault states. Figure 11 shows the FCS of 3 continuous small samples under healthy states.

Table 3. Bearing codes used for experiments

Bearing status	Label	Used bearing code
Health	1	K001, K002, K003, K004, K005
Inner ring fault	2	KA04, KA15, KA16, KA22, KA30
Outer ring fault	3	KI04, KI14, KI16, KI18, KI21

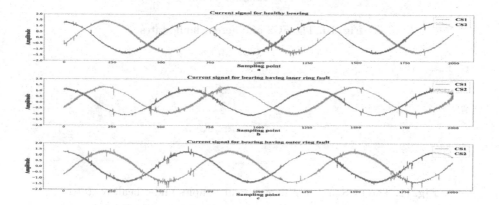

Fig. 9. The phase current of the motor under three conditions

Overall, it can be clearly seen that the fluctuations of FCS under different fault states are different. And although the general trend of continuous FCS of healthy bearings is similar, there are still subtle differences. Therefore, 10 small sample graph networks are fused to enhance the generalization of the model.

Figure 12 shows the nodes and connected edges of the graph network constructed based on two-phase currents of small sample 1. The extremum points in the current signal constitute the nodes in the graph network, where the extremum points without connected edges are seen as invalid nodes. Finally, 10 continuous graph networks are fused as training samples.

Table 4. Dataset of experiments

Working condition	Training samples	Testing samples
A	10800	1200
B	6480	720
C	10800	1200

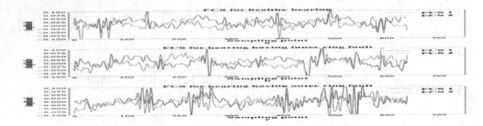

Fig. 10. The FCS of different fault states

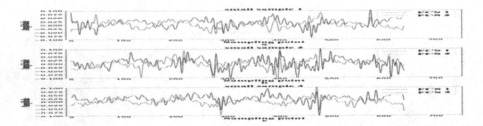

Fig. 11. The FCS of 3 continuous small samples under healthy states.

5.2   Results

We carried out experiments under three working conditions. The results show that the model can stabilize the loss in fewer training batches. The confusion matrixes of diagnosis accuracy of GAT based method and ResGAT based method on the test dataset under three working conditions are shown as Fig. 13 and Fig. 14. All of the prediction accuracies in different conditions reach 97%. Overall, the diagnosis effect of the methods is satisfactory.

Table 5 shows the comparison results [6]. The diagnosis accuracies of our methods are the highest under the three working conditions, especially in working condition B and C. The results of GAT based method and ResGAT based method are similar but the latter accuracy is slightly higher.

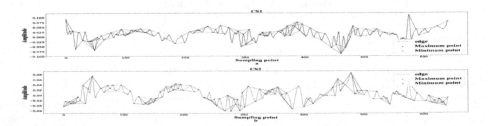

Fig. 12. Diagrams of nodes and connections of graph networks constructed from small sample 1

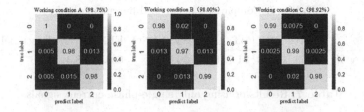

Fig. 13. The confusion matrix diagram of diagnosis accuracy of GAT based method

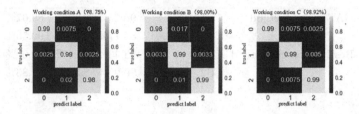

Fig. 14. The confusion matrix diagram of diagnosis accuracy of ResGAT based method

We also compared some diagnosis methods using the same dataset, and the results are shown in Table 6 (the results are obtained from [37] except FCN [36]). These traditional diagnosis methods cannot achieve satisfactory results. Although the accuracy of Ensemble and FCN exceeds 90%, they are still lower than our methods.

In order to prove the effectiveness of multi-phase currents, this paper has done experiments on single-phase current signals. And the results are shown in Table 7. In this experiment, the prediction accuracies are about 90%, which is significantly lower than the results of using multi-phase current signal.

Table 5. Results of different methods

Methods	Accuracy		
	A	B	C
MLP based IF	98.30%	96.70%	96.80%
SVM based IF	98.00%	96.13%	97.86%
KNN based IF	97.07%	96.13%	96.80%
GAT based method	98.75%	98.00%	98.92%
ResGAT based method	**98.92%**	**98.89%**	**99.25%**

Table 6. Comparison between different methods

Model	CART	RF	BT	NN	SVM-PSO	ELM	KNN	Ensembel	FCN
Accuracy(%)	66.7	83.3	81.7	65.8	56.7	69.2	68.3	93.3	91.42

Table 7. Results of using only single-phase current signals

Methods	Current signal	Accuracy		
		A	B	C
GAT based method	CS1	90.25%	91.78%	89.67%
	CS2	87.17%	87.00%	90.50%
ResGAT based method	CS1	93.43%	92.67%	92.00%
	CS2	90.06%	89.11%	91.83%

5.3   Experiment on the Created Dataset

As shown in the Fig. 15, testbed is built to collect current data, which also can create a dataset. The dataset concludes current signal corresponding to one health condition and five fault conditions under four motor speeds (5rps, 10rps, 15rps, 20rps). The current signal of each state contains two-phase current. The data sampling frequency is 10 kHz and lasts for 3 min. Thus, each phase current of each condition contains approximately 1.8 million data. Therefore, not only the period of the current sequence is different and but also the sample size is different, as shown in Table 8. The training and test datasets are divided by 9:1. Each FCS at 4 rotating speeds includes 2000, 1000, 667, 500 data respectively. The abstraction of curve characteristics of the current signals and the FCS are the same with the public dataset.

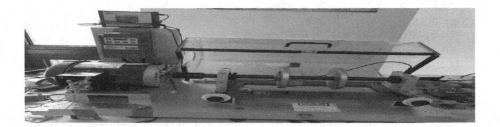

Fig. 15. Data collection testbed

The results of the proposed methods on this dataset are shown in the Table 9. Under the working conditions of 5rps, 10rps and 15rps, the predict accuracies of the methods all reach 100%. And the predict accuracies exceed 99% under the working conditions of 20rps. The methods can achieve excellent results on

Table 8. The sample size of datasets

Rotating speed	5rps	10rps	15rps	20rps
Sample size	4452	8970	13494	18000

Table 9. Results on the created dataset

Method	Accuracy(5rps)	Accuracy(10rps)	Accuracy(15rps)	Accuracy(20rps)
GAT based method	100%	100%	100%	99.78%
ResGAT based method	100%	100%	100%	99.83%

this dataset may be due to that the disturbance when collecting data is small. In addition, we have further studied the results under the working conditions of 20rps. Two comparative experiments are added. One is to increase the number of converged graph networks to 15. The other is to build a graph network using two consecutive small samples, that is, the number of nodes in the graph network changes from 500 to 1000. In these two experiments, the fault diagnosis accuracies both rose to 100%.

6 Conclusion

Although the motor fault diagnosis method based on vibration signals is effective, the installation of vibration sensors increases the cost. The current signal of the motor is easy to obtain, and the cost is low. Therefore, this paper proposes a motor fault diagnosis method based on a graph attention network.

We compare the proposed methods with other models on the same public dataset. The results show that our methods have the highest fault classification accuracy, which indicates that the methods have broad prospects in practical applications.

Acknowledgements. This work was supported by the Key R& D Programs of Zhejiang under Grant(2022C01121).

References

1. Mbo'o, C.P., Hameyer, K.: Fault diagnosis of bearing damage by means of the linear discriminant analysis of stator current features from the frequency selection. IEEE Trans. Ind. Appl. **52**(5), 3861–3868 (2016)
2. Shahriar, M.R., Borghesani, P., Tan, A.C.: Electrical signature analysis-based detection of external bearing faults in electromechanical drivetrains. IEEE Trans. Ind. Electron. **65**(7), 5941–5950 (2017)
3. Jing, L., Zhao, M., Li, P., Xu, X.: A convolutional neural network based feature learning and fault diagnosis method for the condition monitoring of gearbox. Measurement **111**, 1–10 (2017)

4. Nayana, B., Geethanjali, P.: Analysis of statistical time-domain features effectiveness in identification of bearing faults from vibration signal. IEEE Sens. J. **17**(17), 5618–5625 (2017)

5. Maruthi, G., Hegde, V.: Application of mems accelerometer for detection and diagnosis of multiple faults in the roller element bearings of three phase induction motor. IEEE Sens. J. **16**(1), 145–152 (2015)

6. Hoang, D.T., Kang, H.J.: A motor current signal-based bearing fault diagnosis using deep learning and information fusion. IEEE Trans. Instrum. Measur. **69**(6), 3325–3333 (2019)

7. Elasha, F., Greaves, M., Mba, D., Addali, A.: Application of acoustic emission in diagnostic of bearing faults within a helicopter gearbox. Procedia CIRP **38**, 30–36 (2015)

8. Li, C., Sánchez, R.-V., Zurita, G., Cerrada, M., Cabrera, D.: Fault diagnosis for rotating machinery using vibration measurement deep statistical feature learning. Sensors **16**(6), 895 (2016)

9. Lei, Y., He, Z., Zi, Y.: EEMD method and WNN for fault diagnosis of locomotive roller bearings. Expert Syst. Appl. **38**(6), 7334–7341 (2011)

10. Ngaopitakkul, A., Bunjongjit, S.: An application of a discrete wavelet transform and a back-propagation neural network algorithm for fault diagnosis on single-circuit transmission line. Int. J. Syst. Sci. **44**(9), 1745–1761 (2013)

11. Yang, Y., Yu, D., Cheng, J.: A fault diagnosis approach for roller bearing based on IMF envelope spectrum and SVM. Measurement **40**(9–10), 943–950 (2007)

12. Pandya, D., Upadhyay, S., Harsha, S.P.: Fault diagnosis of rolling element bearing with intrinsic mode function of acoustic emission data using APF-KNN. Expert Syst. Appl. **40**(10), 4137–4145 (2013)

13. Qi, Y., Shen, C., Wang, D., Shi, J., Jiang, X., Zhu, Z.: Stacked sparse autoencoder-based deep network for fault diagnosis of rotating machinery. IEEE Access **5**, 15066–15079 (2017)

14. Wen, L., Gao, L., Li, X.: A new deep transfer learning based on sparse auto-encoder for fault diagnosis. IEEE Trans. Syst. Man Cybernet.: Syst. **49**(1), 136–144 (2017)

15. Shao, H., Jiang, H., Zhang, X., Niu, M.: Rolling bearing fault diagnosis using an optimization deep belief network. Measur. Sci. Technol. **26**(11), 115002 (2015)

16. Shao, H., Jiang, H., Wang, F., Zhao, H.: An enhancement deep feature fusion method for rotating machinery fault diagnosis. Knowl.-Based Syst. **119**, 200–220 (2017)

17. Lei, Y., Jia, F., Lin, J., Xing, S., Ding, S.X.: An intelligent fault diagnosis method using unsupervised feature learning towards mechanical big data. IEEE Trans. Ind. Electron. **63**(5), 3137–3147 (2016)

18. Xia, M., Li, T., Xu, L., Liu, L., De Silva, C.W.: Fault diagnosis for rotating machinery using multiple sensors and convolutional neural networks. IEEE/ASME Trans. Mechatron. **23**(1), 101–110 (2017)

19. Lee, K.B., Cheon, S., Kim, C.O.: A convolutional neural network for fault classification and diagnosis in semiconductor manufacturing processes. IEEE Trans. Semicond. Manuf. **30**(2), 135–142 (2017)

20. Lin, L., Hongbing, J.: Signal feature extraction based on an improved EMD method. Measurement **42**(5), 796–803 (2009)

21. He, M., He, D.: Deep learning based approach for bearing fault diagnosis. IEEE Trans. Ind. Appl. **53**(3), 3057–3065 (2017)

22. Sun, W., Chen, J., Li, J.: Decision tree and PCA-based fault diagnosis of rotating machinery. Mech. Syst. Signal Process. **21**(3), 1300–1317 (2007)

23. Ma, F., Zhan, L., Li, C., Li, Z., Wang, T.: Self-adaptive fault feature extraction of rolling bearings based on enhancing mode characteristic of complete ensemble empirical mode decomposition with adaptive noise. Symmetry 11(4), 513 (2019)

24. Ge, M., Wang, J., Xu, Y., Zhang, F., Bai, K., Ren, X.: Rolling bearing fault diagnosis based on EWT sub-modal hypothesis test and ambiguity correlation classification. Symmetry 10(12), 730 (2018)

25. Wang, J., Zhuang, J., Duan, L., Cheng, W.: A multi-scale convolution neural network for featureless fault diagnosis. In: 2016 International Symposium on Flexible Automation (ISFA), pp. 65–70. IEEE (2016)

26. Wang, J., Liu, P., She, M.F., Nahavandi, S., Kouzani, A.: Bag-of-words representation for biomedical time series classification. Biomed. Signal Process. Control 8(6), 634–644 (2013)

27. Xu, G., Liu, M., Jiang, Z., Söffker, D., Shen, W.: Bearing fault diagnosis method based on deep convolutional neural network and random forest ensemble learning. Sensors 19(5), 1088 (2019)

28. Abdeljaber, O., Avci, O., Kiranyaz, S., Gabbouj, M., Inman, D.J.: Real-time vibration-based structural damage detection using one-dimensional convolutional neural networks. J. Sound Vib. 388, 154–170 (2017)

29. Jia, F., Lei, Y., Lin, J., Zhou, X., Lu, N.: Deep neural networks: a promising tool for fault characteristic mining and intelligent diagnosis of rotating machinery with massive data. Mech. Syst. Signal Process. 72, 303–315 (2016)

30. Cho, H.C., Knowles, J., Fadali, M.S., Lee, K.S.: Fault detection and isolation of induction motors using recurrent neural networks and dynamic Bayesian modeling. IEEE Trans. Control Syst. Technol. 18(2), 430–437 (2009)

31. Shao, H., Jiang, H., Zhang, H., Liang, T.: Electric locomotive bearing fault diagnosis using a novel convolutional deep belief network. IEEE Trans. Ind. Electron. 65(3), 2727–2736 (2017)

32. Sun, J., Yan, C., Wen, J.: Intelligent bearing fault diagnosis method combining compressed data acquisition and deep learning. IEEE Trans. Instrumen. Measur. 67(1), 185–195 (2017)

33. Lu, C., Wang, Y., Ragulskis, M., Cheng, Y.: Fault diagnosis for rotating machinery: a method based on image processing. PLoS ONE 11(10), e0164111 (2016)

34. Kang, M., Kim, J.-M.: Reliable fault diagnosis of multiple induction motor defects using a 2-d representation of shannon wavelets. IEEE Trans. Magnet. 50(10), 1–13 (2014)

35. Ding, X., He, Q.: Energy-fluctuated multiscale feature learning with deep convnet for intelligent spindle bearing fault diagnosis. IEEE Trans. Instrumen. Measur. 66(8), 1926–1935 (2017)

36. Karatzinis, G., Boutalis, Y.S., Karnavas, Y.L.: Motor fault detection and diagnosis using fuzzy cognitive networks with functional weights. In: 2018 26th Mediterranean Conference on Control and Automation (MED), pp. 709–714. IEEE (2018)

37. Lessmeier, C., Kimotho, J.K., Zimmer, D., Sextro, W.: Condition monitoring of bearing damage in electromechanical drive systems by using motor current signals of electric motors: a benchmark data set for data-driven classification. In: Proceedings of the European conference of the prognostics and health management society, pp. 05–08 (2016)

Internet Intelligent Algorithm Governance

NILSIC-BERT4Rec: Sequential Recommendation with Non-Invasive and Interest Capturing Self-Attention Mechanism

Haolin Liu[1], Chenhan Luo[2], Rui Zhang[1], Zhenye Liu[2], and Shimin Cai[1(✉)]

[1] University of Electronic Science and Technology of China, Chengdu 611731, China
shimincai@uestc.edu.cn
[2] University of Wisconsin-Madison, Madison 53715, USA

Abstract. Recently, recommendation models based on Transformer have become a hot research topic. Despite the large number of recommendation models proposed in recent years, we argue that the use of invasive fusion when using heterogeneous auxiliary information and mixing multiple different vector spaces results in side effects in existing self-attention models. Additionally, the self-attention layer in Transformer overly focuses on distant items in user interaction sequence, lacking the ability to capture local dependencies of items. Thus, we propose a novel sequential recommendation model, Non-Invasive Long-term Short-term Interest Capturing BERT4Rec (NILSIC-BERT4Rec). NILSIC-BERT4Rec retains the ability of the representation layer and self-attention layer to output in the same vector space. We also introduce a local encoder in the self-attention layer to strengthen the role of item context in the attention function, enhancing the self-attention layer's ability to capture local dependencies. Experiment results show that NILSIC-BERT4Rec can learn a better attention distribution and achieves the best experiment results on all datasets, with an average of 7.36% improvement on evaluation metrics.

Keywords: Recommender System · Sequential Recommendation · Self Attention · Transformer · Interest Capturing

1 Introduction

The rise of sequence-based recommendation algorithms has attracted increasing research attention. Compared to traditional recommendation algorithms, sequence-based recommendation algorithms aim to explicitly model users' sequential behaviour and more accurately represent users' context to make more accurate, customized, and dynamic recommendations. [1,2]. Deep neural networks (DNNs) have a natural advantage in modelling and capturing the complex relationships between different inputs in a sequence, such as users, items, and interaction sequences, which has dominated the subsequent research on sequential recommendation algorithms. DNN usually performs better than traditional matrix factorization-based algorithms [3,4].

Transformer-based models usually perform better in sequence-related tasks, and applying it to sequential recommendation has also demonstrated its superiority [5]. Among all Transformer-based models, BERT [6] achieves higher prediction accuracy than models with unidirectional self-attention mechanism [7]. Although BERT has achieved SOTA performance in many tasks across different domains, we argue that there is still a lack of research on effectively leveraging different types of auxiliary information on top of BERT for sequence-based recommendation tasks. In sequence recommendation, the item ID is the most critical feature, and the effectiveness of its vector representation directly affects the model's performance. Therefore, utilizing auxiliary information, such as ratings and descriptions, to provide a more comprehensive description of items can also improve the model's prediction accuracy. However, BERT is initially designed to accept only one type of input (i.e., item ID), limiting its ability to leverage auxiliary information. In theory, more auxiliary information can be beneficial to the model's prediction accuracy. Existing work based on the BERT framework such as [8], usually takes an invasive approach when utilizing auxiliary information, which does not achieve the desired effect. On the other hand, the attention function is usually non-local, lacking inductive local bias, and therefore unable to capture users' transient interest.

We propose a sequence recommendation model based on non-invasive and long-term & short-term interest capturing self-attention mechanism to address these limitations. It can effectively utilize various auxiliary information in sequential recommendation tasks, avoiding the information overload brought by the premature fusion of item IDs and auxiliary information vector representations in the self-attention mechanism. The model enhances the capture of users' short-term interest preferences in the self-attention layer, allowing Transformer to learn a better attention distribution.

The contributions of our paper are as follows:

- We modify the self-attention mechanism used in the self-attention layer of BERT4Rec by keeping the encoding and decoding of the most important feature in same vector space, and more effectively modeling the user's interest with the help of auxiliary information.
- We introduce a local encoder in the self-attention layer of BERT4Rec, which enhances the ability of BERT to capture transient user interest. By learning better attention distribution in the self-attention layer, we improve its expressiveness in the BERT model.
- We propose a novel model, NILSIC-BERT4Rec, which effectively combines the two aforementioned improvements. We demonstrate the effectiveness of both modifications in the self-attention layer through quantitative analysis.

2   Related Work

Early sequence recommendation models include sequence pattern mining [9] and Markov chain models [10]. These models became intuitive solutions for sequence recommendation because they can naturally capture the dependencies between user-item interactions in the sequence. However, when there is a large amount of sequential data, the time and space costs required for mining frequent patterns also increase dramatically [11].

Deep learning-based recommendation algorithms include algorithms based on DNNs [12,13], recurrent neural networks (RNNs) [14], attention mechanism [15], and graph neural networks (GNNs) [16]. Deep learning algorithms can learn more accurate user and item feature information. In 2015, GRU4Rec [5] is proposed, which utilizes the information from the entire user's interaction sequence, not only focusing on the user's recent behaviours but also comprehensively considering the influence of previous information on subsequent information. GRU4Rec overcomes the problem of dimension explosion in Markov decision processes. In 2018, Caser is proposed byTang et al., which includes a sequence embedding layer for capturing sequential information and a convolutional layer for capturing the relationships between items [17].

Sequential recommendation typically uses a unidirectional neural network to process interactions in a left to right manner, which is not always efficient to capture the sequence pattern inside. Sun et al. propose a sequential recommendation model, BERT4Rec [8]. To avoid information leakage, BERT4Rec trains the model in the form of a cloze task, predicting randomly masked items in the bidirectional context of the item sequence. Therefore, Furthermore, BERT4Rec learns a bidirectional representation model that allows each item in interaction sequence to integrate information from both sides. Zhou et al. propose S3-rec [18], which consists of a sequence cutter and mutual information maximize. In addition, contrastive learning methods have been combined with sequential recommendation in very recent works [19–21]. All of them achieved promising experiment results in comparison to the previous ones.

3   Problem Statement

Let $\mathcal{U} = \{u_1, u_2, \ldots, u_{|\mathcal{U}|}\}$ denote the set of users and $\mathcal{I} = \{I_1, I_2, \ldots, I_{|\mathcal{I}|}\}$ denote the set of items. Let $S_u = [I_1^{(u)}, \ldots, I_t^{(u)}, \ldots, I_{n_u}^{(u)}]$ denote the interaction sequence of user $u \in \mathcal{U}$ sorted in ascending order of time, where $I_t^{(u)} \in \mathcal{I}$ represents the interaction between user u and item I at relative time t, and n_u represents the length of user u's interaction sequence. Given user u's interaction sequence S_u, the goal of the sequence recommendation task is to predict the item I that user u is most likely to interact with at relative time $n_u + 1$. This problem can be modelled as the probability of user u interacting with each item at relative time $n_u + 1$, formally represented as follows:

$$p\left(I_{n_u+1}^{(u)} = I | S_u\right) \tag{1}$$

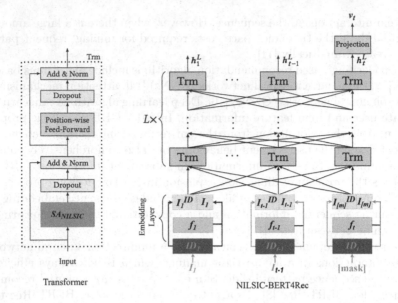

Fig. 1. Transformer layer used in NILSIC-BERT4Rec is on the left, and the architecture of NILSIC-BERT4Rec is on the right.

4   Model Architecture

NILSIC-BERT4Rec modifies the self-attention and embedding layers. As illustrated in Fig. 1, it is built upon the popular sequential recommendation model BERT4Rec. Next, we will introduce NILSIC-BERT4Rec in top-down order.

4.1   Transformer Layer

As illustrated in Fig. 1, for a given user interaction sequence of length t, the l-th layer of the Transformer iteratively computes the hidden vector $\mathbf{h}_i^l$ for each position i. The attention function is parallelly computed for all positions, and the output hidden vectors $\mathbf{h}_i^l \in \mathcal{R}^d$ at the output layer are stacked into matrix form $\mathbf{H}^l \in \mathcal{R}^{t \times d}$. The Transformer (Trm) in the Fig. 1 includes two sub-layers: SA_{NILSIC} and $FPPN$.

Multi-head Self-attention Layer. SA_{NILSIC} is the first sublayer of the Transformer, which consists of global encoders and local encoders with attention functions $f_{att,g}$ and $f_{att,l}$, respectively. Attention functions used in SA_{NILSIC}'s m-th head can be formulated as follow:

$$f_{att,*}\left(\mathbf{Q}_i^{(m)} \to \mathbf{K}_j^{(m)}\right) = \frac{\exp(w_{ij}^{(m)}) \cdot \sigma_{ij}}{\sum_{k=1}^N \exp\left(w_{ik}^{(m)}\right) \cdot \sigma_{ik}} \tag{2}$$

where $\mathbf{Q}_i^{(m)}$ is the query of the i-th item and $\mathbf{K}_i^{(m)}$ is the key of the i-th item in the m-th head of SA_{NILSIC}. $w_{ij}^{(m)}$ is the weight of items i and j in the m-th head's weight matrix. σ_{ij} is the correlation between the pre-defined items i and j.

When we set the σ_{ij} to the value of 1, we consider all the items in the user interaction sequence. Thus, $f_{att,*}$ becomes $f_{att,g}$, which is the weight function in global encoders. Furthermore, we can introduce trainable window parameters with good initialization and rewrite the expression $\exp(w_{ij}^{(m)}) \cdot \sigma_{ij}$ in Eq. 2 as $\exp(w_{ij}^{(m)} + \ln \sigma_{ij})$. This can be achieved by learning weight parameters $p_{ij} = \ln \sigma_{ij}$ to adapt to the correlation between items i and j. The weights can be initialized with a Gaussian-like function, such as $p_{ij} = a \exp(-(i-j)^2/b)$, ensuring that the initial correlation between nearby items is greater than that between distant items. When we pre-define the correlation between items in this way, $f_{att,*}$ becomes $f_{att,l}$, which is the weight function in local encoders.

We project the hidden vector $\mathbf{h}_i$ of each position i in $\mathbf{H}^l$ onto M_g subspaces of the global encoder and M_l subspaces of the local encoder and compute M attention functions in parallel using $f_{att,g}$ and $f_{att,l}$, respectively. This generates vector representations of each attention head in its corresponding subspace, denoted as $\left[\tilde{\mathbf{V}}_{i,g}^{(1)}, \ldots, \tilde{\mathbf{V}}_{i,g}^{(m)}, \ldots, \tilde{\mathbf{V}}_{i,g}^{(M_g)}; \tilde{\mathbf{V}}_{i,l}^{(1)}, \ldots, \tilde{\mathbf{V}}_{i,l}^{(m)}, \ldots, \tilde{\mathbf{V}}_{i,l}^{(M_l)}\right]$. We concatenate these vector representations and use another linear mapping to merge them into a final output vector representation $\tilde{\mathbf{V}}_i$, which can be expressed as follow:

$$\tilde{\mathbf{V}}_i = \left[\tilde{\mathbf{V}}_{i,g}^{(1)}, \ldots, \tilde{\mathbf{V}}_{i,g}^{(m)}, \ldots, \tilde{\mathbf{V}}_{i,g}^{(M_g)}; \tilde{\mathbf{V}}_{i,l}^{(1)}, \ldots, \tilde{\mathbf{V}}_{i,l}^{(m)}, \ldots, \tilde{\mathbf{V}}_{i,l}^{(M_l)}\right] \mathbf{W}_O$$

$$\text{where} \quad \tilde{\mathbf{V}}_{i,g}^{(m)} = \sum_{i=1}^N f_{att,g}\left(\mathbf{Q}_i^{(m)} \to \mathbf{K}_j^{(m)}\right) \cdot \mathbf{V}_j^{(m)} \tag{3}$$

$$\tilde{\mathbf{V}}_{i,l}^{(m)} = \sum_{i=1}^N f_{att,l}\left(\mathbf{Q}_i^{(m)} \to \mathbf{K}_j^{(m)}\right) \cdot \mathbf{V}_j^{(m)}$$

The weight matrix $\mathbf{W}_O$ is used in the linear layer after the multi-head self-attention layer to merge the output results of the multiple heads into the final item vector representation $\tilde{\mathbf{V}}_i$.

The update formulas for the query $\mathbf{Q}_i^{(m)}$, key $\mathbf{K}_i^{(m)}$, and value $\mathbf{V}_i^{(m)}$ as input when the vector representation $\mathbf{R}_i^l$ of the i-th item is projected into the subspaces of the m-th self-attention head, where $\mathbf{W}_Q^{(m)}, \mathbf{W}_K^{(m)}, \mathbf{W}_V^{(m)} \in \mathcal{R}^{d \times d}$ are the weight matrices for the m-th self-attention head, are as follows:

$$\mathbf{Q}_i^{(m)} = \mathbf{R}_i^l \mathbf{W}_Q^{(m)}, \mathbf{K}_i^{(m)} = \mathbf{R}_i^l \mathbf{W}_K^{(m)}, \mathbf{V}_i^{(m)} = \mathbf{R}_i^l \mathbf{W}_V^{(m)} \tag{4}$$

The projection matrices $\mathbf{W}^Q \in \mathcal{R}^{d \times d/M}$, $\mathbf{W}^K \in \mathcal{R}^{d \times d/M}$, and $\mathbf{W}^V \in \mathcal{R}^{d \times d/M}$ for each attention head are learnable parameter matrices. The stacked representation of the output vector representations $\tilde{\mathbf{V}}_i$ from each position through the self-attention layer results in the matrix representation $\mathbf{H}^l \in \mathcal{R}^{t \times d}$, which represents the updated hidden vectors $\mathbf{h}_i$ for each position i in SA_{NILSIC}.

Position-Wise Feed-Forward Network. The $PFFN$ is the second sublayer of the Transformer layer and is applied to the output $\mathbf{H}^l$ of the multi-head self-attention sublayer SA_{NILSIC}. Its main function is to provide the model with non-linearity and the ability to interact between different dimensions. It can be expressed as follow:

$$\text{PFFN}\left(\mathbf{H}^l\right) = \left[\text{FFN}\left(\mathbf{h}_1^l\right)^\top ; \ldots ; \text{FFN}\left(\mathbf{h}_t^l\right)^\top\right]^\top$$

$$\text{FFN}(\mathbf{x}) = \text{GELU}\left(\mathbf{x}\mathbf{W}^{(1)} + \mathbf{b}^{(1)}\right)\mathbf{W}^{(2)} + \mathbf{b}^{(2)} \tag{5}$$

$$\text{GELU}(x) = x\Phi(x)$$

The function $\Phi(x)$ is the cumulative distribution function(CDF) of the standard normal distribution. The matrices $\mathbf{W}^{(1)} \in \mathcal{R}^{d \times 4d}$, $\mathbf{W}^{(2)} \in \mathcal{R}^{d \times 4d}$, $\mathbf{b}^{(1)} \in \mathcal{R}^{d \times 4d}$, and $\mathbf{b}^{(2)} \in \mathcal{R}^{d \times 4d}$ are all learnable parameters. Following the practices in OpenAI GPT and BERT [6], the GELU activation unit used here is smoother compared to the conventional ReLU activation unit. Therefore, it maintains linear growth while also having the smoothing property of the sigmoid function, which can improve the learning ability of the neural network [22].

Stacking Transformer Layer. Generally speaking, stacking self-attention layers is always beneficial to learn more complex item interaction patterns. However, simple stacking can quickly lead to parameter explosion, which is detrimental to model convergence. Following the approach of ResNet [23], residual connections are used to effectively address this issue. Therefore, residual connections are added to each sublayer of the Transformer. Before normalization, each sublayer undergoes a dropout operation [24] to avoid overfitting. Stacking Transformers results in the calculation process of multiple layers of Trm in NILSIC-BERT4Rec as follow:

$$\mathbf{H}^l = \text{Trm}\left(\mathbf{H}^{l-1}\right), \forall i \in [1, \ldots, L] \tag{6}$$

$$\mathbf{H}^{l-1} = \text{LN}\left(\mathbf{A}^{l-1} + \text{Dropout}\left(\text{PFFN}\left(\mathbf{H}^{l-1}\right)\right)\right) \tag{7}$$

$$\mathbf{A}^{l-1} = \text{LN}\left(\mathbf{H}^{l-1} + \text{Dropout}\left(\text{SA}_{\text{NILSIC}}\left(\mathbf{H}^{l-1}\right)\right)\right) \tag{8}$$

Here, $\text{LN}(\cdot)$ denotes the normalization operation, which normalizes the input of all hidden units, stabilizing and accelerating the training of the network.

4.2   Embedding Layer

Let the input item vector representation $\mathbf{h}_i^{0(ID)}$ represents a separate item ID vector representation $\mathcal{E}_i^{(ID)}$, and $\mathbf{h}_i^0$ represents the fused item ID vector representation $\mathcal{E}_i^{(ID)}$ and the item auxiliary information vector representation $\mathcal{E}_i$:

$$\begin{aligned}\mathbf{h}_i^{0(ID)} &= \mathcal{E}_i^{(ID)} \\ \mathbf{h}_i^0 &= \mathcal{E}_i^{(ID)} \bigoplus \mathcal{E}_i\end{aligned} \tag{9}$$

Auxiliary information refers to all inputs except for Item ID, such as item reviews, item categories, etc. Each type of the auxiliary information is embedded through Embedding layer to a vector representation $\mathcal{E}_i^f$, and $\mathcal{E}_i$ is the fused vector representation of $\mathcal{E}_i^f$. The parameter matrices $\mathbf{W}^Q$ and $\mathbf{W}^K$ are trained and updated using $\mathbf{h}_i^0$ in SA_{NILSIC}, while the parameter matrix $\mathbf{W}^V$ is trained and updated using $\mathbf{h}_i^{0(ID)}$. This approach utilizes the item ID and auxiliary information to learn a better weight parameters of SA_{NILSIC}, and then fuses only the item IDs to obtain the final item representation, leading to a non-invasive integration of auxiliary information to the vector representation of the item.

4.3   Output Layer

After passing the input user interaction sequence through the representation layer and L layers of Trm, fully exchanging information at each position, the output matrix $\mathbf{H}^L$ represents each item's embedding in the user's interaction sequence.

Assuming that we need to predict the item I_t that the user is most likely to interact with at relative time t, we can use $\mathbf{h}_t^L$ to make the prediction. During prediction, a two-layer feedforward neural network with ReLU activation is used to calculate and output the probability distribution for the item I_t:

$$P(I) = \text{softmax}\left(\text{GELU}\left(\mathbf{h}_t^L \mathbf{W}^P + \mathbf{b}^P\right)\mathbf{E}^T + \mathbf{b}^O\right) \tag{10}$$

where $\mathbf{W}^P$ is the parameter matrix of the position-wise feed-forward neural network, $\mathbf{b}^P$ and $\mathbf{b}^O$ are the bias terms, and $\mathbf{E} \in \mathcal{R}^{|\mathcal{I}| \times d}$ is the representation matrix of items $\mathcal{I}$. Using the same representation matrix for both input and output can effectively avoid overfitting and reduce the model size to some extent.

Algorithm 1: training process of NILSIC-BERT4Rec

Input: Set of users $\mathcal{U}$, set of items $\mathcal{I}$, set of user interaction sequence $\mathcal{S}$ sorted
by relative time of interaction with items, a number of iterations k.
Output: Set of parameters to be trained in NILSIC-BERT4Rec
for *iter from 1 to k* **do**
    for $\mathcal{S}_u$ *in* $\mathcal{S}$ **do**
        Compute vector representations $\mathcal{E}_{id}$ and $\mathcal{E}_f$ of item IDs and auxiliary
        information for user u's interaction sequence $\mathcal{S}_u$ respectively;
        Calculate input of Trm layer $\mathbf{h}^{0(ID)}$ and $\mathbf{h}^0$ according to Eq. 9;
        Stack item embeddings $\mathbf{h}^0$ into matrix form $\mathbf{H}^l$ and use it as input to
        Trm layer;
        Compute item embedding matrix $\mathbf{H}^L$ after multiple Trm updates using
        Eqs. 3, 5, 6, 7, and 8;
        Predict masked items on training set using Eq. 10;
        Update model parameters using Adam optimizer;
    end
end

4.4   Model Learning

We adopt the Cloze task proposed in BERT4Rec [8] as the training method for our model. The Cloze task involves randomly masking some tokens in the input, and the goal is to predict the original Item ID of the masked tokens solely based on their context. We randomly mask the items in the user's interaction sequence with a proportion of p. These masked items are replaced with a special token "[mask]".

The final vector corresponding to the masked item $[mask]_i$ is used as input to the softmax function over all items. The loss for each masked input in $\mathcal{S}u'$ is defined as the negative log-likelihood function:

$$\mathcal{L} = \frac{1}{|\mathcal{S}_u^m|} \sum_{I_m \in \mathcal{S}_u^m} - \log P\left(I_m = I_m^* \mid \mathcal{S}_u'\right) \tag{11}$$

The training process of NILSIC-BERT4Rec is described in Algorithm 1.

5   Experiments

5.1   Data

We evaluate NILSIC-BERT4Rec on Beauty, MovieLens 1m (ML-1M), and MovieLens 20m (ML-20M). The statistical information is shown in the Table 1. We follow the common practice in [8] for preprocessing.

Table 1. Statistics of Beauty, ML-1m and ML-20m

Datasets	#user	#items	interactions	Avg. length	Density
Beauty	40,226	54,542	0.35 m	8.8	0.02%
ML-1M	6040	3416	1.0 m	163.5	4.79%
ML-20M	138,493	26,744	20 m	144.4	0.54%

5.2   Task Settings and Evaluation Metrics

Task Settings. Leave-one-out evaluation task is used to evaluate NILSIC-BERT4Rec. Leave-one-out is a common method for evaluating performance and has been widely used in [2,7,8]. We leave out one interaction from the sequence of each user in the dataset and use the remaining interactions for model training. The left-out interaction is a test case for performance evaluation. This process is repeated for all interactions in the dataset, and the average performance across all test cases is reported as the model's accuracy.

Evaluation Metrics. The first evaluation metric is the Hit Ratio (HR@K), and the second evaluation metric is the Normalized Discounted Cumulative Gain (NDCG@K). For any of the above-mentioned evaluation metrics, a higher value indicates better recommendation performance of the model. Specifically, the HR@[1, 5, 10] and NDCG@[5, 10] is recorded in the experiments.

5.3   Implementation Detail

We implement NILSIC-BERT4Rec in PyTorch. The model is trained using Adam optimizer, and the learning rate is linearly decayed while gradients are clipped when exceeding a threshold. The parameters used in the BERT4Rec paper are adopted, with the transformer layer set to 2. The number of attention heads in the self-attention layer of NILSIC-BERT4Rec, SASRec, and BERT4Rec is the same, with $M = 2$. However, the difference lies in fact that the self-attention heads in SASRec and BERT4Rec are both global encoders, while those in NILSIC-BERT4Rec are composed of global and local encoders, with $M_g = 1$ and $M_l = 1$, respectively. The dimension size of each head is set to 32. Additionally, the maximum length of interaction sequences that each user can have in different datasets is limited to $N = 200$ in ML-1M and ML-20M, and $N = 50$ in Beauty. The ratio of randomly masking items, denoted as p, followed the values used in the BERT4Rec paper, with $p = 0.6$ in Beauty and $p = 0.2$ in ML-1M and ML-20M.

5.4   Overall Performance Comparison

Table 2. Performance comparison of different methods on next-item prediction

Dataset	Metric	POP	BPR-MF	NCF	GRU4Rec+	Caser	SASRec	BERT4Rec	NILSIC-BERT4Rec	Improvement
Beauty	HR@1	0.0077	0.0415	0.0407	0.0551	0.0475	0.0906	0.0953*	**0.1080**	13.3%
	HR@5	0.0392	0.1209	0.1305	0.1781	0.1625	0.1934	0.2207*	**0.2413**	9.2%
	HR@10	0.0762	0.1992	0.2142	0.2654	0.2590	0.2653	0.3025*	**0.3312**	9.4%
	NDCG@5	0.0230	0.0814	0.0855	0.1172	0.1050	0.1436	0.1599*	**0.1822**	13.8%
	NDCG@10	0.0349	0.1064	0.1124	0.1453	0.1360	0.1633	0.1862*	**0.2114**	13.3%
ML-1M	HR@1	0.0141	0.0914	0.0397	0.2092	0.2194	0.2351	0.2863*	**0.2937**	2.3%
	HR@5	0.0715	0.2866	0.1932	0.5103	0.5353	0.5434	0.5876*	**0.6124**	4.2%
	HR@10	0.1358	0.4301	0.3477	0.6351	0.6692	0.6629	0.6970*	**0.7375**	5.7%
	NDCG@5	0.0416	0.1903	0.1146	0.3705	0.3832	0.3980	0.4454*	**0.4627**	3.7%
	NDCG@10	0.0621	0.2365	0.1640	0.4064	0.4268	0.4368	0.4818*	**0.5026**	4.2%
ML-20M	HR@1	0.0221	0.0553	0.0231	0.2021	0.1232	0.2544	0.3440*	**0.3620**	5.2%
	HR@5	0.0805	0.2128	0.1358	0.5118	0.3804	0.5727	0.6323*	**0.6713**	6.3%
	HR@10	0.1378	0.3538	0.2922	0.6524	0.5427	0.7136	0.7473*	**0.7829**	4.8%
	NDCG@5	0.0511	0.1332	0.0771	0.3630	0.2538	0.4208	0.4967*	**0.5315**	7.0%
	NDCG@10	0.695	0.1786	0.1271	0.4087	0.3062	0.4665	0.5340*	**0.5771**	8.1%

Table 2 reports the best performance achieved by all models on the three datasets. The last column shows the improvement percentage of NILSIC-BERT4Rec over the best baseline model. Bold font indicates the best performance on the dataset, and an asterisk (*) represents the second-best performance. From Table 2, such conclusions can be drawn:

Since POP does not model users' personalized preferences based on their interaction sequences, its performance is the worst among all datasets.

Compared to non-sequence recommendation models (BPR-MF and NCF), sequence recommendation models (including FPMC and GRU4Rec+) perform better on all datasets.

Through comparative experiments, Caser outperforms FPMC, which is verified in all datasets. Caser's performance is particularly outstanding on ML-1m. However, Caser's performance on sparse datasets is relatively poor, especially compared to GRU4Rec+ and SASRec, indicating significant disadvantages in recommendation effectiveness.

Compared to GRU4Rec+, SASRec shows significantly better performance. This result shows that the self-attention mechanism can better model users' interest preferences in their interaction sequences.

Comparative experiments show that BERT4Rec has significant advantages over SASRec in performance. The bidirectional self-attention mechanism has a more vital modelling ability for users' interaction sequences compared to the left-to-right sequential self-attention mechanism.

According to the experiment results, NILSIC-BERT4Rec achieved the best results on all datasets. Especially on the Beauty dataset, the improvement of NILSIC-BERT4Rec in HR@1, NDCG@5, and NDCG@10 is 13.3%, 13.8%, and 13.9%, respectively. NILSIC-BERT4Rec uses non-invasive and long-short interest capturing self-attention mechanism on top of the bidirectional Transformer. This indicates that the fusion of early vector representation and excessive attention to distant items in the self-attention layer weakened the expressive power of the BERT4Rec model.

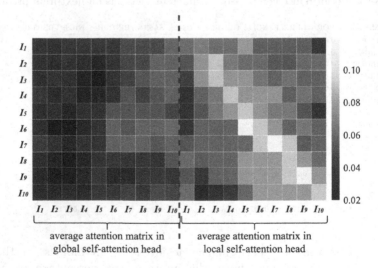

Fig. 2. Average weight matrix. The global encoder and local encoder is split by red line in the middle.

Given that NILSIC-BERT4Rec employs two different self-attention mechanisms, an important question is the role played by each of these mechanisms in the performance of NILSIC-BERT4Rec. To address this question, we conducted comparative experiments between NILSIC-BERT4Rec and several baseline models.

The Role of Long-Term and Short-Term Interest Capturing Self-attention Mechanism. The role of the long-term and short-term interest capturing self-attention mechanism in NILSIC-BERT4Rec can be observed through the average weight matrices of the global and local encoders. For a given user's interaction sequence of the top ten items, the average weight matrices of the global (global attention head) and local encoders (local attention head) in the last layer of the Transformer are considered in the ML-1M dataset and visualized in Fig. 2.

The heatmap shows that the local encoder has higher attention weights (average attention weight of 0.072) for context-relevant items, indicated by lighter colours. In contrast, the average weight matrix of the global encoder is more chaotic (average attention weight of 0.041), suggesting that the global encoder is more inclined to learn weights for all items and is more susceptible to interference from irrelevant items at a distance. The local encoder effectively compensates for the deficiency of the self-attention mechanism in capturing local dependencies, improving the model's overall performance.

Table 3. Performance of applying non-invasive self-attention mechanism on BERT4Rec

model	fusion func.	ML-1M				
		HR@1	HR@5	HR@10	NDCG@5	NDCG@10
BERT4Rec	add	0.2816	0.5762	0.6933	0.4442	0.4791
	concat	0.2863	0.5876	0.6970	0.4454	0.4818
NI-BERT4Rec	add	**0.2891**	0.5916	0.7124	0.4517	0.4883
	concat	0.2885	**0.5940**	**0.7160**	**0.4526**	**0.4904**

The Role of Non-invasive Self-attention Mechanism. Table 3 shows the performance comparison between the BERT4Rec model with and without the non-invasive attention mechanism on the ML-1M dataset. It can be observed that NI-BERT4Rec with the non-invasive attention mechanism achieved significant improvements in all evaluation metrics, with an average improvement rate of 1.91%. This demonstrates that the non-invasive attention mechanism has a positive effect, validating its effectiveness.

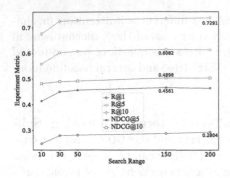 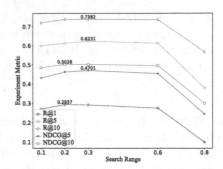

Fig. 3. Experiment results of different user interaction sequence length N

Fig. 4. Experiment results of different masking proportion p

5.5   Impact of Maximum User Interaction Sequence Length N

Figure 3 and Table 4 demonstrate the impact of different user interaction sequence lengths N on the performance of NILSIC-BERT4Rec on the ML-1M dataset.

Table 4. The experiment results of different user interaction sequence length N

N	10	30	50	150	200
R@1	0.2489	0.2804	0.2817	0.2882	**0.2937**
R@5	0.5582	0.6024	0.6082	**0.6136**	0.6124
R@10	0.6761	0.7261	0.7291	0.7352	**0.7375**
NDCG@5	0.4133	0.4501	0.4561	**0.4651**	0.4627
NDCG@10	0.4822	0.4898	0.4914	0.5028	**0.5026**

The model's performance drops in almost all evaluation metrics when N is less than 30, indicating that NILSIC-BERT4Rec struggles to learn the user's true interests from excessively short user interaction sequence. As N increases beyond 50, the performance of NILSIC-BERT4Rec gradually improves in all metrics. The performance difference between $N = 150$ and $N = 200$ is not significant, mainly because the average length of user interaction sequence in ML-1M is 163.5, and $N = 150$ already covers most of the user's entire history of interaction sequence. Thus, increasing N appropriately can improve the performance of NILSIC-BERT4Rec.

5.6   Impact of Mask Proportion P

Figure 4 and Table 5 present the experiment results of the effect of different masking proportions p on the performance of NILSIC-BERT4Rec.

Table 5. Experiment results of different masking proportion p

p	0.1	0.2	0.3	0.6	0.8
R@1	0.2701	0.2937	**0.2914**	0.275	0.1000
R@5	0.5997	0.6124	**0.6231**	0.6123	0.3795
R@10	0.7201	**0.7375**	0.7382	0.7367	0.5664
NDCG@5	0.4312	0.4627	**0.4701**	0.4540	0.2443
NDCG@10	0.4851	**0.5026**	0.5017	0.4955	0.3002

The model achieves the best experiment result when $p = 0.2$ or $p = 0.3$. However, when p is too large, the performance of the model significantly deteriorates. Although a larger masking proportion p can generate more samples for model training to some extent, excessively masking the items will lead to underfitting of the model, making it unable to fully model the user's preference. Therefore, the selection of the masking proportion parameter p needs to be more cautious and should not be too large or too small.

6   Conclusion and Future Work

In this paper, we propose a sequence recommendation model, NILSIC-BERT4Rec, based on capturing the long-term and short-term interests of users. It can effectively model users' interests and preferences and learn more accurate vector representations of item IDs. By adding a local encoder that focuses more on the context of items, NILSIC-BERT4Rec compensates for the overemphasis on distant item information in the global encoder, which means that the expressiveness of the multi-head attention mechanism can be further improved. Through experiments on three widely used datasets, we analyze and compare NILSIC-BERT4Rec with other high-performing recommendation models, verifying its effectiveness.

In future work, it may be considered to completely decouple all heterogeneous auxiliary information, allocate separate self-attention layers for each type of auxiliary information, learn and update the vector representation of auxiliary information, and then fuse the vector representations of each type of auxiliary information corresponding to the output of the self-attention layer through a new self-attention layer. In this way, the weight of each type of auxiliary information in the final item vector representation can be learned, providing more parameter space for the model to further improve the recommendation performance.

Acknowledgment. This work is supported by the Ministry of Education of Humanities and Social Science Project under Grant No. 21JZD055.

References

1. Wang, S., Cao, L., Wang, Y., Sheng, Q.Z., Orgun, M.A., Lian, D.: A survey on session-based recommender systems. ACM Comput. Surv. **54**(7), 1–38 (2021)

2. Chen, X., Xu, H., Zhang, Y., Tang, J., Cao, Y., Qin, Z., Zha, H.: Sequential recommendation with user memory networks. In: Proceedings of the 11th ACM International Conference on Web Search and Data Mining, pp. 108–116 (2018)
3. Koren, Y.: Factorization meets the neighborhood: a multifaceted collaborative filtering model. In: Proceedings of the 14th ACM SIGKDD International Conference on Knowledge Discovery and Data Mining, pp. 426–434 (2008)
4. Koren, Y.: Collaborative filtering with temporal dynamics. In: Proceedings of the 15th ACM SIGKDD International Conference on Knowledge Discovery and Data Mining, pp. 447–456 (2009)
5. Hidasi, B., Karatzoglou, A., Baltrunas, L., Tikk, D.: Session-based recommendations with recurrent neural networks. arXiv preprint arXiv:1511.06939 (2015)
6. Devlin, J., Chang, M.W., Lee, K., Toutanova, K.: BERT: pre-training of deep bidirectional transformers for language understanding. In: Proceedings of the 2019 Conference of the North American Chapter of the Association for Computational Linguistics: Human Language Technologies, pp. 4171–4186 (2019)
7. Kang, W.C., McAuley, J.: Self-attentive sequential recommendation. In: Proceedings of 2018 IEEE International Conference on Data Mining, pp. 197–206 (2018)
8. Sun, F., et al.: Bert4rec: sequential recommendation with bidirectional encoder representations from transformer. In: Proceedings of the 28th ACM International Conference on Information and Knowledge Management, pp. 1441–1450 (2019)
9. Luna, J.M., Fournier-Viger, P., Ventura, S.: Frequent itemset mining: a 25 years review. Wiley Interdiscip. Rev. Data Min. Knowl. Discov. 9(6), e1329 (2019)
10. Shani, G., Heckerman, D., Brafman, R.I., Boutilier, C.: An MDP-based recommender system. J. Mach. Learn. Res. 6(9), 1265–1295 (2005)
11. Chee, C.H., Jaafar, J., Aziz, I.A., Hasan, M.H., Yeoh, W.: Algorithms for frequent itemset mining: a literature review. Artif. Intell. Rev. 52, 2603–2621 (2019)
12. Covington, P., Adams, J., Sargin, E.: Deep neural networks for youtube recommendations. In: Proceedings of the 10th ACM Conference on Recommender Systems, pp. 191–198 (2016)
13. Cheng, H.T., et al.: Wide & deep learning for recommender systems. In: Proceedings of the 1st Workshop on Deep Learning for Recommender Systems, pp. 7–10 (2016)
14. Rumelhart, D.E., Hinton, G.E., Williams, R.J.: Learning representations by back-propagating errors. Nature 323(6088), 533–536 (1986)
15. Vaswani, A., et al.: Attention is all you need. Advances in Neural Information Processing Systems 30 (2017)
16. Scarselli, F., Gori, M., Tsoi, A.C., Hagenbuchner, M., Monfardini, G.: The graph neural network model. IEEE Trans. Neural Netw. 20(1), 61–80 (2008)
17. Tang, J., Wang, K.: Personalized top-n sequential recommendation via convolutional sequence embedding. In: Proceedings of the 11th ACM International Conference on Web Search and Data Mining, pp. 565–573 (2018)
18. Zhou, K., et al.: S3-rec: Self-supervised learning for sequential recommendation with mutual information maximization. In: Proceedings of the 29th ACM International Conference on Information and Knowledge Management, pp. 1893–1902 (2020)
19. Wei, Y., et al.: Contrastive learning for cold-start recommendation. In: Proceedings of the 29th ACM International Conference on Multimedia, pp. 5382–5390 (2021)
20. Yu, J., Yin, H., Xia, X., Chen, T., Cui, L., Nguyen, Q.V.H.: Are graph augmentations necessary? simple graph contrastive learning for recommendation. In: Proceedings of the 45th International ACM SIGIR Conference on Research and Development in Information Retrieval, pp. 1294–1303 (2022)

21. Yang, Y., Huang, C., Xia, L., Li, C.: Knowledge graph contrastive learning for recommendation. In: Proceedings of the 45th International ACM SIGIR Conference on Research and Development in Information Retrieval, pp. 1434–1443 (2022)
22. Hendrycks, D., Gimpel, K.: Gaussian error linear units (gelus). arXiv preprint arXiv:1606.08415 (2016)
23. He, K., Zhang, X., Ren, S., Sun, J.: Deep residual learning for image recognition. In: Proceedings of the IEEE Conference on Computer Vision and Pattern Recognition, pp. 770–778 (2016)
24. Srivastava, N., Hinton, G., Krizhevsky, A., Sutskever, I., Salakhutdinov, R.: Dropout: a simple way to prevent neural networks from overfitting. J. Mach. Learn. Res. 15(1), 1929–1958 (2014)

Rethinking the Robustness of Graph Neural Networks

Tao Wu[1] , Canyixing Cui[1] , Zhuo Zhao[2] , Xingping Xian[1(✉)] ,
Kan Tian[2] , and Xinwen Cao[1]

[1] School of Cybersecurity and Information Law, Chongqing University of Posts
and Telecommunications, Chongqing 400000, China
xxp0213@gmail.com
[2] CQUPT-CCTGM Joint Laboratory of Intelligenct Museum,
Chongqing 400000, China

Abstract. Graph neural networks (GNNs) have achieved tremendous
success in many fields like social networks, citation networks and recommendation systems due to its powerful expression ability and excellent
performance. However, GNNs are vulnerable to adversarial attacks which
can significantly reduce its performance. Meanwhile, researches on the
robustness of GNNs lack the exploration of its underlying mechanism,
leading to the insufficiency of explaining adversarial attack. Thereby, the
reasons for the vulnerability of the model and the process of adversarial
attack need to be explained, which contributes to designing robust graph
neural networks. To achieve this goal, we explore the robustness of GNNs
from three viewpoints. Firstly, from the perspective of data pattern, we
find that the more regular the data, the worse robustness of the model.
Moreover, model factors based on the capacity and architecture are discussed. The results demonstrate that the model with large capacity has
stronger robustness under the circumstance of adequate data, and the
graph attention mechanism is more robust compared with other model
architectures. Finally, in the view of the transferability of adversarial
examples, we observe that adversarial examples are easily transferred
among models with similar architectures, and thus these models are vulnerable to attacks.

Keywords: Graph neural networks · Adversarial attack · Robustness ·
Decision boundary · Transferability

1 Introduction

Recent years have witnessed significant success brought by artificial intelligence
algorithms in industry, agriculture, transportation and other fields. Nevertheless,
there are some security issues in these domains. Only by solving these problems,
artificial intelligence algorithms can be thriving.

Graph neural networks (GNNs) [1], which are the typical artificial intelligence algorithms, have provided an effective method for graph learning, as it

X. Meng et al. (Eds.): BDSC 2023, CCIS 1846, pp. 346–361, 2023.
https://doi.org/10.1007/978-981-99-3925-1_23

can consider graph structure, node features and their relationships at the same time. In spite of its remarkable performance in many fundamental tasks, like node classification, link prediction, graph classification and community detection [2], they are vulnerable to adversarial attack, that is, the attackers can fool the GNNs by manipulating the graph structures or node features with carefully crafted perturbations that individuals are subtle. Adversarial attack on GNNs has caused a wide range of security threats to daily life, for example, spammers add false information to social networks, increasing the spread opportunities of false information [3]; in the credit prediction system, attackers make themselves have high credit by establishing connections with high credit users [4].

Adversarial attack can occur in training and testing stages, which are correspondingly divided into poisoning attack and evasion attack. Between them, poisoning attack is the core of our study. In poisoning attack, the attacker injects carefully crafted poisoning samples into training dataset [5], causing the reduction of model performance and the deviating of decision boundary. Decision boundary is the boundary of correct classification and wrong classification in node classification task [6], and it is the direct embodiment of model classification [7–11]. Perfect decision boundary can improve the generalization ability of GNNs and enhance the robustness of model.

The adversarial attack on GNNs has been widely studied, however, there are still no observations about the in-depth understanding of its underlying mechanism in current research field. Therefore, it is an urgent problem to analyze the influence of adversarial attack on GNNs. In the field of model decision space, the attacker can manipulate the samples by crossing the decision boundary with small perturbations on the node classification task, which makes the node misclassified. Motivated by these observation, we study the robustness of GNNs based on data pattern, model factors and transferability of adversarial examples. Our main contributions are outlined below:

- We analyze the robustness of GNNs from the perspective of data pattern by comparing the data with different regularity. We indicate that a robust model cannot be trained by data with stroity.
- We compare the robustness of GNNs on model capacity and model architecture, and find that with the growth of model capacity, the robustness is improved synchronously with the training data climbing, besides, the robustness of graph attention mechanism is better than that of graph autoencoders.
- We analyze the transferability of adversarial examples by different model architectures and the same model architecture with diverse model capacities. By extensive experiments, we verify that models with the same architecture have great transferability, and thus are easy to be attacked.

2   Related Work

The adversarial attack on graph neural networks can be divided into adversarial attack of node classification task, link prediction task, graph clustering task and graph embedding task. Among them, the adversarial attack of node classification task is the focus of our study.

Researches for adversarial attack on GNNs have been extensively conducted in recent years. Zügner et al. [12] first studied the adversarial attack problem on graph and proposed Nettack towards the semi-supervised classification model. This method based on the prediction loss attacks GNNs , while the obtained perturbation is locally optimal, and the transferability is not considered. To solve the transferability problem, Chen et al. [13] introduced the Fast Gradient Attack (FGA). The core idea is to design an adversarial network generator and attack in accordance with the strong transferability of adversarial attack. However, the target node needs to calculate the gradient with each pair of nodes, which is time-consuming. Faced with the large-scale graphs, Li et al. [14] proposed the Simplified Gradient Attack (SGA) for the scalability of adversarial attack by extracting a smaller subgraph.

Distinguishing from modifying edges mentioned above, adversarial attack can also be achieved by injecting nodes. Considering the difficulty of link disturbance in practical application, Wang et al. [15] introduced the Approximate Fast Gradient Symbol Method (AFGSM). This method approximately linearizes the target GCN, derives an approximate closed-form solution with low time cost, and injects malicious nodes into the graph in sequence. By injecting single node, Tao et al. [16] put forward G-NIA, which reduces the cost of generating multiple nodes for the attack, but it does not consider robustness or whether it is easy to be detected by defense methods.

Other than the above methods, this study first utilizes the decision boundary to analyze the robustness of graph neural networks. This will undoubtedly advance the understanding of adversarial attacks.

3   Preliminary

3.1   Problem Definition

Definition 1. *(Graph). Let $G = \langle V, E \rangle$ represents a graph, where $V = \{v_1, ..., v_N\}$ and $E = \{e_1, ..., e_K\}$ are the set of nodes and edges, respectively.*

Definition 2. *(Decision Boundary). Given an input x with label y_r, the decision boundary is defined as:*

$$D(x) = Z(x)_r - \max\{Z(x)_i, i \neq r\} = 0 \tag{1}$$

The decision function $D(x)$ evaluates the extent to which the correct logit output exceeds the maximum incorrect logit output.

Definition 3. *(Adversarial Attack). Adversarial attack aims to letting the model make a wrong judgement by adding some adversarial perturbations to the input data. The obtained samples are called adversarial examples.*

3.2 Graph Neural Networks

Graph neural networks combine graph with deep neural network, and the typical GNNs mainly include the following categories: graph convolution network, graph attention network and graph autoencoders.

GCN. Graph convolution network uses convolution to fuse features. The propagation rules of each convolution layer can be defined as:

$$H^{(l+1)} = \sigma \left(\tilde{D}^{-\frac{1}{2}} \tilde{A} \tilde{D}^{-\frac{1}{2}} H^{(l)} W^{(l)} \right) \tag{2}$$

GAT. Graph attention network adds an attention coefficient to each edge while aggregating feature. The graph convolution operation can be formulated as:

$$H_i^{(l+1)} = \sigma \left(\sum_{j \in N_i} \alpha \left(h_i^{(l)}, h_j^{(l)} \right) W^{(l)} h_j^{(l)} \right), \tag{3}$$

where $\alpha_{ij} = \frac{\exp(LeakyReLU(e_{ij}))}{\sum_{k \in N_i} \exp(LeakyReLU(e_{ik}))}$ indicates the attention coefficient.

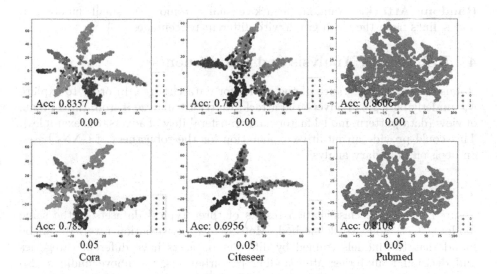

Fig. 1. Classification results with fixed model (GCN) and attack method (Mettack).

GAE. Graph autoencoders use GNNs to represent the nodes as low-dimensional vectors, which using GCN as the encoder to get the embedding of nodes:

$$Z = GCN(A, X) = \hat{A} ReLU \left(\hat{A} X W_0 \right) W_1 \tag{4}$$

After that, the original graph is reconstructed by inner product in decoder:

$$\hat{A} = \sigma \left(Z Z^T \right) \tag{5}$$

3.3   Adversarial Attack on GNNs

The adversarial attack on GNNs can be split into targeted attack, untargeted attack [14, 17–25] and random attack, and their representative methods are Nettack, Mettack, and Random Attack.

Mettack. Mettack takes the graph structure as a hyperparameter, and uses meta-gradient (reflected in the following formula) to meta-update the graph.

$$\nabla_G^{meta} := \nabla_G L_{atk}\left(f_{\theta*}\left(G\right)\right), \theta* = opt_\theta\left(L_{train}\left(f_\theta\left(G\right)\right)\right), \tag{6}$$

where $opt\left(\cdot\right)$ is a differentiable optimization process.

Nettack. Nettack carries out adversarial attack based on the predicted loss of GNNs, and the prediction result of the surrogate model is as follows:

$$L_S(A, X; W, v_0) = \max_{c \neq c_{old}} \left[\hat{A}XW\right]_{v_0 c} - \left[\hat{A}XW\right]_{v_0 c_{old}} \tag{7}$$

The perturbation that maximizing the scoring function is selected.

Random Attack. Random attack casually remove a small number of nodes/links from the clean graph with different percentages [26].

4   Robustness Analysis and Experiments

Robustness is the tolerance of the model for data changes. In order to explore the underlying logic of adversarial attack, we try to analyze it from three points of view (data pattern, model factors and transferability of adversarial examples). This could provide an intuitive explanation for the robustness of GNNs based on decision boundary analysis.

4.1   Data Pattern

Figure 1 shows the classification results of three typical datasets in the same model (GCN) and attack method (Mettack 5% perturbation rate). It can be found that the models trained by different datasets have different categories and decision boundaries; after adding perturbations, the above findings also exist. Accordingly, it is indispensable to further analyze the robustness from the perspective of data pattern.

Taking the task of community detection as the start point, we call the graph with close connections within communities and sparse connections between communities as regular graph data, and those with sparse internal connections and close external connections among communities as irregular graph data. We adopt the LFR benchmark network generation algorithm to create graphs with different regularity. As shown in Fig. 2, the mixed parameter mu determines the regularity of generated graph data. The larger mu is, the more connections between different communities, and the more irregular the graph is.

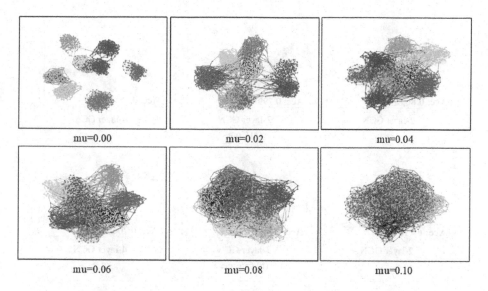

Fig. 2. Graphs of different data patterns generated by LFR algorithm.

Table 1 shows the classification results using these generated graphs under three typical adversarial attacks. In Table 1, the header row is *mu*, from left to right, it indicates that the regularity of generated graph gradually becomes weak, the header column is the adversarial attack methods and their perturbation rate/number. We directly reflected the robustness by means of the accuracy.

Table 1. The accuracy of graphs with different data patterns in typical adversarial attacks under GCN.

Method \ Mu	0.00	0.02	0.04	0.06	0.08	0.10
Mettack (5%)	0.7189	0.7525	0.7695	**0.7894**	0.7603	0.7489
Nettack (2.0)	0.5012	**0.6398**	0.6169	0.6120	0.5699	0.5675
RandomAttack (5%)	0.7214	0.7538	0.7573	**0.7658**	0.7544	0.7517

Interestingly, in Mettack and Random Attack, the accuracy is low when *mu* equals to 0, later it comes to the highest with the mixed parameter rising to 0.06, however, it declines with *mu* increasing. As for Nettack, the accuracy reaches to its peak with the mixed parameter climbs to 0.02, and later goes down. The experimental results indicate that as the complexity of data rises, the accuracy of the model first increases and then decreases. Hence, it can be concluded that the data should not have strong regularity in the process of training a robust model.

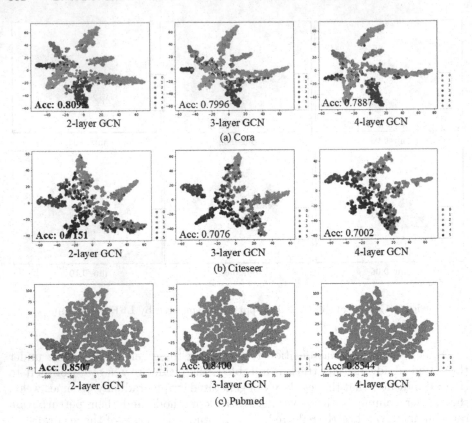

Fig. 3. Robustness of 2-, 3-, 4-layer GCN in Random Attack (5% perturbation rate).

4.2   Model Factors

In this part, we discuss the robustness of GNNs from two aspects: model capacity and model architecture.

Model Capacity Analysis. Model capacity refers to the ability of the model fitting various functions [27]. In GNNs, model capacity is reflected by the layers of model, and the model with more layers has larger capacity. Taking the typical graph neural network GCN as an example, the 2-layer GCN is expressed as:

$$Z = f(A, X) = soft\max\left(\hat{A}\text{ReLU}\left(\hat{A}XW^{(0)}\right)W^{(1)}\right) \tag{8}$$

After increasing model capacity, the 3-layer GCN is described as:

$$Z = soft\max\left(\hat{A}\text{ReLU}\left(\hat{A}\text{ReLU}\left(\hat{A}XW^{(0)}\right)W^{(1)}\right)W^{(2)}\right) \tag{9}$$

Further, the formula of the 4-layer GCN is:

$$Z = soft\max\left(\hat{A}\text{ReLU}\left(\hat{A}\text{ReLU}\left(\hat{A}\text{ReLU}\left(\hat{A}XW^{(0)}\right)W^{(1)}\right)W^{(2)}\right)W^{(3)}\right)$$

$$(10)$$

We compare the robustness of 2-, 3- and 4-layer GCN under the same attack method in node classification task. Figure 3 shows the robustness results under 5% perturbation rate of Random Attack. In Cora, it can be seen that the space between the decision boundaries of 2-layer GCN is more obvious, and thus the robustness of 2-layer GCN is stronger than that of 3- and 4-layer GCN. The above

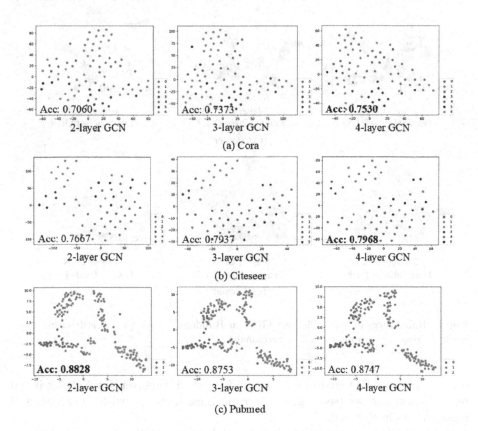

(a) Cora

(b) Citeseer

(c) Pubmed

Fig. 4. Robustness of 2-, 3-, 4-layer GCN in Nettack (2.0 perturbation number).

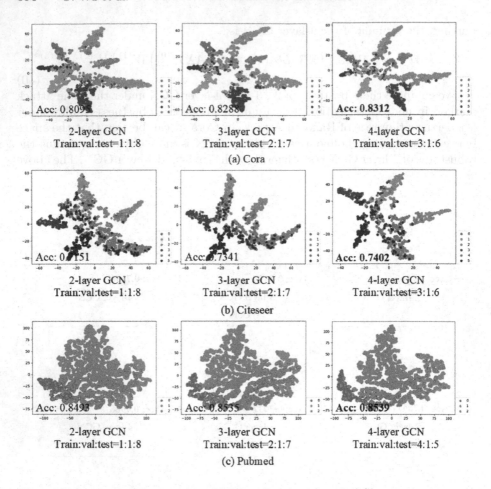

Fig. 5. Robustness of 2-, 3-, 4-layer GCN in Random Attack (5% perturbation rate) while increasing training data synchronously.

findings can also be found in Citeseer and Pubmed. However, for Nettack in 2.0 perturbation number (see Fig. 4), the robustness decreases with the growing of model layers in Pubmed.

Considering that the complexity of model grows with the increasing of capacity, it is compulsory to extend the training data while adding capacity. Figure 5 manifests the robustness of 2-, 3-, 4-layer GCN under Random Attack while rising the training data synchronously. In Cora and Citeseer, when the training data of 3- and 4-layer GCN increases by 10% at the same time, the decision boundaries become clear, and thus the robustness of model grows with the extending of model layers. In Pubmed, only when these increases by 10% and 20% respectively can the effect be produced. Accordingly, with the expansion of model capacity, the robustness climbs synchronously on the condition of enhancing training data.

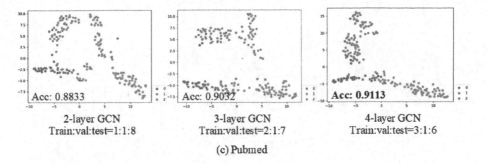

2-layer GCN
Train:val:test=1:1:8

3-layer GCN
Train:val:test=2:1:7

4-layer GCN
Train:val:test=3:1:6

(c) Pubmed

Fig. 6. Robustness of 2-, 3-, 4-layer GCN under Nettack (2.0 perturbation number) while increasing training data synchronously.

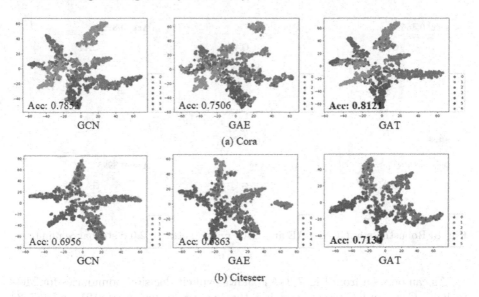

GCN   GAE   GAT

(a) Cora

GCN   GAE   GAT

(b) Citeseer

Fig. 7. Robustness of GCN, GAE and GAT under Mettack (5% disturbance rate).

In the case of Nettack (Fig. 6) in Pubmed, the above conclusions can be obtained when the training data of 3- and 4-layer GCN increases by 10% correspondingly.

Model Architecture Analysis. The study of model architecture can provide an effective theoretical guidance for selecting suitable models. According to the model architecture, graph models can be divided into graph convolution network (GCN), graph autoencoders (GAE) and graph attention network (GAT). Different model architectures have different internal mechanisms, consequently, it is significant to explore the robustness based on model architecture. In the same task, attack method and dataset, we compare the robustness of different model architectures.

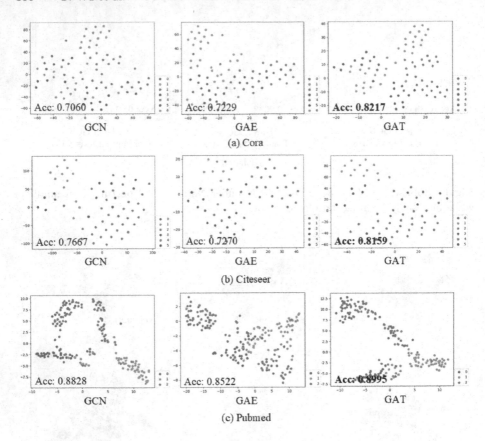

Fig. 8. Robustness of GCN, GAE and GAT under Nettack (2.0 disturbance number).

As can be seen from Fig. 7, GAT shows explicit decision boundaries for Mettack on Cora and Citeseer, and has the highest accuracy (0.8121 and 0.7134 respectively), while Pubmed is out of memory. In Fig. 8, the accuracy of GAT in Nettack is still the highest (0.8217, 0.8159, and 0.8995, correspondingly). As for Random Attack (Fig. 9), Cora and Citeseer can get the above conclusions, while GCN has the strongest robustness in Pubmed, but the difference under diverse model architectures is extremely small (less than 0.01).

By observing the above findings, we can conclude that the graph attention mechanism is more robust than graph convolution network and graph autoencoders on the condition of only changing the model architectures.

4.3   Transferability of Adversarial Examples

The concept of transferability is put forward in [28], that is, the adversarial examples generated from one model can also have some effects on other models. In this paper, the transferability of adversarial examples is analyzed from two

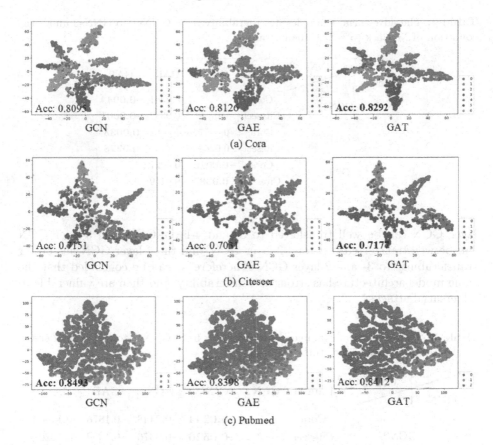

Fig. 9. Robustness of GCN, GAE and GAT under Random Attack (disturbance rate 5%).

aspects, model architectures and capacities. For model architecture, the transferability of adversarial examples produced by GCN, GAE and GAT is analyzed; as for model capacity, we compare the adversarial examples' transferability of 2-, 3-, 4-layer GCN.

The adversarial examples' transferability for Mettack is presented in Table 2, in which the transferability of adversarial examples is reflected by the ratio of the difference of accuracy before and after transferring to the accuracy of original model. And then the positive sign indicates that the accuracy after transferring is bigger than original accuracy. Due to the memory problem of CUDA, we cannot generate adversarial examples from Pubmed, and 3-, 4-layer GCN. As can be observed from Table 2, for different model architectures, the adversarial examples generated by GCN2 can be transferred to GAT well, but the transferability to GAE is exceedingly poor. For graph autoencoders and graph attention mechanism, we can find that GAE can transferred to GAT and GAT can transferred to GCN2 well. According to table 3, in Nettack, the 2-

Table 2. The adversarial examples' transferability from GNNs1 to GNNs2 under the condition of Mettack (5% disturbance rate).

GNNs (2) / GNNs (1)	Dataset	GCN2	GAE	GAT
GCN2	Cora	–	−0.0061	**−0.0044**
	Citeseer		−0.0332	**−0.0001**
GAE	Cora	0.0057	–	**0.0033**
	Citeseer	0.0280		**0.0228**
GAT	Cora	**−0.0015**	−0.0027	–
	Citeseer	**−0.0085**	−0.0449	

layer GCN can be well transferred to 3- and 4-layer GCN, the 3-layer GCN can be well transferred to 4- and 2-layer GCN, and the 4-layer GCN has better transferability to 3- and 2-layer GCN. Therefore, it can be concluded that the same model architecture has stronger transferability, and then are vulnerable to adversarial attacks.

Table 3. The adversarial examples' transferability from GNNs1 to GNNs2 under the condition of Nettack (2.0 disturbance number).

GNNs (2) / GNNs (1)	Dataset	GCN2	GCN3	GCN4	GAE	GAT
GCN2	Cora		**−0.0244**	−0.0448	−0.1878	−0.1350
	Citeseer	–	**−0.0520**	−0.0676	−0.1398	−0.1226
	Pubmed		**−0.0001**	−0.0006	−0.0045	−0.0019
GCN3	Cora	0.0341		**−0.0224**	−0.0851	−0.0807
	Citeseer	0.0372	–	**−0.0079**	−0.0785	−0.0370
	Pubmed	−0.0025		**−0.0006**	−0.0039	−0.0037
GCN4	Cora	0.0222	**0.0213**		−0.0300	−0.0264
	Citeseer	0.0187	**0.0079**	–	0.0371	−0.0234
	Pubmed	−0.0085	**−0.0013**		−0.0102	−0.0024
GAE	Cora	0.0358	0.0180	**−0.0080**		−0.0865
	Citeseer	0.0145	−0.0121	**−0.0119**	–	−0.0467
	Pubmed	0.0018	0.0011	**0.0007**		−0.0037
GAT	Cora	0.0426	0.0393	**0.0355**	0.0650	
	Citeseer	0.0600	0.0199	**0.0020**	0.1179	–
	Pubmed	0.0018	0.0011	**0.0007**	0.0050	

5   Conclusions and Discussion

This study analyzed the robustness of GNNs from three levels (data pattern, model factors and transferability of adversarial examples) based on decision boundary. Our experimental results demonstrated that the robust model cannot be trained by data with strong regularity; with the adding of model capacity, the robustness of the model increases synchronously with the growing of training data; as for model architecture, GAT is more robust; concerning the transferability of adversarial examples, the same model architectures have stronger transferability.

This study provides a new perspective for the interpretability research of adversarial attack on GNNs, and is also helpful to design a robust adversarial attack method. In addition, the features and the evaluation of robustness on GNNs are worthy of further research.

Acknowledgment. This work was partially supported by the National Natural Science Foundation of China under Grant Nos. 62106030, 61802039; Chongqing Municipal Natural Science Foundation under Grant No. cstc2020jcyj-msxmX0804; Chongqing Municipal Postdoctoral Science Foundation under Grant No. cstc2021jcyj-bsh0176; Chongqing Research Program of Basic Research and Frontier Technology under Grant No. cstc2021jcyj-msxmX0530.

References

1. Scarselli, F., Tsoi, A.C., Gori, M., Hagenbuchner, M.: Graphical-based learning environments for pattern recognition. In: Fred, A., Caelli, T.M., Duin, R.P.W., Campilho, A.C., de Ridder, D. (eds.) SSPR /SPR 2004. LNCS, vol. 3138, pp. 42–56. Springer, Heidelberg (2004). https://doi.org/10.1007/978-3-540-27868-9_4
2. Dai, E., et al.: A comprehensive survey on trustworthy graph neural networks: privacy, robustness, fairness, and explainability (2022). https://arxiv.org/abs/2204.08570
3. Wei, J., et al.: Adversarial attacks and defenses on graphs: a review, a tool, and empirical studies (2020). https://arxiv.org/abs/2003.00653
4. Dai, H., et al.: Adversarial attack on graph structured data. In: Dy, J., Krause, A. (eds.) International Conference on Machine Learning. Proceedings of Machine Learning Research, vol. 80, pp. 1115–1124. PMLR (2018). https://arxiv.org/abs/1806.02371
5. Chen, J., Zheng, H., Su, M., Du, T., Lin, C., Ji, S.: Invisible poisoning: highly stealthy targeted poisoning attack. In: Liu, Z., Yung, M. (eds.) Inscrypt 2019. LNCS, vol. 12020, pp. 173–198. Springer, Cham (2020). https://doi.org/10.1007/978-3-030-42921-8_10
6. Yu, F., Liu, C., Wang, Y., Zhao, L., Chen, X.: Interpreting adversarial robustness: a view from decision surface in input space (2018). https://arxiv.org/abs/1810.00144
7. He, W., Li, B., Song, D.: Decision boundary analysis of adversarial examples. In: International Conference on Learning Representations, pp. 1–15 (2018). https://openreview.net/forum?id=BkpiPMbA-

8. Sun, K., Zhu, Z., Lin, Z.: Towards understanding adversarial examples systematically: exploring data size, task and model factors (2019). https://arxiv.org/abs/1902.11019
9. Karimi, H., Derr, T., Tang, J.: Characterizing the decision boundary of deep neural networks (2019). https://arxiv.org/abs/1912.11460
10. Fawzi, A., Moosavi-Dezfooli, S.M., Frossard, P., Soatto, S.: Empirical study of the topology and geometry of deep networks. In: Proceedings of the IEEE Conference on Computer Vision and Pattern Recognition, pp. 3762–3770 (2018). https://doi.org/10.1109/CVPR.2018.00396
11. Lei, S., Zhang, H., Wang, K., Su, Z.: How training data affect the accuracy and robustness of neural networks for Image classification (2019). https://openreview.net/forum?id=HklKWhC5F7
12. Zügner, D., Akbarnejad, A., Günnemann, S.: Adversarial attacks on neural networks for graph data. In: Proceedings of the 24th ACM SIGKDD International Conference on Knowledge Discovery & Data Mining, pp. 2847–2856. KDD 2018, Association for Computing Machinery, New York, NY, USA (2018)
13. Chen, J., Wu, Y., Xu, X., Chen, Y., Zheng, H., Xuan, Q.: Fast gradient attack on network embedding (2018). https://arxiv.org/abs/1809.02797
14. Li, J., Xie, T., Chen, L., Xie, F., He, X., Zheng, Z.: Adversarial attack on large scale graph. IEEE Trans. Knowl. Data Eng. 35(1), 82–95 (2021). https://doi.org/10.1109/TKDE.2021.3078755
15. Wang, J., Luo, M., Suya, F., Li, J., Yang, Z., Zheng, Q.: Scalable attack on graph data by injecting vicious nodes. Data Min. Knowl. Disc. 34(5), 1363–1389 (2020). https://doi.org/10.1007/s10618-020-00696-7
16. Tao, S., Cao, Q., Shen, H., Huang, J., Wu, Y., Cheng, X.: Single node injection attack against graph neural networks. In: Proceedings of the 30th ACM International Conference on Information & Knowledge Management, pp. 1794–1803. Association for Computing Machinery, New York, NY, USA (2021).https://doi.org/10.1145/3459637.3482393
17. Wu, H., Wang, C., Tyshetskiy, Y., Docherty, A., Lu, K., Zhu, L.: Adversarial examples on graph data: deep insights into attack and defense. In: Proceedings of the Twenty-Eighth International Joint Conference on Artificial Intelligence, IJCAI-19, pp. 4816–4823. International Joint Conferences on Artificial Intelligence Organization (2019). https://doi.org/10.24963/ijcai.2019/669
18. Xu, K., et al.: Topology attack and defense for graph neural networks: an optimization perspective. In: Proceedings of the 28th International Joint Conference on Artificial Intelligence, pp. 3961–3967. IJCAI2019, AAAI Press (2019). https://doi.org/10.5555/3367471.3367592
19. Sun, Y., Wang, S., Tang, X., Hsieh, T.Y., Honavar, V.: Node injection attacks on graphs via reinforcement learning (2019). https://arxiv.org/abs/1909.06543
20. Chen, J., Zhang, D., Lin, X.: Adaptive adversarial attack on graph embedding via GAN. In: Xiang, Y., Liu, Z., Li, J. (eds.) SocialSec 2020. CCIS, vol. 1298, pp. 72–84. Springer, Singapore (2020). https://doi.org/10.1007/978-981-15-9031-3_7
21. Bojchevski, A., Günnemann, S.: Adversarial attacks on node embeddings via graph poisoning. In: Chaudhuri, K., Salakhutdinov, R. (eds.) Proceedings of the 36th International Conference on Machine Learning. Proceedings of Machine Learning Research, vol. 97, pp. 695–704. PMLR (2019). https://proceedings.mlr.press/v97/bojchevski19a.html
22. Chen, J., Zhang, J., Chen, Z., Du, M., Xuan, Q.: Time-aware gradient attack on dynamic network link prediction. IEEE Trans. Knowl. Data Eng. 35(2), 2091–2102 (2023). https://doi.org/10.1109/TKDE.2021.3110580

23. Zheleva, E., Getoor, L.: Preserving the privacy of sensitive relationships in graph data. In: Bonchi, F., Ferrari, E., Malin, B., Saygin, Y. (eds) Privacy, Security, and Trust in KDD. PInKDD 2007. Lecture Notes in Computer Science, vol. 4890. Springer, Berlin, Heidelberg (2008). https://doi.org/10.1007/978-3-540-78478-4_9

24. Lin, W., Ji, S., Li, B.: Adversarial attacks on link prediction algorithms based on graph neural networks. In: Proceedings of the 15th ACM Asia Conference on Computer and Communications Security, pp. 370–380. ASIA CCS 2020, Association for Computing Machinery, New York, NY, USA (2020). https://doi.org/10.1145/3320269.3384750

25. Xian, X., et al.: DeepEC: adversarial attacks against graph structure prediction models. Neurocomputing **437**, 168–185 (2021). https://doi.org/10.1016/j.neucom.2020.07.126

26. Malik, H.A.M., Abid, F., Wahiddin, M.R., Bhatti, Z.: Robustness of dengue complex network under targeted versus random attack. CompLex **2017**, 1–12 (2017). https://doi.org/10.1155/2017/2515928

27. Hu, X., Chu, L., Pei, J., Liu, W., Bian, J.: Model complexity of deep learning: a survey. Knowl. Inf. Syst. **63**, 2585–2619 (2021). https://doi.org/10.1007/s10115-021-01605-0

28. Szegedy, C., et al.: Intriguing properties of neural networks. In: Bengio, Y., LeCun, Y. (eds.) 2nd International Conference on Learning Representations, pp. 1–10 (2014). https://arxiv.org/abs/1312.6199

MDC: An Interpretable GNNs Method Based on Node Motif Degree and Graph Diffusion Convolution

Tingting Wang[1], Feng Ding[1], Naiwen Luo[1], Qihang Lei[1], Huafei Huang[1],
Tong Zhang[2], and Shuo Yu[3(✉)]

[1] School of Software, Dalian University of Technology, Dalian 116620, China
ttwang93@outlook.com, dingfeng@dlut.edu.cn, nw.luo@outlook.com,
qihang.lei@outlook.com, hhuafei@outlook.com
[2] Faculty of Humanities and Social Sciences, Dalian University of Technology,
Dalian 116024, China
zhangtong@dlut.edu.cn
[3] School of Computer Science and Technology, Dalian University of Technology,
Dalian 116024, China
yushuo@dlut.edu.cn

Abstract. Graph Neural Networks (GNNs) have achieved significant success in various real-world applications, including social networks, recommendation systems, and natural language processing. One of the challenges in GNNs is their black-box nature, which limits their interpretability and hinders their applications in critical areas such as healthcare and finance. However, existing interpretability of GNNs methods mainly focus on first-hop neighbors of a node and ignores multivariate relationship, resulting in low interpretability and inaccurate predictions. To tackle this challenge, we propose a Motif Diffusion Convolution (MDC) framework with a high-order structure feature augmentation mechanism based on graph diffusion convolution. The mechanism is utilizing multivariate relationship by calculating various node motif degree to enhance the feature channel, which obtains the relationship from a higher-order structure than two directly connecting entities. For better interpretability, MDC automatically learns a set of diffusion coefficients for each feature channel via graph diffusion convolution. We conduct experiments on six real-world datasets with three baselines. The experimental results show that MDC framework can build interpretability of GNNs, and improve accuracy by 2% on node classification benchmarks.

Keywords: Graph Neural Networks · Interpretability · Graph Diffusion · Multivariate Relationship · Motifs

1 Introduction

Graph Neural Networks (GNNs) [22] have achieved great success in a wide range of real-world applications such as social networks, recommendation systems, and natural language processing [14, 16]. However, GNNs are often considered as black-box

X. Meng et al. (Eds.): BDSC 2023, CCIS 1846, pp. 362–374, 2023.
https://doi.org/10.1007/978-981-99-3925-1_24

models [3,4] due to their high non-linearity, resulting in difficulties to interpret their predictions and decision-making process. The lack of interpretability will hinder their applications in sensitive areas such as healthcare and finance.

Extensive efforts have been made to investigate the interpretability of GNNs. Zhang et al. [20] categorized existing GNNs explanation approaches into post-hoc explanation methods and self-explaining GNNs methods (i.e., GNNs with built-in interpretability). Post-hoc methods [11,13,17,18] explain behaviors and decisions of machine learning models after they have been trained. They focus on explaining individual predictions or features of a model, rather than providing a comprehensive understanding of the behavior as a whole. Unlike post-hoc methods, self-explaining methods [3,5,20] are designed to generate explanations alongside predictions. For example, Feng et al. [20] proposed KerGNNs that integrate graph kernels into the message passing process of GNNs. They use first-hop neighbors for propagation in all layers and feature channels (e.g., dimensions) by a fixed update rule to each node at every iteration. If they have different requirements for the neighborhood size to consider high-order structure information, the number of message-passing iterations should be increased. However, when GNNs architecture is deep, the features of nodes become increasingly similar after multiple message-passing iterations.

To address this problem, Graph Diffusion Convolution (GDC) [7] as a type of graph convolutional network [6] was proposed to leverage the concept of graph diffusion to aggregate information. Unlike the traditional graph convolutional network with a fixed number message-passing iterations to update node features, GDC uses graph diffusion to aggregate information from a long-range neighbor. The graph diffusion is based on the kernel function [8], which defines a distribution of information spreading from one node to another. The function is parameterized by diffusion parameters that determine how information propagates through the graph. However, these parameters need to be adjusted manually, resulting in low interpretability.

In this paper, we propose a Motif Diffusion Convolution (MDC) framework with high interpretability of GNNs, which is based on node motif degree and learnable diffusion coefficients. Unlike traditional graph diffusion convolution by tuning diffusion kernel parameters, MDC automatically learn parameters called diffusion coefficients. These learnable coefficients demonstrate partial encoding mechanism of GNNs models, which improve the transparency of original black-box models and realize built-in explanations for GNNs. In addition, MDC can be employed as graph encoders for GNNs models. MDC analyzes the role that specific network motifs play in the overall networks by calculating node motif degree, allowing them to learn high quality representations. Specifically, we design a high-order structure feature augmentation mechanism to replace the adjacency matrix for utilizing multivariate relationship. The adjacency matrix only represents the relationship between two directly connecting nodes of the input graph, which cannot provide a comprehensive understanding of high-order structure information. In order to obtain this information, MDC designs a multi-relationship feature matrix by calculating various node motif degree to replace the original adjacency matrix. The contributions of this work are summarized as below:

- We propose an MDC framework that contains a high-order structure feature augmentation mechanism for utilizing multivariate relationship. We also propose a self-explaining GNNs method by automatically learning a set of diffusion coefficients for specific neighborhoods in each GNNs layer and feature channels.

- We design MDC as a pluggable component that can be applied to any neural networks for obtaining high-order structure information and improving the transparency of neural networks, and we verify the availability of MDC with three GNNs models in this paper.
- We conduct extensive experiments on six real-world datasets with three GNNs models. Experimental results show that GNNs with MDC can improve prediction accuracy compared with the original models.

The rest of this paper is organized as follows. In Sect. 2, we present the related work. In Sect. 3, we prsent some necessary background of GNNs, motifs, and GDC. In Sect. 4, we present the design of MDC. In Sect. 5, we present experiments and their results. Finally, we present the conclusion of this paper in Sect. 6.

2   Related Work

In this section, we present some necessary backgrounds of graph neural networks and their explainable methods. We analyze differences between graph neural networks and graph diffusion convolution. And we also present applications of graph diffusion convolution, which motivates our proposed framework in this paper.

2.1   The Interpretability of Graph Neural Networks

Graph Neural Networks (GNNs) are powerful tools for modeling graph-structured data, and have been successfully applied to a wide range of tasks such as node classification and link prediction. However, the black-box nature of GNNs makes their models less transparency and difficult to be applied to critical areas. Extensive efforts have been made to investigate the interpretability of GNNs, which aim to provide more transparent and interpretable models. Luo et al. [11] proposed a prototype graph generator to generate prototype graphs from learnable prototype embeddings. Neil et al. [12] proposed an interpretable graph convolutional neural network for noisy data on knowledge graphs, which explains the prediction results by visualizing the embedding vectors of each node and edge. Dai and Wang [3] designed the interpretable similarity module to find interpretable k-nearest labeled nodes. Zhang et al. [5] combines prototype learning with GNNs, where explanations are derived from the case-based learning process. However, these methods only consider local direct neighbors, and ignore various highe-order structures (e.g. motifs) to capture multivariate relationships in graphs.

2.2   The Applications of Graph Diffusion Convolution

Graph Neural Networks (GNNs) are based on the principle of message passing, where each node aggregates information from its direct neighbors for several iterations until convergence. On the other hand, Graph Diffusion Convolution (GDC) [7] are based on the principle of diffusion, where information is propagated across the graph through a diffusion process. Compared with GNNs, GDC is able to capture long-range dependencies between nodes across the entire graph. GDC is also a promising alternative to GNNs for processing graph-based data, especially in scenarios where long-range dependencies need to be captured. GDC has been successfully applied to predict traffic flow [19] on road networks, detect traffic incidents, and optimize traffic signals [9]. Li et al. [9] proposed a diffusion convolutional recurrent neural network for traffic forecasting, which uses graph diffusion to model traffic flows on road networks. Zhang et al. [19] proposed a traffic flow forecasting with spatial temporal graph diffusion network, learning the relationship between traffic flow changes from the overall spatial scope in the entire city. Gao et al. [10] proposed a spatio-temporal graph attention network for traffic forecasting, which uses graph diffusion to model traffic flows on road networks. However, GDC typically requires tuning of parameters such as the diffusion coefficients. In order to automatically learn the diffusion coefficients in the diffusion process, we propose a motif diffusion convolution framework to address the limitations of parameter tuning.

3 Preliminaries and Notations

In this section, we introduce notations used in this paper, which are depicted in Table 1. We briefly introduce how GNNs learn the node and graph representations. We also introduce motif representations.

Table 1. Notations

Notations	Implications
v	The node
$\mathcal{V}$	The node set
$\mathcal{E}$	The edge set
$\mathcal{C}$	The node label set
G	An input graph
$M_{(.)}$	A motif instance
$N_{(.)}$	The motif degree
$\mathbf{A}$	The adjacency matrix
$\mathbf{M}$	The message propogation matrix
X	The feature matrix
$H(\cdot)$	The diffusion function
r	The neighborhood radius
L	The layer of GNNs
θ	The learnable diffusion coefficient
$\mathcal{L}$	The normalized laplacian matrix

3.1 Graph Representation

Given an undirected graph $G = \{\mathcal{V}, \mathcal{E}\}$, and each node $v_i \in \mathcal{V}$ has a d-dimensional node feature $x_i \in \mathbb{R}^d$. If a pair of nodes $(v_i, v_j) \in \mathcal{V}$ are connected, edge $e_{i,j}$ of v_i

and v_j equals to one, otherwise $e_{i,j}$ equals to zero. GNNs learn the representation of v_i by iteratively aggregating the information of its neighbors $N(i)$. At the l-th layer of a GNNs model, the v_i's representation $h_i = \text{update}(h_i^{l-1}, h_{N(i)}^l)$, where h_i^{l-1} is the representation of v_i in the previous layer, and $h_{N(i)}^l$ is aggregated from the neighbors of v_i via an aggregation function: $h_{N(i)} = \text{aggregate}(h_j^{l-1}, \forall v_j \in N(i))$. The implantation of the update($\cdot$) and aggregate($\cdot$) can be vairous for different GNNs models. For a GNNs model with L layers in total, h_i^L is the final representation of the node v_i. After aggregating the node representations, the graph representation can be computed by taking the average of all node representations in the graph.

For a node classification task, the goal is to predict the class label for each node in a given graph $G = \{\mathcal{V}, \mathcal{E}\}$. Each node $v_i \in \mathcal{V}$ is associated with a ground-truth node label $y_i \in \mathcal{C}$, where $\mathcal{C} = \{1, 2, ..., c\}$ is the set of node classes. Since only L-hop neighbors of the node v_i will influence h_i^L, we define the L-hop sub-graph of the node v_i as $G_{s(i)}$ which is the computational graph that will be the input of the GNNs model. $A_{s(i)}$ and $X_{s(i)}$ are the related adjacency matrix and feature matrix of $G_{s(i)}$. The trained GNNs model will predict the estimated label $\hat{y}$ for the node v_i as:

$$\hat{y}_i = \arg\max_{c \in \mathcal{C}} P_\Phi(c \mid A_{s(i)}, X_{s(i)}). \tag{1}$$

3.2 Motif Representation

Network motifs refer to graph structures that appear frequently in large-scale networks and have certain biological or functional meanings. Figure 1 shows a schematic diagram of third-order and fourth-order network motifs. As an important high-order structure, network motifs can reveal structure and function of networks. Specifically, network motifs have the following characteristics.

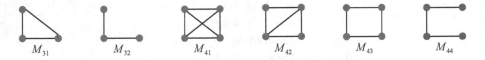

M_{31} M_{32} M_{41} M_{42} M_{43} M_{44}

Fig. 1. Schematic diagram of six network motifs. M_{31} and M_{32} are common third-order network motifs, and the others are common fourth-order network motifs.

- Practical meanings. Network motifs have practical meanings that depend on various structures, types and characteristics of networks. For example, M_{31} as depicted in Fig. 1 is commonly used in social networks, which indicates the interaction among three people.
- High frequencies. Network motifs have higher frequency in real networks than that in random networks. This phenomenon reflects that network motifs have structural characteristics and practical significance. M_{31} occurs frequently in some real networks, compared with the same nodes and edges in random networks.

- Low-order structures. Network motifs refer to a special low-order subgraph structure. Figure 1 shows third-order and fourth-order network motifs commonly used in real networks. The number of nodes in network motifs does not exceed eight, thus the motifs are regarded as low-order structures. Specifically, the motifs containing three or four nodes are called low-order network motifs, while consisting of five or more nodes are called high-order network motifs.

4 The Design of MDC

In this section, we propose a Motif Diffusion Convolution (MDC) framework that designs a high-order structure feature augmentation and learnable graph diffusion coefficients. We firstly find different high-order structures (e.g. motifs) in graphs, and then calculate different node motif degree to enhance feature augmentation of nodes. Finally, we automatically learn diffusion coefficients for each feature channel to realize built-in explanations for graph neural networks models. Similar to the attention mechanism, MDC is a component applied to any neural networks.

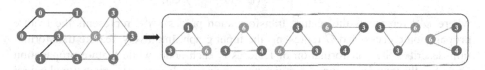

Fig. 2. Schematic diagram of Node Motif Degree (e.g., NMD) in networks. The $M31$-NMD of the orange node equals to 6, which indicates that six $M31$ shown in the box contains this orange node.

4.1 High-Order Structure Feature Augmentation

In GNNs, the edge between two nodes actually reflects a low-order binary relationship that is easily represented by an adjacency matrix. However, the matrix only considers the association between two nodes, not representing high-order information in networks. Therefore, we want to extend the binary relationship to the multivariate relationship that could better extract high-order information for downstream tasks. Such relations commonly exist and are represented by network motifs occuring frequently in real networks. Thus, we use the concept of node motif degree to represent the multivariate relationship of nodes, and it is defined as the number of node in a particular motif as N_{MD}. Figure 2. is a schematic diagram of calculating the $M31$ motif of nodes.

Multi-relationships are diverse in real complex networks. To better represent the relationships, we define a multi-relationship feature matrix X of input graph G to realise feature augmentation. Figure 3 is a schematic diagram of the matrix X. Specifically, we directly extract features of each nodes in graph G, and then integrate each node features into the matrix X of graph G. We calculate N_{MD} based on five network motifs such as $M31$, $M32$, $M41$, $M42$, and $M43$. Finally, we obtain a multi-relationship feature matrix X of graph G.

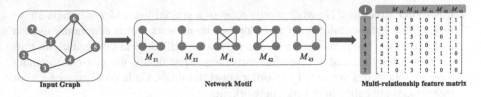

Fig. 3. Schematic diagram of multi-relationship feature matrix X. The left graph in the diagram is the input graph G, and the number i in the node represents v_i. Matrix X have six feature channels, and the first channel represents the original node degree in graph G.

4.2 The Framework of MDC

In order to obtain complex relationships between nodes in a graph, GNNs aggregates neighbors information via message-passing mechanism that iteratively updates the feature representation of nodes. In this process, the attributes of nodes will be passed from one to another by their neighbors. The formulation of the message passing network can be expressed as

$$H^{(l)} = \gamma^{(l)}(\psi^{(l)}(H^{(l-1)}), G), \tag{2}$$

where $\psi^{(l)}$ represents the feature transformation process, $\gamma^{(l)}$ represents the feature propagation process, and G represents the input graph. Intuitively, feature transformation describes the transformation of features at each node, while feature propagation describes the transformation of features between nodes. In a graph convolutional neural network, the feature propagation process can be expressed as

$$\gamma(\hat{H}, G) = \tilde{D}^{-\frac{1}{2}} \tilde{A} \tilde{D}^{-\frac{1}{2}} \hat{H}. \tag{3}$$

In different message passing mechanisms, the distance of quantitative feature propagation indicates the ability of nodes to aggregate other features. The neighborhood radius is defined as

$$r = \frac{\sum_{k=0}^{\infty} \theta_k k}{\sum_{k=0}^{\infty} \theta_k}, \tag{4}$$

where θ_k indicates the influence of a node with a distance of k hops. Through the neighborhood radius, we can quantify the ability of nodes in different GNNs to aggregate features. The larger the neighborhood radius, the more the model is considered to pay more attention to high-order information. On the contrary, it is believed that the model pays more attention to local information. Taking GCN as an example, each layer of GCN can only gather the first-order neighbor information of nodes. If you want to aggregate the information of higher-order neighbor nodes by GCN, you need to design multiple GCN layers to aggregate the features. However, too many stacked graph convolution layers often cause models overfitting and accumulation of multiple nonlinear layers, and reduce the interpretability of models.

To allow GNNs models to maintain interpretability and aggregate high-order neighbor nodes, MDC proposes a message propagation method based on graph diffusion. The pseudocode of the algorithm flow is shown in Algorithm 1.

Algorithm 1. MDC model algorithm

1: **Input:** The adjacency matrix $\mathbf{A}$ of the input graph G, and neighborhood radius r
2: **Output:** Message Propagation Matrix $\mathbf{M}$
3: Initialize the learnable diffusion coefficient $\theta_{ki}^{(0)}, k$
4: Calculate the multi-relationship feature matrix X
5: Compute the normalized Laplacian matrix $\mathcal{L}$
6: **repeat**
7:    Caculate neighbor radius r in equation (4)
8:    Caculate message propagation matrix $\mathbf{M} := \sum_{k=0}^{\infty} \theta_{ki}^{(1)} \mathbf{L^r}$
9:    Update diffusion coefficient $\theta_{ki}^{(l)}$
10: **until** $r <= 10$

Firstly, MDC initializes a learnable diffusion coefficient θ_k for the input graph G based on the propagation distance. Secondly, MDC computes the normalized Laplacian matrix L of the input graph G. Thirdly, MDC computes the message propagation matrix L^r for all messages, using the various of propagation distances of the input graph G. Then, MDC updates the diffusion coefficient $\theta_{ki}^{(l)}$ according to the message propagation matrix L^r. Finally, MDC outputs the feature propagation matrix, using the learned diffusion coefficients $\theta_{ki}^{(l)}$ to weight and sum the message propagation matrix L^r within the various propagation distances.

Specifically, different values of r need to be considered when calculating the propagation message matrix L^r. When r is equal to 10, it is necessary to calculate the first-order message propagation matrix L and the second-order message propagation matrix L^2 respectively, then this process will be repeated. MDC uses the weighted sum of the message propagation matrix and the diffusion coefficient of different domain radius as the new message propagation matrix, so the formula of feature propagation can be written as,

$$\gamma^{(l)}(\widetilde{H}, G)_i = \sum_{k=0}^{\infty} \theta_{ki}^{(l)} L^r \widetilde{H}_i, \tag{5}$$

where $\theta_{ki}^{(l)}$ is the i-th learnable diffusion coefficient of layer l, and the reseult of $\sum_{k=0}^{\infty} \theta_{ki}^{(l)}$ equals to 1. By learning the optimal $\theta_{ki}^{(l)}$, MDC can adaptively learn the features in a certain neighborhood. In addition, the $\theta_{ki}^{(l)}$ can represent the process of the feature propagation, so the whole process is interpretable.

5 Experiments

In this section, we firstly introduce six datasets, three baselines, and experimental parameters in details. Secondly, we compare our proposed MDC framework with another two comparative algorithms. Finally, we present our analysis of the experimental results.

5.1   Datasets

We use six node classification datasets such as CORA, CiteSeer, PubMed, Coauthor CS, Amazon Computers and Amazon Photo, and the details of datasets are shown in Table 2.

Table 2. Dataset statistics.

Datasets	Types	Categories	Features	Nodes	Edges
CORA	Citation Networks	7	1433	2485	5069
CiteSeer	Citation Networks	6	3703	2120	3679
PubMed	Citation Networks	3	500	19717	44324
Coauthor CS	Collaborative Networks	15	6805	18333	81894
Amazon Computers	E-commerce Networks	10	767	13381	245778
Amazon Photo	E-commerce Networks	8	745	7487	119043

The CORA dataset is a common citation network dataset, which contains 2,708 nodes and 1,433 node features. The nodes in the CORA dataset are divided into seven categories. Each node represents a paper, and the citation relationship between two papers is defined as an edge.

CiteSeer and PubMed are citation network datasets as well. The CiteSeer dataset contains 3,312 papers and 3,703 features, and the papers are divided into six categories. The PubMed dataset contains 19,717 papers and 500 features, and the papers in PubMed are divided into three categories.

The Coauthor CS dataset is a collaborative network dataset, which contains 18,333 authors in the computer science field and their cooperative relationships. The feature vector of each author contains the number of this papers and the number of papers citations. Authors are divided into three categories. Each author is represented as a node, and the cooperative relationship between authors is represented as edges.

Amazon Computers and the Amazon Photo are both e-commerce network dataset. The Amazon Computers dataset contains computer products and related review data on the Amazon website. Each computer product is represented as a node, and its feature vector contains information such as the description and price of the product. The Amazon Photo dataset contains photos on the Amazon website and the photos related comment data. Each photo is represented as a node, and the node's feature vector contains information such as the description and price of the product.

5.2   Baselines

We use three GNNs models as basic algorithms. To verify the effectiveness of experiments, we apply another two diffusion methods to the three models. The following are the three basic algorithms, and two diffusion methods.

Basic Algorithm. Graph Convolutional Neural Network(GCN) [6] is a semi-supervised classification method based on graph convolutional networks. Jumping knowledge network (JKN) [15] is a graph neural network based on skip connections, which allows graph neural networks to learn nodes attributes between layers, and effectively captures the interaction between high-order nodes at different layers. Another algorithm is based on convolutional ARMA filters [1], which combines signal processing with the graph theory. It proposes an autoregressive moving average filter to represent the temporal evolution of a signal, and then performs convolution computations in the graph domain.

Graph Diffusion Methods. Graph Diffusion Convolution (GDC) [7] is a graph convolutional neural network, which combines spatial and spectral domain. It also extends the neighborhood range of message propagation, which is an effective alternative to the message propagation process. Adaptive Diffusion Convolution (ADC) [21] improves the GDC by the adaptive learnable neighborhood radius of the message propagation. We use the two graph diffusion methods as baselines to verify the effectiveness of our proposed MDC.

5.3 Experiment Analysis

We conducted experiments in GCN, JKN, and ARMA without graph diffusion methods under the confidence level of 95%. We also applied GDC, ADC and the proposed MDC to the three network separately. The experimental results are shown in Table 3 and Table 4. The best performance on each dataset is in bold, and the suboptimal performance is underlined. The unit of tables is one percent.

Table 3. Bselines Comparison in GCN and JKN

Dataset	Average accuracy (%) of GCN				Average accuracy (%) of JKN			
	GCN	GDC	ADC	MDC(ours)	JKN	GDC	ADC	MDC (ours)
CORA	81.71±0.26	83.58 ± 0.23	83.91 ± 0.63	**84.30 ± 0.23**	82.14 ± 0.24	83.78 ± 0.22	**83.96 ± 0.64**	83.35 ± 0.24
CiteSeer	72.02 ± 0.31	**73.35 ± 0.27**	71.85 ± 0.76	72.81 ± 0.87	70.34 ± 0.38	**72.24 ± 0.31**	69.52 ± 0.73	71.29 ± 0.88
PubMed	78.23 ± 0.40	78.72 ± 0.37	**81.94 ± 1.51**	80.90 ± 0.82	70.34 ± 0.38	79.22 ± 0.32	82.28 ± 1.32	**83.02 ± 0.83**
Coauthor CS	91.83 ± 0.08	**93.01 ± 0.07**	92.69 ± 0.59	92.97 ± 0.70	91.11 ± 0.09	**92.41 ± 0.07**	92.27 ± 0.59	92.10 ± 0.65
Amazon Computers	84.75 ± 0.23	86.04 ± 0.24	86.32 ± 0.70	**86.74 ± 0.56**	83.33 ± 0.27	85.66 ± 0.30	85.51 ± 0.73	**86.13 ± 0.64**
Amazon Photo	92.08 ± 0.20	92.20 ± 0.22	**93.50 ± 0.70**	93.20 ± 0.70	91.07 ± 0.26	92.37 ± 0.22	92.85 ± 0.68	**92.98 ± 0.60**

Table 3 shows that graph diffusion methods have improved the accuracy of prediction, compared with the original method in six datasets. GCN with MDC has achieved the best results in nearly half of datasets, and surpassed GDC, ADC and GCN by 0.72%, 0.39% and 2.59% respectively in CORA. Moreover, MDC outperformed GDC, ADC and GCN by 0.96%, 0.28% and 1.14% in Coauthor CS. In addition, MDC also achieves suboptimal results in the other three datasets, which illustrates the effectiveness of our proposed MDC in GCN. The accuracy of JKN has also been improved when we used graph diffusion methods. Among them, GDC has the best performance in CiteSeer and

Coauthor CS, and ADC achieved the best performance in CORA. MDC performed best in PubMed, Amazon Computers and Amazon Photo, increased by 0.74%, 0.62% and 0.13% respectively. In addition, MDC also achieved suboptimal performance in CiteSeer.

Table 4. Bselines Comparison in ARMA

Dataset	Average accuracy (%) of ARMA			
	ARMA	GDC	ADC	MDC(ours)
CORA	81.62 ± 0.24	83.81 ± 0.21	84.16 ± 0.33	**84.24 ± 0.43**
CiteSeer	70.84 ± 0.32	72.28 ± 0.29	**72.90 ± 0.93**	71.81 ± 0.49
PubMed	77.14 ± 0.36	78.85 ± 0.36	**82.11 ± 1.10**	79.63 ± 0.92
Coauthor CS	91.32 ± 0.08	**92.63 ± 0.08**	91.66 ± 0.60	91.70 ± 0.35
Amazon Computers	84.36 ± 0.26	84.92 ± 0.26	**85.51 ± 0.85**	84.92 ± 0.59
Amazon Photo	91.41 ± 0.22	91.09 ± 0.24	**93.19 ± 0.96**	92.42 ± 0.41

Table 4 shows that ADC achieved best results in CiteSeer, PubMed, and Anazons when ADC was applied to ARMA. MDC achieved best results in CORA, and improved by 2.62%. The prediction accuracy of ARMA has been relatively improved after using these graph diffusion methods. Compared with GDC and ADC, MDC achieved the best results in most cases. ADC determines the neighborhood radius by an adaptive method. GDC has the smallest relative fluctuation, but ADC has the highest relative fluctuation due to the diffusion coefficient based on nucleus.

5.4 Hyper-parameter Analysis

We conducted experiments on six datasets under different neighborhood radius k, and experimental results in ARMA, JKN, and GCN are shown in Fig. 4. We analyzed how prediction accuracy varied from the value of different k. As shown in Fig. 4, the k represents different diffusion radius, equaling to two, five, ten, fifteen, and twenty respectively. The vertical ordinate represents prediction accuracy under various diffusion radius.

Figure 4 shows the prediction accuracy of JKN, ARMA, and GCN models with MDC under different neighborhood radius. It can be clearly seen that large neighborhood radius has better accuracy in JKN, ARMA, and GCN models on CORA and PubMed than small radius. We can also observe that the accuracy of the three models does not always improve with the increase of the neighborhood radius in Amazon Photo and Amazon Computers. CORA and PubMed are relatively sparse datasets. In sparse datasets, increasing the radius can learn more information. Compared with the two datasets, small neighborhood radius achieves better accuracy in Amazon Computers and Amazon Photo. The reasoon is that they are dense datasets, thus the increase of the neighborhood radius will lead to a decline in the accuracy.

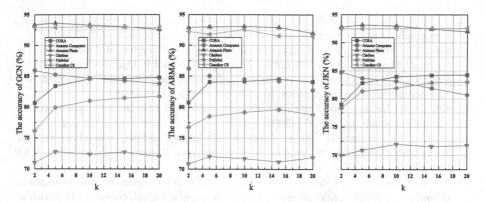

Fig. 4. Comparison diagram of the accuracy of ARMA, JKN and GCN on six datasets. k represents different neighborhood radius.

6 Conclusion

While extensive efforts have been made to explain GNNs from different angles, none of existing methods explain GNNs predictions from graph diffusion convolution perspective, especially in scenarios where multivariate relationships need to be considered. In this paper, we propose a MDC framework that simultaneously provides predictions and explanations based on node motif degree and graph diffusion convolution. We argue that calculating node motif degree can realize feature enhancement and obtain multivariate relationships in networks. For better interpretability, MDC automatically learns a set of parameters called diffusion coefficients for every node in each feature channel and each GNNs layer. Experimental results show that combining node motif degree with graph diffusion convolution can improve the prediction accuracy of GNNs models and enhance their transparency.

Acknowledgment. We would like to thank Muhammad Altaf from Dalian University of Technology for his help with this paper. This work is partially supported by National Natural Science Foundation of China under Grant No. 62102060 and the Fundamental Research Funds for the Central Universities under Grant No. DUT22RC(3)060.

References

1. Bianchi, F.M., Grattarola, D., Livi, L., Alippi, C.: Graph neural networks with convolutional ARMA filters. IEEE Trans. Pattern Anal. Mach. Intell. **44**(7), 3496–3507 (2022)
2. Bruna, J., Zaremba, W., Szlam, A., LeCun, Y.: Spectral Networks and Locally Connected Networks on Graphs. In: International Conference on Learning Representations. ICLR (2013)
3. Dai, E., Wang, S.: Towards self-explainable graph neural network. In: International Conference on Information and Knowledge Management, pp. 302–311. ACM (2021)
4. Dai, E., Wang, S.: Towards prototype-based self-explainable graph neural network. CoRR abs/2210.01974 (2022)

5. Feng, A., You, C., Wang, S., Tassiulas, L.: KerGNNs: Interpretable graph neural networks with graph kernels. In: Conference on Artificial Intelligence, pp. 6614–6622 (2022)
6. Kipf, T.N., Welling, M.: Semi-supervised classification with graph convolutional networks. In: International Conference on Learning Representations, ICLR. OpenReview.net (2017)
7. Klicpera, J., Weißenberger, S., Günnemann, S.: Diffusion improves graph learning. In: Neural Information Processing Systems, NeurIPS, pp. 13333–13345 (2019)
8. Kondor, R., Lafferty, J.D.: Diffusion kernels on graphs and other discrete input spaces. In: Machine Learning, pp. 315–322 (2002)
9. Li, Y., Yu, R., Shahabi, C., Liu, Y.: Diffusion convolutional recurrent neural network: data-driven traffic forecasting. In: International Conference on Learning Representations. ICLR (2018)
10. Lu, Y., Kamranfar, P., Lattanzi, D., Shehu, A.: Traffic flow forecasting with maintenance downtime via multi-channel attention-based spatio-temporal graph convolutional networks. CoRR abs/2110.01535 (2021)
11. Luo, D., et al.: Parameterized explainer for graph neural network. In: Neural Information Processing Systems. NeurIPS (2020)
12. Neil, D., Briody, J., Lacoste, A., Sim, A., Creed, P., Saffari, A.: Interpretable graph convolutional neural networks for inference on noisy knowledge graphs. CoRR abs/1812.00279 (2018)
13. Vu, M.N., Thai, M.T.: PGM-explainer: probabilistic graphical model explanations for graph neural networks. In: Neural Information Processing Systems. NeurIPS (2020)
14. Wu, S., Tang, Y., Zhu, Y., Wang, L., Xie, X., Tan, T.: Session-based recommendation with graph neural networks. In: Conference on Artificial Intelligence, pp. 346–353 (2019)
15. Xu, K., Li, C., Tian, Y., Sonobe, T., Kawarabayashi, K., Jegelka, S.: Representation Learning on Graphs with Jumping Knowledge Networks. In: International Conference on Machine Learning, vol. 80, pp. 5449–5458. ICML (2018)
16. Yao, L., Mao, C., Luo, Y.: Graph convolutional networks for text classification. In: Conference on Artificial Intelligence, pp. 7370–7377. AAAI Press (2019)
17. Ying, Z., Bourgeois, D., You, J., Zitnik, M., Leskovec, J.: GNNExplainer: generating explanations for graph neural networks. In: Annual Conference on Neural Information Processing Systems, NeurIPS, pp. 9240–9251 (2019)
18. Yuan, H., Tang, J., Hu, X., Ji, S.: XGNN: towards model-level explanations of graph neural networks. In: Conference on Knowledge Discovery and Data Mining, pp. 430–438 (2020)
19. Zhang, X., et al.: Traffic flow forecasting with spatial-temporal graph diffusion network. In: Conference on Artificial Intelligence, pp. 15008–15015 (2021)
20. Zhang, Z., Liu, Q., Wang, H., Lu, C., Lee, C.: ProtGNN: towards self-explaining graph neural networks. In: Conference on Artificial Intelligence, pp. 9127–9135 (2022)
21. Zhao, J., Dong, Y., Ding, M., Kharlamov, E., Tang, J.: Adaptive diffusion in graph neural networks. In: Neural Information Processing Systems, NeurIPS, pp. 23321–23333 (2021)
22. Zhou, J., et al.: Graph neural networks: a review of methods and applications. AI Open 1, 57–81 (2020)

Missing Data Imputation for Traffic Flow Data Using SAE-GAN-SAD

Tian Tian[1], Liang Zhang[1], Junqing Shen[1], Yi Jiang[1], Long Zhou[1], Ronghu Chang[1], Shangshang Zhao[1], and Dongwei Xu[2(✉)]

[1] ChinaOly Technology, Hangzhou, China
[2] Zhejiang University of Technology, Hangzhou, China
dongweixu@zjut.edu.cn

Abstract. The traffic data collected from various sensors is easily affected by missing or corrupted data. The presence of missing data poses a significant challenge for various transportation applications such as traffic flow prediction and traffic pattern recognition. In this paper, we propose a deep learning model that leverages stacked autoencoder (SAE) and generative adversarial network (GAN) to impute the missing traffic data. The SAE extracts spatiotemporal features from incomplete traffic data, and GAN is used to generate complete traffic data. The complete traffic data is finally restored using stacked auto decoders (SAD) from the features generated by GAN. We conducted experiments with the traffic data collected from Cal-trans District 7, and the results showed that our proposed model performs better, especially when the loss ratio of traffic data is relatively high.

Keywords: traffic flow · generative adversarial network

1 Introduction

Traffic data filling is an indispensable part of Intelligent Transportation Systems (ITS). The accuracy and completeness of traffic data are vital for traffic management [1, 2]. However, real-world traffic data often have missing value, leading to a significant reduction in data quality [3]. Empirical studies have reported varying levels of data loss rates in different regions [4, 5, 6].

Generally divided into three common types of missing data: Missing Completely at Random, Missing at Random, and Not Missing at Random [7]. In addition, NMAR is the most complex scenario as it indicates that there is a relationship between the likelihood of data missing and its values.

The methods for traffic data analysis include the following: prediction, interpolation, and statistical learning [8]. The first kind is rely on historical data to build a model for predicting the missing or corrupted values [9], including LR [4], SVR [10, 11], ARIMA [12, 13], BNs, and feed-forward neural networks [14]. However, these methods do not consider the information contained in the missing values.

Interpolation methods are commonly classified into two types based on the data information used, namely temporal neighboring [16,17] and pattern neighboring methods [15, 18, 19]. Some of the typical methods include the historical average method [20],

© The Author(s), under exclusive license to Springer Nature Singapore Pte Ltd. 2023
X. Meng et al. (Eds.): BDSC 2023, CCIS 1846, pp. 375–388, 2023.
https://doi.org/10.1007/978-981-99-3925-1_25

k-NN [21–24], and LLS [25, 26]. However, determining the appropriate distance metric to select neighbors is a key challenge for these methods [27]. Interpolation methods may show good performance when the daily data have high similarity. Nevertheless, the practical data are subject to changes in different time.

Traditional Statistical learning methods include the MCMC [5, 29, 30] and PPCA [31, 32] imputation methods. (BPCA) [17], FPCA [33], and KPPCA [34] have also been utilized for missing data imputation. But they may have incorrect results when the data does not obey a certain distribution [35].

As the traffic flow is more and more heavy, precise and full traffic data is essential for the efficient control of ITS. While the aforementioned methods have demonstrated satisfactory performance for imputing missing traffic data, they may not be effective when the missing ratio is significant. To address this, this present study proposes a DL-based model called SAE-GAN-SAD, which exhibits high accuracy even for traffic data with a large proportion of missing data. Initially, the model extracts useful spatiotemporal features from the incomplete traffic data using Stacked Autoencoder (SAE). Subsequently, adversarial training is performed between the generator and discriminator to generate spatiotemporal features of complete data from those of uncomplete data. Finally, the complete data is obtained from SAD.

Our contributions are listed as follows:

(1) We use SAE [36] to extract the useful spatial-temporal features from the missing traffic flow data.
(2) We apply GAN [37] to get the spatial-temporal features of complete data from the features of missing data. And stacked auto decoders (SAD) can recover complete data with the latent features generated by GAN.
(3) The results shows that the SAE-GAN-SAD model performs well even when the traffic data has a high proportion of missing values.

2 Related Work

The stacked autoencoder (SAE) [38] consists of multiple autoencoders [39]. The SAE method includes three main steps [40]. Firstly, the autoencoder is trained to obtain the latent features from the input. Secondly, the latent features are input to the next layer. Finally, the BP algorithm is applied to minimize the cost function. The SAE is utilized to extract the latent features from the input data, while the stacked auto decoders (SAD) are employed to reconstruct the input data from the latent features. Although the denoising stacked autoencoders (DSAE) [3] model has been utilized in data imputation, the experiments have only involved a small percentage of missing data.

The GAN framework comprises two neural networks: a generator and a discriminator. The generator creates data samples from a random noise input, while the discriminator evaluates the authenticity of the generated samples. The competition between the generator and the discriminator is based on the data distribution. The generator learns a map from a low-dimensional latent space to a high-dimensional data distribution of interest, while the discriminator identifies between the generated samples and the real samples. The goal of training the generator is to minimize the error rate.

GAN has been extensively utilized in various fields, such as image dataset synthesis [42], image-to-image style translation [43]. Recently, researchers have used GAN to data imputation, such as GAIN proposed by Yoon J [46], MisGAN proposed by Li SC-X [47], and Chen Y's proposal to use parallel data [48]. However, the most challenging aspect of GAN is training the two NNs to reach a Nash equilibrium and addressing the problem of mode collapse. Surprisingly, none of the mentioned methods addressed these challenges. In this paper, we propose to WGAN [49] to train our model due to its excellent performance in handling these issues during the training process.

3   Methodology

In this part, we give a detailed explanation of the proposed model, which is composed of three parts: Stacked Autoencoder (SAE), Generative Adversarial Network (GAN), and Stacked Auto Decoder (SAD). The framework of the SAE-GAN-SAD model is shown in Fig. 1. The SAE component is responsible for extracting spatiotemporal features from the input data. The GAN component is utilized to get the missing features of complete data, and the SAD component is responsible for restoring the complete data from the generated features obtained by GAN.

3.1   Problem Formulation

Define traffic data as $X = [x_1, x_2, \cdots, x_n]$, and the traffic data of each road denoted as $x_i = [x_{i1}, x_{i2}, \cdots, x_{iT}]$. . Where i is from 1 to n denoted the different roads. Given a mask vector M to indicate whether the data point is missing in some interval. M is a binary matrix which takes values in $\{0,1\}$, and having the same dimension as the X. The traffic data which includes missing data denoted as $\tilde{X} = X * M$. The goal of the proposed model is completing the missing data $\tilde{X}$.

3.2   Auto-encoder

Autoencoders are a class of neural networks that learn a representation of the input data by attempting to reconstruct it after being trained. Autoencoders have gained popularity in recent years and been utilized in various domains like data dimension reduction and feature learning, due to their ability to encode and decode data in a compressed form that closely approximates the input data but is not identical to it.

An autoencoder comprises two parts: an encoder and a decoder. It can be viewed as a feedforward neural network with three layers, consisting of an input layer, a hidden layer, and an output layer. The hidden layer extracts feature from the input data. The mathematical equations for the encoder and decoder are shown in Eq. 1–2:

$$h_1 = a_1(W_{e1}X + b_{e1}) \tag{1}$$

$$X' = b_1(W_{d1} \cdot h_1 + b_{d1}) \tag{2}$$

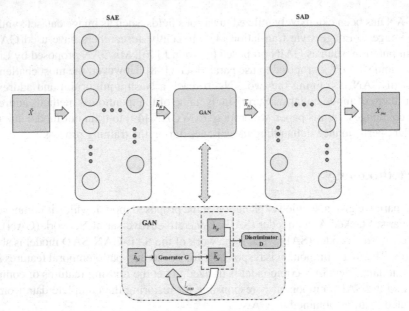

Fig. 1. The Architecture of the SAE-GAN-SAD

where W_{e1} and W_{d1} are the encoding weight matrix and decoding weight matrix. b_{e1} and b_{d1} are the encoding bias vector and decoding bias vector. a_1 and b_1 are the activation functions.

The model error denoted as $L(X, X')$, acquire model parameters by minimize model error, define the model variable as θ, as

$$\theta = \arg\min_{\theta} L(X, X') = \arg\min_{\theta} \frac{1}{2} \sum_{i=1}^{m} \left\| x_i' - x_i \right\|^2 \tag{3}$$

where m denoted the number of the input data X.

3.3 Stacked Autoencoder

A SAE is a NN including multiple layers of sparse autoencoders, where the output of every hidden layer is connected to the input of the successive one. The structure of SAE typically involves several autoencoders stacked on top of each other, with each autoencoder composed of an encoder and a decoder. The encoder maps the input to a hidden representation, while the decoder maps it back to the original input space. The architecture of SAE with three autoencoders is illustrated in Fig. 1. Firstly, the complete data X is input to the SAE to extract the 1st features h_1 by Eq. 1, 2 from 1st autoencoder. Then, the inputs of the 1st autoencoder are the upper layer extracted features h_{i-1}. As shown in Eq. 4, 5.

$$h_i = a_i(W_{ei} \cdot h_{i-1} + b_{ei}) \tag{4}$$

$$h'_{i-1} = b_i(W_{di} \cdot h_i + b_{di}) \tag{5}$$

where i is from 2 to N, N is denoted the number of autoencoders that make up the SAE. The features extracted from i^{th} autoencoder denoted as h_i. W_{ei} and W_{di} are the encoding weight matrix and decoding weight matrix. b_{ei} and b_{di} are the encoding bias vector and decoding bias vector in i^{th} autoencoder. a_i and b_i are the activation functions.

The spatiotemporal features h_N obtained by SAE when the input is X, Meanwhile, the useful features $\tilde{h}_N$ extracted from missing data $\tilde{X}$ by SAE.

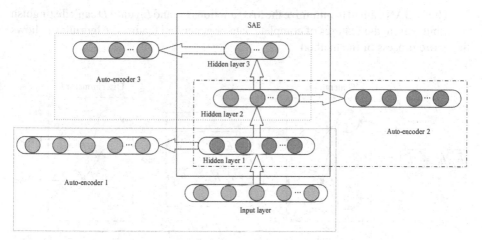

Fig. 2. A simple SAE structure which consists of three autoencoders.

3.4 Generative Adversarial Network

The GAN architecture comprises two key components, the generator G and the discriminator D. The GAN architecture employed in our model is illustrated in Fig. 2. G is trained aiming to rise the error rate of D. However, training GANs can be challenging, and the models may never converge or suffer from model collapses. To address these training difficulties, we adopt the Wasserstein GAN (WGAN), which optimizes the earth mover's distance instead of Jensen-Shannon divergence. Both the generator loss and the discriminator loss are objectives of WGAN. The target of the generator is to get the features of complete data from the features of missing datas. The loss of generator G can be formulated as shown in Eq. 6:

$$L_G = -D(G(\tilde{h}_N)) + \alpha \cdot L_{cons} \tag{6}$$

$$L_{cons} = \frac{1}{S} \sum_{s=1}^{S} (h_N^s - \overline{h}_N^s)^2 \tag{7}$$

where the consistency loss L_{cons} is set to decrease the reconstruction error of the generated features and $\bar{h}_N = G(\tilde{h}_N)$. α is the coefficient of the consistency loss. S denoted the dimension of the generated features.

The discriminator receives either features of complete data or generated features then output a scalar that large values for features of complete data and small values for generated features. And the target of D is to maximize the expected difference between $D(h_N)$ and $D(G(\tilde{h}_N))$. Thus, the loss of discriminator can be denoted as in Eq. 8:

$$L_D = D(G(\tilde{h}_N)) - D(h_N) \tag{8}$$

The WGAN trained to minimize the loss functions L_G and L_D until D can't distinguish the input is from the features of complete data or generated features. Algorithm 1 shows the entire process of the method.

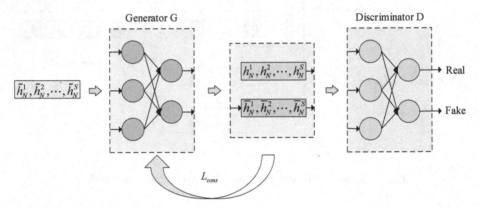

Fig. 3. Architecture of the GAN

3.5 Stacked Auto-decoder

The SAE is employed to extract the features from the input data. On the contrary, the function of SAD is restoring the input data from the extracted features. Thus, the traffic data after imputation can be obtained from the generated features by SAD. The calculation process is as follows:

$$h_{i-1}^* = b_i(W_{di} \cdot h_i^* + b_{di})\, i = 2, 3, 4, \ldots, N \tag{9}$$

$$X_{rec} = b_1(W_{d1} \cdot h_1^* + b_{d1}) \tag{10}$$

where $h_N^* = G(\tilde{h}_N)$, W_{di} and b_{di} are the decoding weight matrix and the decoding bias vector in i^{st} autoencoder in SAE. X_{rec} denoted as the complete data when the missing data $\tilde{X}$ be restored.

Algorithm 1 Generating the features of complete data from the features of missing data with WGAN

Require: number of iterations of the critic per generator iteration $n_d = 5$; the learning rate $lr = 0.00005$; the clipping parameter $c = 0.01$; consistency loss coefficient α; the dimension of features of complete data S;

1: Initialize θ_G, θ_D

2: **while** θ_G has not converged **do**

3:     **for** $i = 0$ to n_d **do**

4:         sample features of missing data $\tilde{h}_N = [\tilde{h}_N^1, \tilde{h}_N^2, \cdots, \tilde{h}_N^s]$

5:         evaluate stochastic gradient of θ_D:

6:         $\delta_{\theta_D} \leftarrow \nabla_{\theta_D}[D(h_N) - D(G(\tilde{h}_N))]$

7:         $\theta_D \leftarrow \theta_D + lr \cdot RMSProp(\theta_D, \delta_{\theta_D})$

8:         $\theta_D \leftarrow clip(\theta_D, -c, c)$

9:     **end for**

10:     fix θ_D

11:     sample features of missing data $\tilde{h}_N = [\tilde{h}_N^1, \tilde{h}_N^2, \cdots, \tilde{h}_N^s]$

12:     evaluate stochastic gradient of θ_G:

13:     $\theta_G \leftarrow -\nabla_{\theta_G}[D(G(\tilde{h}_N)) + \alpha \cdot L_{cons}]$

14:     $\theta_G \leftarrow \theta_G + lr \cdot RMSProp(\theta_G, \delta_{\theta_G})$

15: **end while**

---

4 Experiments

4.1 Data Description

In the experimental study, traffic volume data obtained from Caltrans PeMS are utilized. For the purposes of this study, 22 VDSs in District 7 are chosen, each containing 17,568 data points. Furthermore, the collected complete data are intentionally made to be missing at random, with missing ratios ranging from 10% to 90%, in order to simulate real-world data. The traffic data are split into train and test sets with an 8:2 ratio. Additionally, the data are divided into workday and weekend models to assess the model's performance across different traffic patterns.

4.2 Model Settings and Evaluation Criteria

In the architecture of SAE, the input and output dimensions are set to 288*n. The SAE consists of three autoencoders, each with 3 hidden layers.

Regarding the architecture of GAN, both G and D have three hidden layers. The activation function is basically *ReLU*, while G's output layer uses the sigmoid activation function, and there is no one in D's output layer. The coefficient α for consistency loss is set to 100, and the learning rate lr is set to 0.00005.

To assess the performance, 3 criterias are used to evaluate the error of the generated data: MAE, RMSE, and MAPE. The error is computed between the imputed and the true values of the missing data. The equations for these criteria are given in Eqs. 11–13.

$$MAE = \frac{1}{K} \sum_{k=1}^{K} \left| x_{rec}^{k} - x_{true}^{k} \right| \tag{11}$$

$$RMSE = \sqrt{\frac{1}{K} \sum_{k=1}^{K} (x_{rec}^{k} - x_{true}^{k})^2} \tag{12}$$

$$MAPE = \frac{1}{K} \sum_{k=1}^{K} \left| \frac{x_{true}^{k} - x_{rec}^{k}}{x_{true}^{k}} \right| \tag{13}$$

where K denoted the number of the missing values, and $x_{rec}^{k}, x_{true}^{k}$ are denoted as the kth missing value after imputation and observer value.

4.3 Baseline Methods

To further evaluate the model, several baseline methods have been compared: historical average method(HA) [50], backpropagation network (BP) [51] and k-Nearest neighbors(KNN) [22]. In the historical average method, the missing values have been imputed by averaging collected data at the same time on several past days. The number of past days is set as 4. In the BP model, the structure of BP has the same number of hidden layers and hidden units with genera-tor. In the KNN method, the number of nearest neighbors selected is 5 and ranges from 2 to 15. Meanwhile, the different models have the same missing points when compared to better reflect the superior performance of the proposed method.

4.4 Experiments Results

Experiments on single road

At the beginning of these experiments, the proposed model has been used in the data imputation of a single road. The results of VDS 718155 have shown in Table 1. The results include the error in different missing ratios on workdays and weekends. From Table 1, the error of VDS 718155 is not changed too much with the increase of the missing ratios on workdays and weekends. And the error on workdays is smaller than the error on weekdays. Table 2 shows some other VDS's average error in all missing ratios on workdays and weekends. And the error of VDS 760196 is the biggest. In other VDSs, the error on workdays in also smaller than the error on weekends. The reason considered is that the number of training data on workdays is more than the number of training data on weekdays.

Table 1. The error of VDS 718155 in different missing ratios on workdays and weekends

Missing ratios(%)	Workdays			Weekends		
	RMSE	MAE	MAPE(%)	RMSE	MAE	MAPE(%)
10	12.46	9.06	6.43	19.90	16.76	13.59
20	12.85	9.36	6.17	20.93	17.35	13.36
30	12.75	9.26	6.46	21.17	17.25	13.04
40	12.46	9.17	6.32	21.13	17.09	13.50
50	12.89	9.33	6.20	20.36	16.85	13.01
60	12.86	9.40	6.36	21.69	16.78	12.59
70	12.76	9.29	6.43	20.52	16.93	13.00
80	13.00	9.44	6.37	20.84	16.87	12.70
90	12.95	9.38	6.43	20.74	16.95	13.14

Table 2. The average error of different VDSs in different missing ratios on workdays and weekends

VDS	Workdays			Weekends		
	RMSE	MAE	MAPE(%)	RMSE	MAE	MAPE(%)
716414	26.57	19.66	7.17	28.98	22.87	9.07
760101	30.41	22.40	6.84	33.39	26.10	8.76
760112	31.67	23.41	6.83	37.22	29.64	9.23
716419	34.65	25.94	7.19	37.16	29.38	8.91
716421	33.71	25.60	7.75	37.35	28.70	9.80
760196	22.26	15.02	6.13	44.41	32.88	15.73
716440	32.71	24.12	7.72	48.24	36.93	14.17
716442	25.95	19.48	7.53	35.69	27.32	12.41
760226	26.53	19.72	7.22	37.41	28.33	12.22
760236	28.26	21.15	6.72	45.16	33.38	12.32

Experiments on multiple roads

The experiments on multiple roads have been set after the experiments on single road. Firstly, a comparison experiment has been set to evaluate the effectiveness of SAE and SAD. One experiment has not extracted the useful spatiotemporal features use SAE and directly uses missing data as the input of the GAN when another experiment uses SAE-GAN-SAD to restore the missing data. The error in different missing ratios at workdays and weekends between GAN and SAE-GAN-SAD have shown in Fig. 3–4.

Figure 3–4 presents that the error of SAE-GAN-SAD is significantly smaller than GAN in all missing ratios on workdays and weekends. It is obvious that the error of our model tends to steady and small even the missing ratio is very large. Meanwhile, the error of GAN is gradually increasing. The error on workdays is smaller than the error on weekdays. The above shows that the useful spatiotemporal features can be extracted sufficiently by SAE-GAN-SAD.

Compared to the experiments on single roads, an interesting result have been noticed that the average error of multiple roads is larger than the error of single road on workdays. Considered the possible reason is that the input data contains redundant information and affects the extraction of features.

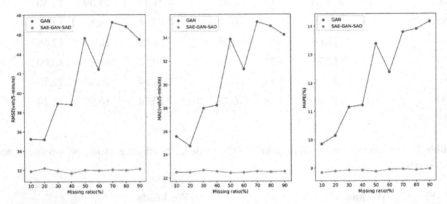

Fig. 4. The error in different missing ratios at workdays between GAN and SAE-GAN-SAD

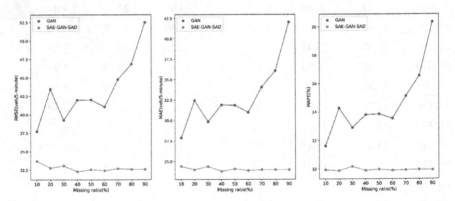

Fig. 5. The error in different missing ratios at weekends between GAN and SAE-GAN-SAD

Then, the results of comparison experiments with different baseline methods have shown in Fig. 5–6. The proposed method gets higher performance than all baseline methods in all missing ratios on workdays and weekends. HA model generally has the worst performance not only on workdays but also on weekends. The performance of BP model is second only to the proposed model when missing ratios are from 10% to 80%. However, in the case where the missing ratio is 90%, the BP model has the biggest MAPE on workdays and weekends. The reason for consideration may be that the BP model can't extract fully valid features when the amount of valid data is small. KNN has a better performance on weekends than on workdays. And the error of KNN is smaller than that of BP on weekends when the error of KNN is larger than the error of BP on workdays. Considered the possible reason is that there is a strong periodicity in the traffic flow on the weekends. In general, SAE-GAN-SAD has the best performance compared to other models.

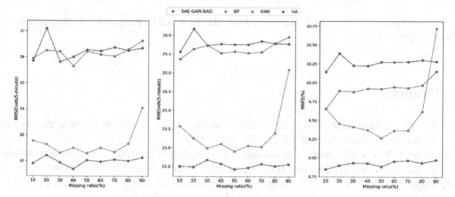

Fig. 6. The error of different methods on workdays

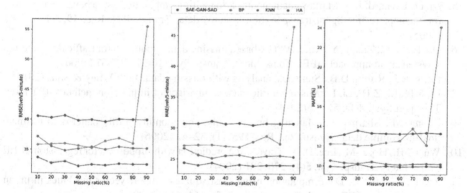

Fig. 7. The error of different methods on weekends

5 Conclusions

This paper proposes a deep learning-based approach for traffic data imputation called SAE-GAN-SAD. The proposed model consists of SAE, GAN and SAD. The SAE is employed to get the spatiotemporal features through missing data. The GAN is mainly to get the features of complete data from features of missing data. And, the restore data is obtained by SAD. To illustrate the superiority of the proposed model, a lot of experiments have been conducted and divided into many different situations. The experiment data was collected from Caltrans PeMS. Meanwhile, the performance of the SAE-GAN-SAD model with that of KNN, BP, and HA was compared. The results illustrated that the SAE-GAN-SAD performs better than the baseline models.

In the subsequent work, the proposed method is expected to be applied in more different data sets to evaluate the model performance. In addition, we are trying to integrate the proposed model with other excellent methods towards performance improvement.

Acknowledgments. This work was supported the Key R&D Programs of Zhejiang under Grant(2022C01121).

References

1. Sharma, S., Lingras, P., Zhong, M.: Effect of missing values estimations on traffic parameters. Transport. Planning Technol. **27**(2), 119–144 (2004)
2. Wang, F.-Y.: Parallel control and management for intelligent transportation systems: concepts, architectures, and applications. IEEE Trans. Intell. Transp. Syst. **11**(3), 630–638 (2010)
3. Duan, Y.J., Lv, Y.S., Liu, Y.L., Wang, F.Y.: An efficient realization of deep learning for traffic data imputation. Transport. Res. C-Emer. **72**, 168–181 (2016)
4. Chen, C., Kwon, J., Rice, J., Skabardonis, A., Varaiya, P.: Detecting errors and imputing missing data for single-loop surveillance systems. Transp. Res. Rec. **1855**(1), 160–167 (2003)
5. Ni, D., Leonard, J.D.: Markov chain monte carlo multiple imputation using bayesian networks for incomplete intelligent transportation systems data. Transp. Res. Rec. **1935**(1), 57–67 (2005)
6. Qu, L., Li, L., Zhang, Y., Hu, J.: PPCA-based missing data imputation for traffic flow volume: a systematical approach. IEEE Trans. Intell. Transp. Syst. **10**(3), 512–522 (2009)
7. Little, R.J., Rubin, D.B.: Statistical analysis with missing data. John Wiley & Sons (2019)
8. Li, Y.B., Li, Z.H., Li, L.: Missing traffic data: comparison of imputation methods. IET Intel. Transport Syst. **8**(1), 51–57 (2014)
9. Zhong, M., Sharma, S.: Matching hourly, daily, and monthly traffic patterns to estimate missing volume data. Transp. Res. Rec. **1957**(1), 32–42 (2006)
10. Wu, C.-H., Ho, J.-M., Lee, D.-T.: Travel-time prediction with support vector regression. IEEE Trans. Intell. Transp. Syst. **5**(4), 276–281 (2004)
11. Zhang, Y., Liu, Y.: Data imputation using least squares support vector machines in urban arterial streets. IEEE Signal Process. Lett. **16**(5), 414–417 (2009)
12. Lee, S., Fambro, D.B.: Application of subset autoregressive integrated moving average model for short-term freeway traffic volume forecasting. Transp. Res. Rec. **1678**(1), 179–188 (1999)
13. Zhong, M., Sharma, S., Lingras, P.: Genetically designed models for accurate imputation of missing traffic counts. Transport. Res. Record J. Transport. Res. Board. **1879**(1), 71–79 (2004)
14. Dia, H.: An object-oriented neural network approach to short-term traffic forecasting. Eur. J. Oper. Res. **131**(2), 253–261 (2001)
15. Yin, W., Murray-Tuite, P., Rakha, H.: Imputing erroneous data of single-station loop detectors for nonincident conditions: comparison between temporal and spatial methods. J. Intell. Transport. Syst. **16**(3), 159–176 (2012)
16. Castro-Neto, M., Jeong, Y.-S., Jeong, M.-K., Han, L.D.: Online-SVR for short-term traffic flow prediction under typical and atypical traffic conditions. Expert Syst. Appl. **36**(3), 6164–6173 (2009)

17. Qu, L., Zhang, Y., Hu, J., Jia, L., Li, L. (eds.) : A BPCA based missing value imputing method for traffic flow volume data. In: 2008 IEEE Intelligent Vehicles Symposium. IEEE (2008)
18. Luo, X., Meng, X., Gan, W., Chen, Y.: Traffic data imputation algorithm based on improved low-rank matrix decomposition. J. Sensors **2019**, 1–11 (2019)
19. Ni, D., Leonard, J.D., Guin, A., Feng, C.: Multiple imputation scheme for overcoming the missing values and variability issues in ITS data. J. Transp. Eng. **131**(12), 931–938 (2005)
20. Al-Deek, H.M., Venkata, C., Chandra, S.R.: New algorithms for filtering and imputation of real-time and archived dual-loop detector data in I-4 data warehouse. Transp. Res. Rec. **1867**(1), 116–126 (2004)
21. Liu, Z., Sharma, S., Datla, S.: Imputation of missing traffic data during holiday periods. Transp. Plan. Technol. **31**(5), 525–544 (2008)
22. Troyanskaya, O., Cantor, M., Sherlock, G., Brown, P., Hastie, T., Tibshirani, R., et al.: Missing value estimation methods for DNA microarrays. Bioinformatics **17**(6), 520–525 (2001)
23. Xu, D.W., Wang, Y.D., Jia, L.M., Zhang, G.J., Guo, H.F.: Real-time road traffic states estimation based on kernel-KNN matching of road traffic spatial characteristics. J. Central South Univ. **23**(9), 2453–2464 (2016)
24. Xu, D.W., Wang, Y.D., Jia, L.M., Li, H.J., Zhang, G.J.: Real-time road traffic states measurement based on Kernel-KNN matching of regional traffic attractors. Measurement **94**, 862–872 (2016)
25. Chang, G., Zhang, Y., Yao, D.: Missing data imputation for traffic flow based on improved local least squares. Tsinghua Sci. Technol. **17**(3), 304–309 (2012)
26. Chang, G., Wu, Q., Luo, L. (eds.): Missing data imputataion for traffic flow based on weighted local least squares. In: IET Conference Proceedings; The Institution of Engineering & Technology (2012)
27. Duan, Y.J., Lv, Y.S., Kang, W.W., Zhao, Y.F.: A deep learning based approach for traffic data imputation. In: 2014 EEE 17th International Conference on Intelligent Transportation Systems (ITSC), pp. 912–917 (2014)
28. Shang, Q., Yang, Z.S., Gao, S., Tan, D.R.: An Imputation method for missing traffic data based on FCM optimized by PSO-SVR. J. Adv. Transp. **2018**, 1–21 (2018)
29. Farhan, J., Fwa, T.: Airport pavement missing data management and imputation with stochastic multiple imputation model. Transp. Res. Rec. **2336**(1), 43–54 (2013)
30. Gilks, W.R., Richardson, S., Spiegelhalter, D.: Markov chain Monte Carlo in practice. Chapman and Hall/CRC (1995)
31. Tipping, M.E., Bishop, C.M.: Mixtures of probabilistic principal component analyzers. Neural Comput. **11**(2), 443–482 (1999)
32. Qu, L., Li, L., Zhang, Y., Hu, J.M.: PPCA-based missing data imputation for traffic flow volume: a systematical approach. IEEE Trans. Intell. Transp. Syst. **10**(3), 512–522 (2009)
33. Chiou, J.-M., Zhang, Y.-C., Chen, W.-H., Chang, C.-W.: A functional data approach to missing value imputation and outlier detection for traffic flow data. Transportmetrica B: Transp. Dynam. **2**(2), 106–129 (2014)
34. Li, L., Li, Y., Li, Z.: Efficient missing data imputing for traffic flow by considering temporal and spatial dependence. Transport. Res. Part C Emerg. Technol. **34**, 108–120 (2013)
35. Yang, H., Yang, J., Han, L.D., Liu, X., Pu, L., Chin, S.M., et al.: A Kriging based spatiotemporal approach for traffic volume data imputation. PLoS ONE **13**(4), e0195957 (2018)
36. Li, Z., Li, J., Wang, Y., Wang, K.: A deep learning approach for anomaly detection based on SAE and LSTM in mechanical equipment. Int. J. Adv. Manufact. Technol. **103**(1–4), 499–510 (2019). https://doi.org/10.1007/s00170-019-03557-w
37. Goodfellow, I., Pouget-Abadie, J., Mirza, M., Xu, B., Warde-Farley, D., Ozair, S., et al. (eds.): Generative adversarial nets. Advances in Neural Information Processing Systems (2014)

38. Rumelhart, D.E., Hinton, G.E., Williams, R.J.: Learning representations by back-propagating errors. Cognitive modeling. **5**(3), 1 (1988)
39. Bengio, Y., Lamblin, P., Popovici, D., Larochelle, H. (eds.): Greedy layer-wise training of deep networks. Advances in Neural Information Processing Systems (2007)
40. Liu, G.F., Bao, H.Q., Han, B.K.: A stacked autoencoder-based deep neural network for achieving gearbox fault diagnosis. Math. Probl. Eng. **2018**, 1–10 (2018)
41. Luc, P., Couprie, C., Chintala, S., Verbeek, J.: Semantic segmentation using adversarial networks. arXiv preprint arXiv:161108408 (2016)
42. Shrivastava, A., Pfister, T., Tuzel, O., Susskind, J., Wang, W., Webb, R. (eds.): Learning from simulated and unsupervised images through adversarial training. In: Proceedings of the IEEE Conference on Computer Vision and Pattern Recognition (2017)
43. Isola, P., Zhu, J.-Y., Zhou, T., Efros, A.A. (eds.) Image-to-image translation with conditional adversarial networks. In: Proceedings of the IEEE Conference on Computer Vision and Pattern Recognition (2017)
44. Ledig, C., Theis, L., Huszár, F., Caballero, J., Cunningham, A., Acosta, A. et al. (eds.): Photo-realistic single image super-resolution using a generative adversarial network. In: Proceedings of the IEEE Conference on Computer Vision and Pattern Recognition (2017)
45. Li, J., Monroe, W., Shi, T., Jean, S., Ritter, A., Jurafsky, D.: Adversarial learning for neural dialogue generation. arXiv preprint arXiv:170106547 (2017)
46. Yoon, J., Jordon, J., Van Der Schaar, M.: Gain: missing data imputation using generative adversarial nets. arXiv preprint arXiv:180602920 (2018)
47. Li SC-X, Jiang B, Marlin B. MisGAN: Learning from Incomplete Data with Generative Adversarial Networks. arXiv preprint arXiv:190209599 (2019)
48. Chen, Y., Lv, Y., Wang, F.-Y.: Traffic flow imputation using parallel data and generative adversarial networks. IEEE Trans. Intell. Transport. Syst. **20**, 1–7 (2019)
49. Arjovsky, M., Chintala, S., Bottou, L.: Wasserstein GAN. arXiv preprint arXiv:170107875 (2017)
50. Allison, P.D.: Missing data: Sage publications (2001)
51. Zhong, M., Sharma, S., Lingras, P.: Genetically designed models for accurate imputation of missing traffic counts. Transp. Res. Rec. **1879**(1), 71–79 (2004)

Scaffold Data Augmentation
for Molecular Property Prediction

Tianyi Jiang[1,2], Zeyu Wang[1,2], Jinhuan Wang[1,2(✉)], Jiafei Shao[1,2],
and Qi Xuan[1,2]

[1] Institute of Cyberspace Security, Zhejiang University of Technology,
Hangzhou 310023, China
jhwang@zjut.edu.cn
[2] College of Information Engineering, Zhejiang University of Technology,
Hangzhou 310023, China

Abstract. Recently, as the applications of machine learning boom in biochemistry, data augmentation has demonstrated its power in molecular generation tasks. Specifically, data augmentation can effectively relieve the problems that insufficient training data results in model overfitting in molecular property prediction, etc. While existing works focus on the rationality of augmented construct but neglect the importance of molecular scaffolds for the task of molecular property prediction. This paper analyzes the contribution of scaffolds in property prediction tasks and proposes a new augmentation technique that preserves functional groups and modifies molecular scaffolds during the augmentation process. By modifying scaffolds, data augmentation can increase the diversity of molecules and thus enrich the dataset. At the same time, by preserving the functional groups, the introduction of noise can be effectively reduced, the quality of augmented data can be improved, and the invariance of labels can be enhanced. We conducted experiments on four benchmark datasets using three baselines with different classification models to test the effectiveness of our proposed method. Our results strongly demonstrate that data augmentation with modifying scaffolds can effectively optimize property prediction performance and improve model generalization.

Keywords: Data augmentation · Molecular scaffold · Molecular property prediction

1 Introduction

Molecular property prediction is a crucial task in the fields of chemistry and medicine [21], as it allows scientists to analyze the properties and reactions of molecules, facilitating the design and development of new drugs or chemical substances [23]. Via the prediction of molecular properties, scientists can predict the toxicity [15], biological activity [20], drug efficacy [24], solubility [8] and thermodynamic properties of molecules, thereby helping drug development and material design [4]. The increasing popularity of machine learning has drawn the attention of researchers to predicting molecular properties with machine learning. These methods can effectively minimize the number of experiments required while providing rapid and precise predictions of molecular properties without the need for expensive and time-consuming trial-and-error [25].

As an essential part of machine learning [32], graph data mining is closely related to molecular property prediction. Researchers usually modeled molecular property prediction as a graph classification task for learning [12,30]. Graph data can effectively process the topology of molecules by representing the elements as nodes and the chemical bonds between elements as edges. Also, graph-based models can capture both local and global information about a molecule through the features of nodes and edges [28]. Furthermore, they can handle missing or incomplete data by inferring the missing information from neighboring nodes [6]. Among them, deep learning methods based on GNNs(GCN [13], GIN [31]) have achieved excellent behavior, while the dependency of GNN models on data also exists in GNN models for molecular property prediction. However, in the real world, labeled data is far less than unlabeled data, and therefore, data augmentation can effectively alleviate this problem.

Data augmentation refers to the methods of adding perturbations to the original data or creating synthetic data from the original data to improve data diversity [40]. Existing research on data augmentation for graph classification tasks is still in its fancy and can mainly be divided into topology-based data augmentation and feature-based data augmentation. Topology-based data augmentation refers to obtaining augmented data by modifying the topology of the graph, such as adding or removing edges or nodes [18,26,41], and so on. However, these methods may not consider the domain-specific information or lack interpretability, and only consider the structural validity of the domain-specific information. On the other hand, feature-based data augmentation refers to methods that mixup the graph representation to generate new data [27] or optimize the representation model [16,33]. However, these methods are often relatively abstract and lack interpretability.

Actually, while data augmentation satisfies the goal of improving data diversity, it also needs to consider the label invariance of augmented data, that is, the augmented data have the same label as the original data. Molecular isomers usually have the same or different physicochemical properties, which have critical applications in various fields, such as drug design, chemical development, and environmental pollution [1,5]. For example, iso-combretastatin A and combretastatin A are molecules belonging to carbon chain isomers, but they have similar biological activities [19]. Therefore, the rational utilization of isomer features can help generate reliable augmented data. In molecular property prediction tasks, the molecular scaffold also plays a fundamental role. Changes in the scaffold structure can affect the properties of the molecule. For instance, in protein engineering, by changing the molecular scaffold of a polypeptide, geometric parameters such as distances, angles, and dihedral angles between amino acid residues can be altered, thus affecting the stability and kinetic properties of the polypeptide and having an impact on the functional and biological properties of the polypeptide [7]. Similarly, carbon chain isomerism and positional isomerism of molecular scaffolds under the same molecular formula can lead to different atomic connectivity, which can have profound effects on the properties of the compound [29]. By using the isomeric variation of the scaffold, we can obtain additional information to improve the diversity of molecules. In addition, functional groups play a crucial role in determining the chemical reactivity, thermodynamic stability, and other properties of the molecule. In fact, for tasks such as chemical reaction and toxicity prediction, the functional groups of the molecule can significantly change its polarity, acidity, basicity, and reactivity [2]. Therefore, during scaffold modification, the position and number of functional groups must be retained. Above all, this paper proposes an augmentation strategy for predicting various molecular properties and explores its effectiveness. Specifically, this paper introduces the concept of augmentation with scaffold variants and molecular isomers and analyzes the importance of molecular scaffolds in property prediction. Furthermore, an augmentation strategy based on isomers is proposed: scaffold-based isomer augmentation (SIA). During the augmentation process, the SIA mainly modifies the scaffold while preserving the structure and connection points of the functional groups. Our main contributions are as follows:

- In molecular property prediction tasks, molecular scaffolds play an important role, and different molecular scaffold structures lead to different physical and chemical properties. Therefore, in order to improve the accuracy of prediction models, this paper designs a data augmentation strategy based on molecular scaffolds.
- In this paper, we propose a new conformation-based molecular data augmentation strategy to increase the diversity of the dataset by modifying the molecular scaffolds. Unlike other data augmentation methods, our method does not change the functional group structures of the molecule and constitutes an isomer of the original molecule by modifying the molecular scaffold.
- By keeping the functional groups constant, our method can effectively reduce the introduction of noise and ensure the label invariance of the augmented data. At the same time, our method can also increase the diversity of the dataset, which can be better adapted to different prediction tasks. Thus, our method provides strong support for molecular design and discovery.
- To validate the effectiveness of our method, we conduct experiments on four benchmark molecular property prediction datasets and compare them with other data augmentation methods. The experimental results show that our method achieves significant performance improvement on different datasets.

2 Related Work

2.1 Molecular Property Prediction

Molecular property prediction is a crucial task in computer-aided drug design workflows [23]. Graph-based molecular property prediction is a kind of method that utilizes molecular topology information to predict molecular properties.

The most mainstream methods for molecular property prediction are based on GNN, with classic representative methods such as GCN [13], GIN [31], Fra-GAT [38], GraSeq [9], MGSSL [37], and Micro-Graph [36], etc. Among them, the GCN and GIN are traditional graph classification methods that achieve effective extraction of graph-level features through neighborhood aggregation, and consideration of graph isomorphism. While FraGAT, GraSeq, and MGSSL take domain information into consideration and extract molecular representations by learning from the functional motif structures in the molecules. Inspired by the exploration of important structures in molecular networks in graph representation, in this paper, we explore the contribution of scaffolds in molecular property prediction and propose a corresponding augmentation method.

2.2 Data Augmentation

Data augmentation is a method of expanding the amount of data to address the problem of insufficient training data in machine learning tasks [40]. It can effectively alleviate model overfitting and improve model generalization, which has received widespread attention from scholars [39,42]. Unlike in the fields of computer vision and natural language processing, graph-based data augmentation is still in the exploratory stage, especially for graph classification tasks. Some of the more classic methods include M-Evolve [41], G-Mixup [10], GraphCrop [26], Graph Transplant [22], Automated augmentation [17], and GLA [34], etc. Among them, M-Evolve, Graphcrop, Automated augmentation, G-Mixup, and Graph Transplant are topology-based augmentation methods, while GLA is a feature-based augmentation method. However, these works lack consideration of domain information, GLA mentioned the issue and introduced label-invariant methods to reduce noise. In this paper, we not only introduce the structural rationality of the augmented data in the corresponding domains but also conduct an exploration of molecular property prediction tasks. We introduce the concept of the importance of scaffolds for molecular properties in the prediction task of molecular network augmentation. In addition, during the augmentation process, we preserve the functional groups to achieve label-invariance and reduce noise.

3 Method

In this section, we propose SIA, a data augmentation framework based on molecular scaffolds. First, we define the graph augmentation problem on graph classification. Then, we analyze the importance of molecular scaffolds and state the main process of our method. The details are described below.

3.1 Problem Definition

We represent a graph G as (V, E, W), where V is the set of nodes, E is the edge set and W is the weight set of edges. For a molecule, the atoms and bonds between atoms form the nodes and edges of the graph. Given a dataset

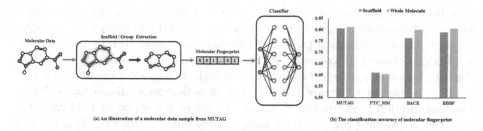

Fig. 1. Classification Performance of Scaffolds and Functional Groups.

$D = \{(G_i, y_i)\}$ that contains a series of graphs and y_i is the label of graph G_i. And it can be split into training, validation, and testing set, denoted as D_{train}, D_{val}, and D_{test}. For a graph data augmentation task, the objective is to design a transformation function $f(G, y) \rightarrow (G_{aug}, y)$ to generate augmented graphs based on D_{train} to relieve the problem of insufficient data and improve the data diversity. Then, problems such as over-fitting can be addressed and classification performance can be improved.

3.2 Importance of Molecular Scaffolds

A molecular scaffold refers to the framework structure composed of atoms and bonds within a molecule, excluding any groups within the molecule. In molecular property prediction, the molecular scaffold can be used as a descriptor to represent the shape, topology, and structural characteristics of the molecule, thus predicting the properties of the molecule. The advantage of using the molecular scaffold for property prediction is that it can reduce feature dimensions and lower computational costs compared to using the entire molecule. Many examples of scaffolds and their relationship to molecular properties have been demonstrated in many studies. For example, for some drug molecules, their pharmacological activity is related to the shape and topological structure of their molecular scaffold [14]. For aromatic compounds, the compactness and number of rings in the molecular scaffold can affect their optical and electronic properties [35]. In addition, the shape and connectivity of the molecular scaffold can also affect the activity and selectivity of the molecule in chemical reactions.

Figure 1 shows the results of graph classification accuracy using only scaffolds on four datasets, with detailed information on these datasets presented in Sect. 4.1. Here we extract the molecular fingerprints of the scaffolds and feed them into the classifier for graph classification. The results show that the accuracy of predicting molecular properties using only the scaffold is comparable to that of using the entire molecule, indicating that the scaffold is an important factor in molecular property prediction. This may be because the scaffold can provide topological information about the molecule, such as the number and size of rings, chain lengths, and branching information, which is essential for describing the biological activity and pharmacological effects of molecules. In some cases, the scaffold may be more representative than the entire molecule. For example, when there are many functional groups in the molecule, these functional groups may interfere with the feature extraction process of the entire molecule, thereby reducing the prediction accuracy. In contrast, the scaffold can ignore these functional groups during extraction and better reflect the topological features of the molecule.

In this work, to increase the diversity of molecular scaffolds and enhance the classification performance of graphs, we adopt a method of modifying the scaffold to generate carbon chain isomers or positional isomers. This method can increase the variety of compounds and enrich the diversity of the dataset by introducing isomers of molecules, thus improving the generalization ability and accuracy of the classification model.

3.3 Graph Data Augmentation

SIA. The main idea of SIA is to keep the molecular functional groups unchanged and generate augmented graphs by modifying the scaffolds. Functional groups are structural units that are closely related to the chemical properties of molecules. By keeping the functional group consistent, similarities between molecules can be more effectively handled. At the same time, we increase the diversity of scaffold structures by changing the molecular scaffold to generate augmented graphs with carbon chain heterostructures or positional heterostructures. SIA first extracts its scaffold graph from the molecular graph and transforms it into a line graph. Then two nodes are selected from the line graph and their corresponding edges in the scaffold graph are swapped to create the augmented graph. Finally, the augmented graph for training is obtained by filtering the graph with chemical rules and molecular fingerprints. An illustration of the process of producing an augmented graph from an original molecular graph with our augmentation model is given in Fig. 2. The specific details of each augmentation step are shown as follows.

- **Line Graph Construction.** To facilitate the data augmentation process, we first construct the line graph of the molecular scaffold graph as illustrated in Fig. 2. Each augmentation process needs to select two edges to swap, in other words, one should select four nodes and apply specific masking rules with the node adjacency matrix to generate a more reasonable augmented graph. However, directly selecting and masking nodes have a high time complexity. According to statistics, the time complexity of using the original graph in the selection operation is $\mathcal{O}(2 \times |V|^2)$, while the time complexity of using the line graph is $\mathcal{O}(2 \times |E|)$. It can be seen that the line graph can greatly reduce the time complexity. Therefore, the line graph construction is introduced here to transform node selection into edge selection.

  Given a graph G, the line graph $L(G)$ is obtained by replacing each edge in the original graph with a node and connecting two of these nodes with an edge if the corresponding edges in G share a common node. Here, we first use

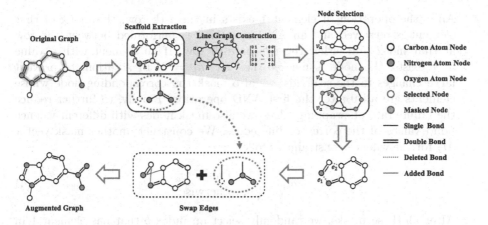

Fig. 2. Overview of Graph Augmentation method.

the open-source toolkit RDKit[1] to extract the scaffold graph G_S and form it into a line graph $L(G_S)$. Specifically, the elements of the adjacency matrix of G_S are defined as:

$$A_{ij} = \begin{cases} 1, & e_s = (v_i, v_j) \in E_S \\ 0, & \text{otherwise} \end{cases} \tag{1}$$

Since the molecular graph is undirected, we convert A to the upper triangular matrix. Then we select out $a_{ij} = 1$ to get the node set V_L of $L(G_S)$. Each element in V_L corresponds to each edge in G_S. By constructing a line graph, the connections between the nodes become simpler and more obvious, and it is also easier for us to modify the edges of the original graph.

– **Edge Sampling**

After constructing the line graph, we select two nodes in $L(G_S)$ to prepare for swapping edges. We first randomly select a node v_a in V_L. Then we introduce the adjacency matrix A of $L(G_S)$. This is because the random operation in the swapping process can easily select edges that share a node or add existing edges, which can cause the augmentation to fail. Therefore, we mask some nodes by combining them with A to reduce the search space.

Let a be the index of the first node selected for edge swapping. First, to ensure that the same nodes are not selected, we define a mask vector $M_1 = [m_1, m_2, \ldots, m_{|V_L|}]$, where:

$$m_i = \begin{cases} 1, & \text{if } A_{ia} = 0, i = 1, \ldots, |V_L| \\ 0, & \text{otherwise} \end{cases} \tag{2}$$

Then we perform an AND operation on the a-th row of A with every other row to avoid rewiring existing edges. This can be expressed as follows:

$$A'_{ij} = A_{ij} \cdot A_{aj}, i, j = 1, \ldots, |V_L| \tag{3}$$

---

[1] https://www.rdkit.org/.

After the operation, if element 1 exists in the i-th row, the index of that element is retrieved and an AND operation is performed between the row at that index and either the i-th or a-th row. If an element with a value of 1 exists, the node is masked, i.e., let $m_i = 0$. In addition, to prevent large changes in the scaffolds, we also mask the corresponding node whose elements are all 0 after the first AND operation. Finally, to further reduce the failure rate of swapping edges, we also mask nodes with different valence bond values of the corresponding edges. We construct another mask vector M_2 for the valence constraint as follows:

$$m_i = \begin{cases} 1, & \text{if } w_i = w_a \\ 0, & \text{otherwise} \end{cases} \tag{4}$$

After all these masks, we randomly select an index b that has element 1 in both M_1 and M_2 as the second node v_b.

- **Swap Edges.** In the previous section, our method selects two nodes v_a and v_b in the line graph used to swap edges. Then, we transform the two nodes into their corresponding edges in the scaffold graph to obtain e_{s1}, e_{s2}. Our ultimate goal is to swap edges on the original molecular graph, so here we need to correspond e_{s1}, e_{s2} to the edges in G to get $e_1 = (v_1, v_2, \omega), e_2 = (v_3, v_4, \omega)$. After that, we break e_1, e_2 and rewire $e_1' = (v_1, v_4, \omega), e_2' = (v_2, v_3, \omega)$.

Finally, we perform a chemical rule check on the generated graph using RDKit. The above is a single modification in the graph network. During data augmentation, it is possible to modify several times until the modification ratio is reached or the number of failures exceeds the number of edges in the graph network.

Data Filtration. In machine learning, data filtration is a key pre-processing step to select representative data samples from the original dataset to be used for training the model. In the above step, we generate more training data by data augmentation. However, during data augmentation of the graph data, noise may be introduced due to some transformation operations. In this work, based on the field of cheminformatics, molecular fingerprints are introduced and used as a criterion for data filtration. The molecular fingerprint is a way to describe the structural information of a compound by converting the structural information of a molecule into a series of numerical vectors [3]. Compared with traditional filtering used for graph data augmentation, molecular fingerprints can capture chemical information such as structure, function, and properties of molecules, thus allowing better processing of molecular graph data. In addition, the molecular fingerprint is a fixed-length encoding method, which can reduce the computational complexity and thus improve the efficiency of classifiers.

Here, we introduce a concept of label reliability [41] to measure the matching degree between the molecular fingerprints of the augmented graphs and the labels with the graph classifier. We first transform the graph data of D_{train} and D_{val} into molecular fingerprints. Each molecular fingerprint of graph data in D_{val} will be fed into the pre-trained classifier to obtain the prediction vector $p_i \in \mathbb{R}^{|Y|}$. The class average probability matrix $Q \in \mathbb{R}^{|Y| \times |Y|}$ will be also calculated. Then, we can obtain label reliability r_i of each graph in the training set. When r_i is larger, it means that the classifier can correctly predict examples with greater probability using molecular fingerprints. If r_i is higher than the threshold we set, it will be used as the final augmented graph.

4 Experiments

In this section, we perform a series of experiments on various molecular datasets to verify our method. First, we give the details of the datasets, baseline, and experimental setup. Next, we conduct the experiments with two different GNN architectures: GCN [13] and GIN [31] and compare our method with other graph augmentation methods. We also conduct a parameter study to analyze the sensitivity of our method to the modified edge ratio.

4.1 Experimental Setup

Datasets. To demonstrate that our method brings consistent improvement across various datasets, we conduct the experiment on four benchmark datasets in chemical and biological domains, which include: MUTAG, PTC_MM, BACE and BBBP. All the dataset statistics are summarized in Table 1. In this table, $|V|$ and $|E|$ denote the average number of nodes and edges in each graph.

Table 1. Summary of datasets.

Dataset	Graphs	$|V|$	$|E|$	Features	Labels
MUTAG	188	17.9	19.8	7	2
PTC_MM	336	14.0	14.3	19	2
BACE	1513	34.1	36.9	8	2
BBBP	2050	23.9	25.8	10	2

Baselines. We compare our method with the following baseline methods, including:

- Edge perturbation (PermE) [11], which randomly adds and removes a certain ratio of edges. We tune the perturbation (add/remove) ratio to 0.2.
- Attribute masking (MaskN) [11], which stochastically masks a certain ratio of node features. We tune the masking ratio to 0.2.
- Graph Transplant [22], which leverages graph rewiring to mix two dissimilar-structured graphs by replacing the destination subgraph with the source subgraph.

For a fair comparison, we use the same hyperparameter setting in training classification models for all methods.

Table 2. Performance across GNN architectures and four benchmark datasets.

Model	Method	MUTAG	PTC_MM	BACE	BBBP
GCN	original	0.750	0.669	0.710	0.773
	PermE	0.753	0.666	0.695	0.761
	MaskN	0.749	0.666	0.714	0.787
	Graph Transplant	0.781	0.667	0.727	0.793
	SIA	**0.796**	**0.696**	**0.746**	**0.795**
GIN	original	0.840	0.634	0.765	0.769
	PermE	0.845	0.590	0.778	0.782
	MaskN	0.828	0.655	0.759	0.791
	Graph Transplant	0.839	0.661	0.776	0.795
	SIA	**0.919**	**0.692**	**0.791**	**0.804**

Settings. We evaluate the model with 10-fold cross-validation. For each dataset, the experiments are repeated five times, and the different train/validation/test splits with a ratio of 8:1:1. The Adam optimizer with a learning rate of 0.001 is used for the training of all models. For classification models, we employ GCN and GIN models as GNN encoders, where the GCN model has 3 layers and the GIN model has 4 layers, with a hidden size of 64 for all layers. And, training is conducted for 100 epochs with a batch size of 64 for MUTAG and PTC_MM, and 256 for BACE and BBBP. In addition, during the augmentation process, we set the modified edge ratio to $\alpha = 0.2$ for our augmentation method.

4.2 Performance Comparison

Table 2 summarizes the performance of our proposed method compared to baselines on all four datasets. From the results, our method can improve the performance of different GNN models on various datasets. It is worth noting that our method consistently outperforms other baselines, with the MUTAG dataset showing the most significant gain on GIN, which is a good illustration of the importance of the molecular scaffolds described in Sect. 3.2. This phenomenon is reasonable that scaffolds contain important information about molecules. By swapping edges, new structural information similar to the original graph can be introduced to better reflect the chemical features and increase the sample size of the features.

Compared with other methods that randomly perturb edges and mask node features, our method only operates on the scaffolds and does not modify or delete atomic features, thus not easily introducing additional noise information, which can better preserve the basic structural information of the original molecules and prevent information loss and confusion caused by random perturbations. Moreover, compared with feature-based augmentation methods such as MaskN, our method only needs to consider the topology of the molecule, i.e., the way the atoms and bonds are connected. By changing the positions of atoms and bonds,

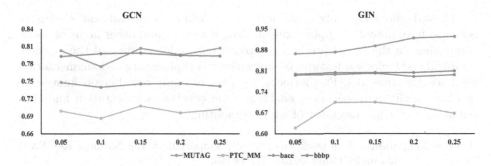

Fig. 3. Parameter Sensitivity Evaluation on Graph Classification.

we can generate different molecular graphs. In this process, we do not need to consider the features of each node and edge. This method is not only faster in computation but also does not require feature encoding, thus reducing training time and computational resources.

4.3 Parameter Sensitivity

In this section, we analyze the parameter sensitivity of our method on four datasets, our method includes one parameter, modified edge ratio α. We vary the parameter α among $\{0.05, 0.1, 0.15, 0, 2, 0.25\}$ and evaluate the graph classification performance on GCN and GIN. Figure 3 reports the results on four datasets, it is not difficult to conclude that our data augmentation method is not very sensitive to α. Although the performance on the MUTAG and PTC_MM datasets fluctuates slightly under the modification rate of augmentation, this is mainly due to the relatively small size and simple molecular structures of these datasets, as well as their fewer model parameters and lower complexity, making the data augmentation method have a greater impact on the model generalization. Generally, when the augmentation modification rate is set to 0.2, good performance can be achieved in most cases.

5 Conclusion and Future Work

In this work, we propose SIA, an augmentation method based on scaffolds. SIA considers swapping the edges on molecular scaffolds for augmentation. To reduce the search space, SIA constructs a line graph of the scaffolds and uses it for the operation of masking nodes. In addition, we analyze the importance of scaffolds for the classification of different datasets by masking some of the node features. Through extensive experimental studies, our method can achieve better performance than many existing graph augmentation methods on graph classification tasks, and the importance of scaffolds for the classification of different datasets is well reflected in GCN and GIN.

These findings not only contribute to the field of computational chemistry but also have potential applications in drug discovery and other areas of social computing. In the future, we aim to further our understanding of the physico-chemical and biological features of molecules and explore targeted augmentation methods for molecules. Furthermore, we plan to apply our domain knowledge to other application scenarios, enabling more effective augmentation and contributing to the advancement of social computing.

Acknowledgement. This work was partially supported by the National Key R&D Program of China under Grant 2020YFB1006104.

References

1. Arenas, M., Martín, J., Santos, J.L., Aparicio, I., Alonso, E.: An overview of analytical methods for enantiomeric determination of chiral pollutants in environmental samples and biota. TrAC, Trends Anal. Chem. **143**, 116370 (2021)
2. Bader, R.F.W., Popelier, P.L.A., Keith, T.A.: Theoretical definition of a functional group and the molecular orbital paradigm. Angew. Chem. Int. Ed. Engl. **33**(6), 620–631 (1994)
3. Cereto-Massagué, A., Ojeda, M.J., Valls, C., Mulero, M., Garcia-Vallvé, S., Pujadas, G.: Molecular fingerprint similarity search in virtual screening. Methods **71**, 58–63 (2015)
4. Chen, D., et al.: Algebraic graph-assisted bidirectional transformers for molecular property prediction. Nat. Commun. **12**(1), 3521 (2021)
5. Clayden, J., Moran, W.J., Edwards, P.J., LaPlante, S.R.: The challenge of atropisomerism in drug discovery. Angew. Chem. Int. Ed. **48**(35), 6398–6401 (2009)
6. Daminelli, S., Thomas, J.M., Durán, C., Cannistraci, C.V.: Common neighbours and the local-community-paradigm for topological link prediction in bipartite networks. New J. Phys. **17**(11), 113037 (2015)
7. Daura, X., Gademann, K., Jaun, B., Seebach, D., Van Gunsteren, W.F., Mark, A.E.: Peptide folding: when simulation meets experiment. Angew. Chem. Int. Ed. **38**(1–2), 236–240 (1999)
8. Feinberg, E.N., et al.: Potentialnet for molecular property prediction. ACS Cent. Sci. **4**(11), 1520–1530 (2018)
9. Guo, Z., Yu, W., Zhang, C., Jiang, M., Chawla, N.V.: GraSeq: graph and sequence fusion learning for molecular property prediction. In: Proceedings of the 29th ACM International Conference on Information & Knowledge Management, pp. 435–443 (2020)
10. Han, X., Jiang, Z., Liu, N., Hu, X.: G-Mixup: graph data augmentation for graph classification. In: International Conference on Machine Learning, pp. 8230–8248. PMLR (2022)
11. Hu, W., et al.: Strategies for pre-training graph neural networks. In: International Conference on Learning Representations (ICLR) (2020)
12. Kearnes, S., McCloskey, K., Berndl, M., Pande, V., Riley, P.: Molecular graph convolutions: moving beyond fingerprints. J. Comput. Aided Mol. Des. **30**(8), 595–608 (2016). https://doi.org/10.1007/s10822-016-9938-8
13. Kipf, T.N., Welling, M.: Semi-supervised classification with graph convolutional networks. In: International Conference on Learning Representations (2017). https://openreview.net/forum?id=SJU4ayYgl

14. Klebe, G.: Recent developments in structure-based drug design. J. Mol. Med. **78**(5), 269–281 (2000). https://doi.org/10.1007/s001090000084
15. Liu, J., Lei, X., Zhang, Y., Pan, Y.: The prediction of molecular toxicity based on BiGRU and GraphSAGE. Comput. Biol. Med. **153**, 106524 (2023)
16. Liu, S., et al.: Local augmentation for graph neural networks. In: International Conference on Machine Learning, pp. 14054–14072. PMLR (2022)
17. Luo, Y., et al.: Automated data augmentations for graph classification. In: The Eleventh International Conference on Learning Representations (2023). https://openreview.net/forum?id=vTb1JI0Gps_
18. Magar, R., et al.: AugLIChem: data augmentation library of chemical structures for machine learning. Mach. Learn. Sci. Technol. **3**(4), 045015 (2022)
19. Messaoudi, S., et al.: Isocombretastatins a versus combretastatins a: The forgotten isoCA-4 isomer as a highly promising cytotoxic and antitubulin agent. J. Med. Chem. **52**(14), 4538–4542 (2009)
20. Nantasenamat, C., Isarankura-Na-Ayudhya, C., Prachayasittikul, V.: Advances in computational methods to predict the biological activity of compounds. Expert Opin. Drug Discov. **5**(7), 633–654 (2010)
21. Nigam, A., et al.: Assigning confidence to molecular property prediction. Expert Opin. Drug Discov. **16**(9), 1009–1023 (2021)
22. Park, J., Shim, H., Yang, E.: Graph transplant: node saliency-guided graph mixup with local structure preservation. In: Proceedings of the AAAI Conference on Artificial Intelligence, pp. 7966–7974 (2022)
23. Shen, J., Nicolaou, C.A.: Molecular property prediction: recent trends in the era of artificial intelligence. Drug Discov. Today Technol. **32**, 29–36 (2019)
24. Tarcsay, Á., Keseru, G.M.: Contributions of molecular properties to drug promiscuity: miniperspective. J. Med. Chem. **56**(5), 1789–1795 (2013)
25. Walters, W.P., Barzilay, R.: Applications of deep learning in molecule generation and molecular property prediction. Acc. Chem. Res. **54**(2), 263–270 (2020)
26. Wang, Y., Wang, W., Liang, Y., Cai, Y., Hooi, B.: GraphCrop: subgraph cropping for graph classification. arXiv preprint arXiv:2009.10564 (2020)
27. Wang, Y., Wang, W., Liang, Y., Cai, Y., Hooi, B.: Mixup for node and graph classification. In: Proceedings of the Web Conference 2021, pp. 3663–3674 (2021)
28. Wigh, D.S., Goodman, J.M., Lapkin, A.A.: A review of molecular representation in the age of machine learning. Wiley Interdiscip. Rev. Comput. Molecular Sci. **12**(5), e1603 (2022)
29. Woodward, R.B., Hoffmann, R.: The conservation of orbital symmetry. Angew. Chem. Int. Ed. Engl. **8**(11), 781–853 (1969)
30. Wu, Z., et al.: Moleculenet: a benchmark for molecular machine learning. Chem. Sci. **9**(2), 513–530 (2018)
31. Xu, K., Hu, W., Leskovec, J., Jegelka, S.: How powerful are graph neural networks? In: International Conference on Learning Representations (2019). https://openreview.net/forum?id=ryGs6iA5Km
32. Xuan, Q., Ruan, Z., Min, Y.: Graph Data Mining: Algorithm. Springer, Security and Application (2021)
33. Xuan, Q., et al.: Subgraph networks with application to structural feature space expansion. IEEE Trans. Knowl. Data Eng. **33**(6), 2776–2789 (2019)
34. Yue, H., Zhang, C., Zhang, C., Liu, H.: Label-invariant augmentation for semi-supervised graph classification. In: Oh, A.H., Agarwal, A., Belgrave, D., Cho, K. (eds.) Advances in Neural Information Processing Systems (2022). https://openreview.net/forum?id=rg_yN3HpCp

35. Zhang, D.W., Zhao, X., Hou, J.L., Li, Z.T.: Aromatic amide foldamers: structures, properties, and functions. Chem. Rev. **112**(10), 5271–5316 (2012)

36. Zhang, S., Hu, Z., Subramonian, A., Sun, Y.: Motif-driven contrastive learning of graph representations (2021). https://openreview.net/forum?id=qcKh_Msv1GP

37. Zhang, Z., Liu, Q., Wang, H., Lu, C., Lee, C.K.: Motif-based graph self-supervised learning for molecular property prediction. Adv. Neural. Inf. Process. Syst. **34**, 15870–15882 (2021)

38. Zhang, Z., Guan, J., Zhou, S.: FraGAT: a fragment-oriented multi-scale graph attention model for molecular property prediction. Bioinformatics **37**(18), 2981–2987 (2021)

39. Zhao, T., Liu, G., Günnemann, S., Jiang, M.: Graph data augmentation for graph machine learning: a survey. arXiv preprint arXiv:2202.08871 (2022)

40. Zhou, J., Shen, J., Xuan, Q.: Data augmentation for graph classification. In: Proceedings of the 29th ACM International Conference on Information & Knowledge Management, pp. 2341–2344 (2020)

41. Zhou, J., Shen, J., Yu, S., Chen, G., Xuan, Q.: M-evolve: structural-mapping-based data augmentation for graph classification. IEEE Trans. Netw. Sci. Eng. **8**(1), 190–200 (2020)

42. Zhou, J., Xie, C., Wen, Z., Zhao, X., Xuan, Q.: Data augmentation on graphs: a survey. arXiv preprint arXiv:2212.09970 (2022)

Author Index

Printed in the United States
by Baker & Taylor Publisher Services